Utopia in the Anthropocene

Utopia in the Anthropocene takes a cross-disciplinary approach to analyse our current world problems, identify the key resistance to change and take the reader step by step towards a more sustainable, equitable and rewarding world. It presents paradigm-shifting models of economics, political decision-making, business organization and leadership and community life. These are supported by psychological evidence, utopian literature and inspirational changes in history.

The Anthropocene is in crisis, because human activity is changing almost everything about life on this planet at an unparalleled pace. Climate change, the environmental emergency, economic inequality, threats to democracy and peace and an onslaught of new technology: these planetwide risks can seem too big to comprehend, let alone manage. Our reckless pursuit of infinite economic growth on a finite planet could even take us towards a global dystopia. As an unprecedented frenzy of change grips the world, the case for utopia is stronger than ever. An effective change plan requires a bold, imaginative vision, practical goals and clarity around the psychological values necessary to bring about a transformation.

This book will be of great interest to students and scholars of the environmental humanities, sustainability studies, ecological economics, organizational psychology, politics, utopian philosophy and literature – and all who long for a better world.

Michael Harvey is a London-based organizational psychologist and leadership coach with extensive experience in personal and organizational change. A former literary academic and entrepreneur, he's also a trained psychotherapist and author of *Interactional Coaching* (2012) and *Interactional Leadership* (2015).

Routledge Studies in Sustainability

Fore more information on this series, please visit: www.routledge.com/
Routledge-Studies-in-Sustainability/book-series/RSSTY

Utopia in the Anthropocene

A Change Plan for a Sustainable and Equitable World

Michael Harvey

Routledge
Taylor & Francis Group

LONDON AND NEW YORK

earthscan
from Routledge

First published 2019
by Routledge
2 Park Square, Milton Park, Abingdon, Oxon OX14 4RN

and by Routledge
52 Vanderbilt Avenue, New York, NY 10017

Routledge is an imprint of the Taylor & Francis Group, an informa business

British Library Cataloguing-in-Publication Data
A catalogue record for this book is available from the British Library

Library of Congress Cataloging-in-Publication Data
A catalog record has been requested for this book

ISBN: 978-1-138-31111-4 (hbk)
ISBN: 978-0-429-45905-4 (ebk)

Typeset in Baskerville
by Wearset Ltd, Boldon, Tyne & Wear

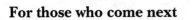

For those who come next

Contents

About the author

Michael Harvey was born in London and grew up in the Surrey Hills.

For the past two decades, he has helped to develop organizations across Europe, coaching corporate leaders and promoting creativity, teamwork and open communication among employees at every level.

His other career roles include university teacher (specializing in literature and cultural theory), radio producer, media manager and entrepreneur (pioneering online, interactive services ahead of the internet revolution). In the early 1990s, he trained as a psychotherapist (working in the NHS and privately) and as organizational psychologist.

He has degrees in English Literature, Sociology, Psychology, Psychotherapy and Organizational Psychology. He lives in London and is married with three children. He can be contacted at mdbharvey@gmail.com.

His recent publications include *Interactional Coaching: Choice-focused learning at work* (Routledge, 2012) and *Interactional Leadership: The art of the choice-focused leader* (Routledge, 2014).

Introduction
The case for utopia

Thomas More's *Utopia* is strangely out of its time. At least that's how it always struck me during my first career, as a student and teacher of radical approaches to literature and culture. The book was published in 1516, the best part of a century before Shakespeare's greatest works and 200 years before the Augustan era of Alexander Pope and Jonathan Swift, and yet it still seems so strikingly modern. It calls for greater equality between classes and genders, espouses a belief in human rationality and a faith in our ability to achieve the common good in a more peaceful, better managed world. In reimagining the present, it looks to the future in an extraordinarily innovative way, as well as seeking to preserve what it reveres about the past.

Revisiting *Utopia* many years later I began to see the origins of the book's unique two-way vision. What's more, I began to realize what it, and the great tradition of utopianism which it initiated, has to say to us today in the twenty-first century. More's belief that a rational management of humanity can create stability and human flourishing has never been more relevant. Five hundred years on the case for a better, more equitable world is stronger than ever. And, as I'll explain later in this chapter, I believe my current occupation of organizational psychology can provide a compelling, contemporary way to make that case.

First, let's try to understand the unique historical moment which *Utopia* occupies, for it's this which lies at the heart of its relevance today. Just as on the edges of an ecosystem – where water reaches land, for example – we find the most interesting phenomena (Mulligan, 2015), so it's on the margins of history where one era meets another that the most profound creativity often occurs. *Utopia* occupies such a position, standing on the threshold of modernity, between the new world and ways of life which had existed for thousands of years during the Holocene epoch.

For More, part of this momentous change was happening very close to home. *Utopia* is a plea for a form of spiritual and community life, which was under threat from a new wave of materialism and elitism. Following the devastation caused by the Black Death, the fifteenth century had brought good times to ordinary people, with high wages, available land, increased social mobility and an aristocratic elite shrinking in power and size (the number of peers fell from 200 in 1300 to just 60 in 1500 (Scheidel, 2017)). But the enclosure of common lands was gathering pace – hence More's satirical jibe that 'your sheep ... swallow up people: they lay waste and depopulate fields, dwellings and towns' (More, 1516/2012:33) – and this practice would end the long-held rights of ordinary people to farm communally and efficiently through open-field farming (Fairlie, 2009). Soon forests and woodlands, where for thousands of years villagers had been free to obtain firewood and game to support their families, would become the private property of the nobility, turning peasants into poachers. More's London was still a place of communal property, housing many monasteries and nunneries and the hospitals, almshouses, libraries and places of learning run by religious orders. But these too would soon be transferred into the ownership of the rapidly reviving elite, in Europe's first great wave of economic privatization, the English Reformation. More's resistance to this project, which was master-minded by none other than his employer, Henry VIII, and his refusal to accept the king's unconditional supremacy over the Church of England, would ultimately cost him his life.

The great unlevelling

Utopia also has a powerful global dimension. Its creation was influenced by accounts of the hitherto unknown civilizations Western Europeans were encountering in the course of their voyages of discovery, especially Amerigo Vespucci's descriptions of the indigenous peoples of the New World (Cave, 1991). Utopia is a premonition of a world that is about to change in an unprecedented way. As the flat-earth theory of geography was disproved, something else began to occur, the sloping of world power towards a tiny minority of European countries with Atlantic seaboards. In this, *Utopia* anticipates a dramatic state of global imbalance that continues to this day.

Although in More's world, sharp economic inequalities existed within nations, the relationship between nations was more level than today. (In that sense the Flat Earthers were right.) The late medieval world moved slowly, in time with the changing seasons, spiritually and materially in balance with nature. The vast majority of people earned their living through agriculture and skilled crafts and lived on the land or in small towns or villages (even as late as 1800, only 2% of the global population lived in cities (UN, 2001)). Life expectancy between Western Europe and the rest of the world was relatively equal: although overall it was lower than today, in part due to high infant morality. There was, of course, far less technology and science than today, although both existed outside Europe, especially in the ancient civilizations of China and India, as Kenneth Pomeranz shows in *The Great Divergence* (2001). For example, it took

Western Europe until 1700 to catch up with the level of iron production of eleventh-century China, which had possessed an advanced civil service since 200 BCE. Medieval sub-Saharan Africa also had well-established iron and copper metallurgy and international trading empires, as well as efficient, decentralized agrarian societies, and the Islamic world could boast a long history of scientific innovation in mathematics, astronomy and medicine.

This world order was already changing by the time *Utopia* first appeared, as the nations of Europe began to assert their competitive advantage in seafaring, advanced weaponry and an aggressive sense of entitlement that was unparalleled in world history. Columbus's arrival in Hispaniola in 1492 had resulted in the enslavement or death from disease of the vast majority of its indigenous population, and by 1500 the Portuguese had claimed Brazil, an area larger than all of Europe (Stannard, 1992). In the following decades the arrival of Cortés and Pizarro in what is now Mexico and Peru would slope the world even more dramatically, as the sophisticated and highly organized Aztec and Inca civilizations were destroyed by small bands of ruthless European invaders. The vast quantities of gold and silver which the conquistadores began shipping home transformed the European economy, creating the basis for the capital which would later fund the Industrial Revolution (Hickel, 2017).

The great unlevelling had started, and from the eighteenth century it would intensify, dizzyingly tilting the world towards the West. In 1700, the great civilizations of India and China still produced almost half of the entire world's GDP, but by 1950 this share had shrivelled to just 9% (Maddison, 2007). Colonization by Western Europeans vastly increased the productive land available to them at the expense of the indigenous inhabitants who had occupied these countries for thousands of years. Africa's civilizations suffered most, as its economy – half the size of Europe's in 1500 but just a twelfth of it by 1870 – was plundered, with millions of its people turned into slaves and its lands occupied in an increasingly frenzied rush. When *Utopia* was published, Britain had a mere 1% share of the world economy (and still under 3% of it in 1700), but by 1870 it had metastasized into the British Empire and was churning out a quarter of the global GDP. Perhaps the most tragic example of this grotesquely distorted map of the world was the Belgian Congo, a vast area 80 times bigger than Belgium, which until 1908 was the personal property of King Leopold II. Western civilization would undoubtedly bring the rest of the world advances in education, healthcare, science and, eventually, democracy but the price paid in plundered cultures, destroyed civilizations, enslavement, oppression and deaths that run into tens of millions has no parallel in history.

The nation that came out on top after this staggering period of global rebalancing didn't even exist in More's time. By 2008 the United States of America had an 18.5% share of global GDP – and perhaps an even greater cultural, ideological and political grip on the world, in spite of never having more than a twentieth of the global population. Its economy had grown 755-fold since 1820 and by a factor of around 35,000 since the publication of *Utopia* (Maddison, 2007). Even Thomas More couldn't have seen that one coming.

From *Utopia* to *Ecotopia*

I also doubt whether More realized just what his book had unleashed: a powerful utopian tradition of imagining a better future, which would continue to gather strength for hundreds of years. In the seventeenth century visions of an ideal world began to be charged with the idea of scientific progress, for example, in Francis Bacon's benevolent and tolerant *New Atlantis*, published in 1627, and Margaret Cavendish's phantasmagorical *The Blazing World* of 1666, the first utopia written by a woman. In the following century, Daniel Defoe's hugely popular *Robinson Crusoe* (1719), a kind of utopia by default, offers a beguiling vision of human resourcefulness in accord with the natural environment. In 1754 Jean-Jacques Rousseau went further in his novel, *Emile*, depicting a defiantly rural utopia which unites the individual and the communal. Rousseau's protest that it was 'manifestly contrary to the law of nature … that a handful of people should gorge themselves with superfluities while the hungry multitude goes in want of necessities' (Rousseau 1754/1984:138) was an inspiration for real revolutions, in France and elsewhere.

However, it was in the nineteenth century that utopianism fully emerged as an intellectual and political force to be reckoned with, as utopians reacted to the grotesque injustices and imbalances in European societies caused by industrialization. (In Britain, for instance, the richest 1% saw their share of national wealth increase from 37% in 1700 to 69% in 1910 (Scheidel 2017:104)). The cry for a more rational, humane and equitable way of organizing humanity would reach its peak in the works of numerous utopians, including the influential philosophies of utopian socialists Charles Fourier and Henri de Saint-Simon and the religion of humanity of Auguste Comte (Manuel and Manuel, 1979). In fiction, William Morris's *News from Nowhere* (1890) presented an alluring alternative to the harsh industrial realities of Victorian life, in the form of a peaceful, mutually supportive society, based on a skilled crafts economy and ordinary people's ability to organize themselves. Edward Bellamy's *Looking Backward* (1888) envisaged a more centralized, socialist society, in which all adults served their turn in an 'industrial army', providing citizens with plentiful time for leisure and culture and all the consumer goods they require.

Before the dark horrors of the First World War, largely provoked by European nations fighting to maintain their position in the sloping world, H.G. Wells's *A Modern Utopia* (1905) presented an ebulliently liberal, democratic and scientific vision of the future. It envisaged mass university education, universal enfranchisement and a world government. After that, utopian experimentation moved beyond theory and fiction, notably in the Russian Revolution and other attempts to turn Marx and Engel's ideal of a world beyond capitalist exploitation into a social and economic reality. Orwell's *Nineteen Eighty-Four* (1949) was one damning verdict on the result, matched in popularity by *Brave New World*, Aldous Huxley's dystopian satire on American consumerism. But utopia would flourish again in the counterculture of 1960s and 1970s, in works like Ursula Le Guin's feminist, egalitarian society in *The Dispossessed* (1971) and in *Island* (1962), Huxley's own attempt at an ideal world inspired by environmentalism and Eastern meditation.

What's also striking about this period is the emergence of a fully fledged ecological utopia. In *Walden* (1854), Henry David Thoreau had presented a defiantly radical, real-life account of Rousseauian rural simplicity in the woods of Massachusetts, but Ernst's Callenbach's *Ecotopia* (1975) is the first fictional utopia to combine modern ecology and progressive politics in a wholly new form of social and economic organization. The novel offers a vision of a breakaway society which returns to many of More's classic themes but with a new emphasis on gender equality, environmental management and open, honest, loving relationships. It's a model which restores the equilibrium between humanity and nature at the heart of the utopian vision, and which we'll explore along with other utopian fictions in Chapter 15.

The beliefs of utopianism

As these works indicate, the utopian tradition has always stood against the disequalizing forces of modern history. It uses the power of imagination to try to correct the imbalances between nations, classes, races and genders, as well as between humanity and nature. Its values challenge a status quo which can seem incontestable in its insidious ubiquity and defiantly assert a vision of what life could be at its best. Utopianism is the opposite of fatalism. It's the refusal to accept that the future just happens and there's not much you can do about it. It's an encouragement to articulate a better world, not simply a less bad version of what we already have. Utopia is a paradigm shift towards the greater good rather than the acceptance of a lesser evil.

This best-case scenario for humanity is always based on the belief that people are essentially driven by a desire for cooperation rather than a lust for power, if they are only given the social and economic conditions to realize this benevolence. That doesn't imply naivety or a simple-minded belief that human beings can return to a mythical state of nature: utopia is not Elysium or a supernatural state of bliss. The term 'utopian' is often misused to indicate something like this, an impossible state of human perfection, a lotus-eating idyll. On the contrary, utopia can be hard work, but it's work that liberates human beings rather than degrading or enslaving them. Utopias offer models of social and economic management which bring out the best in humanity, in stark contrast to the top-down forms of absolute control to be found in dystopias. In that sense, utopias are always radical rather than reformist. They argue that what's needed is not just a modification of the existing system but a completely different system.

That requires a profoundly different, holistic way of looking at the world. The word 'utopia' derives from the ancient Greek for 'no place'. This was More's ironic acknowledgement that his world lies somewhere between the real and the ideal (and a prudent defence against his political opponents). But it can also be interpreted to mean 'no place in particular', in other words, 'every place'. Certainly, utopianism has always been concerned with humanity as a whole, regardless of geographical location, and over the centuries it has become increasingly universal, espousing a plan for the entire planet. If utopia were a film it would mainly be shot using a wide-angle lens, although with some mid-shots and close-ups as well. This big-picture approach sees the whole not as an extension of one part but as an interconnected totality which is greater than the sum of its parts. That also means a vision in time, looking forward and back, using long historical horizons, in a way that's impossible for short-termist cultures. Visionary in space and time: this is utopianism at its best.

It also requires something else, a profound faith in human rationality, a conviction that we can look at reality without flinching and then make the decisions that we need to make. It's a belief that we are capable of making informed choices that will lead to the common good of humanity. This confidence in human decision-making has never been needed more than today. Because once again we've arrived at a critical crossroads of history.

Utopia in the Anthropocene

Half a millennium after the appearance of *Utopia*, we stand at another historical edge – but today the stakes are even higher. For this time we stand not simply between historical phases but in the transition of geological epochs, between the Holocene in its entirety, which stretches back 11,700 years to the end of the last Ice Age, and a wholly new phase of human and planetary history. The Anthropocene is recognition that human influence over our planet has undergone a step change, which now extends to the very rocks below our feet (Ellis, 2018). Scientists have not yet confirmed the precise starting date of this new interval of geological time, although it's likely to be 1945, the year of the first thermonuclear bomb tests. It's only in the new millennium that the full meaning of the Anthropocene has started to become apparent, as public awareness catches up with the profound human impacts on the planet which have occurred since the Second World War. The rate of change is such as would make the inhabitants of the Middle Ages gasp with incredulity. Look in any direction in our world system and we see human activity creating changes which the planet has not experienced for millions of years. And new technology promises to transform aspects of our daily lives which throughout history have been considered immutable realities of human existence.

Now we can see both ways – just as Thomas More could – with a heightened sense of a turning point in history. A double vision of the past and the future is possible, between what is and what could be, both positive and negative. It's a unique moment where hindsight, insight and foresight can all come together. Taking responsibility for the Anthropocene, changing the way we interact with each other and our environment is the biggest challenge humanity has ever had to take on. In the Holocene it was possible to treat nature with indifference: whatever we did to it, it somehow seemed to bounce back (or so we thought), but now things are far more precarious. We are not on a solid steady platform that we can take for granted but on a swaying tightrope, with below us a rapidly shrinking safety net. The sloping world is more perilously balanced than ever before and the implications for humanity as a whole are enormous. The dangers are without precedent, but so is the opportunity. When have we ever had such a chance to put humanity on the drawing board, to redesign and take full responsibility for how we live with each other and our planet? It is, of course, an opportunity that most utopians could only dream of.

And yet just as the point where the utopian vision is most needed, humanity seems have abandoned it. Since the 1970s the great stream of utopian literature has gradually dried up. In our still-new millennium we seem to have forgotten how to imagine a rational alternative world that is convincingly better than our own. At the same time, our ability to imagine a world that is much worse has grown immeasurably. In recent decades dystopia seems to have conquered the human imagination. New forms of dystopian fiction have flourished, taking over existing cultural platforms and inventing new ones. A host of genres have sprung up, such as feminist dystopias and techno-dystopias, many specifically targeted at younger readers. Incredibly, this century, dystopian novels outnumber utopian fictions by about a hundred to one (according to those listed by Wikipedia (2018a). I firmly believe that the spirit of utopianism is still alive, but the cultural expression of it seems to have come to a complete dead end.

A change plan for utopia in the Anthropocene

So what form can a utopia in the Anthropocene take? How can we not only imagine it but think it through in evidence-based detail? The case for it may be stronger than ever, but, without a suitable emotional and intellectual framework, the chances of rising to the challenge of our historical

moment are reduced. Change on any scale can be anxiety provoking, but
the degree of change represented by the Anthropocene is without parallel.

That's where I believe clinical psychology, psychotherapy and organizational psychology can help. These are fields which I've been working in
and writing about for the past 20 years. I've always seen psychology as utopianism in action (this is perhaps why I was attracted to it in mid-career)
in that it promotes a better balance between the ideal and the real and
tries to equalize the imbalances which prevent individuals and groups
from achieving what they want. Like utopia, psychology is all about
change. It is, in effect, the science of human change and as such contains
a vast storehouse of theory and research, experimental evidence and practitioner experience, drawn from across the entire spectrum of change situations. Large-scale organizational change is an area which I, like many
other practitioners, have worked on extensively. So why not bring this
background to planning the biggest change event of them all?

Of course, the transformation of the world is several orders of magnitude beyond anything ever achieved at a personal or organizational level –
and some might even say there's a touch of utopian irony about my project
– but there's a clear case for bringing tried-and-tested tools to what might
otherwise seem to be an insurmountable task. Practical organizational
change starts with a clear vision of the change it aims to bring about. A
change plan also needs bold, measurable goals and a definition of the
means by which it intends to achieve its desired end. It requires a holistic
grasp of the current system and a description of the way its parts interact.
And it needs to clearly analyse the problem it aims to overcome, who will
resist the change and who will champion it. So that's what I'll attempt to
provide in this book.

The plan of the plan

The book is in four parts. Part I begins with an analysis of the problem of
our current world system, which I call the 'Anthropocene crisis', an unprecedented, hydra-headed complex of challenges, which we have extreme
difficulty in even identifying, let alone managing.

In Part II, I try to describe the 'growthist' world plan behind this crisis,
which is based on the pursuit of infinite economic growth that has created
our sloping world. I identify those in charge of it and the irrational values
and assumptions which drive it. I also look at the way these values have
become embedded in the primary institutions of our age, economics, business and politics. An increasingly seamless system of reinforcement has
spread to all forms of culture, affecting our everyday psychology in profound ways. All this means that, at this crossroads of history, the path to
dystopia could be beckoning.

Part III describes a 12-step utopian alternative, aimed at capitalizing
on the opportunity offered by the Anthropocene crisis to create a world

based on sustainable, equitable wellbeing planetwide. In the first step, I outline a vision, a logic and a model of balance to correct the sloping world. The next step is to describe concrete goals and a set of values, based on cooperation, democracy and reverence for nature to counter the competitivist and materialist assumptions of our current world system. In subsequent chapters, I look at alternative disciplines and institutions which can rebalance economics worldwide, revitalize our dysfunctional democracy and create a new purpose for workplace organizations, based on pro-social goals, rather than profit. I argue that utopian internationalism can help solve complex practical problems, such as the danger of overpopulation and war, and stimulate greater global intergovernmental cooperation.

The second half of the change plan explores this values revolution, illustrating very different practices of decision-making, teamwork and leadership, which can spread from the workplace to wider society. Psychology has a significant role in providing practical methods for encouraging cooperative behaviours, weaning us off excessive individualism and restoring faith in democracy, internationalism and the positive power of nature. We can also learn from the utopian imagination, adopt utopian styles of thinking and behaving and take heart from the lessons from history which show that a world transformation is possible.

In the end, as I suggest in Part IV, it's always a matter of choice whether a change plan is implemented. We are at a unique historical moment when a two-way vision of the past and future is possible, but which road will we choose to take and how long do we have to decide?

Throughout the book, I'll try to offer encouragement through many examples of practice and theory which suggest that the foundations for a more balanced and better world already exist. By the end of the book I hope to persuade you that the best case scenario for the Anthropocene is a real possibility. At the same time, we have to face up to the fact that something much worse could also lie down the road. The case for utopia has always been compelling. But 500 years after Thomas More's great work first appeared, utopia may no longer be an enlightened dream but an urgent necessity.

Part I

The burning platform

1   The Anthropocene crisis
Change mismanaged

In change-management circles a crisis in urgent need of a solution is known as 'a burning platform'. When two geological epochs meet we can expect something even greater – a conflagration of crises. For some time, social scientists have recognized that precarious volatility is an essential aspect of the modern world, christening it a 'risk society' (Beck, 1992), but the full range of hazards and uncertainties that we face at the beginning of the Anthropocene have probably never been fully acknowledged.

So be prepared for a rocky ride through our current world situation. I ask for your patience in advance because I know that some of this won't be easy. But our tendency to ignore the negative is usually most pronounced when there is no positive alternative to it or if it's seen as being impossible to change. That's not the case here. Like every crisis, the Anthropocene crisis is made up of dangers and opportunities. In fact, the carrot and the stick have never been bigger. This analysis of our current world situation is not presented from a pessimistic perspective, or out of a desire to sensationalize or alarm, but from the conviction that unless we frankly and fully recognize the dangers of the Anthropocene we will not be in a position to take advantage of the immense opportunities it offers. Real change requires the truthful acceptance of 'what is'.

I'll focus, as briefly as I can, on the following areas of risk in our world system.

- Climate change
- Attrition of natural resources
- Population issues – especially overpopulation
- Income and wealth inequality
- The challenge to democracy
- The dangers of war
- The gamble on new technology

All these areas represent challenges which are virtually without historical precedent. They are closely linked together but usually dealt with as though they were separate; they are treated as though they occupied their own individual time dimensions, yet they all bear down on us simultaneously: here and now. Together they reveal the current, precarious state of the sloping world, tilting perilously on one axis. But as in any change plan, we need to calmly analyse the problem if we are to move towards a solution. Let's look at each factor in turn.

Climate change

Global warming represents one of the biggest imbalances humanity has ever created in its relationship with its environment. Since 1750, the concentration of CO_2 and other greenhouse gases such as methane and nitrous oxide has increased from the average for the Holocene of 280 parts per million (ppm) to over 400 ppm today. These emissions have risen by over 90% since 1970 which has already been enough to cause an increase of 1°C in global air temperature since the pre-industrial period (IPCC, 2014). Average air temperatures conceal more extreme differences between land and sea, cities and the countryside and different regions of the world. The Arctic, for instance, which plays a critical role in the weather systems of the Northern hemisphere, is experiencing alarmingly rapid warming, with temperatures as much as 20°C hotter than average. Globally, the 20 warmest years on record have occurred in the last 22 years, including the hottest ever year in 2016 (WMO, 2018). The incidence of extreme weather has increased five-fold since the pre-industrial period. Events such as floods or droughts, violent hurricanes or days of extreme heat, which used to occur once in a century, now happen with alarming frequency.

The world has been attempting to manage the climate crisis for over three decades now. In 1992, at the Rio Earth Summit, humanity, through the agency of the United Nations and its International Panel on Climate Change (IPCC), committed itself to 'stabilize the concentration of greenhouse gases in the atmosphere at a level which prevents dangerous anthropogenic interference in the climate system' (UNFCCC, 1992). In 2007 this level was set at 2°C, even though this would involve a degree of climate disruption unprecedented in the Holocene. However, the world's governmental leaders failed to agree anything of note in the shambles of the UN climate conference in Copenhagen in 2009, leaving it until Paris in December 2015 to breathe new life into global climate management. The Paris Climate Agreement set a new 'aspirational' target of 1.5°C, and at least proved that 194 nations can work together, but it was never going to be able to make up for lost time or counter the political and corporate influences on the IPCC (as many of us protesting in the streets of Paris at the time feared). The accord's emissions targets were too low, it was over-reliant on unrealistic assumptions about non-existent 'negative-emissions' technology and it lacked legal consequences for individual countries which breach their targets (more in Chapter 7). 'There is not a cat in hell's chance' of meeting the Paris targets was the damning verdict of one climate scientist (Simms, 2017).

Sure enough, in 2018, alarmed by the existing evidence of climate breakdown, the IPCC issued a special report which lowered its official target to 1.5°C, aiming for a 45% reduction in CO_2 emissions by 2030 (compared to 2010) and net zero emissions by 2050. It acknowledged that this would require 'rapid, far-reaching and unprecedented changes in all aspects of society' (IPCC, 2018). But the December 2018 UN climate talks in Katowice failed to endorse the IPPC report (largely due to the resistance from oil-producing giants, the USA, Russia and Saudi Arabia), let alone set new, ambitious emissions targets. The fact remains that as of January 2019, the planet is on course for global warming of 3–4°C by the end of the century, according to the vast majority of climate scientists. This would be true even if the entire world adopted the EU's current emissions trajectory, while if every nation on the planet followed the example of the United States the result would be over 4°C of global warming by 2100. Emulating the greenhouse-gas pollution of China, Russia or Saudi Arabia would lead to a planetary temperature rise of over 5°C (Robbiou du Pont and Meinshausen, 2018).

Warming in the region of 3–4°C would be a catastrophe which could take many parts of the planet close to collapse. It would mean that extreme weather events become 65 times more frequent than in 1750. Superstorms could rage from pole to pole, as James Hansen warns (2009), with heavy and longer bouts of rainfall, disrupting the monsoons on which so much of the Asian economy depends. Deserts will expand even faster, while rainforests contract – and with it their ability to absorb CO_2, further intensifying the warming effect. Sea levels could rise by between 0.5 and 1.3 metres by 2100, threatening the hundreds of millions of people worldwide who live in coastal areas and many of the world's mega cities from Mumbai and Dhaka to New York, Miami and Shanghai (Potsdam, 2016). An increase in sea levels of 1 metre would put 74,000 square kilometres of land in East Asia and the Pacific region at risk of permanent inundation – displacing up to 40 million people (Dasgupta, 2018) – and if ice cliffs continue to collapse in Antarctica and Greenland considerably greater rises could be expected (NOAA, 2017).

Incredibly, it could be even worse. A recent study, based on an analysis of sediment and ice samples rather than computer modelling, argues that warming in an interglacial period such as ours could result in a temperature rise of over 7°C by the end of this century (Friedrich *et al.*, 2016). Even at lower temperatures, the danger of runaway climate change is very real, in particular due to the possible release of large quantities of methane gas from the frozen seabed or tundra permafrost (methane being much more effective at trapping heat than CO_2 in the short term). Continuing on our current business-as-usual trajectory is a reckless gamble that could transform the Earth from the comparatively temperate planet which has enabled humanity to grow by the billion into an environment far more hostile to human life.

The effects of climate change beyond 2°C will be as tragically uneven and unfair as anything in our sloping world. Hardest hit will the global South rather than the global North which is largely responsible for human-made climate change. Over half of the roughly 40 billion tons of CO_2 which the world pumps into the atmosphere every year is produced by just three emitters (China, the USA and the EU), while the bottom 100 countries only account for 3.5% (World Resources Institute, 2017). Likewise, Europe and North America – less than a sixth of the world's population – are responsible for 60% of global private consumption, while the poorest third of the world who live in Africa and Asia only account for 3.2% of consumer spending and are reliant on local, small farming for almost all of their food (Worldwatch, 2012). Agriculture is highly sensitive to climate change and even small variations in temperature can devastate harvests. Melting glaciers and reduced snowfalls will disrupt water supplies and threaten the hundreds of millions of people who already have limited access to clean drinking water. Famine, drought and disease could lead to a phenomenal increase in mass migrations, adding to the 21 million refugees who are currently displaced by weather-related hazards such as floods, storms and wildfires, with Asia suffering the most (UNHCR, 2016). A recent World Bank estimate forecasts that there will be 143 million climate refugees by 2050 – and the total thereafter could be much higher (Rigaud *et al.*, 2018).

Shocking as this picture is, the situation is not hopeless. In spite of opposition from the fossil-fuel industry, the 2018 UN Climate Change Convention in Katowice made some progress towards a rulebook for implementing the Paris Climate Agreement. Efforts to ratchet up national and local emissions targets to a realistic level continue, with scientists and campaigners throughout the world determined not to give up on preventing climate collapse. Green technology and sustainability initiatives are laying down the foundations for the radical changes which we'll have to make in order to protect the precious equilibrium of our climate, as we'll see in Part III. But for now we need to stick with the big picture, for climate is one only aspect of the Anthropocene crisis.

The attrition of nature: the environmental crisis

The truth is that we've been falling out of balance with nature for a good while. In the Holocene, when natural resources were abundant, it was perhaps understandable that we should treat the fertile land, nutrition-rich marine species and the vast forests of our planet as though they were inexhaustible. But in the Anthropocene, acting as though 'we're only passing through', as Janine Benyus puts it (1997:249), turning a resource into a wasteland and then moving on, is no longer an option. We are now, almost literally, destroying the ground under our feet in a reckless frenzy of environmental destruction that has no precedent.

Researchers in Stockholm, studying the earth systems necessary to sustain the conditions in which humanity has been able to flourish, have identified nine planetary boundaries. Of these, at least four are already in a state of 'increasing or high risk': climate change, genetic diversity, land exchange use and biochemical flows (Steffen *et al.*, 2015). Geographer Jared Diamond (2005) outlines other ecological threats that arise from the destruction of natural habitats, such as the invasion of alien species of weeds and pests and even a possible ceiling to the Earth's ability to create photosynthesis, on which all life depends. The scale of air, soil and water pollution being experienced by China alone, perhaps the country with the greatest influence on our future, is staggering.

Planetwide, we face non-climate related threats to food production, through the depletion of almost a third of the world's topsoil, which takes 1,000 years to regenerate itself nutritionally. Marine life, the source of 20% of the world's animal protein (and up to 50% in parts of Asia) is severely threatened by overfishing. According to the UN, less than a third of fish species are currently harvested at a biologically sustainable level and the ten most productive species are now all fully fished or overfished (FAO, 2016). Acidification due to warming seas also threatens marine species, already menaced by millions of tons of non-degradable plastic deposited in our oceans each year. Dead zones in coastal waters, such as the giant area in the Gulf of Mexico linked to pollution from the meat industry, have increased ten-fold since 1950, threatening the 350 million jobs dependent on fishing (Breitburg *et al.*, 2018). The Great Barrier Reef, the largest living structure on the planet, suffered one of its biggest bleaching events ever in 2016, and the IPCC (2018) forecasts that 99% of corals would be destroyed by 2°C of warming.

Throughout history, trees have been one of our greatest natural resources but they continue to be decimated. Half of the planet's original great forests have disappeared over the last 8,000 years, with a quarter of what remains likely to follow suit in the next 50 years (Diamond, 2011). Deforestation of an area the size of India by 2050 could be on the cards, with Indonesia, for example, destroying twice as much forest as Brazil (Morgano *et al.*, 2014). As legal and illegal logging marches on, the inestimably valuable 'ecological services' which trees perform, including mitigating climate change and reducing the ambient air pollution that currently kills 4.2 million people a year worldwide, will decline (WHO, 2018b).

Another precious resource for life, clean water, is also being used up fast, as aquifers and wells sink to perilously low levels. And we are ransacking the Earth's store of precious minerals at an alarming rate. A Club of Rome report (Bardi, 2014) finds that, in addition to easily accessible oil, which is almost exhausted, we are 'hollowing out the Earth', depleting it of many minerals vital to modern life. As writer Nafeez Ahmed (2014) notes,

> US Geological Survey data analysed by the report shows that chromium, molybdenum, tungsten, nickel, platinum-palladium, copper, zinc, cadmium, titanium, and tin will face peak production followed by declines within this century.

What this all adds up to is a catastrophe for biodiversity, as flora and fauna which have taken millions of years to evolve vanish forever. A total of 468 vertebrates have gone extinct since 1900, compared to a normal, background rate of nine (Caballos *et al.*, 2015). According to the World Wildlife Fund (2018a), there are now 60% fewer animals in the world than in 1970. This represents a rate of decrease in animal populations of 2% a year, caused by agriculture, deforestation, climate change and the hunting of species to near extinction. In just the past 50 years a staggering 89% of vertebrates have been eliminated in Latin America, prompting the World Wildlife Fund to warn that 'nature is dying' (2018b). Freshwater fish populations are also massively down, by 83%. Three-quarters of flying insects have disappeared in Germany over the past 30 years, and, across Europe, similarly devastating rates of disappearance of bees and other vital pollinators and contributors to the food chain are being recorded.

No wonder, then, that scientists say we that are now experiencing 'the sixth mass extinction' of species. But whereas the five previous mass extinctions were the result of natural causes and took place over thousands of years, the Anthropocene extinction rate is much faster, and it's humanity which is bringing it about. The current trend is 1,000 times faster than it would be without human impact, which, if it continues unabated, will lead to the extinction of one in six species by 2100, according to evolutionary biologist Mark Urban (2017), who calls for the launching of 'a biological Manhattan Project' of international species protection.

It's hard to be optimistic about such an initiative because attempts to manage the environmental crisis across the world are constantly thwarted by the prevailing economic and management philosophy. Even the simplest legislation can have significant ameliorative effects – like the UK government's introduction of a small charge for plastic bags which reduced their use by 85% virtually overnight – but these measures always seem to be 'too little, too late' (which is really just a euphemism for chronic mismanagement). In the meantime, the depletion of our greatest human resource, our planet and the life it sustains, accelerates.

Population

The climate and environmental crises are both related to another source of imbalance: the fact that there are so many of us now on this planet. It took humanity over 200,000 years to reach the half a billion mark at the beginning of the Industrial Revolution. Since then the population has grown by 1,500% to 7.5 billion and it's now rising by about half a billion every six years. The United Nations' projections through the century see a continued rise to 9.7 billion by 2030 and 11.2 billion by 2100. This assumes a medium fertility rate. A low rate would reduce the totals, while a higher rate would increase them, producing an end of the century estimate of 16.6 billion (UN, 2015a).

Of course, predictions of doom about overpopulation have been with us since Thomas Malthus's time but the interwoven challenges of the Anthropocene mean it's time to take the possibility of population catastrophes more seriously. For some ecologists, the Earth's sustainable 'carrying capacity' is inherently limited, but for me, the question that really matters is how the world's resources are managed. The biggest concern is overpopulation in the poorest parts of the world. The majority of the UN's projected global population growth comes from Africa. The continent is forecast to increase its population from its current total of 1.1 billion to 2.4 billion in 2050 and 4.3 billion in 2100. This means that by the end of the century almost 40% of the world's population will be in Africa, whereas Europe's share will have shrunk to just 6%. Other rapid growth is predicted among the 48 nations which the UN designates as the 'least developed countries'. Here populations will more than triple in size by 2100, creating massive challenges for governments in eradicating poverty, reducing inequality and promoting sustainable development.

Rapid rates of growth have undermined the certainty of demographic forecasters that population will stabilize in the course of the century and then gradually decline, based on the patterns of declining fertility in developed and developing countries since the 1970s. If this unexpectedly persistent correlation between high poverty and high fertility continues, it could be a recipe for disaster. Famines, droughts and other calamities could take on a wholly new degree of malevolence in parts of the world that are sadly already no strangers to them. Yet, as we'll see in Chapter 11, progressive, evidence-based solutions involving contraception, female education and gender equality can bring about the stabilization of the world population, if only we can make the necessary changes in our values and our world plan.

A new approach is also needed to address another disparity in the demographics of the Anthropocene, which is being chronically undermanaged, the ageing of humanity. Already a quarter of Europe's population is over 60 (UN, 2015a), in the UK alone there are projected to be 280,000 centenarians by 2050; and by 2100 the over-60s are forecast to number 3.1 billion worldwide. This is another unprecedented phenomenon, the appearance for the first time in history of societies with potentially too few working-age citizens to look after the older population. This is already creating intergenerational tension, as the under-35s have to work harder and longer to support parents who are richer than they will ever be.

Visionary global leadership on this issue is urgently needed but is seemingly absent in a world increasingly obsessed with ethnic divisions, border controls and racist interpretations of population issues. Like most people, I find it impossible to visualize the 300,000 babies across the globe who have been born this very day – let alone the billions yet to be born this century. But I'm sure of one thing: they deserve a new sense of responsibility from their elders to ensure that they inherit a planet on which there is a place for them.

Inequality of wealth

Many of the imbalances of today's world have their root in the disequalization of wealth and income, which, as we've seen, has slanted the economic balance towards Western nations over the past 500 years. The gains of a relative period of levelling which took place in the post-war period have been reversed, with economic inequality in the UK increasing by 8% from 1975 to 2008, as judged by the rise of its Gini coefficient, which measures relative income distribution after tax (Bellfield *et al.*, 2016). Since the Great Recession, inequality has actually increased further with the richest 1,000 people in Britain now owning as much as the poorest 40% of the population (Equality Trust, 2017). In the USA, the most economically unequal rich country in the world, the recent disequalization has been even more emphatic. Since the early 1980s, the wealth share of the richest 1% has almost doubled to 41%, while the share of the bottom 90% has almost halved to just over 20% (Saez and Zucman, 2014). In 2012, for the first time ever, the richest 10% of Americans earned over half of the country's entire pre-tax income (Piketty and Saez, 2012).

According to the 2018 World Inequality Report, compiled by economist Thomas Piketty and his colleagues, since 1980, 'income inequality has increased in nearly all countries', with the share of the of the richest top 1% rising by a quarter to 20% (Alvaredo *et al.*, 2017:9). (Credit Suisse (2018) puts this share even higher, at 43%). The gap has also widened between the global North and the majority of the world who live in the global South. Some metrics conceal this disparity, but anthropologist Jason Hickel (2016) shows that it is clearly revealed by focusing on regional differences in wealth:

> The best way to do this is to measure the gap, in real terms, between the GDP per capita of the world's dominant power (the United States) and that of various regions of the global South. Using World Bank figures, we see that since 1960 the gap for Latin America has grown by 206%, the gap for sub-Saharan Africa has grown by 207%, and the gap for South Asia has grown by 196%. In other words, the global inequality gap has roughly tripled in size.

This gargantuan rise means that over the last 30 years the incomes of the poorest 10% in the world have increased by less than $3 a day, while those of the richest 1% went up 182 times (Hardoon *et al.*, 2016). Half the world's population still live on less than $5.50 a day, while 800,000 live in dire poverty, chronically malnourished, experiencing hunger much of the time. Meanwhile, the planet's class of billionaires swells by about two a week. In 2018, it comprised 2,208 individuals, who are collectively worth over $9 trillion (*Forbes*, 2018), following their record-breaking year of 2017 when they added 20% to their wealth (UBS, 2018). The richest eight individuals on the planet now possess as much wealth as the poorest 3.5 billion (Hardoon, 2017). This wealth will create more multi-generational dynasties, as over the next 20 years 500 people hand over in excess of $2 trillion to their heirs (Pimentel *et al.*, 2018). At the current rate, it's only a matter of time before the world's first trillionaire strides on to the world stage.

Inequality of wealth within developing countries is even more stretched than in the developed world, especially in countries that never experienced relative post-war equalization. The richest 10% of Chinese own 41% of their country's total wealth, the figure for Russia is even larger at 46%, in Sub-Saharan Africa it's 54%, in Brazil and India 55% and in the Middle East an astronomical 61% (Alvaredo *et al.*, 2017). Many developing countries have more unequal Gini coefficients than France before the French Revolution. In fact, twenty-first-century economies are beginning to look less like modern societies committed to the Enlightenment ideals of democracy and equal opportunity and more like feudal hierarchies or the empires of antiquity.

Economically unequal societies are bad for everybody, as Richard Wilkinson and Kate Picket (2009) and other equality scholars have shown. From the rates of teenage pregnancy and mental illness to levels of crime and the size of prison populations, the greater the inequality, the greater the damage to society. Among rich countries, inequality also correlates with lower levels of educational attainment and social mobility. People trust each other less in unequal societies and are less civically engaged than in more equal societies (Jordhal, 2007). Inequality, also influences life expectancy. For instance, in the UK, longevity in some areas of Glasgow is almost 15 years lower than in the most affluent areas in London. This kind of imbalance in wellbeing is a massive drag on society as a whole, which even the rich don't necessarily benefit from. We've known for some time that happiness doesn't grow with increased GDP (Easterlin, 1974) and extreme wealth can even be a source of deep discontent, a condition I'll explore further in Chapter 4.

The challenge to democracy

Growing economic inequality also manifests itself as a crisis of democracy, as the superior wealth of the few is translated into political power at the expense of the many. Politics in the twenty-first century wasn't meant to be like this. In the post-Cold War 1990s, many people went along with the 'end of history thesis' of historian Francis Fukuyama (1992), who saw the future as an eternal debate between different variations of liberal democracy, all based on free-market capitalism. But since the optimistic turn of the millennium, the challenges to liberal democracy in the West have come thick and fast: the 9/11 terrorist attacks, the US-led invasions of Afghanistan and Iraq, the 2007/8 financial crash, the Great Recession, public spending cuts, the Syrian war, European migration emergencies, Brexit, the election of Donald Trump and the apparent break up of the rule-based international order. As a result, in 2017, 'democracy faced its worst crisis in decades', according to US NGO Freedom House (2018), whose annual report, entitled 'Democracy in crisis', charts a 12th consecutive year of 'decline in global freedom'.

In many developed countries, representative democracy has failed to progress, succumbing to the influence of multinational corporations and leaving many citizens disenchanted and effectively disenfranchised, including 'the unheard third' who don't vote in general elections. A recent online, global survey of 125,000 respondents found that 51% of people 'feel like they have no voice in politics'.

> Almost two thirds (64%) of people living in democracies think their government 'rarely' or 'never' acts in the interests of the public, compared with 41% living in non-democracies.
>
> (Alliance of Democracies, 2018)

It's a dispiriting situation which in the early 2000s the political scientist Colin Crouch (2004) called 'post-democracy'. One of the most powerful reactions to this dysfunctional, crisis situation is now coming from nationalist populists, whose anger is mainly directed at corrupt elites, economic migrants and foreigners in general.

Although worldwide progress on democracy has undoubtedly been made since 1945, the fact remains that only 5% of the global population live in what in the Economist Intelligence Unit (EIU) calls 'full democracies' – and most of these are in Europe. Using five criteria (electoral process, the functioning of government, political participation, political culture and civil liberties), the EIU (2017) finds that 88% of the world's countries have regimes which it categorizes as 'flawed democracies', 'hybrid states' or 'authoritarian' states. For two years running, the report has classified the United States, the self-proclaimed beacon of democracy, as one of these electorally 'flawed' states, largely due to a decline 'in popular confidence in the functioning of public institutions, a trend which predated – and aided – the election of Donald Trump.'

Across the world, the mechanisms for majorities to get their voices heard seem to be deteriorating. Kleptocratic dictators, hereditary absolute monarchs and military juntas still hold sway over many of the world's nations, with some even dispensing with the corrupt, rigged elections by which other leaders claim political legitimacy. At worst, some authoritarian regimes rely on political and legal systems which explicitly reject the principle of human equality, especially on grounds of gender, as in several regimes in the Middle East.

All in all, the precariousness of democracy is one of the most acute aspects of the Anthropocene crisis. Never before have there been so many choices to make about how to manage the changes affecting every aspect of human life, and yet the political systems intended to facilitate majoritarian decision-making seem to be rapidly disintegrating. If we can't transform our political processes in time to create genuinely participatory democracies, we risk following the logic of post-democracy to its bitter conclusion and leaving plutocratic, self-interested elites to make all the important decisions about the future of humanity.

The risk of war

Failed democracies can lead to war. Sadly, this Horseman of the Apocalypse still looms over us. Some progress has been made since the bloodletting of the Second World War in Europe, but war still rages across the world – some of it sponsored by the West – with new lows being recorded in mass brutality against civilians. The Global Peace Index (IEP, 2018) reports a decline in peacefulness across the world since 2008 with only 13 countries actually free of conflict. Political leaders acting in ways that contradict the peaceful interests of their people are nothing new, but the quantity and quality of the weapons at their disposal are. There are now over 15,000 nuclear weapons in the world located in 14 countries, 1,800 of them 'on high alert and ready for use at short notice' (Kristensen and Norris, 2017).

At the same time, armed drones can kill enemies thousands of kilometres away from their operators and a new breed of Lethal Autonomous Weapons System (LAWS) provides something even more deadly, humanoid robots which potentially make their own decisions about killing humans (CTSKR, 2018). Delegating military aggression to machines may sound like a good idea to the anguished relatives of soldiers across the world, but it could make it even more difficult to put an end to war. The secrecy surrounding rapidly developing forms of cyber warfare doesn't help either, making conflicts less democratically accountable and potentially unmanageable even for government leaders. And all the while, terrorists, increasingly delocalized, fragmented and surfing on waves of internet propaganda, continue to offer a violent, non-state reaction to state-sponsored violence, a vicious cycle that we seem as far as ever from breaking.

New technology

Finally, as we move across the fire-strewn platform of the Anthropocene crisis, we come to potentially the biggest balance-changer of them all: the development of new technology in the coming years. Here's what futurist, inventor and Google director of engineering, Ray Kurzweil has to say on the subject:

> We won't experience one hundred years of technological advance in the twenty-first century; we will witness on the order of twenty thousand years of progress ... or about one thousand times what we achieved in the twentieth century.

(Kurzweil, 2005:11)

For Kurzweil this is all positive, but for many people what this reveals is an unprecedented degree of risk. All new technology brings potential dangers for human health, the environment and economic stability. It can take a long time to understand these dangers: consider, for instance, the three-quarters of a century it has taken for the problems of non-biodegradable plastic to reach public awareness. A phase of technological development faster than anything humanity has ever experienced threatens us not only because of its pace but due to its unprecedented scope. It's scarcely an exaggeration to say that virtually everything about being human is now up for grabs. It's one of the biggest challenges ever presented to humanity from the point of view of public safety and wellbeing and yet so far our attempts to manage it are puny.

Take the assault on the world's human jobs. An influential Oxford report (Frey and Osborne, 2013) suggests that fully 47% of all existing jobs are at risk of replacement by automation in the coming decades. This includes jobs at all levels, whether white collar or blue collar. In the knowledge industry alone, some 140 million jobs worldwide could be at risk in the next 10 to 20 years. In the UK public sector, 250,000 jobs could disappear by 2030, according to one report, including 90% of all administrative posts in Whitehall (Hitchcock *et al.*, 2017). A report by Nomura Bank (NRI, 2015) goes further, asserting that that '49% of the Japanese working population can be replaced by artificial intelligence and robots' as soon as 2035. The much heralded advent of driverless vehicles could destroy tens of millions of driving jobs across the world, with huge implications for workers and their families (for instance, truck driving is the biggest male occupation in the USA).

Automation threatens to change not only the meaning of work, as we know it, but many other cornerstones of what it is to be human. For instance, human decision-making is increasingly being delegated to machine intelligence, in everything from equity trading to medical procedures and air traffic control. This potentially puts complex management beyond our control, especially as systems are developed which can learn from their own mistakes and innovate in ways which humans can't necessarily understand. Nothing is more central to our basic sense of human identity than sexual intercourse, but this, too, could be automated, if the growing (male-dominated) sex-robot industry has its way, and traditional sexual encounters between humans are relegated to 'special occasions', as some experts predict (Bodkin, 2016).

There is little public debate about these momentous changes and virtually no governmental planning commensurate with managing them. In fact, the automation of everything, also known as 'the fourth industrial revolution' (Schwab, 2016), has now gone to the top of the West's corporate and political agenda. Regulation for the artificial intelligence (AI) at the core of this proposed transformation is virtually non-existent. An open letter signed by over 150 scientists has warned of the 'potential pitfalls' of unregulated AI, with entrepreneur Elon Musk calling it 'our biggest existential threat' (Hern, 2015). Physicist Stephen Hawking stated that we need to 'employ the best possible practice and management', otherwise AI could turn out to be 'the worst event in the history of civilisation' (CNBC, 2017). These urgent admonitions are being almost totally ignored, however. As Nate Soares of the Machine Intelligence Research Institute puts it:

> There are thousands of person-years and billions of dollars being poured into the project of developing AI. And there are fewer than ten people in the world now working full-time on safety ... basically no one is working on containment.
>
> (O'Connell, 2017:91)

When it comes to automation, it seems blind faith rules.

Medicine and biotechnology could also be on the threshold of dramatic changes with unknown consequences for humanity. Of course, some of these developments could be extremely positive, such as possible breakthroughs in oncology centring on drugs that use the human immune system to fight cancer. But the ambitions of some proponents of biological technology go well beyond repairing the existing human body. They aim to replace human organs with synthetic versions, strengthen limbs with bionic technology, introduce nanorobots into the human body for monitoring purposes and even use neurotechnology to insert computerized implants in the brain (Kurzweil, 2005). For so-called 'transhumanists', the project is to transcend human biology altogether, seeking 'the continuation and acceleration of intelligent life beyond its current human form' (More, 2013:3).

The fast-developing 'life-extension' industry thinks in similar terms, aiming to extend human ageing to 150 years and eventually to transcend the ultimate limitation on human life, death. High-tech billionaire entrepreneur Peter Thiel is planning to 'overcome the state of nature' by making human death a thing of the past (Brown, 2014). To say that the abolition of death would change the fundamental meaning of being human is an understatement. For existential philosophers like Martin Heidegger (1927/1962), death is the only absolute fact of human existence, the one thing of which we can all be sure, whatever our relativistic beliefs and moral codes. A contrary threat could come from entirely new life forms escaping from the world's synthetic biology laboratories, which former astronomer royal Martin Rees (2003) considers the number one threat to our survival in the twenty-first century. But in the Wild West of biological innovation, the only law that seems to count is whether an investor is prepared to fund a project.

Even in areas of biotechnology where international regulations have been introduced, they are in constant danger of being breached by market-driven forces. Take the booming area of gene editing. Germline modification, which involves changing an embryo destined to become a human, is currently illegal in most countries. But there is increasing pressure from commercial and scientific interests to relax the law in order to prevent diseases being passed on. Marcy Darnovsky, director of the Center for Genetics and Society, argues that if this form of genetic modification was allowed, it would quickly lead to designer babies:

> We'd end up in a world of genetic haves and have-nots, and risk introducing new kinds of inequality when we already have shamefully way too much.... People say it is a slippery slope. I don't call that a slippery slope, I call that jumping off a cliff.
>
> (Sample, 2015)

This is the sloping world at its most extreme, potentially creating inequalities of a qualitatively different kind to anything we've seen over the past 500 years. Anti-ageing techniques could widen the already considerable longevity gap between the rich and the poor – for example, almost 40 years separates average life expectancy in Monaco (89) and Chad (50) (CIA, 2018). This rift could increase even further, if access to this new medical technology is solely regulated by the free market – and bear in mind that the private US healthcare industry represents half of the entire world's healthcare market. This could be a prelude to the biological differentiation of the rich and the poor, and the opening of a new horizon on global inequality, where those at the top and bottom of the wealth distribution graph are physically and mentally distinct. This is only one of the many nightmarish risks which are emerging from the Pandora's Box of technological innovation that we seem determined to force open.

Conclusion

Untrammelled, exponentially fast, technological and scientific development completes the picture of a headlong rush towards a future with virtually no safeguards, few areas of adequate control and very little real attempts at risk management. It's a world system that has thrown away its safety net and is engaged in a gamble on everything, a bet on whatever the future holds. Where future risks are absolutely known, through climate science or the ecology of biodiversity, they are too often ignored, as the world's leaders obfuscate and deny the truth, before (at best) opting for a policy that is too little and too late. Natural resources are being ransacked, and our life-support systems depleted with wilful disregard for the generations to come and the interests of the most vulnerable people in the planet. Economic inequality condemns billions to live in, or perilously close to, poverty and weakens the politics systems intended to protect the majority. And when democracy is in crisis, war is usually not far behind. All of which makes the dawn of the Anthropocene look like just about the most recklessly unhinged and dangerous period in the entire history of humanity.

Misconduct in public office includes the charge of 'reckless indifference', a phrase which seems to sum up the current high-risk mismanagement of our world. But is this apparent stampede towards the cliff edge of the unknown as irrational as it seems? Or is it actually part of a plan which has its own bizarre rationality? If so what are the goals and values that support this plan and who is behind it? These are the some of the questions which we need to answer if we are to give ourselves a chance of bringing the Anthropocene crisis under control.

Part II
The growthist world system

2 The goals and values behind our 'mad' world plan – and who's behind it

In describing our current world situation as a recklessly mismanaged crisis, I am, of course, making a series of value-based judgements. But I don't think I'm alone in holding these values. I suspect they are broadly shared by many of the 15,364 scientists from 184 countries who recently issued their 'Second warning to humanity' 25 years after their first, urging us to move rapidly towards real environmental sustainability and effective climate management (Ripple *et al.*, 2017). Many people probably share my view that growing inequality is a major problem and are concerned by the current state of democracy. They do so because we have many goals and values in common. These may include the belief that nature is valuable in itself; that the interests of the majority matter and should not be secondary to those of a global elite or to people living in the West; that we need to look to the long term and discharge a moral reasonability to those who are most vulnerable in the world and to generations who are not yet born; and that we still have active choices about how the future can be managed.

It's important to make this point about values, because the truth is that many of those making the decisions that are shaping our world do not accept my interpretation of our historical situation. They may see some of the threats I describe, but others they dismiss as irrelevant, exaggerated or of low urgency. Other risks they simply do not see at all. What I may interpret as a problem they see as a solution – and vice versa.

This is what the gap between paradigms or value systems looks like. What seems like mismanagement of the world system to me is just business as usual to those in charge of it. Where I see chaos, they see a different kind of order. Where I'd charge them with the wilful denial of reality, they'd accuse me of alarmism or sensationalism. Where I see an ultra high-risk gamble on new technology, and almost everything about being human, they see a plausible investment strategy. In short, what seems to me like the complete absence of a plan is for them the plan itself.

All this adds up to a major problem from a change perspective, because a plan is always more difficult to shift than mere chaos. That's especially true if the plan is underpinned by widely held priorities, theories and assumptions which are embedded in the major institutions of the world.

Until we understand these values and beliefs, we'll have little chance of replacing them with something better.

The growthist world plan

Our current world plan is growthism – or at least that's why I'm proposing to call it – and it's been evolving ever since Thomas More's *Utopia* first appeared. A sloping world has to have sloping values, an unbalanced system has unbalanced goals. The core objective of our current world plan is simple: to increase economic growth – indefinitely. The material expansion of the world economy is intended to go on forever. It's measured by GDP, which since the Second World War has become the universal yardstick for evaluating national progress and much else besides.

Regarding economics as the explicit basis of politics would once have been regarded as left-wing, but nowadays nobody attempts to conceal the secret of gaining political power: 'it's the economy, stupid', as Bill Clinton's 1992 US presidential campaign slogan put it. Tied to this proposition are many more long-standing assumptions about the sacrosanct value of private property and some surprising assumptions about the natural world in modern economics. I'll return to this in the next chapter, but let me say now that for me one of the most astonishing revelations in researching this book has been the extent to which modern economics ignores the value of natural resources. The effects of human activity on the environment or climate are totally excluded from growthist economic accounting and treated as an irrelevant 'externality'.

Wiser heads have known about this for some time. As early as the 1960s, economist Kenneth Boulding (1966) was warning that the Earth was a closed resource system and to treat it as if it were endlessly open was to encourage a reckless 'cowboy economy'. 'Anyone who believes that exponential growth can go on forever in a finite world is either a madman or economist', he famously remarked. In the Club of Rome *Limits to Growth* report, Donella Meadows and others (1972) calculated for the first time that we were in imminent danger of overshooting the material capacity of our planet. More recently, it's been estimated that the amount of biomass, minerals, metals that we can sustainably consume globally is 50 billion tons a year but that we are on course to use 3.5 times that much a year by 2050 (Dittrich *et al.*, 2012). When have you ever heard a politician or economist talking about an economy reaching the right amount of economic expansion and then stopping? Instead they promise that GDP will keep on growing forever (even at a modest 2% annual rate that means quadrupling the size of an economy by 2090). This is the 'mad' contradiction between economic expansion and the limited natural resources of our planet on which our current world plan is based. Growthism's solution to the runaway processes of change threatening life on Earth is the breathtakingly irrational imperative of 'go faster, go further, get bigger'. It's as though a doctor advised a patient suffering from lung cancer to move to a city with dire air pollution and start smoking 50 cigarettes a day.

The growthist irrationale

The goal of never-ending economic expansion which is at the heart of growthism has no parallel in reality. Nature produces nothing which grows exponentially. Andrew Simms (2013) cites the case of the hamster, which if it continued its normal rate of growth every week from birth to puberty, would weigh 9 billion tonnes after a year. A similarly monstrous human equivalent might occur if we didn't end our physical growth in our teenage years. In the natural world, growth is limited and combined with phases of degrowth. In history, too, civilizations tend to follow a cyclical pattern of rise and fall, often with an undulating plateau in between. But it seems that the empire of growthism expects to rise and rise forever. Whereas development in nature and human history curves between ascent and descent, the projected growthist graph is linear, constantly slanting to the top right, like a rocket taking off on a flight to infinity.

This implies a very unique interpretation of time, among other things. The idea of the future being radically different from the past is itself a relatively new assumption: it probably only became widely established in the Victorian era, expressed in the 'melioristic' belief that things would keep improving. Most generations throughout the last 200,000 years have seen the future as being broadly similar to the past – and certainly not conspicuously better. Many utopians agree with this notion of time as circular rather than rocket-like and aim to create a stable society in which constant improvement would be unnecessary.

In recent years, the growthist ideal of change has been refined under the rubric of 'creative destruction', indicating a perpetual state of disruption of the economic status quo. The idea has its origins in G.W.F. Hegel's philosophy of history, in which social formations creatively destroy each other over time, culminating in a state of synthesis which is intended to embody human freedom. The originator of the term, economist Joseph Schumpeter (1942), shared Karl Marx's scepticism about whether capitalism could survive its own creative destructiveness, especially as regards job automation. But that has not stopped the belief that economic growth can go on forever, as long as innovation continues, from becoming a key article of growthist faith. Creative destruction means what it says, a determination to eliminate almost anything, for which a more profitable alternative can be found.

The idea that 'change is the only constant' – to borrow a much-used business phrase – has many implications but one is that long-term management becomes extremely difficult. If you don't know what's going to happen in the next year, how can you realistically plan for a decades or even centuries ahead? (It's a psychological barrier climate containment is constantly bumping up against). Almost by definition, the effects of the kind of exponential growth welcomed by futurists like Ray Kurzweil are impossible to control: it's hard enough to predict the known unknowns, let alone the unknown unknowns. So, on the one hand, growthist time arcs towards a benign future of endless economic expansion; on the other hand, grab what you can today, because who knows what tomorrow will bring. The short termism symbolized by the frenzied stampede towards the annual bonus, which contributed to the 2007/8 financial crash, is just óne manifestation of this widespread temporal myopia, which is far removed from the visionary, long-term consciousness required to take up the challenge of the Anthropocene.

Another effect of a system of constant change is that it shuts down choices. There is a widespread fatalism about the future among some of the most perceptive analysts of the future. In *Homo Deus*, historian of the future Yuval Noah Harari admits that nobody knows where the world system is heading 'in such a rush' but that 'if growth ever stops, the economy won't settle down to some cosy equilibrium, it will collapse' (2016:59). It seems that we're being swamped by the unstoppable tide of history, and all we can do is go with the flow (and perhaps hope for the best). This feeling of helplessness stiffens the status quo's resistance to change and provides one of the biggest obstacles to any positive change plan. It's one of growthism's most subtle but powerful defences to say that there is no alternative to it, although the implications for democracy of this evisceration of choice are deeply disturbing.

The beliefs behind our 'mad' world plan do indeed promote a kind of irrationality, familiar to psychologists working with patients who have high-risk lifestyles. Compulsive behaviours such as gambling, alcoholism, drug abuse, sex or work addiction, fall into this category. They are often characterized by impulsiveness, a short attention span and a penchant for immediate gratification and thrill-seeking. Often a jaunty sense of immortality goes along with this recklessness, a sense of immunity to health hazards or financial risks. Moral exceptionalism is another part of the pattern, a belief that ethical rules only apply to other people. In this fashion, the blatantly irrational is rationalized, in much the same way as it is in the growthist world plan. Of course, in the end these behaviours cause unhappiness, shame and bitter self-reproach, but they are hard to give up until a better alternative seems to be attainable. Only then can the pseudo-solution represented by irrational, self-destructive behaviour be seen for what it is.

The CIMENT values

There is another set of values which underlies the growthist irrationale and adds to its insidious persuasiveness. I have in mind a series of beliefs and attitudes which we will have to be overcome if the revolution of values necessary to bring about utopian change is to occur (I'll say more about this in Chapter 7). At its most basic, I suggest that this group of values can be summed up in the mnemonic CIMENT, which stands for: competitivism, individualism, materialism, elitism, nationalism and technologism. As their mnemonic implies, the CIMENT norms are heavy, viscous and binding, forming a vital part of the emotional and conceptual infrastructure of growthism, in which so many of us seem to be stuck fast. I'll explain each value separately and briefly outline its role in the current mismanagement of the Anthropocene.

Competitivism: battlefield logic

Tackling the problems of the Anthropocene requires a new era of human cooperation, but growthism takes it as axiomatic that economic progress – and hence all other development – can only be made through perpetual competition. According to this view, the world consists of nations competing with each other and life is 'a war of all against all', as philosopher Thomas Hobbes, in his 1651 classic *Leviathan*, imagined the human state of nature to be: 'Because the way of one competitor, to the attaining of his desire, is to kill, supplant or repel the other' (1651/1968:161). Today it's increasingly assumed that human competition is a positive force. The central trope of free-market economics which now dominates economic thinking is that of life as a market, in which everybody and everything is in competition over price.

In fact, Hobbes feared that without regulation people would tear themselves to pieces, and, to a certain extent, neoliberal founding father Milton Friedman agreed, advocating that the role of government is to do what 'the market cannot do for itself, namely, to determine, arbitrate and enforce the rules of the game' (1962:27). The problem is that in neoliberal economic theory, the tax-deprived government has been so scaled down that it's hard to see how it can regulate domestic businesses, let alone mighty transnational corporations.

This is a crucial omission, not only from free-market economics, but from growthism in general. Regulated competition is a state which can bring out the best in cooperation and competition, combining justice with dynamism. Fair competition creates rules which give each party an equal chance, as long as they are impartially arbitrated and enforced by a referee or judge. Games provide outstanding examples of a positive synthesis between cooperation and competition, not least because the score is always reset to zero after each event. No matter what has happened before, every game starts from a position of equality. And, as in tennis, your 'opponent' is also your 'partner', without whom there would be no game.

That's a long way from our current sloping world in economic and international relations where accumulated advantage is never given away, the rules are often rigged and arbitration skewed in order to ensure that inequality is maintained. That's not healthy competition but the opposite, the deeply unhealthy attitude which ecological philosopher Joanna Macy calls 'life as battlefield' (2007). For the hyper-competitor, cooperation is itself seen as form of competition to be resisted, avoided or circumvented, as reality is always a zero-sum game in which there can only be a winner and a loser. Compromise is seen as defeat and a win–win outcome an illusion. In this dog-eat-dog world, the only choice appears to be to dominate or to be dominated.

This raises the psychological stakes. It affects communication: competitors tend to talk over others or talk them down, seeing conversationalists as rivals. Rather than listening, empathizing and making connections, a strategy often favoured by women rather than men (Tannen, 1992), competitors prefer monologue to dialogue and regard every verbal exchange as an argument to be won or lost. Also, if life is a high-stakes race, losing becomes intensely painful; it's not an experience to be learned from, as in trial and error, but a shameful humiliation. This powerful emotional vicious circle can often sanction any action that offers the prospect of winning rather than losing.

Competitivism has become so rooted in growthist international relations, business, politics and even popular culture that it seems like an incontestable norm. And it still persists as a fundamental belief about human evolution, a hangover from Social Darwinism, which misinterpreted the theory of natural selection as the survival of the morally fittest. So it's worth reminding ourselves that life on earth is unthinkable without cooperation, as biologist Martin Nowak emphasizes:

> Cooperation was the principle architect of 4 billion years of evolution. Cooperation built the first bacterial cells, then higher cells, then complex multicolour life and insect superorganisms. Finally cooperation constructed humanity.
>
> (Nowak, 2011:280)

Individualism: sloping away from society

The second CIMENT value is individualism. Growthism is based on a prioritization of the interests of the individual, which potentially tips the social balance away from the interest of the majority. The rights of the individual were first articulated in the seventeenth century by John Locke and closely linked to property ownership. Nevertheless, 'individualism' was still a term of general approbation in 1848, when Charles Dickens made 'looking after number one' the credo of the villainous Fagin's criminal gang in *Oliver Twist*. By the 1880s, however, this value was becoming thoroughly institutionalized, with one of the founders of modern economics, F.Y. Edgeworth, insisting that 'the first principle of economics is that every agent is actuated only by self-interest' (quoted in Bowles and Gintis, 2011:

9). And a century later, Margaret Thatcher's (1987) belief that 'there's no such thing as society, only individual men and individual women' had more or less become official government policy.

Looking after number one means making self-interest the key factor in human development, at a personal and historical level. It can involve putting the enterprising individual on a pedestal, as in Ayn Rand's (1957) novel *Atlas Shrugged*, much loved by free-market economists, in which heroes of 'ethical egoism' and 'rational selfishness' defy the 'looters' and 'moochers' who depend on social welfare. This also means putting responsibility for positive changes to the system on consumers rather than producers. For instance, action on climate change has been held back by an excessive concentration on individuals reducing their ecological foot-print at the expense of governments taking decisive action.

Extreme self-interest destroys the generosity and concern for others which accompany cooperative acts. It can leads to extreme selfishness and a tendency to blame those in need for their own situation, which can be used to justify almost any kind of unethical behaviour. In fact, the entire concept of morality becomes more or less impossible without a strong element of altruism.

For the individualist, the group is often seen as a threat. Of course, groups can be oppressive and some forms of collectivism can vitiate indi-vidual freedom, but individualism is not the same as individuality. In order to develop as an individual you have to be able to trust others and open yourself up to different social influences. This can help you to move from looking after number one to looking out for the other eight billion people on this planet.

Materialism: the rule of things

Materialism is the third CIMENT value and it follows inevitably from the prioritization of economic growth above all other goals. This distinctly modern belief in the positive value of material possessions frames many of the unwritten rules of growthism. It's in the rule of money that encour-ages you to see yourself in terms of what you earn: the more you earn, the more you are. It's in the rule of consumerism which dictates that you are what you buy. Through advertising, the possibility of consumption is per-manently with us, and shopping is presented not as a transactional way of meeting subsistence needs but as a transformative act of self-fulfilment. Another materialist rule states that quantity is superior to quality. Bigger is better, regardless of what it involves. The creed of 'productivsim' states that the more you produce, the more the economy will prosper, even if what you are producing has no real value or is actually causing harm (Latouche, 2009).

For growthism, the rule of ownership means you are what you possess. And what can be possessed increases all the time: land, buildings and treasure have long existed, but now there are new forms of property, such as securities, bonds, financial investments of bewildering complexity and all manner of collectibles from wine to antique cars, and, potentially most lucrative of all, intellectual property, such as patents and copyright. In the age of aggressive possessiveness, what any individual can have is unrestricted: the world's rich list has no upper limit. For the Buddhist, the possession of things is the sin that prevents any possibility of achieving the good life, but growthism is based on the assertion that wealth is a source of liberation rather than a prison. And what the wealthy have they hold, aided by a legal systems which tend to confirm the adage that 'possession is nine tenths of the law', another clear indication of why the sloping world is so hard to correct.

Elitism: the rule of the minority

The next value in the growthist ethos, elitism, is one that has been around throughout the Holocene. Minority-ruled hierarchy remains a stubborn reality today. In the past, elites were justified by divine ordinance, as in the medieval great chain of being which descended from God to the monarch, down through the predestined ranks of humanity to the lower orders of nature. Now instead of God, we have fame, capital or celebrity – or even the vestigial remains of feudalism such as the British monarchy – but the pyramidal shape of society still looks strangely similar, even if not everybody knows their place as precisely as they were once expected to. Elites are as effective as ever at incorporating would be opponents, seducing them with titles, awards, qualifications and marks of social status that bring minor increments of power and prestige.

Right-wing populists are trying to reverse the equalizing, socially levelling processes that have occurred recently and return to traditional Holocene hierarchies, usually ones which tend to put white, male heterosexuals at the top of the heap. And many states in the world do not even pay lip service to equality, criminalizing LGBTQ relationships and granting sharply differential rights to men and women and to members of different ethnic groups.

The growing economic gap between the richest and the poorest can make elitism seem like the natural order of things. This myth is also reinforced by the popular view of history as the creation of kings, queens and emperors, and by the top-down organization of political parties and the hierarchical structures which dominate many workplaces.

Nationalism: heading in the wrong direction

The fifth CIMENT value is another hard-to-eradicate set of beliefs which derives from the nation state. The Anthropocene reveals that the most crucial borders on this planet are not national but natural. There are no frontiers, flags or custom posts in the stratosphere: whichever national jurisdiction greenhouse gas comes from, its potentially calamitous effects will be felt across the planet. Yet precisely when history cries out for a new era of internationalism and cross-border collaboration, nationalism is remerging as a global force, as a simplistic set of solutions to problems that are more complex than ever before.

Nationalism is another form of zero-sum thinking, which narrows rather than widens, reinforcing the competitivism which sees conflict between nations as the norm. As a personal value, it needs enemies to subjugate – symbolically or actually – in order to fully express itself. This makes it easy to exploit by unscrupulous politicians for their own purposes, stoking up anxiety about foreigners, often among people who have little actual contact with them. Nationalist beliefs tend to correlate very highly with anti-foreigner prejudices and what psychologists call 'collective narcissism', a form of extreme exceptionalism in which a person's nationality gives them a unique status (for some this may be all that they feel they have left). According to one study, predictors of xenophobia were the biggest factors explaining the Brexit vote in the 2016 British EU referendum, far more than other demographic factors such as age, region or educational attainment (De Zavela *et al.*, 2017).

Nationalism should not to be confused with patriotism or regionalism. Familiarity with, and fondness for, the places, people and culture you grew up with can be a source of positive change, but elevating the nation above all other values can put global progress into reverse.

Technologism: conquering nature

The final value in growthism's unbalanced value system is technologism, the myth that all human progress can be equated to the progress of technology. It involves an uncritical reverence for new technology which borders on blind faith. Whereas the very existence of the Anthropocene is an indication that we need to moderate our impact on nature, fully fledged technologism wants to dominate nature and even conquer it altogether. As we've seen, for transhumanists, this battlefield logic goes so far as to envisage the complete transcendence of human biology.

Compared to this, the worldwide consumerist religion of gadgets, celebrated in rituals such as queuing overnight for the new iPhone, seems harmless enough, but the view that technology is the solution to everything, even if it is not a problem (Morozow, 2013), is one of the biggest dangers we face. The breezy confidence of today's techno-optimists might make even Voltaire's Pangloss blush. One of them claims that 'the twenty-first century will be a magnificent time to be alive', as the 'flame of innovation' ensures that

> prosperity spreads, technology progresses, poverty declines, disease retreats, fecundity falls, happiness increases, violence atrophies,

freedom grows, knowledge flourishes, the environment improves and wilderness expands.

(Ridley, 2010:359)

In fact, the author of this declaration, Matt Ridley, has already made a significant contribution to the mismanagement of our current world system, as chairman of Northern Rock, the former building society whose calamitous collapse marked the beginning of the 2007/8 financial crash.

But Ridley is far from being unique in his zeal for technological change, whatever the consequences. Computer science dean Andrew Moore states, 'many of us believe there's a moral imperative to get the technologies out there. I find it offensive to deliberately hold back from this' (quoted in Waters, 2017). This idea of technologism as an ethical duty (which suggests that attempts to regulate technology amount to acts of gross immorality) is another expression of the new morality of growthism. It's why the pursuit of 'disruptive technology' has now become the stated aim of many governments and the core strategy of some of the world's biggest companies. But 'disruption' is what it says: its synonyms include 'separation', 'splitting' and 'severance'. What technologism separates, splits and severs us from is not explained: it could well be jobs, privacy, democracy or the viability of parts of our planet as human habitats. For growthism the fourth industrial revolution is the ultimate glamour project and the next phase in the competitivist's battlefield mission to conquer nature. What happens after that is rarely discussed, perhaps because it's completely unknowable. All of this makes technologism a shockingly poor basis for managing the unprecedented challenges which we face in the Anthropocene.

Who's in charge of the growthist world plan?

The global elite

So who is behind these values and this deeply irrational world plan? The answer is two groups: one is very large, one is very small, and we'll start with the latter, for it actively executes our world plan. We can call it the global elite, the leadership class, the CEO society: many definitions exist for this aggregation of people in positions of power in our world. They are the super-rich investors, the leaders in the political and commercial spheres, the bureaucracy and the media who shape and make the key decisions which structure our world, now and in the future. Some of these decisions are made openly, in full public view, some much more secretly in the world's boardrooms, penthouses and governments chambers. I've some familiarity with this leadership class, having spent many years trying to help them improve their choice-making. So it's not with any pleasure that I say that this group is more responsible than anyone else for the mismanagement of our current world system, although, naturally, they wouldn't see themselves in these terms.

The Occupy movement shocked the world by showing how unrepresentative this elite is, when it popularized the phrase 'the One Percent', a miniscule percentage of the world's population, which works out as about 75 million people (in 2018). This number would certainly account for the world's 2,200 or so billionaires, its many centi-millionaires (worth $100 million or more) and 42 million millionaires, as well as all our governmental, corporate, financial and administrative leaders, plus a significant chunk of the developed world's upper income earners (Credit Suisse, 2018). But is the global elite even smaller? After all, 0.1% of the global population, 7.5 million people, would easily accommodate all the world's super-rich and their families, the senior managers of the world's largest 100,000 companies and every high-ranking politician, civil servant and mover and shaker on the planet.

However, even this tiny fraction of humanity is far too inclusive for *Forbes* (2015) the in-house magazine of the super-rich, which declaims,

> Forget about the 1%. The men and women who are featured on Forbes annual ranking of the world's most powerful people are the 0.00000001% – the global elite whose actions move the planet.

The writer here may have got slightly carried away with his decimal points but the group of 75 'planet movers' he describes is plausible enough. Sixty per cent of the group consists of corporate multibillionaires and most of the remainder are politicians, split more or less equally between leaders of democratic countries and authoritarian regimes, plus some central bankers and the pope.

However you define the global elite, one thing about it is absolutely indisputable: the vast majority of humanity is excluded from it. Whether you define that majority as 90% of the world's population or 99% or 99.9999999%, the message is the same. A tiny proportion of the billions of people alive today are making the decisions which determine not only our present but our futures and those of our children and grandchildren. These decisions include choices affecting climate change, which over the past 150 years have been made by a handful of leaders. Richard Heede (2014) suggests that just 90 investor- and state-owned corporations are responsible for almost two-thirds of the carbon dioxide and methane emissions produced over the period 1854–2011. The small group of executives running these organizations could have made different executive decisions in the past – and they still can – but they chose to follow the path of infinite economic growth.

I'm not suggesting that all leaders making decision are incapable of acting for the common good. There are many splits within the leadership elite, as the bitter battles around Brexit and the Trump presidency show.

Just how progressive-minded leaders will act in the coming decades will be a crucial factor in determining humanity's fate. However, when push comes to shove, the attraction of defending your own immediate interests, including those of your family and friends, is very powerful. This is especially true when you live and work in a cocooned, privileged environment, increasingly remote from the lives of ordinary people, in a moral and cultural atmosphere saturated in competitivism, materialism and elitism. Many members of the global elite have grown up in environments entirely shaped by wealth, which as, we'll see in Chapter 4, powerfully stimulates self-interest and weakens altruistic decision-making.

We also have to realize that many decisions made at the top of organizations are often not in the personal gift of executives. For all the swagger and pomposity of the leadership class, the core principle of growthism is an impersonal force which can transcend individual agency, In fact, the number one value of growth capitalism is capital itself. It may sound boringly mundane but the real engine of the modern world is ROI, the 'return on investments' which shareholders gain. ROI is the invisible king reigning over our world plan. It's the law by which business live and die, which increasingly overrides the interests of employees, customers, citizens and other stakeholders. The clue is in the name. Capitalism was once a term of criticism, even abuse; now it's a proud boast, used by the leaders who ardently promote it. After all, it's not called 'welfare-ism' or 'poverty-reduction-ism' or 'mass-education-ism' (although it can sometimes advance these causes).

Since the 1980s, growthism has stealthily taken capitalism back to basics, towards the late nineteenth century, when the sloping world was at its steepest. Then industrialists' pursuit of profit was rarely inhibited by considerations about the wellbeing of their workers, and globalists (then called imperialists) could occupy almost any country with scant regard for international law (which was on their side anyway). This is the 'liberalism' revered by neoliberal economists, who through their policies of privatization, reductions in public spending and massive tax cuts for the wealthy, have helped to reverse the relative economic equalization of the post-war period.

This economic reassertion of the number-one value of capitalism, combined with the insidious ubiquity of the CIMENT ethos, bathes the growthist elite in a glowing light. Not only do they have wealth – and all the supposed benefits this exposes them to – but they can claim that they deserve this because they are the fittest competitors and the best exemplars of individualist self-development and morality. As for technologism, this designates the elite as the new subjects of history, marching under the banner of market freedom. Who did Schumpeter anoint as the heroes of creative destruction, engaged in the constant process of innovation which prevents the current world systems from collapsing? You guessed it. It was the entrepreneurial class, made up of business executives, technologists and politicians and the investors who back them, pursuing the chimera of perpetual economic growth with undying fidelity.

The mass conspiracy: us

Growthism is not only about this small group, however. Even if the number one rule of capitalism can sometimes seem like an almost impersonal process, there has to be a much larger group making it possible. It's us. Unless a considerable portion of the world's population shared many of the goals and values that prioritize economic growth, our current world plan would collapse. Growthism not only requires the active, public participation of hundreds of millions of men and women, it also needs their private consent. The true cunning of growthism lies in its ability to persuade the majority – at least the majority in the global North – that infinite economic growth is possible and in our interest. (I readily confess that it persuaded me for some of my adult life.) Across almost the entire political spectrum, it seems that the only cure for the ills of our world is to boost our national GDP, increase our personal wealth and speed up the rate of technological development. If only everybody could be richer, life would so much better, even if that means working even harder. For most people, the only valid political question seems to be how to distribute this increased wealth.

Add to the reasons I've already given for why growthism is so seductive, its ability to create an apparently insatiable appetite for novelty. This is creative destruction as an everyday reality, an endless fascination for new things, new products, new lifestyles, gadgets, body shapes, fashions and ideas. What is new today is old tomorrow, a constant shape-shifting which continuously changes our perception of reality. The cycle of novelty is a moving walkway that obliterates all fixed points and keeps us entranced by the spectacle of moving forward. It's a powerful distraction which prevents us from realizing that many things are not getting better, they are only becoming different, and often not in a good way.

If the magic pie of economic growth stops expanding infinitely, so does the prospect of our slice getting a bit bigger. If this happened, we'd become less tolerant of those who already have such a large slice of the pie that it's impossible for them to ever eat it all. This realization would be terminal for growthism. That's why we need to be persuaded that there is always something new and wonderful just around the next corner. The future is all we have left, it seems, and ever onwards is our only choice.

Greed and fear

The philosophy of the new opens us up to the philosophy of more. The material gain offered by growthism is its most obvious and visceral source of attraction, which is stoked by continuous advertising and the

360-degree, wrap-around environment of marketing and popular culture. It's an all-encompassing way of being that is brilliantly captured in Gordon Gekko's famous 'greed is good' speech in Oliver Stone's film *Wall Street* (Stone, 1987). The specific context of the speech is highly significant – Gekko is trying to persuade a group of shareholders to betray their old-fashioned beliefs in stakeholder value – but it's best known for the idea that greed should no longer be seen as a sin but embraced as a virtue, indeed the primary human virtue:

> Greed is right, it works. It clarifies, cuts through and captures the essence of the evolutionary spirit. Greed in all forms; greed for life, for money, for love, knowledge has marked the upward surge of mankind.

It's hard to find a more cogent, succinct summary of growthism than this. In equating material acquisitions with human evolution, it unites the conquistadores with the financial masters of the universe. Growthism, it proclaims, is about having not only more money but more of everything that is good and valuable in life. Gekko's promise of a nirvana of improvement expresses itself in a crescendo of rhetoric which expresses the vertiginous quality of ever-increasing gain. Who among us can be entirely immune to this? And yet we know where it leads. The ancient Greeks called it hubris, pride before a fall, Christopher Marlow depicted Dr Faustus selling his soul to the devil and Jean Paul Sartre (1956) called the human desire to be God a tragic, 'futile passion'. Even Gordon Gekko ends up in jail for fraudulent financial misconduct (he's a fictional character, after all).

However, there is another even more powerful reason why growthism continues to grip so many of us. At times, the carrot may look illusory, but the stick is all too real. Growthism is about not only gain but loss, which psychological research shows we are acutely sensitive to at a pre-reflective, bodily level (Damasio, 1994). Interfering with economic growth portends the most basic losses we can imagine – the loss of our income, our jobs, our ability to support ourselves and our families. This sword of Damocles hangs above the head of every adult alive today – and children often become aware of it at a painfully early age. If growth capitalism fails, the immediate consequences would seem to be dire. Even the most seemingly irrational thinking is driven by this logic, the true rationality behind the growthist irrationale.

It goes some way to explaining why we consent to growthism, whatever our conscious doubts. American novelist Upton Sinclair put his finger on it when he said: 'It is difficult to get a man to understand something his salary depends on his not understanding' (1935: 109). Fear can make us reluctant to voice criticisms against our employers – real or potential – because of the effect this might have on our subsistence prospects. (And, again, this is something I can easily identify with). It can penetrate deeper, at a prereflective level of consciousness, destroying potentially rebellious ideas at source, so they never even surface. This can lead individuals to make moral choices they never thought they'd make or politicians to support industries they disapprove of, such as oil or tobacco or defence, on the basis that they protect jobs. The lesser evil can easily become the major criterion of our choices, eviscerating the possibility of the greater good. Alternatives start to look like versions of each other, all complicit in varying degrees with growthism, which condemns well-meant efforts at reform to failure. Greed and fear can make conspirators of us all.

Conclusion

Our current world plan reveals why we are recklessly failing to manage the Anthropocene crisis. The plan is based on the frankly crazy goal of unlimited economic expansion on a limited planet. This is unleashing an uncontrollable torrent of creative destruction, which makes it impossible to manage the planet in the interests of humanity as a whole. We are failing to see this because growthism is so ubiquitous, popping up in the most unexpected places, especially our unconscious thoughts and feelings where a bad-cop/good-cop routine of fear and greed can turn us into obedient conformists. It lurks in the CIMENT values based on competition, elitism and materialism which maintain the growthist irrationale. Combined with the weird time dimension of growthism and its mesmerizing stream of novelty, this ethos seems to justify the actions of the minuscule global elite who are making the decisions about the present and the future that matter – with our apparent consent.

Our collective inattentional blindness to what is happening in our world is largely due to the success of growth capitalism in effectively colonizing the primary institutions of the modern world. So let's now examine our current economic, business and political systems and see what more they can tell us about what stands in the way of a utopian future.

3 What keeps the system going?
The economics, business and politics of growthism

The key to the survival of the 'mad' growthist world plan is its ability to translate values into social institutions and to bind these institutions together in a mutually reinforcing system. In systems theory, a system consists of interactions between 'reinforcement cycles', which on their own will increase exponentially and destroy the system, and 'balancing cycles', which prevent this from happening. In fact, the reinforcement cycle of growthism is so unbalanced that it leads to constant break downs, resulting in the regular economic recessions and depressions that have occurred in Britain almost every decade since the 1850s. But, as we've just seen, the determination of the elite to pursue their material goals and the continued consent given by the majority through their expectations of the future has enabled the growthist system to survive these frequent collapses.

Another crucial factor in this resilience is the claim, contrary to appearances, that growthism actually promotes balance. After all, what better way to disguise a sloping world than to suggest that it's actually the very opposite, a system that constantly levels itself? This fake equilibrium operates throughout the institutions of economics, business and politics that form the foundation of growthism, which I want to examine in this chapter. Unless we understand how these key institutions work, we'll have little chance of developing a viable utopian alternative.

Economics: the balancing of imbalance

Towards the end of the nineteenth century, the heyday of the sloping world, economists set out to turn their ancient discipline into a modern science, along the lines of Newtonian physics. As alternative economist Kate Raworth (2017:130–7) recounts, these intellectual pioneers provided economics with mechanistic metaphors, such as the pendulum and gravity flow, as well as mathematical formulae which only experts could decipher, and, crucially, attempts to define 'the laws of equilibrium'. Later, graphs were created to show the interaction of elements in the system, such as supply and demand (the so-called price pendulum). The key to the model was its supposed ability to correct itself, to achieve a state of perfect balance which would prevent it from collapsing. Sometimes a little tweaking by economists would be needed, perhaps to the money supply or interest rates, but this should be enough to restore a state of equilibrium.

However, the price paid for the construction of this ostensibly scientific model was the rejection of many of the principles of science and the inclusion of numerous untenable assumptions and myths. One-time champion of economy growth theory, Robert Solow realized this early this century, as Raworth (2017:135) explains

> The general equilibrium model, [Solow] pointed out, depends on there being just one single, immortal consumer-worker-owner maximising their utility into an infinite future with perfect foresight and rational expectations, all the while served by perfectly competitive firms.

In this interwoven fantasy, even more drastic omissions were necessary. If a model is to serve a preordained purpose, some things just have to be kept out of it. In the case of modern economics, these absences not only include a realistic description of the human subject and how business markets actually work but nature itself. And recessions and depressions are also outside the scope of the equilibrium model: such massive disturbances to economic equilibrium are simply not supposed to happen. This reinforces the strange sense of time which is integral to the growthist project and explains why economists are so poor at forecasting the future.

As International Monetary Fund researchers Ahir and Loungani (2014) wryly observe, among economic professionals 'the record of failure to predict recessions is virtually unblemished'. Only two of the 60 recessions that occurred worldwide during the 1990s were predicted by economic forecasters a year in advance and even in March 2008 the vast majority of UK economists were predicting annual growth of up to 5% before the September 2008 crash brought about a 5% decrease in GDP. In the past, necromancers, readers of runes and other official diviners guilty of such inefficiency would have been harshly treated, but the extreme myopia of economists as regards the future plays a key role in the current mismanagement of the world and so is not only forgiven but often generously rewarded.

The algorithms of capital

A much better description of the growthist economic system than equilibrium theory is provided by non-profit entrepreneur and commons scholar Peter Barnes, who compares our present economic world order to the software running a computer:

Our current operating system is dominated by three algorithms and one starting condition. The algorithms are (1) maximize return to capital, (2) distribute property income on a per-share basis, and (3) the price of nature equals zero. The starting condition is that the top 5 percent of people own more property than the remaining 95 percent.

(Barnes, 2006:51)

The first algorithm is the instruction which impels our economy on the path of ever greater growth, regardless of the real cost to ourselves and our planet, something I've been referring to as the number one value of capitalism. If managers of major corporations obsess over profit, it's partially because they have a fiduciary duty to do so, and because their jobs and level of remuneration depend on it. If the return on their capital is inefficient, shareholders will take it elsewhere, potentially causing a company's share price to plummet or even go into bankruptcy. 'For all practical purposes', Barnes notes, 'the publicly traded corporation is a slave to its algorithm' (2006:51).

Unlimited private property

The second of Barnes's algorithms of capitalism refers to the high value of private property, which has always been central to growthist materialism. John Locke in his 1689 labour theory of property claimed that as long as you worked and improved land you had a right to it (since, in his view, nature provides little value of its own), an argument which has been used to legitimize almost any form of land appropriation, from Native Americans and many other indigenous peoples. A similar hierarchy of private over public has been used to justify the massive transference of state assets in countries across the world since the 1980s. The distribution of the vast amount of this property to the ruling elite, initially through dividends or other forms of shareholder income, prevents its dilution. The result is an increasingly unequal distribution of all property across the world that probably would have troubled even John Locke, who insisted that 'enough and as good' property should always be made available to others.

Nature as zero

Barnes's third algorithm, the zero value put on nature, is the most extraordinary omission from equilibrium economics and the most disturbing aspect of the growthist world plan. As ecological economist Herman Daly says, mainstream economics only measures the value which human activity adds to natural resources: 'That to which value is added' is regarded as 'inert, undifferentiated, interchangeable and superabundant, very dull stuff indeed' (1996:83). A stable climate, drinkable water, non-renewable resources, the value of undegraded topsoil and unpolluted air – none of these are included in economic accounting. They are technically classified as 'externalities', which can be excluded from the balance sheet. As a result, real resource costs are totally ignored. For instance, if the 10,000 litres of water needed to produce a pair of jeans was priced into the product, accountants might conclude that it was being sold at a loss to its country of origin, not a profit. Whereas classical economists like Adam Smith, David Ricardo and Karl Marx, in different ways, recognized the importance of nature to an economy, the category was expunged from economics at the same time as it was being set up as a 'science'. This conceptual banishment was partially due to the very practical efforts of large-scale landowners like J.P. Morgan to thwart a proposed US land tax, according to Brian Czech's (2013) illuminating account. The balancing of imbalance had started in earnest.

The fallacy of the GDP game

Another type of false equilibrium in the smoke-and-mirrors world of mainstream economics is provided by GDP. Most of us know little about micro-economic theory but everybody knows the rules of the GDP game. The first rule is that the level of GDP reveals the real strength of an economy. When GDP increases this is positive, when it decreases this is negative, and when it decreases below zero for two quarters in a row, this is very negative, because you're in a recession. GDP also tells you where a nation is in the world league table, overriding its population size, geography or any other criteria. The USA is at the top of the GDP league – one reason why it is the model which all growthist nations want to emulate, while the UK is sixth. Going up the league table is good, going down is bad. Simple enough, it seems.

Except that it's almost completely wrong. GDP is a very crude, inaccurate measure of the real strength of an economy because it only measures the amount of money circulating in it. The more crimes, accidents, environmental disasters and corporate malpractice in a nation, the higher its GDP, because they all promote money-based activities, such as insurance pay outs, replacement of damaged property, environmental restoration, consumer compensation, and so on. GDP is blind to the difference between quantity and quality. It makes no distinction between economic goods and economic bads or between what nineteenth-century cultural critic John Ruskin (1860/1985) called wealth and 'illth'. It's as though in a football game the number of fouls you committed were added to your goal tally.

In fact, the lack of balance in GDP is deliberate. It was introduced as an emergency measure in the US and the UK during the Second World War to ensure that food and armament production could be properly managed. In these extreme circumstances, every other aspect of economic life could be legitimately ignored: the war effort took precedence over human wellbeing, environmental integrity and even civil rights. But a bias which was justified in war has no place in peacetime, you might think, except that it's too useful to growthism for it to relinquish it (and anyway for the CIMENT, battlefield mindset, war is permanent).

Once you introduce a more balanced, holistic measurement of economic life, the true shape of the sloping world is revealed. The Happy Planet Index (HPI), for example, which measures life expectancy, wellbeing, inequality and a nation's ecological footprint alongside its economic activity, turns the GDP league table upside down. The UK which is constantly referred to by establishment politicians as 'the sixth richest country in the world' – its GDP league rank – drops to 34th place in the HPI table (NEF, 2018). Even more astonishingly, the USA, the acknowledged world leader in almost everything economic, doesn't even make the top 100 of the 140 countries that the HPI analyses. It's ranked 108th, largely because of its depressingly low scores on equality and ecological sustainability. Top of the HPI list is Costa Rica, which only comes 76th in the GDP league table, and the Scandinavian countries also perform well.

When the first threatens to become last and the last first, you know something is very wrong. Holistic measures of economics – and there are several of them which have been extensively researched for decades, such as the General Progress Indicator – provide dramatic confirmation of the irrationality of growthism's pursuit of crude material expansion over everything else. Mainstream economists claim that increased efficiency can eliminate the negative impact of economic growth on natural resources, but this 'decoupling theory' has been proved to be another aspect of the GDP myth (Jackson, 2009). From 1990 to 2007, expanding economies in the UK and the USA increased their material footprint by 30%, in Spain and the Netherlands it was 50% (Raworth, 2017). In a business-as-usual scenario, even the most widespread use of green technology would only reduce our current over-consumption of the planet's biomass and minerals to twice sustainable levels by 2050 (Dittrich *et al.*, 2012). Only economic recessions reduce the real drain on natural resources (as in China in 2009), but temporary, unplanned, destructive contractions of this sort are no way to create a more sustainable world.

The truth is that the algorithms of capital lead to a pyrrhic victory, in which the real cost of winning is far higher than the cost of 'defeat', at least when calculated in terms of what matters to most people on this planet. Yet the myth of GDP penetrates every level of economic activity from global macroeconomics to the operation of micro-businesses and dominates our political discourse. It's a confusing, distorting fallacy which, for the time being at least, immensely strengthens growthism's resistance to change.

Running on debt

The myth of GDP also cunningly distracts us from the lack of balance between the value of money and what most people would see as real collateral. In fact, as ecological economist Tim Jackson states, 'the capitalist economy runs on debt' (2009:21). Only 3% of the money in circulation is the stuff you can put in your purse or wallet, the other 97% is debt, largely existing on the spread sheets of commercial banks (which play a much more integral role in public finances than is generally known). If everyone paid off their debts at the same time, banks would collapse. They only hold in reserve about 10% of what they lend out. Growth capitalism is debt capitalism. Its weird sense of time relies on people consistently spending more than they have, mortgaging their future, sacrificing tomorrow for today.

If too many people save rather than spend, an economy becomes stagnant – it's been happening in Japan for decades. The more we are in debt the more we have to earn, so that we can spend more and get further into debt. If we all lived within our means, the entire system would break down. This all goes against a feeling which many people have that debt is wrong, that it's a form of exploitation and even enslavement. 'Neither a borrower or a lender be' Shakespeare's Polonius urged Hamlet (*Hamlet*, I iii 75), but that advice wouldn't get you far today. Recent words for borrowing, such as 'gearing' and 'leveraging', have normalized – and even glamourized – the credit business, enabling it to become a huge global industry in its own right.

In fact, making money out of money has become one of growthism's favourite activities, creating an immensely lucrative sphere which is almost completely severed from the real economy. Elaborate betting – going long or short on equities or currencies, for example – means that huge profits can now be made out of any financial activity, without the bother of actually supplying goods or services to real people. Foreign exchange trading has mushroomed since financial deregulation, increasingly conducted by AI programmes which can arbitrage the minutest currency fluctuations in micro-seconds. In 1975, about 80% of foreign exchange transactions were related to legitimate business functions, such as providing companies with the means to import or export. By 1997, that figure had shrunk to around 2.5%, according to former currency trader Bernard Lietaer (2002), and today the overwhelming majority of FX trades can be described as exchange-rate speculation. And the sums involved are head-spinningly large: as much as $5.1 trillion in daily trades, adding up to some $2 quadrillion a year in 2016 (BIS, 2016). Regular scandals around LIBOR and other exchange rates, along with insider trading and billion-dollar 'rogue trader' frauds have underlined the risks to the entire world economy of making money out of money.

Wellbeing minimized

As we've seen, GDP doesn't measure wellbeing, which is rather convenient for growthism's claims that it promotes ever-increasing progress. In fact, GDP has grown by over 200 times since 1500 but people are hardly 200 times happier than when *Utopia* was first published (Maddison, 2007). And are we even less poor? Poverty reduction is often touted as one of the main justifications for never-ending economic growth, with economists frequently claiming that billions worldwide are being 'lifted out of poverty', to use their quasi-evangelical phrase. However, ecological economists Robert Dietz and Daniel O'Neil (2014:17) suggest that much of the growth in wealth over the past century has simply come from the increase in world population. From 1900 to 2008, global GDP (inflation-indexed) rose from $2 trillion to $51 trillion, a 25-fold increase, but income per capita only increased six-fold. Yet around the world about 2 billion people still live on less than $3.20 a day and 800,000 people on $1.90 a day, according to the World Bank (2018b), in a condition of 'extreme poverty, a condition characterized by severe deprivation of basic human needs' (UN, 1995). Can anyone really have lived on six times less than $3.20 a day, let alone a sixth of $1.90? And are well-paid economists, sitting in front of their computer screens in opulent World Bank or IMF offices, really best placed to define what poverty is?

In fact, Jason Hickel (2017) suggests that a more realistic estimate of the number of people living in extreme poverty could be close to 4 billion, once factors such as the high calorie consumption required by the lowest paid jobs are taken to account. If this staggeringly high figure is the real outcome of 500 years of industrial 'progress', it's unlikely to have impressed the citizens of the late Middle Ages, when the entire human population was 300 million, even if the proportion of them living in poverty may have been higher than today.

Perhaps the best indication of the power of growthism to confuse and distract lies in its hold over supposedly oppositional economic theories. Once your enemy starts speaking the same language as you, you really have won. For example, the pump-priming economics of John Maynard Keynes are often seen as the alternative to neoliberalism, and, to be fair, its focus on redistribution does offer something different. But fundamentally Keynesianism is not an alternative economic theory but a fix for growth capitalism, a temporary balancing cycle to repair a GDP cycle which has gone bust. 'Returning the economy to a condition of consumption growth is the default assumption of Keynesianism', confirms Tim Jackson (2009:118). As I'll suggest in Part III, an economic theory which is capable of bringing about the changes demanded by the Anthropocene has to be based on an ecological paradigm shift much more radical than this.

The myth of *Homo economicus* and the science of selfishness

The complete disregard for human wellbeing displayed by growthist economics is demonstrated by the bizarre portrait of the human subject at its core. *Homo economicus* is a bloodless calculator of personal gain, 'a human robot, a mere production and consumption unit' (Sedlacek, 2011:22), who makes his decisions on the basis of perfect rationality. The very embodiment of the 'rational selfishness' championed by Ayn Rand, this creature has total free will and complete information about his purchases.

Having spent many years working with people to improve their personal and professional choices, I've never come across a decision-maker who vaguely resembles *Homo economicus*. Indeed, if any psychologist encountered someone so obsessed with personal gain at the expense of emotional experience and social relationships, they would probably suspect them of suffering from a personality disorder or even a form of serious brain injury. Indeed, neuroscientific research has shown that emotions play a major role in our everyday choices and that damage to the emotional brain can make functional decision-making impossible (Damasio, 1994). Nor does *Homo economicus* makes any sense in terms of how businesses actually function. Why, for instance, would it be necessary to spend billions on advertising and marketing to persuade consumers if they are going to choose what they want anyway? However, this myth of a consumer endowed with perfect free will does conveniently shift the burden of responsibility away from the seller and on to the buyer: if consumers want to buy polluting cars or pay ruinous interest rates, that's their fault, the argument runs.

In fact, it's more realistic to see *Homo economicus* as a self-portrait of growthist economists themselves, a projection of their inner values on the rest of us. As a plethora of studies have demonstrated, mainstream economics seems to encourage the self-interested materialism, which I've described as part of the CIMENT ethos. In one study, for instance, first-year university students of economics rated values like helpfulness, honesty, loyalty and responsibility much the same as students of other subjects, but by their final year they considered these values far less important (Gandal *et al.*, 2005). Professors of economics give less to charity than professors of other disciplines, and economics students are less likely to engage in cooperative behaviour than other students (Frank *et al.*, 1993). They also have a more positive attitude to greed and the supposed benefits to society of self-interest (Wang *et al.*, 2011:643) and seem to be more open to corruption than is the norm, judging by their willingness in experimental conditions to bribe a tradesperson to give them preferential treatment (Frank and Schulze, 2000). Economics, it seems, has not succeeded in becoming a natural science comparable to Newtonian physics but has developed into the science of selfishness. This is significant, as it's not only the master academic discipline of the growthist plan but central to the business studies and MBA courses which form the education of many of the global elite's corporate and political leaders.

Multinational corporations: the engines of growthism

Another illusory form of balance in neoliberal economic theory comes in the form of the fair competition which the free market is supposed to provide. As we've seen, this requires a strong government to enforce 'the rules of the game', in Milton Friedman's words (1962), something that could only happen if domestic states were far more powerful than neoliberals recommend and closely linked together across the world to prevent nations from undercutting each other on tax regulations (as they do today). As it is, the myth of the free and fair market offers excellent cover for what growthism really thrives on, the growth of monopolies. The main institution of growthism, the globe-straddling multinational corporation, has mushroomed in size and power in order to maximize shareholder value, often with disastrous consequences for the environment and human wellbeing.

Since the early 1980s, neoliberal polices of deregulation, privatization and corporate-tax reduction have turned corporations from sleepy leviathans into giant killer whales, apex predators for whom every other creature is prey. Lax anti-competition regulation has made it easier for cash-rich companies to swallow up upstart competitors, often killing innovation in the process and bringing in huge profits for financiers specializing in M&A (mergers and acquisitions). Big is beautiful for such commercial giants, enabling them to form powerful worldwide oligopolies, which are the complete opposite of fair markets. In almost every commercial sector, from banks, accountancy and energy to seeds, grains and fertilizers, there is a Big Four or a Big Six, pushing up prices to consumers and squeezing suppliers. Notoriously, by the time the economic cycle finally implodes, they may even have made themselves 'too big to fail'.

Privatization has allowed the corporate sector to swallow up huge chunks of what used to be non-profit, public-sector activities, such as administration, security and welfare. Combine this with the selling off of publicly owned infrastructure, natural resources and intellectual property, and it's easy to see why 132 of the world's most valuable companies are former state enterprises (Wilks, 2013). In fact, the biggest corporations are now richer than all but the world's richest countries. Sixty-nine of the 100 largest economic entities on the planet are companies, not states, according to Global Justice Now (2016), with the turnover of the ten biggest corporations exceeding the combined revenues of the world's 'poorest' 180 nations. Fossil-fuel giant ExxonMobil commands revenues greater than those of India and has it own foreign affairs department, enabling its CEO to deal directly with heads of government. In effect, sovereignty has switched from nations to multinationals.

Giant companies only advance the algorithms of capital if they produce gigantic investment returns. And this they have succeeded in doing to an extent which even corporate raiders like Gordon Gekko could not have imagined. Since the 1980s, tax cuts, financial deregulation and innovations such as stock buybacks – where a corporation uses its profits to buy its own shares – have brought about a massive shareholder bonanza. From 2003 to 2012, S&P 500 companies used 54% of their profits in stock buybacks, and another 37% went in shareholder dividends. In other words, only 9% of corporate profits were available for investing in future business development, which is often put forward as the main justification for profit-making (Lazonick, 2014). In 2018 *The Financial Times* reported that US banks were about to pay out more in shareholder payouts than they'd made in annual profits (Gray and McLannahan, 2018). Shareholder greed is now officially good.

How corporations mismanage the world's natural and human resources

What many large corporations actually do to earn their stratospheric shareholder returns is often frankly shocking. They transgress natural boundaries, harm environments, put human health at risk and endanger overall human wellbeing, creating many of the imbalances which are at the core of the Anthropocene crisis. They get away with it because they don't have to rely solely on economic theory or the political system's willingness to forgive corporate scandals: they have another, much blunter weapon: secrecy. One of the main purposes of the huge legal department which a corporation maintains is to keep knowledge of its immoral, anti-social or overtly illegal acts out of the public eye, by silencing whistleblowers and intimidating victims or campaigners working on their behalf in legal processes that can continue for decades. If all else fails, claimants can be bought off with non-disclosure contracts that ensure the public is kept in the dark. Think for example of the numerous out-of-court settlements which prevented *The News of the World* phone-hacking scandal from coming to light for years (Davies, 2014). So the corporate crimes which I mention in what follows are those that slipped through the net, legal department failures, some of which made it all the way to court and resulted in real penalties. As such they probably represent the tip of the iceberg of what really goes on in the corporate world.

When it come to the corporate war against truth, fossil-fuel corporations lead the way. The dangers of anthropogenic climate change only become known to the general public in 1988, when NASA scientist James Hansen presented a stark warning to the White House. But this was not news to the giants of the oil-and-gas industry, including the nation-unto-itself that is ExxonMobil. As environmentalist and writer Bill McKibben (2015) points out:

ExxonMobil, the world's largest and most powerful oil company, knew everything there was to know about climate change by the mid 1980s, and then spent the next few decades systematically funding climate denial and lying about the state of the science.

In fact Exxon executives had been briefed as early as 1977, with remarkable accuracy, that the planet was on course for warming of 2°C, unless carbon emissions decreased dramatically (Banerjee *et al.*, 2015). At this time, Exxon was the largest and most profitable company in the world with immense financial, strategic and marketing resources. A positive, early response to its top-secret scientific evidence could have changed the entire course of planetary history – and helped to avert the Anthropocene crisis. But its reaction was purely in line with the algorithm of capital. It turned its back on the interests of humanity in order to protect the short-term interests of its shareholders. It embarked on a relentless campaign of climate denial, pouring millions of dollars into stealthy, lobbyist operations, some of which tried to cast doubt on the reliability of any form of scientific evidence.

Other fossil-fuel majors also knew about the dangers of global warming from early on. In 1991, Shell actually commissioned a glossy educational film warning about them. Why wouldn't these companies be in the know? Unlike many business people, oil-and-gas executives tend to have scientific backgrounds. They also employ large numbers of geologists and other natural scientists and have close links with academia.

In addition, companies like Shell and BP have long had a reputation for sophisticated strategic planning that looks much further into the future than most commercial operations. Oil exploration has always required patience, with some oil fields necessitating decades of investment before any yields are returned (Yergin, 1991). If anyone has a grip on the future, it's the fossil-fuel companies. But instead of taking the opportunity to lead the world into a new era of renewable energy, oil companies uniformly decided to throw their weight into betting against governments' ability to limit climate change to safe levels. And they're still doing it. Two months after 195 countries signed the Paris Climate Agreement, BP's projection for oil consumption by 2035 implied that the European Union would miss its emissions targets for both 2020 and 2030 (Carbon Brief, 2016). In 2018, as the IPCC announced that the world had just 12 years to reduce its CO_2 emissions in order to avoid a 1.5°C rise in global temperatures, the annual report of the Organization of Petroleum Exporting Countries bullishly predicted a rise in global oil and gas production by 2040 to an all-time high of 112 million barrels a year (OPEC, 2018). The global elite's contempt for the world's public officials and elected representatives couldn't be more clearly illustrated.

As far as the attrition of nature is concerned, the destructive role played by business enterprises is inseparable from the long history of industrialization. Over the centuries, most environmental crimes have gone unpunished but one remarkable sequence of violations by General Electric (GE), once the largest and most prestigious company in the world, gives us a flavour of the damage done to nature by big business. Between 1990 and 2001, GE's publicly acknowledged legal breaches included:

- contamination of soil and groundwater in South Carolina
- pollution at Silicone Products plants in New York
- dumping of industrial chemicals in California
- contamination of sediment in the Hudson River
- air pollution in New York
- contamination of groundwater and the public water supply in New Hampshire
- asbestos use and related pollution in the UK
- PCP pollution in the Housatonic River

Other violations over this period by GE included money laundering, the illegal sale of fighter jets, overcharging on defence contracts, unfair debt collection, design flaws at nuclear plants and discrimination against workers reporting safety issues. (For the astonishing full list see Joel Bakan's *The Corporation* (2004:75–9)). All this occurred during the 'legendary' stewardship of CEO and chairman Jack Welch, under whom GE's market value swelled 40-fold, and who after his retirement became a major figure in leadership consultancy.

Corporations versus human health

The assault of transnational corporations on our mental and physical health is another astonishing feature of growthism. Take tobacco companies, which from the 1950s onwards were faced with the prospect of commercial extinction, so firm was the scientific evidence linking smoking to lung cancer and other life-threatening diseases. We now know that cigarettes cause at least 25 diseases and kill 50% of their users (Oreskes and Conway, 2010.) Yet today there are more smokers than ever, over a billion of them, and tobacco revenues have increased by more than a quarter this century to $700 billion (Tobaccofreekids, 2018). Tobacco corporations have protected their shareholders' investments by aggressively investing in science denial, fighting anti-smoking legislation and exploiting emerging markets where little or no such legislation exists. Above all, they've focused relentlessly on attracting young smokers, who, once addicted, find it particularly hard to give up and without whom the industry has no long-term future. The result, according to one estimate, is that tobacco will kill 1 billion people this century, to add to the nicotine death toll of 100 million in the twentieth century (Jha, 2009).

This preventable harm to health is now joined by a newer threat, the obesity epidemic sweeping the world. Worldwide, a staggering 1.9 billion people are now overweight and 650 million of them are obese, a three-fold increase since 1975 (WHO, 2018a). Obesity is the ultimate product of the growthist irrationale. Only a system determined to put profit before people could engineer a new source of life-threatening diseases such as diabetes, heart disease and cancer. Some gains have been made in reducing the evils of poverty, but here is a new one: malnourishment caused by excess. In fact, according to the World Health Organization, in most countries you're now more likely to die from being overweight than being underweight. Addictive high-fat, high-sugar, high-salt diets now blight poor countries as well as wealthy ones and are having a devastating effect on healthcare.

Obesity particularly affects children, with 41 million children under 5 now overweight or obese, a situation they cannot be expected to have any personal control over. This is a terrible tragedy going on right under our noses, because overeating is an extremely difficult habit to throw off in later life. Research published in *The Lancet* (Ochner *et al.*, 2015) suggests that obesity may cause biological adaptations, which lead the body to permanently interpret reduced eating as a starvation threat.

Eating and drinking more healthy products is one obvious solution to the global obesity crisis, but that's not a course of action favoured by the multi-trillion-dollar food-and-beverage industry. As medical doctor Deborah Cohen (2007) notes:

> [The food industry] spends billions of dollars each year to develop products, packaging, advertising and marketing techniques that entice us to buy more food because selling more food means making more profits.... Food marketers test whether the color, the font size of words and the images used to market food will grab our attention by studies of eye movement.

Cynically, food-and-drink corporations also spend billions sponsoring sporting events such as the Olympics and the FIFA World Cup to promote a healthy image for unhealthy products. Even more disturbing are the actual changes to the structure of what we are eating, as food production and farming become increasingly industrialized. 'Ultra-processed' food (of which the UK is Europe's largest consumer) is low in nutritional content but high in chemical additives designed to increase addictiveness. According to professor of nutrition, Jean-Claude Moubarec, the aim is no longer to simply make food and drink that people like: 'It is beyond liking. We are entering the world of craving' (Bosely, 2018). Meanwhile, we see supermarkets act like 'control freaks', dominating the food-and-drink supply chain, often squeezing small farms out of business and encouraging poorer countries to depend on single crops (Simms, 2007). Genetically modified seeds, licensed to farmers annually, reduce the usefulness of local knowledge and the seed diversity which is the best protection against variable weather. All this gives even more power to large food and agriculture oligopolies, ruthlessly concentrating all food production on the needs of the richest parts of the world, with potentially disastrous consequences for the global South.

Addiction capitalism is not confined to narcotics and food and drink. It's busting out all over, as turning consumers into addicts becomes a central strategy of the growthist irrationale. As a result of deregulation, gambling, which used to be a marginal activity, has become a major business and, on fast-expanding online platforms registered in tax havens, virtually impossibly to regulate. Fixed-odds betting terminals are programmed to exploit a player's vulnerabilities and advertising relentlessly hounds problem gamblers. Hardcore pornography, once only available underground, has now gone mainstream, available gratis on any smartphone. This is changing the sexual attitudes of some younger people, often encouraging sexism, misogyny and unreal expectations of sex that will possibly pave the way for the widespread use of sex robots.

Meanwhile, social media is turning people's desire for social connection and approval into a highly profitable addiction. As the co-founder of Facebook, Sean Parker, has admitted, the site's 'like' function was designed to exploit 'a vulnerability in human psychology' by proving regular 'dopamine hits': adding, 'God only knows what it's doing to our children's brains' (Allen, 2018). Video-game designers are also increasingly using AI to hook players. No wonder that the WHO has now identified 'gaming disorder' as a public health hazard and the NHS has opened its first internet addiction clinic (Bridge, 2018).

We could look at almost any industry and see this unheeding, self-interested disregard for mental and physical health, but let's focus on the automotive industry, responsible for the production of the 1.2 billion motor vehicles with which we currently share this planet. Like oil corporations, car-makers could have made much greater efforts to combat climate change and reduce the air pollution which causes millions of premature deaths every year. Electric alternatives to the internal combustion engine have been available since the late nineteenth century. As recently as 2000, General Motors stopped production of its popular EV1 electric vehicle in California, after auto industry pressure forced the state to drop its zero-emissions mandate, a scandal vividly described in Chris Paine's documentary, *Who Killed the Electric Car?* (2006). Far from being proactive about protecting the planet and human health, we know now that car-makers have unscrupulously cheated existing regulations. Notoriously, Volkswagen has so far been fined over $18 billion for creating software which temporarily reduces the toxicity of a diesel car's exhaust emissions once it detects that it is being tested (McGee, 2017). Other major manufacturers are currently under investigation for using similar 'defeat devices'. Another disturbing use of machine intelligence to outwit consumer protection regulations was Uber's Grayball software, which identified possible municipal-standards inspectors posing as ordinary customers, so that Uber drivers knew not to pick them up.

Unfortunately, there's nothing new about big corporations using their own sophisticated technology to cheat regulators, abuse customers and illegally promote their own business interests. Economist Joseph Stiglitz (2012:57). describes one of the underhand ways that Microsoft in the 1990s contrived to crush Netscape, a popular, technically superior, non-profit rival to its Internet Express web browser:

> [Microsoft] deployed a strategy known as FUD (fear, uncertainty and doubt) creating anxiety about compatibility among users by program-ming error messages that would randomly appear if Netscape was installed on a Windows computer.

Over the past two decades Microsoft has also engaged in similar cam-paigns to destroy DR-DOS, Word Perfect, Java, rival media players and operating systems in ways that have directly and indirectly harmed con-sumers interests, according to the non-profit ICT-industry association ECIS (2009). The company has been fined billions of euros by the Euro-pean Union for anti-trust offenses, including failing to pay previous fines, but this is a small price to pay for the monopolistic market posi-tions it has gained by them. Newer Big Tech corporations are revealing a similarly single-minded ruthlessness, exploiting the non-profit, counter-culture ethos which founded the internet to make vast personal fortunes. For instance, under the banner of 'bringing people together' and making the world a better place, the billionaires of Facebook have sold the personal information of millions of unsuspecting users to third parties, enabling advertisers to develop algorithms that can covertly predict consumers' preferences. So far, the company's CEO, Mark Zuck-erberg, has been forced to acknowledge 'a major breach of trust' in at least one case of illegal data mining (AP, 2018).

Free-market economics is supposed to be about maximizing citizens' choices, but in reality it has enabled big business to wage a war against choice. Corporations seem to do everything they can to prevent citizens from making real, free, informed decisions about what they want to buy and the consequences of doing so. Indeed, Big Data is now being used to undermine the biggest of all exercises in collective choice-making, general elections. Cyber technology and psychometrically designed mes-sages which target individual voters, often based on illegally harvested data, are being used to subvert the most basic democratic processes (Cadwalladr, 2017). It's a disturbing development but only the latest in a long-standing campaign by big business to tilt the political system in its own favour.

Democracy under growthism: the slanted political system

The danger of a political minority dominating the majority goes back at least as far as ancient Athens. As Aristotle shrewdly observed, 'in democracies all share in all things, in oligarchies the opposite practice prevails' (*Politics* VII 9). The modern pendulum theory of democracy suggests that there is a constant alteration between alternatives chosen by the electorate and constitutions have built-in 'checks and balances' designed to prevent the oligarchy – or, as we might call them now, the plutocracy – from gaining hegemony. But growthist elites have become increasingly effective at reducing the span of the policy pendulum and bypassing all checks and balances; so much so that that the majority is in danger of being shut out of its own political system.

In fact, the 'post-democracy' phenomenon, which I referred to in Chapter 1, tends to marginalize any area of political and public life which challenges growthist goals and values. Government departments, representing a huge variety of different social sectors and interests, from school and universities to healthcare and farming, have become secondary to the needs of a single ministry, the Treasury. A political manifesto is increasingly nothing more than an exercise in costing. The civil service, which was once considered an impartial, public policy-making alternative to the private sector, is now seen as a pale imitation of it, sharing the same results-driven culture but not its sense of purpose. The 'revolving door' between the civil service and corporations ensures that business executives are present in every major government department. Google has made some 80 revolving-door moves in Europe over the past decade and has over 250 public appointments of this kind in the USA, helping them to influence upcoming legislation, specifically regulation relating to new technology, and reducing the amount of tax they have to pay (CfA, 2016). Aggressive, lavishly funded political lobbying provides a similar corporate service, in addition to much needed employment for out-of-work politicians.

The inauguration of Donald Trump as US president in January 2017 ripped the mask off what remained of this relatively discreet connection between business and government. It's as if the super-rich have grown weary of delegating the economy to accommodating politicians and have decided to take direct control of it themselves. The initial Trump cabinet was unashamedly elitist, largely consisting of corporate CEOs, wealthy investors and Wall Street financiers (especially from investment bank Goldman Sachs, colloquially known as 'Government Sachs'). The net wealth of this cabinet of plutocrats has been estimated as between $3.5 billion and $14.5 billion, considerably greater than that of the poorest third of the American population (Politifact, 2017). In 2018, this group duly delivered the biggest tax cuts to corporations and upper-rate tax payers since the Reagan era. History's capacity to surprise may seem to have surpassed itself with Trump's presidency, but it only confirmed the increasing intolerance of growth economics to anything that impedes the working of the algorithms of capital. This can be seen more subtly in the practice of British minsters taking up lucrative consultancies on leaving public office or more bluntly, and even brutally, in the inseparable intertwining of politicians and oligarchs in Putin's Russia.

Attempts to rebalance the Anglo-American system in favour of the majority are often thwarted by the political establishment itself. Proportional representation or other electoral reforms which would reduce the monopoly power of the two parties are rejected, as are calls to extend the franchise to voters under 18 years old or create more direct democracy through referendums or electronic voting. The 'first past the post', 'winner takes all' system suits growthism's preference for competition over cooperation. It maintains political parties as ideological 'broad churches', encompassing many distinct and opposing political positions, which means that the real decision-making is made behind closed doors, often though feuding and infighting among party leaders. This maximizes the influences of private donors who subsidise the party system and the wealthy owners of the overtly political press and media.

Party membership, which has shrunk hugely since its post-war heyday, also provides another form of influence, in the case of the Conservative Party one tilted towards a wealthy, ageing minority. This makes a 'pro-business' agenda a *sine qua non* for electoral success, even for the British Labour Party and US Democrats, ensuring what Colin Crouch called 'the maximum amount of minimal variation' (2004:112). So far, any attempts to offer programmes which don't assume economic growth, and focus on pro-people or pro-planet manifestos have failed to loosen the establishment's hold on power. This pro-business, circular logic ensures that whichever party gets elected, the algorithm of capital will be served.

The voter reaction: more democracy or less?

The reaction of many members of the public to this sealed system only seals the system further. Instead of creating a new balancing cycle, voter apathy reinforces the status quo. The whole idea of political choice-making is undermined, as voters stop trusting politicians or giving any credence to what they say. In a recent 'veracity poll', in which the public is asked how much they trust various occupations to tell the truth, politicians scored a miserly 17%, whereas nurses, doctors, teachers and scientists all scored above 80%. Interestingly, at 64%, 'the ordinary man or woman in the street' is trusted almost four times more than politicians and considerably more than bankers and business leaders (Ipsos MORI, 2017).

A consequence of this failure of trust is that many citizens are, in effect, disenfranchising themselves. Whereas in the four UK elections of the 1970s voter turnout averaged 75% (with a high of almost 80%), the four elections between 2003 and 2015 averaged just 63% (with a low of 61%). In the USA, the figures are even more dismal, with only 56% voting in the 2016 election (and a recent low of 49% in 1996). At a local level the alienation is even worse, with only a third of British voters generally turning out to vote in council elections. The growing influence of older UK voters – for example, in tipping the balance in favour of leaving the EU in 2016 – is another problematic aspect of democracy today. It's also another symptom of plutocracy, since older people are now the wealthiest cohort in the population.

But the crisis of twenty-first-century democracy goes much further than the indifference of the 'unheard third'. Some young adults are turning against the very idea of democracy. In the USA, only 30% of millennials (born since 1980) now state that 'it is essential to live in a democracy' (compared to 72% of those born before the Second World War). Almost a quarter of young Americans now say democracy is 'a bad' or 'very bad way to run the country'. In fact, almost a third of all Americans said that it would be better to have 'a strong leader who does not have to bother with parliament and elections' (Foa and Munk, 2016:13). This trend of rejecting democracy is not quite as strong in Europe, although the recent rise in right-wing populism and anti-immigrant authoritarianism suggests it could be catching up fast.

All this indicates that a major correction to the current political system could be on its way. The prime question is: will it reinforce growthism or break free of it? For some the dysfunctions of democracy prove that a wholly new paradigm is needed, which can deliver genuine participation and liberation from the power of the wealthy, ideas which we'll explore further in Part III. For others, however, it could mean abandoning even the pretence of democracy, severing the connection between expanding capitalist economies and advances in democracy, which the neoliberal, 'end of history' model saw as inseparably linked. This decoupling is likely to be accompanied by explosive increases in authoritarian irrationality, as the lowest forms of prejudice are preferred to evidence, raw emotions elevated above informed decision-making and vast waves of fake news discredit the very notion of truth. This reaction to the crisis of democracy is already gaining force across the world: time will tell how long we'll have to wait before the pro-democratic response has its turn.

Conclusion

The linking of economics, big business and the political system into an apparently impenetrable, seamless institutional process is central to the current world plan. It provides growthism with one of its greatest assets, the ability to present itself as a rational system of balance, when it manifestly operates as the opposite, in the short term as well as the long term. The perfect crime, after all, is the one that nobody knows has been committed. The epochal significance of the Anthropocene is obscured behind the recklessly irrational need to continue doing business as usual. But however smoothly impersonal this ingenious institutional process seems to have become, we need to remember that it can only function because people persist in giving their consent to it. I've suggested that the CIMENT values can help us understand the mindset underlying the 'madness' of growthism but let's now turn to some even more startling evidence about the psychological and cultural factors that can turn the algorithm of capital into a compulsive, everyday reality.

4   The wealth fallacy
The psychology and culture of growthism

At the centre of the growthist world plan is a very simple assumption about wealth. Contrary to the New Testament's assertion that 'love of money is the root of all evil', growthism claims it's the root of most virtues. The belief that wealth makes you better is the tacit justification of the pursuit of economic growth and the assent which so many give to this. This betterment is supposed to come not only in the form of the satisfaction of material needs but through greater happiness and wellbeing. The assumption that those who have wealth are morally superior to the poor is the most direct challenge to the Christian contempt for money, shared by many religions (Islam, for example, still bans usury) and the utopian tradition (Thomas More ridiculed gold by declaring it was only fit for making chamber pots). But wealth creation is not simply tolerated by modern society, it's the main goal of it, and 'wealth creators', a new term for the business and investor elite, are its true heroes. This minority are seen to be most fit to exercise leadership of society and make the highly consequential decisions which shape our future.

But what if the age-old religious suspicion of wealth was right? What if instead of making you happier, wiser and more moral, wealth has the very opposite effect? It would pull away the entire foundation of the modern world plan. We'd have to add this wealth fallacy to the other values-reversing tendencies of the growthist irrationale, such as presenting the unequal as equal. But that's exactly what a growing body of social scientific evidence suggests we should do. The positive qualities of wealth are at best limited, and at worst, affluence can lead to selfish, anti-social and unethical behaviour, as well as unhappiness and poor decision-making. In this chapter, we'll explore how the wealth fallacy affects everyday psychology, as well as corporate and popular culture, providing another powerful set of reasons why growthism is leading to the mismanagement of our world.

The psychology of wealth

Wealth doesn't make you happier

As I've already suggested, there is a good deal of evidence that the economic growth which our world plan prioritizes doesn't necessarily lead to growth in personal happiness. In the 1970s, economist Richard Easterlin (1974) established this proposition in what has come to be known as the Easterlin or Life Satisfaction Paradox. He found that in spite of a tripling of GDP in the USA and other developed countries from 1946 and 1970, self-reported levels of happiness had remained static, and even declined somewhat. Later Easterlin and his colleagues (2010) extended this study to emerging economies in Latin America and the former Soviet bloc and found similar results. At low levels of income, a rise in earnings usually increases life satisfaction but, according to economists Eugenio Proto and Aldo Rustichini (2013), once a country's average national income reaches $17,000 rises in happiness are fairly marginal (and at $30,000 life satisfaction actually starts to decline somewhat). In fact, the World Happiness Report 2018 concludes that people are no happier in China than they were 25 years ago, in spite of huge GDP per capita increases. It also finds that in rich countries 'mental illness is the biggest single source of misery' (although war surely comes close) and that most of the variance in happiness across the world occurs within societies (Helliwell *et al.*, 2018). As we've seen, in spite of higher GDP, the economically unequal USA and UK rate considerably lower on wellbeing than Costa Rica and the Scandinavian countries.

One of the reasons for the wealth fallacy is that people with high materialistic values – which include the need for high social and job status and a desire for their appearance to be admired – seem to experience lower levels of wellbeing and psychological health than those who hold non-materialistic values. Summarizing his own work in this field, and that of many other researchers, psychologist Tim Kasser (2002:22) writes:

> The studies document that strong materialist values are associated with a pervasive undermining of people's well-being, from low life satisfaction and happiness, to depression and anxiety, to physical problems such as headaches, and to personality disorders, narcissism, and antisocial behaviour.

In fact, extreme wealth can be profoundly disappointing, leading not to the nirvana that consumerism portrays but to an overwhelming sense of emptiness, dissatisfaction and often to dangerous behaviours and addictions. Leadership coach Manfred Kets de Vries (2014), in a blog post ironically entitled 'Pity the super-rich', describes the condition of 'affluenza' or 'extreme wealth syndrome', as experienced by many wealthy people:

In spite of all their accomplishments and material possessions, they remain bored and deeply unfulfilled. There are very few things that make them really feel alive. Given this sense of void, they may even engage in self-destructive activities.

Extreme wealth can create a miserable bubble of isolation and loneliness, as the lofty position in the hierarchy that elitists long for turns into a kind of prison, locking them out of the best things in life. In a sense, this is the ultimate hubris, the revenge of economic equality on those who reject it, and a clear indication of the utter futility of pursuing wealth as the primary human goal.

Wealth can make you more selfish

A second sustaining assertion of growthism is that wealth can make you ethically superior to others in the sense of promoting considerate, responsible, law-abiding behaviour. This at least would provide some form of moral justification for the economic and power imbalances of the sloping world. But a growing body of evidence suggests that it's simply not true. For instance, one recent observational study in California showed that drivers of upmarket cars are four times more likely to cut up other drivers at a road junction than people driving inexpensive cars. When it came to stopping for a pedestrian at a crossing (as required by Californian law) the results were even more alarming. All the drivers of the least expensive cars yielded to pedestrians, whereas almost half of the drivers of the most expensive vehicles simply ignored them and drove on (Piff *et al.*, 2012).

Several studies show that the poor are more generous than the rich, even though they have far less disposal income. An analysis of UK survey data from the recessionary period of 2010/11 found that the poorest 20% of households gave proportionally three times more of their income to charity than the richest 20%. The most generous ethnic group in the entire survey were people of Pakistani and Bangladesh origin, many of whom are in the country's lowest income bracket (Manchester University, 2013). And it seems the richer you are, the meaner you can become. According to research reported in *The Financial Times*, so-called high-net-worth individuals in the UK, who have £1 million to £10 million in investable assets, give just £500 a year to charitable causes, while the ultra wealthy, who have more than £10 million, give a measly £240 (Ross, 2018). An experimental economic game confirms this tendency for upper-class individuals to act selfishly. In the game, they kept more credits for themselves, shared fewer credits with a stranger and were less trusting than lower-class participants, whose pro-social behaviour was attributed to 'a greater commitment to egalitarian values and feelings of compassion' (Piff *et al.*, 2010).

The tendency for wealth to reduce altruism can also be observed at an international level. Levine and colleagues (2001) gauged the responses of passers-by in 23 major cities around the world to non-emergency situations such as assisting a blind person to cross the road or helping an injured pedestrian. The four countries in which people showed the most help for others were Brazil, Costa Rica, Malawi and India, which, according to the World Bank (2018a), had a per capita income of under $4,000 at the time of study. By contrast, the average income of the least altruistic nations, the USA, Singapore and the Netherlands, was between $21,000 and $37,000 (all in 2001 values).

Wealth breeds unethical and anti-social behaviour

The impact of wealth on people's honesty can also be startling. Paul Piff and his colleagues (2012) found that upper-class individuals are more likely than lower-class individuals to take valuable goods from others, to cheat in order to increase their chances of winning a prize and to endorse unethical behaviour at work. Wealthy participants in this study also displayed a greater proclivity than their poorer counterparts to lie and engage in deceptive, untrustworthy behaviour when involved in a negotiation exercise. In another experimental study, powerful people were found to be more morally hypocritical than powerless people, being more likely to condemn others for cheating but also cheating more themselves (Lammers *et al.*, 2010).

Even more astonishing evidence comes from an experiment which required a group to conduct an anagram task in a room with a table piled high with money, while another group performed exactly the same task in another room but without any visible signs of wealth. The mere presence of money seemed to cause the first group to cheat far more in evaluating their performance than the second group, even though they gained no reward for it. The researchers suggest that the presence of signs of abundant wealth created perceptions of negative inequity, 'which induce feelings of envy that motivate unethical behaviours such as theft and deceptive overstatement of performance' (Gino and Pierce, 2009:142). That the possibility of wealth acquisition produces envy underlines the folly of relying on increased wealth to reduce economic inequality. It even suggests that the worst perpetrators of the 'politics of envy', an argument often used to defend the privileges of the rich, are in fact the rich themselves.

Wealth impairs decision-making

Wealth may not make you happier or more ethical, but surely it increases your ability to make good decisions, so justifying the position of the wealthy at the helm of our world plan. Not according to the evidence. People of high socio-economic status often lack a key leadership skill: empathy. Not only are they less able to recognize other people's suffering than poorer people and exhibit less distress when confronted with evidence of suffering (Van Kleef *et al.*, 2008), they often find it more diffi-cult to put themselves in other people's shoes. In one ingenious study, sub-jects who had been asked to recall situations when they felt powerful were required to write the letter 'E' on their own foreheads. Subjects in a high-power condition tended to perform this task in a way that corresponded to their own perspective. By contrast, low-power participants formed the letter in a way that anticipated other people's point of view, which of course meant that the 'E' was much easier to read (Galinsky *et al.*, 2006).

Powerful people are also weaker than powerless people at forming assessments of what a outgroup thinks of the in-group, in other words, answering the question of 'how do *they* see *us?*' (Lammers *et al.*, 2008). People lacking in social power are better at this kind of perspective switch, in part because they are less prone to 'objectivation' (the tendency to see people as things) than the powerful, (Greenfield *et al.*, 2008). Indeed, the research of Jons Lammers and Diederik Stapel (2010) suggests that the experience or possession of power increases 'dehumanization', which they define as 'the process of denying essential elements of "humanness" in other people and perceiving them as objects or animals'. This can reduce the pain involved in difficult decision-making but it says nothing positive about the quality of these decisions.

Other cognitive deficiencies displayed by the rich and powerful include their greater use of stereotypes when evaluating others, which can bias their impression of subordinates (Goodwin *et al.*, 2000). In some circum-stances, high-status people are also more comfortable with abstract think-ing than people of lower status. For example, government officials describing the aftermath of the 9/11 attacks were far more likely to use abstract terms than volunteers and victims and were particularly poor at differentiating between out-groups (Magee *et al.*, 2010). This compelling evidence of the impaired judgement of the powerful suggests a real inability to see the big picture and to make impartial decisions which balance the interests of all parties – a kind of inattentional blindness to anything except self-interest.

Of course, it's not only the rich who engage in anti-social behaviour: David Dubois and his colleagues (2015:438) suggest that upper-class indi-viduals break ethical rules for themselves, while lower-class individuals do it for the benefit of others – a kind of Robin Hood effect. And the distin-guishing factor is power:

> Whereas power gives the powerful the freedom to pursue their own interests with fewer constraints (i.e. greater agency), the powerless are dependent on others, and often require communion to achieve their goals.

In other words, the best bet for members of a powerless group is to stick together, communicating closely with one another, because they do not have a realistic option of achieving their own individual goals, which the powerful do. This could be further psychological evidence of how poorly equipped the wealthy are to make decisions which benefit everybody in society.

Wealth can act like a drug

This wide-ranging research strengthens the idea that wealth is not so much a source of enlightenment, as a kind of drug, inducing irrational behaviour – broadly the outcome we'd expect growthism's 'mad' goals and values to produce. More evidence is provided by those who make money out of money, a cornerstone industry of growthism, as described in the previous chapter. A psychological study of City of London traders in foreign exchange and commodities, responsible for trading trillions of dollars daily, suggests that it's levels of testosterone rather than rational calculation that best predict the success of their trades. The extremely volatile levels of this hormone, in combination with cortisol, can put a trader's ability to 'engage in rational choice' severely at risk, researchers Coates and Herbert (2008:6167) conclude. This testosterone-fuelled 'Gekko syndrome' becomes self-reinforcing, as risk-prone people are attracted to this high-profit, high-pressure (and overwhelmingly male) environment. As former investment bank employee Laurence Knight (2012) explains:

> For many traders, their sense of self-worth is defined almost uniquely by their 'P&L' – the profit and loss they make for the bank – and, by implication, the size of their bonus. Making a profitable trade shows that they are right. And the bigger the profit the more right they are.

Unrestrained profit-seeking may just be one of the most the most addictive drugs humanity has ever come up with. As an entrepreneur in the 1980s, I had some exposure to this myself. It's a physical and mental force that can take over one's life – and it's present throughout our modern world as never before. Free-market economics has spread this intoxication, as it has increased other addictive activities such as gambling and the heavy use of alcohol and Class A drugs often associated with the professional's lifestyle.

You may think that the algorithm of capital is far too abstract a concept to be real, but the drug of wealth can pump it straight into the human bloodstream, creating the highs and lows, the ecstasy and agony that drive so many ordinary, everyday profit-junkies. It personalizes the number one value of capitalism in the most compellingly visceral way. It also makes it clear why cooler heads are needed to guide us towards a better future.

Inside the corporation: the culture of CIMENT

If there's one arena where the addiction to wealth and the entire panoply of CIMENT values flourish most freely, it's the multinational corporation. Here, in the engine room of the growthist world, we see the Janus-faced culture of the irrational pursuit of infinite wealth pushed to extremes. Big businesses are not democracies: that's the first thing anybody working within one discovers. Corporations are top-down hierarchies, which in the political sphere would probably not even be categorized as 'flawed' or 'hybrid' democracies but as 'authoritarian'. They are sleek pyramids of power, where those at the bottom, and even in the middle, have no votes and little say in what the organization does.

This hierarchy enables a separation of powers, between those who are seen to directly contribute to maximizing shareholder value, the executive class, and those necessary to keep the organization running. The distinction between these two groups of employees often boils down to their values and especially their attitude to competitivism. In my experience, the majority of workers in large organizations are more interested in cooperation than competition. They come to work in order to work with others, serving customers, suppliers and the general public, rather than to climb the corporate ladder. They may be involved in back-room functions such as facilities management, finance, administration or human resources or customer-facing roles. Their principal goal is not remuneration in itself but the means to support themselves and their families. Most people in banks, for example, are not highly paid executives, vying for six figure bonuses, but clerks and counter staff in branches on or below the average wage.

Unfortunately the lot of those classified as non-revenue earners and (wrongly) seen as 'a cost to the business' is increasingly bleak. It's characterized by high pressure and often extreme anxiety about job security. Providing stress management was what brought me back into the corporate world in the 1990s, but stress has turned into an epidemic since then. UK government statistics suggest that 12.5 million working days were lost due to stress, depression and anxiety in 2016, almost half of all health-related absences. The main causes of stress were overwork, lack of support and violence or threats of bullying (HSE, 2018). According to a recent survey, stress now affects a third of workers at least one day a week (Forth, 2018).

As numerous studies show, a sense of powerlessness intensifies the stress reaction. For example, a US survey of daily life found that people experienced considerably more stress, mental exhaustion and feelings of helplessness in low-power situations than in high-power situations (Smith and Hoffman, 2016). Those at the bottom and in the middle of organizations generally have the fewest discretionary decisions to make over their jobs and hence the least power.

Add to this a high degree of precariousness, as the job security which used to be a feature of large organizations vanishes. It has been replaced by part-time work, short contracts and even zero-hour contracts, which demand total loyalty from the employee but no guarantees of work by the employer. Long hours and people holding down several jobs have become common, and bullying at work is now reported by a third of all UK workers, three-quarters of it by managers (TUC, 2015). Indeed, some of the working conditions in highly profitable new corporations resemble those of the Victorian workplace. That's the verdict of a British parliamentary committee, reviewing what happened behind the closed doors of retailer Sports Direct's cavernous warehouses. Employees had their work timed 'to the second', with lateness penalized by a 'strike' (six strikes and they're fired) and were often so terrified of losing their jobs that they worked when they were physically ill or injured, necessitating a total of 110 ambulance calls to one warehouse over a two-year period. One woman was so fearful of being sacked that she gave birth in a warehouse toilet (House of Commons, 2016). It's a return to nineteenth-century work standards that must shock even some neoliberal economists.

Life at the top: a hothouse of CIMENT values

At the top of the hierarchy, the culture is very different, for those pledged to engage in a 'war of all against all' in pursuit of fabulous earnings. For these executives, success is excess, more is more and less is definitely less. The corporate hierarchy has to be strong enough to keep these hyper-competitive executives focused on the corporation's number one purpose. If people were really a company's biggest asset, as is often claimed by senior managers, what would happen to the shareholders' investments? Rather like the authoritarian leviathan which was Thomas Hobbes solution to extreme competitivism, the corporate hierarchy prevents unfettered competition from tearing the organization apart. But only just. Executive creative destruction drives businesses to the edge of collapse – and sometimes over it. In this, it models the entire world plan and provides another insight into the high-risk brinkmanship of growthism.

For both aspiring and actual executives, the twenty-first-century corporation is a fertile hothouse for individualism, materialism, elitism and the other CIMENT values. Oliver Stone intended his 'greed is good' speech as a bitter denunciation of the ethos of Wall Street, but it was taken at face value by his intended targets and celebrated as a triumphant vision of the new corporate culture. For executives, that means focusing on any action which helps you get to the top by drawing attention to yourself and advancing your claims ahead of your rivals. Coaching psychologist Marshal Goldsmith (2007) describes some of these behaviours: making destructive comments, not listening, telling the world how smart we are, speaking when angry, withholding information, claiming credit that we don't deserve, failing to express regret, shooting the messenger and passing the buck. This is the battlefield mentality at its most single-minded. It means making a religion of looking after number one and turning your career into an entrepreneurial entity in its own right. Influential management consultant Tom Peters (1997) calls this embracing 'the brand called You' and making yourself 'CEO of Me Inc'. All this often entails rejecting another model of equilibrium which growthism claims it promotes, namely 'work–life balance', as you ruthlessly subordinate your personal relationships to the demands of your career.

Greed and fear in the executive suite

The wealth drug also plays a huge part in executive culture. Executive salaries have grown inordinately over the past 40 years in relation to average earnings, driving a further wedge between executives and the rest of the workforce. Much of this is related to performance-related pay and bonuses against targets. Rapidly increasing earnings can convert executives who are not already hooked on materialism into consumerist junkies, chasing more expensive clothes and accessories, a faster car, a better holiday, a bigger house. Grade by grade, as you rise up the executive ladder, you are lured into a more expensive lifestyle, which inescapably leads to higher pay demands.

After a while, gain and pain become inseparable. As suggested in Chapter 2, greed is most effective in motivating human affairs when it's combined with the fear of loss. The higher you go, the more terrifying the fall. For executives, the potential losses which come from failing to achieving their targets are not only financial. A corporate sales director once told me he 'motivated' his sales team by urging them to buy more expensive houses ('There's nothing like a massive mortgage to wake you up in the middle of the night in a cold sweat!' he observed). In a sales culture – and every executive culture is a sales culture – everything is always at stake: your earnings, status, promotion, the job itself and with it possibly your house, your marriage, even access to your children. The pressure can be so intense that at the highest level executives become desperate to earn enough money to abandon business altogether and retire early – the lure of so-called 'fuck-you money'. It's the corporate equivalent of the gangster whose crimes are driven by his longing to 'go legit'.

Fear and greed are two sides of the same coin which spell out the harsh message: grow or die. Emotionally, they create a formidable dialectic, a perfect vicious circle of motivation. Jean-Paul Sartre (1958) called this kind of existential condition 'flight-pursuit', a situation in which you can't tell the difference between chasing or fleeing. Is wealth the reward you are pursuing or are you running as fast as possible to escape the consequences of losing it, running for your life, in fact? For a hyper-competitor, the humiliation of losing can outweigh any possible satisfaction of winning. The more you have, the more you have to lose.

'Greed and fear syndrome' is simply zero-sum logic translated into the most visceral gut feelings. It goes some way to explaining why wealth can be so addictive and why it produces the morally warping effects, which psychological experiments are beginning to reveal. It's not that executives are inhuman – many are all too human – but the system they are in has another set of rules which supersedes normal moral considerations. This morality switching can happen almost instantaneously, as one experimental study in letter-writing to victims showed: the mere mention of economic terms caused executives to lose empathy and write less compassionate letters than they were planning to (Molinsky *et al.*, 2012). The shadow of *Homo economicus* seemed to rear up out of nowhere, freezing their human emotions and turning the rich phenomena of life into a cold set of symbols on a balance sheet.

Elitism and technologism

Other CIMENT values reinforce executive culture. Elitism plays a central role, as corporate climbers become familiar with a hierarchy that can contain a dozen or more managerial levels and grades of remuneration that can run into the hundreds. Job titles also try to maximize the minutest differences in status. This differentiation accustoms you to think differently from the outside world, which is supposed to be committed to horizontal, equalizing relationships. It also separates executives from the everyday lives of ordinary people as they move around in limousines between exclusive clubs, private schools and gated communities. Many think they are at the top because they deserve it – and superior to those who didn't make it. 'Tough decisions' which affect the lives of others, such as mass redundancies, become easier to make in the closeted, mutually reinforcing environment of confident Social Darwinists. It's another part of the explanation for how corporate executives can make choices which disregard the interests of vulnerable people across the world. It's also a possible answer to that question perplexed climate change campaigners often ask, 'Don't fossil-fuel company bosses have children and grandchildren?'

Another key CIMENT value is technologism, which increasingly dominates corporate culture, as all businesses turn themselves into high-tech companies, forced to constantly reinvent themselves through technological innovation. The executive is both the victim of creative destruction and its perpetrator. New technology can survey, record, measure and judge every minute of an executive's working life and perhaps wake her up at night, so fearful is she of missing out on a vital email. But her role is increasingly to force through initiatives on her subordinates which turn them into semi-robotic administrators of computer screens.

Through technology, big corporations are shrinking in terms of employee size. Google is one the largest companies in the world, with ten times the market capitalization of traditional manufacturers like Volkswagen, but it has only a tenth of its workforce (although VW is robotizing fast). High-tech hedge funds that earn billions in profit often have only a dozen or so employees. The 'post-employee' organization could be just around the corner, if technologism has its way. It might consist only of executives making strategic decisions, working in innovation and sales while most of the other human jobs are performed by intelligent machines. In Japan, the post-employee company is already a reality, with an AI system based on IBM's Watson – advertised as 'cognitive technology that can think like a human' – replacing the entire workforce of an insurance company (BBC, 2017).

The employee-free corporation could be a paradise for many executives. Intelligent machines don't need offices, washrooms or canteens, let alone holidays, maternity leave or pay rises. For technocratic executives, who struggle with the human side of management – and in my experience that's a significant proportion of the management class – this could be a dream come true. All those emotionally awkward review sessions, tricky remuneration discussions and painful dismissals, not to mention stormy stand offs with trade unions – all of these could disappear from the executive's diary leaving him free to concentrate fully on maximizing shareholders' earnings – and his own. But how long until he is himself replaced by a cheaper, more efficient decision-making, strategy-forming algorithm? Technologism's preference for machines over people could eventually turn out badly for almost everybody.

Psychopaths in the board room?

Given all this, should we describe the psychology of our current leadership class as 'psychopathic'? It's certainly tempting to classify growthist irrationality as a personality disorder, characterized by self-aggrandisement, ruthless cold-heartedness, charming manipulativeness and a lack of empathy, guilt or remorse. Industrial psychologist Paul Babiak and criminal psychologist Robert Hare (2006) claim that this description applies to only 1% of the general population but to 3–4% of senior executives. Psychologist Kevin Dutton (2012) suggests that CEO is the most popular occupation for psychopaths, while leadership coach Manfred Kets de Vries (2012) is a little more circumspect, describing this executive profile as 'SOB (seductive operational bully) or psychopath-lite' but agreeing that it's widespread. In my experience, leaders often exhibit anti-social personalities, but we also need to take into account the system they are serving, rather than seeing their mindset as a psychological anomaly which can be 'cured' in isolation (as I once thought). The danger of describing growthist leadership as a personality disorder is that it turns it into a case of 'abnormal psychology', making an exception of what is now the norm in the business world. Leaders obsessed with wealth creation are simply doing what shareholder society demands of them.

The real 'psychopathic creature' is the corporation itself, as professor of law Joel Bakan points out:

Nothing in its legal makeup limits what it can do to others in pursuit of its selfish ends and it is compelled to cause harm when the benefits of doing so outweigh the costs.

(Bakan, 2004:51)

Given that we allow this legal entity to dominate our society, and our values and expectations of the future, perhaps we should apply the psychopathy test to ourselves. The madness of growthism can be described in many ways but until we see it as the product of a system rather than an exception to it, we'll have little chance of relegating psychopathic behaviour to the extreme margins of society where it belongs.

Growthism in popular culture

Finally, let's turn to the effect of the wealth fallacy on popular culture. Since economic growth is embedded in every modern institution, it's no surprise to find that CIMENT values have entered the bloodstream of popular culture. Here, in those periods of entertainment and leisure when people are supposedly outside the workplace and 'off duty', they are actually most vulnerable to the influence of growthist values. In part, this is simply a reflection of the values of the entertainment and leisure corporations, which have grown into worldwide enterprises constantly searching for greater profits, and the consumerist messages that advertising sublimi-nally transmits to us. The result is that people's imaginations are invaded, occupied and colonized by growthism from the earliest age.

For instance, growthist values have swept through TV programming, transforming staid family quiz shows into coliseums of competitive mate-rialism. Game shows, which in the UK used to be limited to a maximum prize of £1,000, now aspire to be prime-time block busters creating instant millionaires and offering life-changing opportunities to the tiny minority who win them. Reality TV goes even further, providing shows in which the winner takes all and the loser is placed in the full glare of the spotlight to be ritually ridiculed and humiliated. *The Weakest Link* was the first British programme to trash the traditional fair-play ethos of quiz shows. Now shows like *The Apprentice*, with its pugilistic catch phrase 'You're Fired!', regularly celebrate the fact that for every winner there are many losers and that losing can be the most compelling form of entertainment of all. For 'the greed is good' message to become univer-sally acceptable, people have to lose all inhibition about humiliating losers, because this is what a zero-sum society is really about. *The Appren-tice* is a camped-up celebration of big business as the realm of unscrupu-lous, Machiavellian go-getters. The fact that the show's original American host could go on to develop a new career as US president would be comical if it weren't so tragic.

Craft as competition and the destruction of the value of play

Reality TV has also sunk its teeth into traditionally non-competitive areas of life beyond the economic market such as hobbies, craft-based pastimes or other leisure activities. In William Morris's *News from Nowhere*, a utopian society is constructed around people working lovingly and carefully at skilled crafts, often on a non-profit basis. It's a vision which turned upside down the harsh reality of nineteenth-century wage-slavery, imagining work as a form of play and communally orientated cooperation, which also had a moral discipline to it. Today's marketized idea of craft on TV is the very opposite, urging everybody to transform their hobby into a job and find a route to instant fame and fortune. TV production companies turn to virtually every leisure activity, including singing, dancing, cooking, baking, pottery and every known form of sport, in search of the next ratings-topping format. And, if they can survive the cutthroat competition, show winners can pick up big money prizes and a well-paid new career, usually in the media.

Yet pastimes and hobbies are expressions of adult play and as such have an intrinsic value. Play is what we'd probably choose to do if we didn't have to work all day. It has a spontaneous freedom and a self-defining pleasure which doesn't have to obey any rules. Hobbies often involve the patient mastery of skills, as well as active, rather than passive, entertainment. Activities like this are also, a matter of give and take, win–win rather than win–lose, in which learning is freely given and partnership is more important than rivalry.

These intrinsic and cooperative values are given short shrift by TV shows that focus relentlessly on an elimination process which whittles down the hopeful many to the increasingly nervous few before the winner enjoys their instant celebrity and the losers are returned to obscurity. The idea that people can engage in solitary pastimes or communal activity without an economic motive or the need for competition is just too much of an affront to our dominant culture. The trend towards 'competitive leisure', reflected in the growing popularity of triathlons, ultramarathons and other extreme sports, seems remorseless, especially among younger people increasingly hooked on perfectionism (Godwin, 2018). Turning the intrinsic into the extrinsic, the cooperative into the competitive, confirms the superiority of the CIMENT ethos, even if it threatens to destroy the whole meaning of leisure.

Nor are children exempt. They are, in fact, a prime target for growthist values and subjected to a continuous blitz of often sexualized advertising, seemingly designed to deprive them of the openness and innocence of childhood and turn them into sharp-eyed, avaricious consumers as quickly as possible. This rampantly materialist and individualistic culture is profoundly changing children's outlook, as one penetrating piece of research illustrates. Psychologists Yalda Uhls and Patricia Greenfield (2011) studied the values contained in US TV shows over a 40-year period, focusing on those most popular among 9- to 11-year-olds. In 1967 the predominant values displayed in the two TV shows most watched by this age group (as judged by a panel of adult experts) were 'community feeling' and 'benevolence'. But by 2007, these collectivist values had plummeted to 14th and 15th in the list of that year's most popular programmes (*American Idol* and *Hannah Montana*). They were replaced at the top by the values of 'fame' and 'achievement', with 'financial success' moving up the list to 5th (from 15th in 1977). The creation of a generation strongly addicted to growthist beliefs, at the expense of what Uhls and Greenfield call 'traditional, familialistic and communitarian values', seems to be well under way. A survey of pop songs from 1980 to 2010 traces a similar retreat from pro-social values which emphasize working together. Lyrics which relate to 'other-focus, social interactions and positive emotions' were found to have decreased significantly, as had the use of the pronoun 'you', while there was a sharp rise in 'me-focused' songs (DeWall *et al.*, 2011).

The culture of dystopia

This consistent valuation of individualism and materialist values over pro-social, communitarian attitudes surely lies behind the spectacular rise of dystopia in the popular imagination, which, as I suggested in the Introduction, is an integral part of the Anthropocene crisis. Following a brief renaissance in the 1960s and 1970s, utopian fiction has all but petered out in this century, swept aside by a growing tsunami of dystopian narratives. According to Wikipedia (2018a) – the most comprehensive and up-to-date guide I could find – only 13 dystopian novels were published before 1900 but 145 in the twentieth century and over 100 since the turn of the millennium, more than half of them for young adults. Dystopian representations of the future are flooding every form of popular culture, from popular music to graphic novels and films. Whereas only a handful of utopian films are listed on Wikipedia (2018b), there are almost 200 dystopian movies named, half of them produced since 2000. Sub-genres are proliferating, for example techno-dystopias, such as *Blade Runner*, *Terminator* and *Robocop* or 'bio-dystopias', in which genetic engineering has created separate classes of humanity. Feminist dystopias are also growing fast (*The Handmaid's Tale*), as are other political dystopias, including TV versions of alternative histories imagining a Nazi victory in the Second World War, such as *The Man in the High Castle*.

The fastest growing dystopian cultural category of all appears to be video games, with about 120 developed since 2000 (Wikipedia, 2018c). The following selection of titles gives a vivid impression of the catastrophic future gamers are invited to participate in: *Battlefield 142*, *BattleTanx: Global Assault*, *Beneath a Steel Sky*, *Bioshock*, *Deus Ex: Mankind Divided*, *Kikokagai: The Cyber Slayer*, *The Moment of Silence* and *Year Zero*.

On this evidence, it's no exaggeration to call the twenty-first century the era of dystopian culture. Whereas in the past people daydreamed about utopia, now nightmares about dystopia seem to fill our waking hours. The sheer force of human innovativeness may be impressive, but its direction is deeply troubling. It all suggests that the only alternative to growthist values is a collapse of civilization altogether – greed and fear syndrome taken to the most extreme. If the best-case scenarios become less easy to imagine – and representation of pro-social behaviours disappear from our screens – doesn't the worst case become more thinkable? It's almost as though growthism is preparing us for the advent of a real dystopia.

Conclusion

Hard evidence about the effects of values and beliefs on behaviour is never easy to come by. But here I've presented a wide range of research which underpins the wealth fallacy and the irrationality of making wealth-seeking the main goal of our world plan. Far from producing enlightenment, happiness and sound leadership abilities, the pursuit of money can instil selfishness, dishonesty and immorality and makes little improvement to life satisfaction beyond a relatively low level. It can actively promote irrational decision-making, a frenzied, almost psychopathic organizational culture and a popular culture which immerses people in cockpits of competitive individualism and me-focused materialism from the earliest age. It's more evidence of how the reinforcement cycles of growthism translate values into institutions, which in turn shape the intimate feelings, thoughts and assumptions that guide our actions.

No wonder then that the very idea of utopia is becoming unthinkable. Images of dystopia have captured the popular imagination to such an extent that the possibility of a worst-case scenario for the sloping world has become increasingly normalized. So let's now take this bitter logic to its historical conclusion and speculate on the where the dark mindset of growthism might lead us in the coming decades, if the full force of the Anthropocene crisis is allowed to reach land.

5 The worst case scenario
Dystopia in the Anthropocene

This book is mainly about utopia and the positive opportunities that the Anthropocene offers but it's important to be clear about what the negative consequences of continuing with our current world plan could be. The business-as-usual trajectory of growthism will lead to increased instances of climate breakdown and environmental degradation and growing threats of famine and overpopulation in the world's poorest regions, leading to mass-migration movements. How will our current global elite react to these immense shocks? How can democracy, which is already under threat in a way that few anticipated at the turn of the century, cope with these unprecedented global and domestic crises? And what will be the results of the unbridled, exponential technological development which even its most fervent champions admit is unknowable in its outcomes?

The possibility of a dystopian response to these problems, I believe, is all too real. In fact, it could even be the logical end point of the growthist irrationale. Dystopias take the sloping world to its most extreme point, institutionalizing inequality by eliminating all pretences of democracy and giving the elite permanent, legally binding privileges over the majority. Flagging up the possibility of such a dire turn of events may seem alarmist, but throughout history dystopias never seem possible until they happen – and by then it's usually too late to do anything abut them. Growthism relies on a mythical sense of the future in which everything will work out for the better, as long as we maintain our current trajectory. So we need to be especially wary of what German philosopher Günther Anders called 'apocalypse blindness', which he attributed to 'a belief stretching back generations in the supposedly automatic progress of history' (quoted in Welzer, 2012:137). In truth, the possibility of dystopia is inherent in utopia. It's utopia's dialectical opposite, its real and conceptual evil twin, without which utopia can never be fully understood.

Stretching the imagination to its utmost to anticipate the future, both good and bad, is also thoroughly part of the utopian tradition. That's true as well, of any change plan worth its salt, which needs to construct worst-case scenarios to have any credibility. Only in this way can we hope to strike the right balance between optimism and pessimism and accurately assess the probabilities of change. A serviceable map of the future also has the advantage of containing clear signs for what to watch out for. So here are four ways the Anthropocene crisis could take a dystopian turn.

Scenario 1: drifting into dystopia

How much of a push is needed to propel the world into a state where authoritarian nationalism becomes the dominant political form? Asking this question in the spring of 2015, when I started researching this book, might have seemed rather far fetched. Who then could have anticipated the crisis of immigration in Europe which began in the summer of 2015, causing some of the most democratic counties to erect barriers against immigrants; the Brexit referendum vote in 2016, in which nationalist, anti-foreigner sentiments played such a major role; the election of an avowed climate denier as US president five months later; and the socially reactionary authoritarianism spreading like wildfire in Europe and elsewhere, prompting many to talk about a return to the 1930s?

These unanticipated events have strengthened the competitivist CIMENT ethos to an extraordinary degree, resurrecting nationalism and a new regressive elitism which attempts to restore the white, male heterosexual to some of his former cultural and political supremacy. In the coming years, this reaction against the gains made in equal rights over the past decades could become even more confidently aggressive. Climate deniers might gain a new lease of life, causing climate and environmental regulation to go into reverse. Climate mitigation efforts could be left entirely to the whims of market forces. As increasing environmental disasters occur in the global South, they could be dismissed as natural and inevitable or perhaps blamed on corrupt leadership or the general feck-lessness which the wealthy ascribe to the poor. Ever larger fences would be erected to protect wealthy nations and immigrants treated with ever greater hostility.

You might think that mass refugee crises and famines would provoke a massive humanitarian reaction on the part of the West. Perhaps it will, but building vast refugee camps is not a real solution to the problem. This response may not occur at all, if censorship conceals or distorts reality and accurate news is replaced with fake news. In the Syrian war we've already seen Russian state-owned TV claim that verifiable film footage of alleged government chemical attacks on the town of Douma was fabricated and the entire incident staged, using child actors (ABC, 2018). In the future, reports of environmental or refugee disasters may be hotly disputed and aid donations accused of funding corrupt politicians or terrorists.

Bear in mind that dystopia is all about controlling information. The government of Orwell's *Nineteen Eighty-Four* tried to restructure all language to the point that there were no words to express political opposition, so it becomes literally unthinkable. Today post-truth politics has already started down this path, providing 'alternative facts' and so many fake news stories that almost half of the public admits to having been fooled by at least one of them (Ipsos MORI, 2018a). Some people are being urged to dismiss the very idea of impartial evidence and instead place blind faith in their leaders. In the near future, decades of corporate truth denial may reap the whirlwind, as the tactics of FUD – fear, uncertainty and doubt – go mainstream, making informed decision-making seem impossible. The truth may become so difficult to ascertain that self-interest takes over and people end up believing whatever it suits them to believe. In this way, the most dystopian consequences of our recklessly irrational world plan would simply be erased from public consciousnesses, as are so many of its disturbing realities today.

Scenario 2: war and dystopia capitalism

Another response to the extreme pressures of the coming decades would be for the authorities to go to war. That's always been a solution to intractable domestic political problems ('busy giddy minds with foreign quarrels' Shakespeare's Henry IV advises (*Henry IV, Part 2* IV v 212–13)). The competitivist logic of nationalism can make military conflicts almost inevitable, as leaders seek to shore up their popularity at home by stoking up tensions abroad. In the years since 1945, the world has had little difficulty in finding pretexts for war, even before militarist, anti-foreigner nationalisms remerged on the world stage. Now the rise of economic protectionism creates the possibility of trade wars, which have a nasty habit of leading to real wars. The growing environmental crisis will only intensify the possibility of conflict between, and within, nations.

Climate change may already have contributed to the Syrian war, with abnormally extreme droughts in the region having led to high levels of urban migration and food shortages (Kelley *et al.*, 2015). Conflicts for resources will exacerbate tensions in many other parts of the world. Military historian Gwynne Dyer (2008) sketches a possible confrontation over water between India and Pakistan (both nuclear nations), leading to the collapse of the Indus river and up to 100 million casualties. Another dire scenario he outlines is multinational conflict in the Arctic over scarce oil and gas reserves. As the century progresses, resources for populations in the poorest countries could lead to mass migrations on a scale hitherto unknown in world history. In 2017, for the first time ever, refugees made up 1% of the world population (forming the 'other 1%'), a 12-fold increase on 1950 (IEP, 2018), and this number could swell to 200 million refugees or more by 2050, according to the UN (IOM, 2018). Job automation can add to these numbers, with new industrialized agricultural techniques forcing more of the billions who still live in the country to migrate to cities, at the same time as robotics deprives existing city dwellers of traditional urban jobs in manufacturing, retail and transport.

One result of declaring war is that democracy can disappear almost overnight. Even terrorist threats can be enough to erode basic civil rights in the most democratic countries (as shown by the draconian response of France's socialist president to the terrorist attacks in Paris in November 2015). But countries engaged in total warfare go much further, turning into authoritarian regimes, in which compliance with top-down authority becomes a matter of life and death. We sometimes forget that during the Second World War, a period rightly hailed for its heroic social solidarity, Britain was in effect a dictatorship, albeit a dictatorship by consent. Elections were cancelled, civil rights disappeared, people were conscripted into the armed forces or compelled to change occupations, while some leftists and pacifists were locked up without trial. Even private property rights were abrogated, as land, houses and businesses were pressed into war service.

Once taken, there is no guarantee that democracy will be given back, as it was in Britain in 1945. A temporarily suspended democracy in the future could disappear permanently, as its promised restoration is deferred so often that eventually all memory of it is erased. When a war is over the ruling elite can take advantage of an economically devastated and psychologically shattered majority to maintain radically unpopular measures indefinitely. Or perhaps the war will never be allowed to end: it will remain perpetually – and conveniently – unwinnable, the situation which the global powers conspire to create in *Nineteen Eighty-Four*.

How the global elite react to potential war situations will be crucial. Will they act coherently as a group or split into different factions, for example, liberal and authoritarian? Some corporate leaders may take a back seat, allowing politicians to make the key decisions about military conflict, but others are likely to take the initiative themselves. Indeed, for many existing corporations, conflicts, disasters and other crises are not only good for profit-making but essential to it. Without wars, for example, the vast sums of public spending devoted to the military-industrial complex are at risk of being diverted elsewhere. In *The Shock Doctrine*, Naomi Klein makes a convincing case that since the 1970s American corporations, politicians and economists have actively encouraged military conflict and economic crises in Latin America and elsewhere. The goal of this 'disaster capitalism' is to introduce unpopular but highly profitable, neoliberal policies which in normal times would be rejected by the electorate. 'Crises are democracy-free zones', Klein says, 'gaps in politics when the need for consent and consensus do not seem to apply' (2007:140).

One recent such crisis was the 2003 US-led invasion of Iraq, a disaster-escalating event which was itself a reaction to the disaster of 9/11. The trillions of dollars of tax payers' money spent on the war created a profit bonanza for corporations like Halliburton, which saw its share price jump 300% as a result of the services it provided to the vast military camps built in Iraq. One of Halliburton's major shareholders was its former CEO, Vice

President Dick Cheney, a leading advocate of the war, who retained his shares in the company and a deferred salary throughout his tenure in government (Klein, 2007:313). Other corporations which profitably went to war in Iraq include Pizza Hut, Burger King, McDonalds, Pepsi and Coca-Cola, an obesogenic coalition which constituted a significant invasion in its own right (Crowley, 2011).

In the context of disasters caused by increased military conflict, such as disease and famine, as well as mounting climate and environmental breakdowns, it's not unreasonable to expect that disaster capitalism will develop into dystopia capitalism. More and more businesses could join the queue of corporations already 'making a killing out of catastrophe', to borrow Anthony Lowenstein's (2015) acerbic subtitle to his book on disaster capitalism. Not all will actively lobby for the creation of wars and other crises but few will have any great commercial incentive to prevent them from happening.

Scenario 3: the barbaric road to global apartheid

An even gloomier future is one of several astute forecasts produced by the Global Scenario Group, a team of international scholars led by Paul Raskin. In *The Great Transition* (2002), the group envisage that the early decades of the century would be dominated by a worldwide regime which benefits the world's 20 wealthiest countries and the top 20% of income earners in the rest of the world, a so-called 20/20 Club (which provides another interesting definition of the global elite). For this minority, consumerism flourishes, but the billions who are left out of this largesse suffer increased depravation, only partially mitigated by international bodies such as the United Nations. As the gulf between rich and poor increases, all foreign aid dries up:

> Multiple stresses – pollution, climate change, ecosystem degradation – interact and amplify the crisis. Disputes over scarce water resources feed conflict in regions with shared river basins. Environmental degradation, food insecurity and emergency diseases foster a vast health crisis.
>
> (Raskin *et al.*, 2002:26)

In these circumstances 'the excluded billions grow restive'. Mass emigration to more affluent areas becomes a life or death issue, criminality thrives and 'a new kind of militant emerges – educated, excluded and angry – to fan flames of discontent'. New types of terrorism emerge, with the possibility of chemical and nuclear weapons. This state of 'barbarization' weakens national borders, as ethnic, tribal and religious tensions grow, and nationalism becomes a force to be reckoned with. Poor countries fall apart, with organized crime moving into the vacuum. In affluent countries, infrastructure starts to decay, as the global economy falters.

Published at the relatively optimistic turn of the century this scenario seems to accurately predict today's world with the ever-present global threat of Al-Qaeda, Daesh, Boko Haram and other terrorist organizations with the ambition and (at least temporary) capacity to set up states. The erosion of national frontiers in the Middle East, Libya and parts of sub-Saharan Africa may already have begun, as intensified sectarian and ethnic rivalries are deliberately unleashed, for example, between Shia and Sunni Muslims. Robert Kaplan (2000) presents a cartography of this barbarized world, 'a last map', in which national boundaries have vanished and vast shanty towns and slums dominate what used to be cities. Militias, drug cartels and private armies fight for scant resources, as failed states implode, perhaps inevitably since they were never states in the first place but lines drawn on a map by colonial powers. Only a little imagination is needed to see this systemic chaos extending to other parts of Africa and Asia, to a fragmenting Europe and even an increasingly secessionary, anti-federal USA.

This state of incessant conflict, terrorism and borderless anarchy eventually causes the world's leadership class to say 'enough is enough'. In one of the scenarios Raskin and his colleagues construct, the global elite use the UN as a platform to declare a state of global emergency. There follows 'a campaign of overwhelming force, rough justice and draconian measures' which descends on the world's hot spots of conflict and restores stability. What emerges is 'planetary apartheid', a rigid hierarchy in which,

> the separate spheres of the haves and have nots, the included and the excluded, are codified in asymmetrical and authoritarian legal and institutional frameworks. The affluent live in protected enclaves in rich nations and in strongholds in poor nations – bubbles of privilege amid oceans of misery.
>
> (Raskin *et al.*, 2002:27)

This 'fortress world' is a police state that mires the majority in poverty and denies it basic freedoms. High-tech weaponry is used to protect precious environmental resources, if necessary by 'old-fashioned brutality'. Presumably, legislation would be enacted to segregate various categories of human beings and enforced through surveillance and control over every aspect of life.

As in *Nineteen Eighty-Four*, the distinction between the health of the state and the health of the individual will cease to exist, as will the possibility of privacy or subjective space (at least for those who cannot afford its sky-high market price). Life beyond the fences might be possible for some, perhaps in separate colonies or homelands, but this would be a denial of the democratic direction of our history since the Enlightenment. Global apartheid would be a terrible fate — but can we really rule it out if growthism is mortally threatened and those who own the most are faced with the prospect of giving up what they have and hold?

In one sense, this imagined condition of separation is simply a reversion to the state of international law at the end of nineteenth century (the era of free-market capitalism which neoliberals revere). Until the First World War, a rigid, tripartite, global hierarchy governed the legal status of nations, according to their supposed 'standard of civilization', a stratification which historian Mark Mazower (2012:71) describes as follows:

> At the top were assumed to stand the civilized – European or former European settler colonies. Below them stood 'barbaric' powers like the Ottomans and the Chinese that had institutional history and some state capacity. At the bottom were the 'savage' peoples of Africa and the Pacific.

'Savage' nations had virtually no rights under international law. For instance, the 1914 British Manual of Military Law states that 'the rules of war apply only to warfare between civilised nations' (Mazower, 2012:77). In a fortress-world scenario, a reversion to these relatively recent norms cannot be ruled out.

Insidious separation

To this extreme forecast, I'd add a less violent, more subtle scenario which would see a form of apartheid emerging less formally but just as effectively, under cover of free-market capitalism and the rule of democracy. It involves the global elite using their wealth to build separate enclaves and to protect themselves from environmental chaos and social unrest. Extensive acquisitions of land in northern parts of the globe would lead to new exclusive cities, defended by robot security armies, perhaps under high-tech domes to protect inhabitants from the ravages of climate change. Elsewhere gated estates would turn into gated communities and gated towns. Billionaire-owned private islands would become private countries, with absolute rights to admit only those who share the values of their owners. In high-density urban environments the rigid separation between the rich and poor may be extended by sky bridges and the soaring 'horizontal skyscrapers', which are already being built in some Chinese megacities (Shen, 2018). These airy enclaves, replete with upmarket restaurants, opulent leisure facilities and luxury offices ensure that the penthouse level never needs to meet the street level.

The global elite's possession of the means of information – in the form of Big Data, Big Tech and Big Finance – open the way for the manipulation of citizens increasingly compromised by job automation and a world system run by intelligent machines. Vigilance and privatized healthcare means that those in power will know more about you than you know your-self, making the coercive powers of previous totalitarian dystopias seem unnecessarily crude. All this could enable a stealthy elitist coup to take place almost before anybody realizes it has happened – the ultimate triumph of the algorithms of capital.

Genetic apartheid

If anything like global apartheid arrives, whether formally or informally, another alarming possibility is that it would accelerate the transhumanist project of transcending human biology which I described in Part I. The patchy regulation which currently exists around biotechnology, the immortality industry and genetic engineering could disappear entirely and a free-market race to accelerate human augmentation would ensue. The result could be an effective division of the human race, dominated by those who can afford healthy lives which last many times longer than those of the have-nots, aided by computer-augmented brains and synthetically rejuvenated bodies. Bi-speciation could even occur, if genetic engineering is allowed to advance beyond the point where interbreeding is possible. Geneticist Lee Silver (1998) warns that human cloning and genetic engineering could easily spiral out of governmental control in the future, leading to the creation of a new master race. He calls them the 'Genrich', a 'modern hereditary class of genetic aristocrats', whose combination of selected and synthetic genes enables them to dominate the 90% of popu-lation who are merely 'Naturals'. Stephen Hawking (2018:81) also pre-dicted that some people will be unable to resist the temptation to genetically redesign themselves, warning that

> Once such superhumans appear, there are going to be major political problems with unimproved humans, who won't be able to compete. Presumably they will die out, or become unimportant.

Again, genetic apartheid may seem like an exaggerated fear, but it's con-sistent with the goal of never-ending economic growth of our current world plan, at a time when the pace of scientific progress could be thou-sands of times faster than ever before. It certainly chimes with the elitist individualism of growthist values and provides a logical conclusion to com-petitivist, 'us and them' beliefs and the economic creed of' rational selfish-ness'. Indeed, the transhumanist master race could be seen as *Homo economicus* made flesh. What's for sure is that if we can't bring about a revolution of values to replace the CIMENT ethos, there's a huge risk that human destiny will remain in the hands of those who see the technolo-gical conquest of nature as the ultimate goal of humanity. And that leads us to our final scenario.

Scenario 4: techno-dystopia

Where could the massive concentration of resources currently being deployed on developing artificial intelligence take humanity? We've noted the reckless disregard surrounding AI safety, and the many doubts that experts have about whether it's even possible to programme robots and other intelligent systems to be 'human friendly' (Bostrom, 2014). Already sophisticated AI is controlling 70% of trades in equity markets, running payrolls, energy grids and sewage systems, guiding the world's air and road traffic and playing an increasing role in every aspect of government, commerce and healthcare. Every month more systems are automated, many of which do more than simply follow instructions: they can learn, innovate and solve problems by themselves. 'Genetic algorithms' can now create complex electronic circuits which we know work – but we don't know how. Supercomputers can defeat world champions not only at rule-bound chess but also at poker, in which human bluff and counter bluff play a significant part. AI has now even triumphed at the ancient, highly intuitive game of Go, using extraordinary winning moves, which, in the view of one expert player, no humans would ever make (Bridle, 2018:149).

This suggests that the aim of many AI developers to match the capacity of human intelligence has already been reached in some limited areas. Hotly debated is the time lapse between achieving human intelligence and the next stage, the advent of so-called superintelligence, in which machines are smarter than humans by an unknown factor (how could we ever calculate it?) Superintelligence could take decades or even centuries to develop but as James Barrat (2013) points out, it could happen much sooner. In fact, it could be almost instantaneous, especially if newly human-intelligent machines are able to access the internet and connect with each other.

It sounds like science fiction, but it's quite logical, when you think about it. We are the top dogs on the planet, not because we are bigger, stronger or faster than other species but because we are smarter. Why would we give away this priceless advantage to machines? It's as though chimpanzees had created human brains and then wondered why they'd ended up living in zoos. And our brains are only four times bigger than a chimp's, whereas superintelligent entities may be more intelligent than us by a factor of thousands or even millions.

What the superintelligent machines running all of the world's life systems would decide to do with humanity is anybody's guess. They might be benign and help us with the management of the problems of the Anthropocene which we're currently finding so painfully difficult. Or they might decide we're a lost cause and get rid of us altogether and use our atoms for something more interesting, like intergalactic colonization. The real question is: do we want to take that risk? Growthism says 'yes, we have no choice' but that's simply not true. What is true is that if we – humanity as a whole – are content to leave our destiny to those who currently own and direct machine learning, it might be machines themselves who make the final decision. The ultimate dystopia would be a strangely fitting act of human hubris, technologist megalomania attaining its logical transhumanist end, the rocket of growthism taking humanity on a flight to extinction. This would be a terrible fate but it has one consoling aspect, an egalitarianism which is palpably absent from all the other dystopian scenarios. As humans, at least we'd all be in it together – if only for the very last time.

Conclusion

Drifting into authoritarian nationalism, succumbing to dictatorship in a constant state of war, global apartheid, the splitting of the human race or even the replacement of humanity by intelligent machines: all these scenarios are possible outcomes of our irrational pursuit of economic growth at the expense of our planetary and human wellbeing. Like many worst-case scenarios they seem incredible, and yet history is always a series of events which flows from a chain of unexpected decisions. What starts as a range of choices is gradually narrowed down. For instance, in the 1930s the many options that Britain had to contain the power of the Nazi Germany eventually turned into a starkly binary choice: war or surrender. As the sunk costs of previous decisions add up, it's hard to ever go back. The unthinkable gradually becomes the possible, then the probable, and finally the inevitable.

But if you are thinking that we're still a long way from any of my worst-case scenarios I agree with you, and so, by the way, does the Global Scenario Group. If only we can act quickly enough, there are many positive ways in which we can change the direction of history. There is a much better solution to the Anthropocene crisis than any dystopian response can provide. It's time to explore it.

Part III
The change plan
12 steps towards a people-planet utopia

In Parts I and II I've tried to describe what I think we're up against. Our current, growthist world plan seems incapable of even acknowledging the Anthropocene crisis, let alone managing it. Climate change, species extinction, population issues, persistent economic inequality, the crisis of democracy and exponential technological development: all these inter-twined issues threaten to spiral out of control, taking life on earth, including human life, to breaking point. The foolhardy irrationality of pursuing economic growth at any cost protects those who have most but threatens disaster to those who have least. And, at the very worst, the current trajectory of growthism could turn our world into a full blown dystopia.

It's high time to invoke the spirit of the utopian tradition which has always stood against the sloping world. The opportunity for a better way of living exists, if only we can take it, by backing rationality against economic madness and cooperation against destructive competition. That requires us to put our faith in our ability to live in peace with ourselves and our environment. In short, it's time to believe in the best of humanity, not only in our capacity to protest against the worst but also in our creative ability to make something better.

That's not to suggest that creating a practical alternative to our current world plan will be easy – we need to be clear about that from the outset. It requires something close to a seismic change in our institutions and con-sciousness, a paradigm shift comparable to a great scientific revolution, such as Einstein's theory of relativity, which changed Newtonian physics forever. Thomas Kuhn described this kind of transformation as 'a recon-struction of the field from new fundamentals' (1970:89), a step change that can occur 'only if an alternative candidate is available to take its place' (1970:77). Paradigm shifts can be painfully slow and then suddenly break through. Kuhn noted that many scientists in the physics establishment ini-tially rejected the theory of relativity, but when it was empirically con-firmed during a solar eclipse in 1919 Einstein became a worldwide celebrity overnight.

I know from my business career in innovation and my time in organiza-tional change that being ahead of the curve can be an uncomfortable place. The process of turning radical ideas into everyday reality can bring out a good deal of defensiveness in others. Organizations sometimes cling on to what they've got, however palpably unsatisfactory that may be, simply because moving towards the unknown can create such extremes of anxiety. Indeed, in psychotherapy it's often said that every therapy client wants two things: to change and to stay the same. Charting a course through these paradoxical straights is what the epic journey of change involves.

So be prepared to disagree with some of what I'm going to propose. You may feel challenged, perturbed or provoked by some of the ideas I'll advance but, in my view, such reactions are probably a necessary consequence of the scale of the problem we are facing. Big problems require big solutions and surely no problem has ever been bigger than the Anthropocene crisis and no solution is greater than utopia. Resetting the algorithm of our world from maximizing shareholder value to promoting peace, rationality and human flourishing may involve some leaps into the unknown and some apparent losses, at least at first glance. But without risk and loss there is no change. So be ready to believe in the power of possibility. Utopia is possible if we are prepared to make it so.

With these provisos (and this respectful advice), let's move on to the change plan for utopia in the Anthropocene. Every effective change plan involves new objectives and values, together with practical systems which facilitate new forms of behaviour. Here's a reminder of the 12 steps involved:

Step 1: Define the utopian vision (the SEWP model)
Step 2: Set goals and clarify values
Step 3: Support an ecological revolution in economics
Step 4: Put wellbeing and community first
Step 5: Build circular democracy (and champion a transvaluation of politics)
Step 6: Embrace utopian internationalism
Step 7: Help to grow post-growth organizations
Step 8: Manage yourself to utopia (by democratizing leadership and other organizational practices)
Step 9: Put psychology to work on transforming our values
Step 10: Learn from the utopian imagination
Step 11: Think and act like a utopian
Step 12: Take heart from history

6 Step 1
Define the utopian vision
(the SEWP model)

An effective change plan, like all great projects, starts with the future. It needs a vision, a picture of where we are heading and a map to the new destination. To cross the chasm of the unknown, we need to draw on one of our greatest strengths as human beings: our ability to imagine a future that is different from our present.

Outline of the people-planet vision

Let's begin with a very ancient story about change, as told by Ovid in his book of transformations, *The Metamorphoses*. Daedalus and his son, Icarus, find themselves trapped in a tower on an island, the coast of which is closely guarded to prevent escape. Daedalus, who is a brilliant engineer and master craftsman known for his inventiveness and foresight, is not deterred by this. He crafts two superb sets of wings for himself and his son but before launching themselves into the air, he issues Icarus with this stern warning: 'Follow a course midway between heaven and earth. Fly too close to the sea and the water will make the wings too heavy. Fly too high and the sun will melt the wax that holds them together.' But Icarus is headstrong and ambitious. He can not resist the temptation to fly as high as possible until, in the end, he crashes to his death in the sea (Ovid, *Metamorphoses* VIII).

The moral is obvious: to escape to a better world we need to be like the visionary genius, Daedalus, and get the balance right between human ingenuity and our respect for nature, rather than imitate Icarus whose self-centred rashness led to his downfall.

Let's put this positive vision in a more literal form:

> To create a sustainable, equitable world in which wellbeing can flourish planetwide.

Or more poetically:

> To live together securely, fairly and beautifully.

At the core of this vision of utopia in the Anthropocene is the following simple proposition: We are one people on one planet. For too long, we've behaved as though this was not the case. We've acted as though we are many different peoples, with fundamentally different, often opposed values. We've built an entire world order based on competing with other humans, subjugating some and elevating others and, when it comes to war – as, tragically, it so often does – on eliminating many of them. We now have a golden opportunity to change this – or the consequences could be unimaginably destructive.

We've also acted as though our natural resources are endless. That's another profound lesson of the Anthropocene. We've taken for granted the extraordinary abundance of nature on planet Earth, which seems almost infinite when compared to the other known planets in the universe, but it has its limits. In the developed world, we cannot continue to act as though we had several planets' worth of natural resources available to us and to future generations, still less aspire to a luxury lifestyle that would require even more resources. We need to manage the precarious fragility of our biosphere or lose it. We are one people on one planet – not many peoples on many planets.

We are also at a unique moment in history, as I suggested in the Introduction. We can see the momentous changes of the Anthropocene all around us, yet we act as though we were still in the Holocene. We have the chance to redesign our world order, not simply to avert ecological catastrophe but to create the social equality, peace and human flourishing which has always been part of the human dream. So it's back to the drawing board for humanity. Except when have we ever really been there before? Nobody designed our current world plan: it simply evolved, largely guided by those who were already in power and keen to protect the wealth which it gave them. For a short time – perhaps for no more than a decade or so – we have the unique chance to create a new world plan which is fit not only for the twenty-first century but for as long as the Anthropocene endures.

People-planet propositions

Here are some of the further implications of the people-planet vision.

First, it facilitates a holistic approach which always sees the part in the context of the whole. This eclipses the fragmentary, biased, self-centred thinking of growthism, which turns the most proximate part into the whole and confines everything else to the shadows. It forces us to think in terms of the whole planet, not simply that part of the globe which we happen to occupy. It can help us see 'invisibles', such as people in the poorest parts of the world. We need this kind of global vision to counter the phenomenon of growthism, which has penetrated every major institution worldwide. To tackle the interconnected crises of the Anthropocene we need to operate planetwide, even if many actions will have to be achieved locally. Uniting the macro- and the micro-levels will be key to achieving a people-planet transformation.

Second, a people-planet vision means seeing humanity as a relationship rather than a self-defining entity. To define humanity in isolation from our natural environment, segregating people and planet, has always been a philosophically incoherent act of human vanity. New research is showing just how many people share a feeling of connectedness to humanity with a connectedness to nature (e.g. Lee *et al.*, 2015). This mindset sees the goal as cooperation with the biosphere, rather than conquest of it (which would be ultimate Pyrrhic victory for humanity).

This 'people first, planet first' dialectic also acts as a powerful corrective to the competitivism which so easily divides us, countering our all-too-human tendency to form into opposing groups and replacing an 'us and them' with a 'we' vision. This extra-human dimension also gives us a new ability to see ourselves – as if for the first time. At the moment we still seem to rely on aliens and extraterrestrial beings in science fiction to give us a glimpse of humanity as a unified species. The Anthropocene requires us to develop a planetwide consciousness, which sees the interaction of humanity and its environment as primary, not as a secondary issue buried somewhere down the agenda.

Third, people-planet awareness can also bring us a new sense of positivity and gratitude for nature and the gift of life, which might be called 'planetude'. We are lucky to be alive, which is almost always better than the alternative, and to be born human, which is probably better than other species options. We are in this fortunate condition because we inhabit a lucky planet, which specializes in life in a way that is completely unique in our solar system. That perspective in itself should move us away from the grim desperation which always seeks something more, which sees humanity as a lack, an insufficiency, guilty of the pride of original sin and in need of redemption, instead of the miracle of evolution that we are. In the face of this pessimism, which prepares us for dystopia, people-planet awareness proclaims the basic optimism which should come from being human.

Fourth, the interaction of people and planet changes our sense of time. It not only enables us to grasp the uniqueness of our historical moment, but also to embrace much longer time horizons. It opens a sense of deep history, which can help us see the long vistas of planetary evolution and the extraordinary resilience of humanity, which can stand us in good stead for the struggle ahead. It's a temporal paradigm shift which can enable us to learn from societies which trace their roots back to our pre-Holocene, hunter-gatherer history, as well as create a new sense of responsibility for generations who have not yet been born (more of this in Step 12). This pivotal vision I'll refer to as 'remoderning', a purposeful going back to the past in order to find a better way to the future.

All this creates the opportunity for the long-term planning which is essential to solving the Anthropocene crisis and ending the reckless mismanagement which has brought it about. Our Western obsession with the short term, which leaves us stumbling from one disaster to the next, is no longer a realistic option. We got away with the piecemeal, reactive, self-serving management of the Holocene – to the extent that we did – purely because it was based on smaller populations using less advanced technologies. But almost 8 billion of us living in an ecologically unbalanced world, amid an explosion of untested technologies, is a very different proposition. We can't rely on reaction any more, we need pro-action. We must learn to see the future before it arrives, if we are to restore the equilibrium between humanity and its environment which we have lost. It may be the greatest challenge of decision-making which humanity has ever faced but it gives us the chance to create the stability and cohesion out of which utopia can emerge.

The logic of balance: the circularity of enough

Although the people-planet vision seems to take us into a wholly new dimension of being, utopia relies on something much more familiar: the logic of balance. This is the alternative to the vicious circularity of grow-thism with its mad, impossible vision of never-ending material expansion. The logic of balance is the logic of return, the logic which reunites the past and the future. It's the karma popularly expressed in the phrases, 'what goes around comes around' and 'what you sow so shall you reap'. It's rooted in Daedalus's philosophy of moderation. 'Nothing in excess' was inscribed above the Apollo of Delphi in ancient Greece and it's a piece of wisdom we desperately need to recognize today. Achieving moderation creates a virtuous circle. For example, the right amount of exercise increases your fitness, enabling your muscular power and cardio-vascular capacity to expand amazingly. But too much exercise can cause you an injury and exercising with an injury only intensifies the damage (as every marathon runner knows).

The circle is the symbol of utopia. It's what we see when we gaze at the famous image of Earth taken from space, the spherical 'blue planet' made up of a three-dimensional multiplicity of circles. Compare this to the shape of our current sloping world, with its steep hierarchical lines, pyramids of power and the illusory diagonals of infinite economic growth. Circularity is not just a visual image of utopia, it's also one of its key operating principles, a force which can reshape the current institutions of the world, from economics to politics to international relations and culture. Virtuous circles can drive out vicious circles, in an ever-correcting state of balance.

This circular logic can also be described as the rationality of enough. Focusing on enough not only tells us that 'too much' can trap us in cycles of dissatisfaction but that it's also probably somebody else's 'too little'. In other words, utopianism is not outrageous idealism but simple realism. It only seems extreme when confronted by the irrational excesses of our current world plan. As Freud (1920/1984) suggested, the reality principle may seem less exciting than the pleasure principle, but in the end the gently undulating plain of satisfaction is a better basis for mature psychological life than an alpine landscape of highs and lows. Indeed, the Latin etymology of the word 'satisfaction' tell us all we need to know: together *facere* and *satis* mean 'making enough'. Working within rational limits, achieving the right ratio between less and more, this is the satisfaction utopia brings, and 'making enough' is as good a way as any to sum up its mission.

The beauty of 'enoughism' is its simplicity. Thomas Princen calls it 'the logic of sufficiency', explaining that 'by asking how much is enough, and how much is too much, one necessarily asks what is excessive, what the risks are ... both for the immediate and the long term' (2005:9). We need this commonsense, intuitive approach on our drawing board of humanity to guide us through the bewildering, interconnected complexity and knotty 'wickedness' of the Anthropocene crisis. It can give us a map which shows how close we are to a transformed world, where enough is enough and less is genuinely more (at least for most people). It's all a matter of getting the scale right, up-scaling those areas which don't receive enough resources (like health, equality, peace), and down-scaling those which receive too much (luxury goods, tax havens, fossil fuels). It means growing what we really need and degrowing what we can't afford. Utopia is sufficiently challenging without making it more complex than it needs to be. The logic of balance will be more than enough.

SEWP: the balance model

Supporting this vision of a people planet utopia are four pillars, which are intended to give this change plan the detail that will help to make it operational. These fundamentals are sustainability, equitability and wellbeing planetwide and together they make up the SEWP model.

Pillar 1: Sustainability

Sustainability is the maximum growth which a closed system can allow without threatening its viability. Sustainable systems are able to regenerate themselves, to diversify within limits and have high degrees of resilience which enable them to bounce back from shocks (Mulligan, 2015). Sustainability is the logic of enough in action, represented by the complex, self-organizing interactions by which nature attains a steady state of equilibrium. Your body is working to achieve this condition of homeostasis at this very minute, keeping your temperature neither too hot nor too cold, by means of mechanisms like shivering or perspiring or other subtle biochemical and neurological adjustments.

At its best, sustainability has the perfection of a circle: endless in that what comes around keeps going around but also constrained by its closed structure. That's why it's associated with actions and concepts beginning with the prefix 're-', like 'regenerating', 'recycling', 'renewing' and 'restoring', because it stands for doing something again, although each time it repeats itself it adds something new.

To understand this better, we need to draw on systems theory, which tells us that all systems organize themselves through the interaction of two cycles. Reinforcing cycles promote growth or decline, while balancing cycles bring about stability (Meadows, 2008). If reinforcement flows are not checked by balancing flows, they can lead to exponential growth which in turn leads to rapid decline and the collapse of the system. The aim of sustainability is to prevent this breakdown and instead promote the maximum amount of growth the system can tolerate.

Take global warming, which at the moment is driven by a reinforcement loop in which the expanding amounts of greenhouse gas in the atmosphere prevent more and more heat from escaping the earth's surface. This impairs natural balancing cycles like the albedo effect, the tendency for white ice to reflect back the sun's rays. As ice melts and is replaced by dark water, the ocean's temperature increases, creating another reinforcing cycle which further accelerates global warming. The aim of climate containment is to introduce new balancing flows – for instance, by eliminating the use of fossil fuels in energy production – to alter the current reinforcement cycles, which otherwise will result in climate chaos.

Sustainability focuses on the quantity and quality of human activity necessary to achieve a new state of equilibrium in which the biosphere can regenerate all the energy it has lost. Achieving and maintaining this point of total sustainability planetwide will require a revolution in what we produce and what we waste and substantial changes to our consumption and life styles. This degree of people-planet circularity calls for a totally new approach to the design, planning and engineering of our world and ultimately for an economic levelling of poor and rich economies until their ecological footprints match. This, in turn, creates the opportunity to address humanity's most outstanding piece of unfinished business: how to live together equitably.

Pillar 2: Equitability

The desire for equitability, for a just, fair and equal society, is another core element of the utopian ideal. Ever since the Enlightenment, the Rousseauian principles enunciated in the American Constitution of 1776 – 'all men are created equal' – and the French Revolution's Declaration of Human Rights of 1789 – 'men are born, and remain, free and equal in rights' – have been the theoretical cornerstones of the West's political and juridical systems. The long overdue challenge of a twenty-first-century utopia will be to turn this theory into practice and not just for the West (or only for men). It means making equitability the principle governing all human relationships, regardless of gender, ethnicity, sexuality or able-bodiedness. Now, under the growing pressure of the Anthropocene crisis, we may have our best chance to fully realize one of the most powerful ideas humanity has ever created.

Equitability is the logic of balance applied to the human world. It involves the ability to see yourself in a delicate, reciprocal relationship with others, which may well be an innate human quality. Psychologists have found that 15-month-old infants display 'the rudiments of a sense of fairness in that they expect resources to be allocated equally when observing others' (Schmidt and Sommerville, 2011). It's certainly a moral principle that can be found across the world in virtually every major religion, public philosophy and ethical code. It's often referred to as the Golden Rule. Confucius summed it up 2,500 years ago when he was asked for the single principle needed to guide a person's conduct in life. 'It is perhaps the word "shu" ', he replied. 'Do not impose on others what you yourself do not desire' (*Analects* XV 24). 'What you wish done to yourself do to others' is how it was phrased more recently in the Declaration towards a Global Ethic, signed by 200 leaders from over 40 different faith traditions, which describes this principle as the 'unconditional norm for all areas of life' (Parliament of the World's Religions, 1993). This simple, seemingly universal, ethical position stands in stark opposition to the individualism and elitism of growthism and represents a concise refutation of the entire CIMENT ethos.

The most pure, social expression of the law of reciprocity is egalitarianism, a form of organization which still exists today among some pre-modern societies, which can help us understand equality as a lived practice. As Christopher Boehm's (1999) invaluable survey reveals, traditional egalitarian societies usually have little use for private possessions and often all their property is held in common. Redistribution rituals like potlatch and elaborate gift-giving ensure that nobody builds up too much wealth and power. In egalitarian societies, decision-making is often taken by the whole community, and a constant effort is made to prevent individualistic leaders from taking over and developing power bases which would lead to structural inequality. These 'reverse dominance' tactics include overt humour, mockery, covert criticism (gossip), denunciation, banishment and, in extreme cases, assassination. It's a reminder that egalitarianism is not an easy or lazy option: it requires vigilance and commitment from the whole group to prevent competitive, self-interested leaders from gaining a hold.

Even in traditional egalitarian societies, equality is not literal in the sense that everybody is seen to have the same needs and the same ability to contribute to society. Among humans, differences inevitably exist in personality, aptitude and energy and some will also be more vulnerable than others, especially the old, the young and the infirm. This notion of differential needs and abilities is most famously captured in the phrase 'from each according to his ability, to each according to his needs', which Karl Marx adapted from French utopian writers and which became a major source of inspiration for some of the boldest revolutionary experiments of the twentieth century (Manuel and Manuel, 1979).

The principle of 'equality within difference' not only respects individual human variability, it actively seeks to maximize diversity. This means recognizing people for their humanity, regardless of their class, gender identity, ethnicity, sexual preference or any other trait that can be stereotyped. It means making forms of sexual or ethnic violence in word or deed punishable and socially repellent. The progress recently made by campaigns like 'Me Too' show that cultural awareness can spread rapidly but transforming the way people of different genders relate to each other requires systemic change. As we'll see in Step 7, post-growth enterprises are already attempting to establish structural equality, using methods such as wage ratios, diversity quotas and other new rule-based systems. And new forms of company ownership are bringing 'equity', in the sense of 'fairness', into alignment with its other meaning of 'shareholding'.

The scales of justice are another long-standing symbol of human desire for equilibrium (the ancient Egyptians believed that after death the god Anubis would weigh your heart against a feather to determine your fate). The courage and persistence of groups campaigning for justice show how powerful the need for fairness is in our world. It's a profound human need, which can be pursued over many generations, as in the case of colonial injustices, for example, or other crimes of the sloping world. The desire for a better balance between right and wrong, has always been at the heart of utopia and making real progress on social equality is as central to managing the Anthropocene crisis as eliminating ecological imbalances.

Pillar 3: Wellbeing

The third pillar of the people-planet plan is human wellbeing. This is a condition of existence which we explore every day in the typical exchange, 'How are you?' 'I'm well, and you?' and through concepts such as happiness and life satisfaction. It's long been a staple of utopia and, in fact, for many centuries was at the heart of political economy. For Aristotle, eudaemonism, or human flourishing, was the very point of politics and ethics. For Thomas More, Utopia was the 'happy place', as well as 'no place' (a pun on the prefix *eu-* which can mean 'good' or 'happy' (More, 1516/2012:9)). The same priority of values emerged again in the late 1700s in the philosophy of Jeremy Bentham, who saw life as a perpetual tussle between pleasure and pain and argued that public policy should be guided by the principle of 'the greatest happiness of the greatest number'. However, when economics took its fake turn towards science in the late 1800s, wellbeing was relegated to the margins of public planning. In the early twentieth century even the emergent discipline of psychology tended to be focused on the unsunny lowlands of the human condition, where self-control was the best one could hope for, before humanistic psychotherapy and latterly positive psychology put human flourishing back on the agenda. Now some economists have taken up the baton again, restoring happiness as an indicator of economic success (more of this in Step 3).

As a result, there are a number of increasingly sophisticated approaches to wellbeing that we may draw on (e.g. Ryff and Krueger, 2018) but I propose to employ here a relatively simply definition, which I've found useful in everyday practice. It's based around six terms: health, education, love, involvement, originality and sense of purpose. Together these make up the mnemonic HELIOS, the ancient Greek word for the 'sun', which, apart from being the major source of life on earth, has long been associated with human happiness.

Health

Good health is a vital constituent of wellbeing, without which it's extremely difficult to live life to the full. To be healthy is to be whole (or 'hale'), which requires the active functioning of the totality of biophysical and biochemical systems in the human body. This, in turn, depends on a positive interaction with your environment, which needs to meet your basic subsistence needs, such as food, water and shelter. It also needs to provide the social and cultural fulfilment necessary for robust mental health and the avoidance of depression, anxiety and other psychological disorders which are the biggest source of human unhappiness. Ultimately, then, robust physical and mental health is another instance of the logic of enough, one that implies a state of reciprocal balance with the totality of society.

Education

Education is another core element of wellbeing and a long-standing goal of utopians. In *The Shape of Things to Come* (1933), for example, H.G. Wells imagined a world in which tertiary education was universal, producing a population of polymaths. We're still a long way from that. Worldwide only 7% of people have a college degree and a quarter of a billion people on the planet remain illiterate (UNESCO, 2016). Education is one of the few areas which can expand almost infinitely without increasing humanity's material footprint. And once the current educational bias towards an educated minority is removed – the disequalizing effect of so-called 'cultural

capital' (Bourdieu and Passeron, 1990) – an explosion in diverse knowledge and creativity can be expected.

A wellbeing-based society will be a total learning society, prioritizing
life-long learning for everybody over formal qualifications. This will free
up teachers as well as learners, as for many, teaching is as much a passion
as it is a profession. Liberated from the constraints of institutionalized,
monetized education, a learning society will nurture a whole range of new
and old life skills, vastly improving people's ability to participate creatively
in their social and natural environments.

Love

According to a Ministry of Justice report, almost a third of UK prisoners
have experienced emotional, physical or sexual abuse in childhood (Williams *et al.*, 2012), and for a long time psychologists have known that much
of the violence in society is perpetrated by those who have been deprived
of love at an early age (e.g. Miller, 1985). Human love should start at the
moment of birth, as parental love is the first and most important reciprocal bond for humans. Without this early attachment, happiness and fulfilment in later life can be hard to come by, which is why love, in every sense,
is at the heart of a wellbeing society. This includes the emotional ties of
kinship, friendship, communal fellow-feeling and even the utopian idea of
humanity as a single family ('the brotherhood of man'). Love also involves
the free play of adult sexuality. That's another utopian theme, the idea
that humanity can only achieve true sexual liberation through social and
economic emancipation.

Put all these lines of desire together, and we have another definition of
utopia, as 'the democracy of love'. We can't always choose who we love or
who we are loved by, but we can chose how we relate to our loved ones in
thought and deed. In this union of rational choice and our deepest emotional desires, the democracy of love can reach the highest and most fulfilling state humans are capable of – one that makes techno-utopias seems
shallow and tawdry by comparison.

Involvement

Being actively involved with others in the world around you is another key
to human flourishing. Social alienation, isolation and a lack of social
support and connectedness are some of the most destructive aspects of
growthism – loneliness now kills more people than obesity and it can
increase the risk of coronary heart disease or stroke by 30% (Valtorta *et al.*,
2016). And yet the communitarian spirit can still prevail. It's often most
visible in disasters, such as the Grenfell Tower conflagration in my area of
West London in June 2017, when the entire community seemed to spring
to the help of the victims, while the authorities struggled to organize

anything. Involvement with others involves sharing. In Ubuntu, the Zulu philosophy of communal life, this interactional principle is expressed in the phrase, 'I am a person through other persons.' Involvement is also key to 'flow', a significant element in the psychology of happiness, which we experience when we're so absorbed in an activity that time seems to pass in a flash and decisions appear to make themselves (Csikszentmihalyi, 1992).

Originality

Wellbeing also involves the ability to engage in creativity. In his important taxonomy of human needs, economist Manfred Max-Neef (1991) includes creation and idleness, characterized by such qualities as curiosity, day-dreaming, imagination, passion, skills and productive feedback. Psychologist Abraham Maslow wrote that 'creativeness and the concept of the healthy, self-actualizing, fully human person' (whom he placed at the pinnacle of his well-known hierarchy of needs) 'are coming closer and closer together and may perhaps turn out to be the same thing' (1971:55). Creative originality can express itself through the learning of existing skills, as in crafts, but it can also denote the ability to make a difference, to define one's own contribution and add something to the world. This involves a commitment to openness and inquisitiveness, and, if necessary, repeated experimentation. Originality requires the right to imagine and to soar beyond the confines of the status quo (which often reinforces itself by trying to crush the imagination).

Sense of purpose

A sense of purpose creates a vital trajectory towards the future, without which our wellbeing can suffer and unhappiness, apathy and addictive recklessness set in. As Nietzsche wrote, 'if we possess our *why* of life we can put up with almost any *how*' (1889/1968:33). Clear, confident objectives are crucial for informed choice-making. Growth capitalism has been extraordinarily effective in capturing people's sense of the future and persuading them that there is no alternative to it. An equally powerful sense of purpose is crucial for utopia and for the choices which can resolve the Anthropocene crisis in a positive manner.

Pillar 4: Planetwide consciousness

The final pillar of the SEWP model is a reminder of the need to raise our theory and practice to a truly planetwide plane. Anthropocene consciousness needs to be holistic and inclusive, putting systems thinking at the forefront of our approach to our analysis and planning, and rejecting the fragmentation of knowledge in the free-market economy. It means making internationalism a primary value and literally and imaginatively stepping up to seeing ourselves as one people on one planet (more of this in the next step).

This whole-world approach can bring together natural science, social science and the humanities in a synthesis that transcends the current domination of individual specialisms, which fiercely protect themselves from other provinces of learning. People-planet thinking implies a knowledge revolution that breaks down the walls of academia which prevent us from seeing what is really going on in our new epoch. For the informed, people-planet generalist, synthesis is the highest value. Philosophically, it creates the possibility of transcending the splits and the dualisms of conventional thought, which privilege the private over public, or men over women and the West over the rest, biasing our thinking at the deepest, most unconscious level. Holistic thinking is our best hope for restoring the shattered mirror of our current political world, where some are proclaiming 'the death of truth' (Kakutani, 2018) and evidence-based discourse seems to have been abandoned.

In contrast to the cul-de-sac of human infighting, planetude is a delta: it widens rather than narrows. It can open us up to the inspiration of nature. Even as we recognize our stewardship of nature and our responsibility to preserve it, we can see in a new light the innovation the natural world has created over millions of years. For example, biomimicry studies reveal incredibly complex yet simple phenomena such as the creation of colour through light rather than dyes (as in the butterfly's wing) or the silk which a spider produces, which pound for pound is the strongest thread in the universe (Benyus, 1997:135). This recognition could even bring within reach a reconciliation between science and many forms of spirituality, perhaps the ultimate state of utopian synthesis.

Planetwide thinking can also bring a much-needed ethical dimension to public policy and private choice-making. It puts human flourishing at the centre of all its concerns but extends this to all sentient beings, highlighting the reverence for animals that is part of being human, whether expressed in the earliest human art in cave paintings or the animism of young children, who are unable (or unwilling) to distinguish between humans and animals.

Finally, it's worth repeating, that the people-planet perspective can give us new confidence in decision-making, creating a new context and new imperatives for the bold choices which urgently need to be made in the coming years. This planning on a visionary scale circularizes top-down policy through a commitment to the self-organizing principles by which nature has always functioned. In short, a new vision for our new epoch can enable us to see humanity not as a horde of violent competitors, dominated by a tiny elite, but as peace-loving, creative cooperators, all worthy of an equal right to exist and well capable of managing our planet so that all can share in its amazing abundance.

Conclusion

In a nutshell, Step 1 is about embracing a grand vision of where we are, where we have been and where we need to go. We need to get the balance right, like Daedalus, and not fly to destruction by ignoring the power of nature, like Icarus. That means creating a clear path to the future which enables us to rectify the irresponsible mismanagement of our world which the twenty-first century has so alarmingly revealed. The SEWP model of sustainable, equitable wellbeing planetwide can bring us closer to fulfilling humanity's ancient, utopian dreams of equality, peace and happiness. In other words, the opportunity could not be greater. So let's move on to the goals and values which can help to turn this vision into a reality.

7 Step 2

Set goals and establish values

A people-planet utopia may be a shining vision, but it's going to take some tough structural changes to transform the SEWP model into a functional social system. That's the task for Step 2. And in order to replace our growthist current world plan, we'll also need a transformation of the values and beliefs which underpin it.

Let's start with the structural changes. The first move is to set some clear, wide-ranging goals which will focus our thoughts and actions. Goal-setting is one of the most powerful resources in the change-management toolbox. The strategic decision-making involved in establishing targets can itself have a transformative effect, which is one reason why it has been claimed that goal-setting is organizational psychology's best candidate for 'elevation to the lofty status of a scientific law of nature' (Mento *et al.*, 1987:74). What works for organizations is also true of individuals. A clearly ranked list of specific goals is far more likely to bring rewards than a rambling agenda of vague, wished-for outcomes. So we need to make full use of this often miraculous source of change if we are going to have a real chance of turning our new world plan into a reality.

Some planetwide goals already exist for changing the world over the next decade. The UN's 2030 Sustainable Development Goals were finalized in 2015 in its 'Transforming our World' programme (UN, 2015b). They are a useful start and represent a significant act of international collaboration, but they are still too patchy, contradictory and rooted in Holocene economics to be up to the task of managing the Anthropocene crisis. If we are to achieve total sustainability, the point where we begin to live within our ecological means, in a time scale which does not lock us into irreversible environmental damage, more ambitious goals are needed up to 2030. These may seem extreme but that's a characteristic of any authentic paradigm shift and in reality they simply represent the logic of balance in action. What's more, as we'll see in Step 3, many of them are grounded in the long-established theory and practice of ecological economics.

Containing climate change

As Chapter 1 made clear, if we don't significantly reduce greenhouse-gas emissions in the coming decade, it will be impossible to contain climate change at 1.5°C. The pledges currently made by 194 countries in the Paris Climate Agreement are not enough to prevent global warming of 3–4°C or more by 2100, which would have catastrophic consequences for all life on earth (including human life). To do this, we need to take stringent measures, such as ensuring that three-quarters of all existing reserves of fossil fuel remain in the ground (Berners-Lee and Clark, 2013).

Realistic goals around climate change have to get the timescale right and focus on creating zero emissions in the rich countries which are the highest emitters of greenhouse gas by 2030. Targets of 2050 or even 2100 are too distant to be of use. We also need targets beyond the end of the century, as the risk of global warming will not suddenly end. These goals are missing from the IPCC reports, an inexcusable omission, as many children alive today will live well into the twenty-second century.

In any change plan, goals that are absent undermine existing goals. So we also need tough targets for the emissions-producing sectors that are excluded from the Paris Climate Agreement, such as shipping, responsible for 2.5% of greenhouse-gas emissions and aviation, pollution from which is set to triple by 2050 (IMO, 2014). We also urgently need to eliminate the illusory targets based on the use of biofuels and unproven negative-emissions technology, the so-called BECCs (they can be re-instated if technologies such as carbon storage and capture ever come into existence). And finally, we still need mechanisms around monitoring the progress of climate targets and legally enforceable penalties for countries failing to meet them, although some progress was made in these areas at the 2018 UN Climate Change Conference in Katowice. Goals without consequences are mere aspirations, so it was no surprise to find that two years after the Paris Climate Agreement, not a single major industrialized nation was living up to its emissions pledges (Victor *et al.*, 2017). This was confirmed in late 2018 in a comprehensive review by Climate Transparency (2018) which found that 82% of energy needs in the G20 countries were still being met by fossil fuels and that the planet was on course for warming of 3.2°C by 2100.

Ending the attrition of nature

Rigorous goal-setting of a similar kind is required to preserve biodiversity and move towards global ecological balance. The nine measurable planetary boundaries, first articulated by Will Steffen, Katherine Richardson, Johan Rockström and others in 2009, have not yet been formally included in the UN's Sustainable Development Goals, but they may well represent humanity's best chance for halting our mad rush towards the destruction of our planetary home.

New worldwide goals around preserving the integrity of the biosphere (a boundary which has already been breached) can start the task of returning the world to the levels of biodiversity enjoyed for thousands of years prior to the industrial revolution. We urgently need to curtail the mass extinction of wildlife which has seen humanity, a mere 0.1% of the biomass of this planet, wipe out 83% of all mammals and half of all plants since the dawn of the Holocene (Bar-On *et al.*, 2018). Biodiversity goals will also help to preserve threatened environmental habitats, such as forests, grasslands and tundra, and marine biomes, like coral reefs and mangrove swamps. Ocean acidification targets will aim to stop our oceans being starved of oxygen by chemical pollution and littered with millions of tons of plastic waste each year.

Once goals for chemical pollution are universally set we can expect to see the decline of intensified chemically-based agriculture in unsuitable regions, which are accelerating soil depletion and water withdrawals. They will also help to prevent other potential dangers posed by the more than 100,000 chemicals currently in commercial use – many of them completely untested (Urbina, 2013). As we start to manage the planet's aquifers, underwater rivers and lakes, we can protect our reserves of one of our most precious finite resources, freshwater, from overuse and the invasion by salt water to which it is currently subjected. Targets will also help to reduce the reckless use of phosphates and nitrogen in agriculture and other threats posed by profit-seeking industrialized farming. Rigorous auditing of the planet's minerals will maintain the metals and the other minerals which are heading for irreversible decline this century. And land-conversion targets can help to bring about widespread reforestation, the replenishment of soils and slow down the creeping advance of the world's deserts.

All this is doable, but it won't be without cost. To manage our climate and our environment in the way that the Anthropocene requires will mean abandoning many of the illusions of never-ending wealth accumulation. The growthist economics of the Holocene will have to be left behind, something the UN's Sustainable Development Goals unfortunately are not yet ready to do. They assume continued GDP growth in all countries, support the concept of economic decoupling and set goals of at least 7% annual increase in GDP for the least developed nations (UN, 2015b). It will take a fundamental rethinking of economics, of the kind we'll examine in the next chapter, if we are to achieve real progress towards global sustainability in the time we have left.

Other goals for managing the Anthropocene crisis

Brave, honest goal-setting can also help with many of the other seemingly intractable problems on the burning platform caused by growthism. The inequality issue is a good example of how our language around goals can be confusing and lower our ambitions. We need to stop talking about reducing inequality and start talking about increasing equality. As we saw earlier, the notion of 'lifting people out of poverty' is not only highly questionable in reality, it's actually quite compatible with *increased* economic disparities between the top and bottom income distributions. Once 'raising equality' becomes the measurable target, this distracting manoeuvre will be more difficult to make and it becomes easier to introduce equality goals around such issues as social mobility, health outcomes and educational attainment.

Likewise, goals around improving democracy will dispel some of the complacency about past achievements, which masks the real deficits in representation and popular engagement, especially in the Anglo-American sphere. Self-congratulatory rhetoric around civilized values also turns attention away from the slow progress of democracy around the world this century and the major regressions taking place: for example, as 'emerging democracies' like Russia and Turkey turn into electoral dictatorships.

The goal of eliminating war is at the forefront of a utopian consciousness but finds little resonance in the battlefield logic of contemporary geopolitical reality. It may seem incredible in the twenty-first century that the invasion of Iraq by the Western coalition caused hundreds of thousands of violent deaths and the Syrian war killed half a million people (many of them civilians) and drove over ten million from their homes. Just as disturbing is the Second Congo War in which 5.4 million people are estimated to have died between 1998 and 2007, a humanitarian catastrophe which has been largely ignored by the rest of the world (International Rescue Committee, 2007). This egregious indifference to human suffering couldn't happen if we had explicit, internationally agreed peace goals, effective monitoring of conflicts worldwide and much more emphasis on peace-building.

We'll return to this issue in Step 8, where we'll also look at concrete measures to combat another symptom of our current world crisis, overpopulation in some of the world's poorest regions. Setting targets around population levels is a highly controversial subject, especially among progressives, because it seems to invite nationalist and overtly racist interpretations of the problem. But we cannot duck this responsibility if we are to achieve sustainability on our finite planet. Growthism simply kicks the can down the road, making a dystopian reaction to increased mass migrations from crisis-torn areas all the more likely. As we'll see, the solution lies not in forced sterilization or even more extreme 'population reduction' methods but the voluntary birth control which occurs when adequate contraception is available and girls have more secondary education and women greater empowerment. Setting explicit, evidence-based goals of this type is by far the best rejoinder to CIMENT-style polices.

Containing technology

That brings us to one of the most pressing and challenging set of goals a utopian transformation needs to put into place. Unless we can contain and redirect the vast tide of new technology coursing through the world, achieving total sustainability will be impossible. The first stage to accomplishing this containment is to believe that it can be done. Many intelligent and persuasive analysts seem to be convinced that advances in roboticization, AI and biotechnology are unstoppable and that all we can do is hope for the best (while perhaps secretly expecting the worst). The UN's Sustainable Development Goals don't include any targets around regulating technology, a sign of just how deeply a reverence for innovation is rooted in the modern psyche.

Yet technology has been made by us and so it can be remade by us to serve purposes appropriate to our historical moment. The Holocene culminated in the age of machines, but we are now on the threshold of the age of life. Life is what machines do not have, although some people seem to be determined to give them this, even if the ultimate cost to humanity could be horrific. In the age of life, that which is living takes precedence over all arrangements of metal, plastic and digital code. If that entails rewriting the algorithm of capital so that it no longer rewards a minority of investors but benefits all of society, future and present, so be it. Breaking taboos has always been the business of utopia.

One way of setting goals around innovation would be to create what we might call a SEWP charter, which would enable us to ask the following type of questions of all existing and potential technology:

- How ecologically sustainable is this proposed technology (i.e. how much does it contribute to achieving a steady state in the biosphere?)
- To what extent does it promote human equitability and equal opportunity and outcome?
- Does it potentially enhance or reduce human wellbeing?
- What are its possible implications planetwide?

This last question is crucial. A new universal precautionary principle is required to replace growthism's 'bring it to market and see what happens' approach. We need to rigorously assess the potential harm that new technologies can cause, not simply in developed countries but for the two thirds of the world's population who don't live in the global North.

Once broad sustainable technology development goals are established, there are many measures which will help to implement them. Here are just a few:

1   Set up regulatory bodies to monitor all developments in technology, medicine, gene editing and biotechnology, armed with effective

powers for shutting down inappropriate research and penalizing offending parties. We need much more public control over the huge investments being made into artificial intelligence by the world's biggest corporations. At the moment, only a tiny fraction of research into AI is dedicated to safety (O'Connell, 2017). Legislation could compel all organizations researching AI to demonstrate that their intelligent machines will remain under full human control. Only if this can be satisfied should further developments be permitted.

2   Apply SEWP principles to all taxpayer-funded research. For example, 84% of pharmaceutical research is government funded (Hickel, 2017) as have been two thirds of the most influential US technologies of the past half-century, including smartphones, autonomous cars and personalized medicine (Brookings Institute, 2017). The public should also receive a return on successful taxpayer investments.

3   Initiate anti-trust legislation. This is increasingly being called for by mainstream politicians and commentators as a way of reducing the near-monopoly on power over new innovations which the high-tech colossuses currently enjoy. Even Apple CEO Tim Cook has said, 'we have to admit when the free market is not working. And it hasn't worked here' (Allen and Fried, 2018). Breaking up these corporations (two of which hit the trillion-dollar valuation mark in 2018) would create a host of opportunities for smaller, local, employee-owned organizations. Bringing technology corporations into public ownership could also be an option (using sophisticated, organizational methods developed since the disappearance of the clumsy, nationalized behemoths of the past).

4   Introduce new incentives for commons-based technology developers, open-source programmers and non-profit, cooperatively run and community-based enterprises (more on post-growth organizations in Step 7).

5   Consider banning the practice of using technology and science to induce compulsive and addictive behaviour, whether in the consumption of food or drink or through gambling, entertainment and social media.

6   In the end, a moratorium on all new technology may be necessity in order to staunch the almost unimaginably rapid flow of innovation this century. Severely regulating Silicon Valley will not be easy but a 'techno-pause' will allow us to take stock of what is really compatible with authentic sustainability goals. In fact, it's a small price to pay to prevent the algorithms of capital from driving creative destruction to a wholly new level and creating changes to virtually everything about being human, without any public debate or agreement. And, realistically speaking, is there any other way to guarantee that we don't commit the ultimate human hubris of endowing machines with such intelligence that they decide to solve the Anthropocene crisis in a

manner that suits them rather than their (former) masters? Also bear in mind that new breakthroughs which do not breach SEWP boundaries will almost certainly occur – the long-heralded nuclear fusion revolution might be a case in point – and these will bring dramatic benefits to everybody.

The great transvaluation: the CANDID ethos

Setting transformational targets can help to channel utopianism in the right direction, but a new world system is unlikely to come about without a similar paradigm shift in our values system. New choices require a new consciousness. Values can provide the experiential and philosophical guidelines to help us set out on a new journey and tell us how close we are to reaching our destination. They can also connect us to psychologically meaningful beliefs that we already hold.

New values are vital to challenge a growthist reality which comes at us from every side at once. As we've seen, the competitivism, individualism and materialism of the CIMENT ethos are deeply rooted in our institutions, relationships and thinking. To replace this system we need to expose its outdated values and offer alternative beliefs, better arguments and richer forms of motivation. In fact, nothing less than a people-planet revolution in consciousness is called for, akin to what Nietzsche termed 'a transvaluation of all values' ('Umwertung aller Werte') (1889/1954:72).

So here is the CANDID transvaluation, a utopian alternative to the beliefs which shore up the growthist irrationale. It's a set of values based on cooperativism, altruism, non-materialism, democracy, internationalism and deference to nature. As the CANDID mnemonic suggests, these norms are transparent and open and aim to shatter the inauthenticity and secrecy which keep our current world plan in place.

For illustration purposes, I present the contrast between CANDID and CIMENT values in the form of a grid in Figure 7.1. However, the revolution of values the grid implies should not only be seen as a binary choice but as a potential synthesis which brings out the best in both sets of beliefs.

Cooperativism

The lead value in the CANDID ethos is cooperation, a core principle of sustainability and equitability and an expression of the logic of balance. Real-world competition entails systemic imbalance: in a zero-sum game, someone has to end up on top and someone on the bottom. For cooperation, by contrast, a non-zero outcome is not simply a possibility but the whole object of the exercise. This kind of win–win solution is the precondition for rebalancing the world. It's based on a give-and-take strategy, where you relinquish some things in order to gain others. Growthism can't understand the cooperative spirit because it's never satisfied and never has

People-planet utopia

Growthism

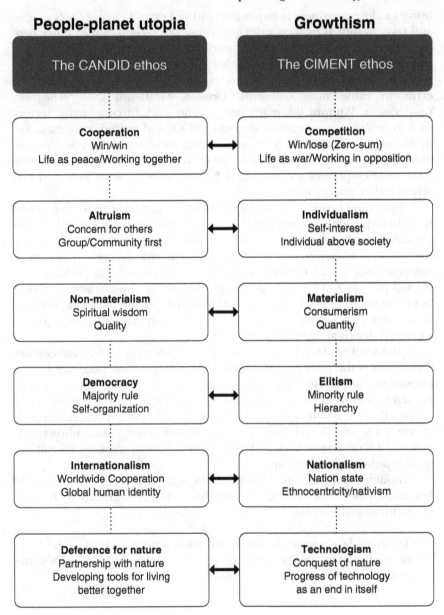

Figure 7.1 The CANDID/CIMENT values grid.

enough; whereas the cooperator can always settle for less if it means more in the end.

Cooperativeness is sidelined by our current world plan, but it still thrives in every walk of life. A modern conurbation of millions of people living in close proximity is impossible without countless quiet acts of give and take, as well as explicit rules governing the recognition of other people's needs. The highways of the world are sites of intense, high-stakes cooperation, as drivers interact with each other in complex formations, often at lethally high speeds, where it takes only the smallest individual error to cause mass collisions. Growth capitalism itself relies on cooperation. Without the many people who work in cooperative sectors such as healthcare, education, charities, NGOs and reproductive care, for-profit corporations would have no economy in which to operate. And, as previously stated, my experience is that even in hyper-competitive corporations most employees are motivated by the desire to work with, and for, others rather than against them.

Cooperation is not about replacing all forms of competition: that would be both impossible and undesirable. In fact, competitive games which are regulated, fairly arbitrated and reset to zero after every event provide a fine example of how to endow cooperativeness with the creative energy of competitiveness. Life is not a game, but in utopia we can perhaps start playing politics and business as though they were: in other words, bound by fair, equal rules. And why have the virtues of 'playing the game' become so unfashionable? Once winning becomes the only reason for engaging in a game, defeat is always certain to follow.

At the level of deep history, one the most exciting twenty-first-century discoveries is the growing realization of how important cooperation is to human evolution. Biologist and mathematician Martin Nowak defines human beings as 'super-cooperators' who are capable of a wider array of cooperative behaviours than any other species. These include direct reciprocity ('I'll scratch your back and you scratch mine') and indirect reciprocity ('I scratch your back and someone will scratch mine because of the good reputation I've built up').

Although competitiveness has played a significant role in human evolution, Nowak echoes my sense that the Anthropocene has to be very different, when he writes:

> Today we face a stark choice: we can either move up to the next stage of evolutionary complexity, or we go into decline, even become extinct.
>
> (2011: 281–2)

Asserting the cooperative strategies and behaviours which many people intuitively favour is one of the surest ways to bring about utopian change. Game theory shows that the majority of people prefer to cooperate rather than compete. In the in the oft-repeated Prisoner's Dilemma experiment, where subjects can either show solidarity with a partner and receive a short prison sentence or betray them and get off scot-free, it's the former, cooperative option that is the usual choice (Fehr and Fischbacher, 2003).

Altruism

As a value, altruism (from the Latin *alter*, meaning 'other') is part of a cooperative consciousness, which sees being with others as the condition of human existence. Against individualistic self-interest, CANDID pitches selfless, other-directed emotions and behaviour. Altruism is the motivating force behind parenthood – we take it for granted that parents will sacrifice almost anything for their children – and in this sense it's what drives human evolution. It's probably hard-wired into us, as even babies seem to be able to empathize with the distress of other babies, and toddlers show a range of spontaneous sharing and helping behaviours, immediately responding to appeals to help from other children and adults (Tomasello, 2009).

Altruism often emerges when it really matters. In natural disasters, for example, we see it in the number of people who, literally and metaphorically, move towards danger rather than running away from it (Solnit, 2009). Many in the emergency services routinely risk their own lives in order to protect others, even when their own chances of survival are minimal. Anyone who doubts this quality should visit Postman's Park in London, a moving memorial to human altruism, with particularly heartbreaking accounts of children who gave their lives trying to save other children.

The challenge of utopia is to make altruism the norm. Other-directed behaviour is the highest form of morality, but, if it's not reciprocated, it's unlikely to be durable. If my acts of generosity are not met by yours, at some point I'm likely to give up on acts of kindness. Indeed, a survey by the Common Cause Foundation (2016) found that 74% of respondents prefer compassionate values to selfish values and yet 77% thought that their fellow citizens consider selfish values to be more important. As Step 9 will show, a propensity for individual kindness can be reinforced quite easily, but it will take a sustainable, equitable society to make it the condition of everyday behaviour.

Once this happens we can expect individuality to flourish. As people become more confident in their own identity, the herd mentality of mindless collectivism will wither away and with it the justification for aggressive individualism which can only express itself in defiance of others. In this sense, altruism is a self-interested value, in that my ability to develop myself and yours are ultimately the same. Only when the entire social and material environment is built around reciprocity can we can truly become ourselves.

Non-materialism

Achieving non-materialist ways of understanding the world is one of the great tasks of a people-planet utopia. Growthism worships the material power of things and predicates our wellbeing on what we have rather than who we are and how we interact with others. This puts us at the mercy of the CIMENT values and could force us down the dark road to dystopia. I'll return to the subject of spiritual ways of interpreting the world in Step 9, but here I just want to say that there are many traditional wells of non-materialist wisdom which we may need to draw on in order to adapt to the Anthropocene. Religions such as paganism or Shinto have a reverence for the phenomena and rhythms of nature, and Buddhism has a deep under-standing of life without material possessions. Christianity, like many reli-gions, has a moral code for good living, where altruistic and self-denying behaviour is rewarded, if only in what to non-believers is an imaginary afterlife. Secular non-materialism may even be on the rise. While claims that the growthist economy is 'dematerializing' must be treated with extreme scepticism, there are some signs that young adults are rejecting 'stuffocation', preferring to invest in experiences rather than consumer goods (Wallman, 2013).

Art is another door that has always taken us beyond an obsession with possessions. Human communities without music and dance have probably never existed, whereas most societies in history have managed to get by without burglar alarms or personal insurance. The world of ideas is another realm of non-materialism, driving the work of writers, thinkers and scientists far more than material rewards. Philosophically, this can even lead to a quasi-religious appreciation of being alive, as in the intense experience of the here and now, which phenomenologist Maurice Merleau-Ponty (1962: xiii) called 'wonder in the face of the world'.

Democracy

Democracy is the strongest value we have to combat the elitism which nor-malizes the sloped world of growthism. Democracy as the practical rule of the majority still has a long way to go worldwide and is even in danger of retreating in some developed countries. That is why the people-planet paradigm has to be committed to strengthening it. More democracy is the only viable alternative to less democracy.

At the core of the democratic idea is the practice of majoritarian decision-making. Increasingly, this is essential to taking on the historically unparalleled range of choices which our new era forces on us. Democracy needs to become more responsive, flexible and confident and engage people far more than simply putting a cross on a ballot paper once every few years.

New forms of practical choice-making need to find their way into every aspect of life, from the local to the national and from work to education and family life, contesting the top-down control which elitism regards as natural. As Martin Nowak says, 'we need to place more faith in citizens not leaders. Cooperation has to come from the bottom up and not be imposed from the top down' (2011:281–2).

Either we take choice-making to a new level of sophistication and develop a new social technology around it, or the current mismanagement of the world will persist. Vital decisions will continue to be made for us by the leadership class, except that these decisions will become increasingly life-changing, such as choices around the future of work and the biochemical structure of the human body. Over the past 400 years, achieving parliamentary democracy has been one of humanity's greatest achievements. Turning democratic choice into the lived reality of everyday experience, for everybody across the entire planet, is the true challenge of utopia in the Anthropocene.

Internationalism

'Internationalism' is a word that didn't exist until the late eighteenth century (we've Jeremy Bentham, again, to thank for it), and it still struggles to establish itself as a system of belief. It's hounded today by a revived nationalism, which blames some of the emerging problems of the Anthropocene crisis on foreigners of one sort or another and promotes a nostalgic, toxic nativism as a catch-all solution. This reinforces the competitivist mentality of 'the war of all against all' at the very time when we need a huge leap forward in international cooperation to take control of the unprecedented hydra of problems facing us.

The structural measures that can help promote global coordination will be examined further in Step 5, but, to become a genuine value, internationalism also has to fully enter into the personal sphere. Already, there are many people for whom internationalism is part of their core identity – one reason why so many in the UK found the Brexit vote in 2016 such a profoundly traumatic shock. As someone of Irish and German parentage, growing up in the English Home Counties, the idea of having a single national identity always seemed curiously alien to me. Around the world today growing numbers of people with multi-ethnic, multicultural heritages feel the same. Post-national identity is not about abandoning a 'patriotic' love for your country or region. On the contrary, it's about freeing up regionalism, getting closer to the town or area in which you live, and at the same time seeing the bigger, global picture.

Anthropocene belonging is a form of consciousness that goes beyond the either/or compartmentalization nationalism favours. It's an attitude quite distinct from the 'the citizens of nowhere' of global neoliberalism, whose home is wherever their capital is likely to extract the maximum returns. It's where the citizen of somewhere (a region or a town) meets the citizen of everywhere, who is open-minded, multicultural and resourceful, a global member of the people-first, planet-first world. It's the beginning of the sense of species-wide human identity which our new epoch demands.

Deference to nature (detechnologism)

Finally, how do we encourage a new psychological awareness to contest the blandishments of those who proclaim that untrammelled new technology is the only way to solve a world crisis which it has done so much to create? That's where placing the interaction of people and planet at the forefront of our thinking can pay off. Against those who see humanity's destiny as surmounting nature, fuelling a possible transhumanist nightmare, we need to rediscover our deference to nature. Among other things, that involves prioritizing earth science over psychics, placing less faith in space travel as a way of getting us out of our current planetary mess and adopting a more grateful and gracious attitude to our place in the cosmos.

This deference to nature can also be described as 'detechnologism', an attitude which flows from seeing new technology through the filter of the SEWP criteria. Detechnologism draws heavily on the concept of 'degrowth' (*decroissance*), which emerged as a concept and a social movement in France in the 1970s (Latouche, 2009). Degrowth is much more than a single value but a cluster of values which prioritize quality over quantity, ecology over conventional economics, self-organization over top-down power.

Like degrowth, detechnologism focuses on social technology, human-made instruments such as laws, rules, theories, moral codes and narratives which guide how people interact with one another. These fundamental tools of social existence predate anything that could be called a machine by hundreds of thousands of years. The technology of living, in contradistinction to living though technology, also means getting the most out of our social being, celebrating what we have already as humans and sharing in the abundance which potentially comes from being alive on this exceptional planet.

At the same time, fears that detechnologism means the end of new technology, a kind of total Ludditism or a literal 'going back to nature', are utterly unfounded. On the contrary, it's about expertise in technology selection, like a horticulturist working in an overgrown garden, identifying the plants that have value – because they are beautiful or aromatic or fruit-bearing – and freeing them from the weeds that choke their growth. Detechnologism is not about undiscovering aspirin or penicillin or uninventing electricity or the internet, even if that was remotely possible. Detech may be low-tech, less-tech and (in some cases) no-tech, but it's also more-tech when it comes to the innovations that really improve people's lives. It's about putting technology in its place as humanity's servant rather than its master. Detechnologism questions who and what economic growth is really for, rather than allowing the market to decide. In this sense, degrowth is actually 'right-growth', focusing on what is good or bad for us to expand in the qualitatively different epoch we now inhabit.

Conclusion

Step 2 is about having the courage to set bold goals that can help us turn the SEWP model of planetwide, sustainable, equitable wellbeing into a viable world plan. Breaking the grip of growthism on our hearts, minds and social structures will also require a revolution in values. The CANDID ethos could provide this, directing us towards the international cooperation and altruistic, democratic respect for nature which we need to manage the Anthropocene crisis and put us on the road to utopia. And, as we'll now see, it can also help us create a viable alternative to the intellectual linchpin of the growthist irrationale, mainstream economics.

8 Step 3

Support an ecological revolution in economics

Step 3 of the utopian change plan brings us up against the key institution of our current world: economics. Growthism is, at root, a system of economic mismanagement based on the contradictory assumption that infinite economic expansion is possible on a finite planet. In prioritizing the interests of shareholders, this unnatural economics ignores the devastating impact that unchecked economic activity is having on our planet and our chances of surviving on it. To operationalize the people-planet vision, we'll need a revolutionary new economic theory and practice, which brings the logic of balance to bear on the unparalleled challenges of our new epoch.

A natural economics is already here

Thankfully, the foundation for an economics for the Anthropocene already exists. Since the early 1970s economists have been laying the groundwork for an ecological economics which utterly changes the way we think about markets, supply and demand, production and consumption. The big idea of ecological economics is simple; it's that we should see ourselves as subject to the laws of nature. As pioneer US ecological economist Herman Daly (1996:48) puts it:

> Just as the micro unit of the economy (firm or household) operates as part of a larger system (the aggregate or macroeconomy), so the aggregate economy is likewise a part of a larger system, the natural ecosystem.

As we saw in Chapter 3, classical economists accepted that humanity is constrained by the limitations of nature, but since the nineteenth century neo-classical economics has recklessly declared that there are no natural limits, only the limits of human technology. In effect, mainstream economics sees nature as a subsystem of the economy and for Daly (2008) that means it's more like a religion than a science. One of the implications of this was first expressed by Romanian economist Nicholas Georgescu-Roegen, who emphasized the economic significance of the second law of thermodynamics, entropy, which, put simply, says that in the end everything wears out. Growthism in the industrialized era has been supported by the almost miraculous energy boost provided by nature in the form of fossil fuels, which vastly improves on the energy of muscle power on which humans have always had to rely. But this energy source, like everything else in nature, is finite. Easily accessible, high-quality oil has already peaked, and in any case the environmental cost of continuing to use fossil fuels is now impossibly high.

Ignoring the laws of natural science has created a global economy which is mainly focused on consumption – the market – and unconcerned with the impact of the production that precedes it and the waste disposal that follows it. A natural economics makes planetary sustainability its number one goal, a steady state in which we live within our ecological means, constantly replacing the energy we use. That entails putting production, consumption and waste into a single balanced cycle, which forces society to take account of what it leaves behind – and what it leaves for those who come next. As Daly says (1996:48), it's a 'necessary change in vision', a big bang in economics, as it were, so expect to see transformations at each stage of the circular economy.

The circular economy

Making production and consumption sustainable

One way to transform our current production-and-consumption cycle into a sustainable system is very straightforward: a comprehensive repricing of its key components, a literal transvaluation. Growth capitalism radically underprices natural resources, even to the point of assigning them a zero valuation which makes them virtually free, 'there for the taking'. At the same time, it heavily taxes the labour it takes to produce goods and underprices the environmental costs of producing them – CO_2 emissions, toxins in streams, soil degradation – and in consuming them – litter, plastic packaging and so on. For centuries natural resources have been 'underpriced assists' – that much loved category of asset-strippers – as are so many of the ecological services which keep our world going, from pollination to cleansing rivers and absorbing CO_2.

'The polluter pays' principle can assist this economic transformation. For example, 'cap and share' schemes compel emission-producers to pay for energy permits which could be distributed free to citizens in the form of vouchers (Matthews, 2010). (To be effective, legislators need to guard against conservatives who try to keep the cap as low as possible, as Fatheuer and colleagues (2017) point out). Fair pricing in a circular economy taxes 'bads', such as non-organic fertilizers, not 'goods' and would price all natural resources in line with their scarcity, protecting resources such as the cobalt used in lithium batteries and other rare metals. We also urgently need to change the economic value of that most precious natural resource, land, a category which, as we know, disappeared from mainstream economics in the late nineteenth century, partially as a result of the explicit intervention of robber barons, who were also major landowners. At that time Henry George – sometimes referred to as 'the most famous economist no one has heard of' – championed a land value tax (LVT), which he claimed could act as a 'single tax', doing away with the need for all other types of taxation (Czech, 2013). Forms of LVT have already been introduced in countries like Denmark and Hong Kong. A relatively low rate of 5% can be enough to bring land back into the heart of economics and help to prevent the widespread land-grabbing currently being conducted by transnational corporations and states such as China.

Another circular economic measure is to bring production and consumption closer together by shortening supply chains. For example, fossil fuel has to be transported thousands of kilometres, using high-emission tankers or cross-continental pipe lines. Manufacturing has even more complex supply chains with thousands of different parts criss-crossing borders. In food production produce is often flown halfway around the world to get from field to fork. Only 20% of the energy used in industrial agriculture is actually related to growing crops or raising livestock; the rest goes in packaging, transport, marketing and storage (Mulligan, 2015), so huge gains could be made here.

The most pressing task for a circular economy is to eliminate the potentially destructive effects on our climate of carbon-based production. Ending the astoundingly large public subsidies given to fossil-fuel producers – currently worth over $5 trillion a year or 6.5% of total world GDP, according to a group of IMF researchers (Coady *et al.*, 2015) – will help to accelerate the transition to renewable energy and non-petrol-based transport. Banning coal mining and the exploration and drilling of new gas and oil resources will accelerate the financial divestment from the industry which is already under way. By investing in the unglamorous task of improving the energy efficiency of existing homes through insulation – and introducing appropriate legislation on all future house building, governments can reduce energy wastage and create as many as a million new jobs, according to an influential report by the Campaign against Climate Change (2014).

This kind of change is vital, but it will not be enough to produce people-planet equilibrium. Civil and environmental engineer Mark Jacobson and his international team of experts argue that it's still possible to decarbonize the entire global economy in time to avoid the devastating effects of global warming of more than 1.5°C (2017). They argue that the world's total energy supply (including all cooling and heating) could be 80% converted to renewable energy by 2030 and 100% converted by 2050. Their study examines 137 countries and is based wholly on the use of wind, water and solar power. It excludes nuclear power from the energy mix and doesn't rely on the use on the negative-emissions technology targets which so distort the Paris Climate Agreement. Achieving this energy transformation would require unparalleled political will and international coordination but would be possible with the kind of community involvement which has led to almost half of Germany's renewable energy installations being citizen-owned (Morris, 2016).

However, such heroic changes are unlikely to get worldwide go-ahead in the time needed. Almost certainly, we will also need managed economic contraction to achieve and maintain planetary sustainability but by how much is open to question. As noted in the landmark Stern report on climate change (2006), decarbonizing by more than 3–4% a year is incompatible with economic growth, but, according to leading climate scientists Kevin Anderson and Alice Bows (2011), rich counties will have to reduce emissions at the rate of 8–10% to have a reasonable chance of meeting the 2°C target (let alone 1.5°C). That could mean downscaling production and consumption by as much as 6% a year for rich countries, followed by developing countries by 2025, according to one estimate (Hickel, 2017:288).

Bringing production and consumption into a sustainable cycle will probably cause initial difficulties in countries used to over-consumption, although most people tend to underestimate just how resilient they are. Some rationing of energy may be expected in rich countries, although this may well be less than that which many citizens in the developing world live with every day, to say nothing of the hundreds of millions who have never had electricity. (In any case, an occasional free digital detox will do nobody any harm, as the growing number of people going through this therapeutic process can testify.) Food production will also probably contract, at least until the sustainable farming revolution is completed, but this may also bring unexpected health gains. Food rationing is unlikely to be as severe as it was during the 1940s in Britain but the health benefits which resulted at that time (mainly to the least well off) were so great that Labour campaigned to continue it after the war (it was the Conservatives who ended it in the 1950s). The potential for solving the current global obesity crisis is obvious, as are the trillions of dollar which can be saved in related healthcare costs.

Integrating waste

Rectifying the exclusion of waste from mainstream economics is the third stage of the circular economy. Nature doesn't produce waste, it regenerates and recycles everything, but the growthist world economy is recklessly indifferent to what it throws away. Reducing and reclaiming the mountains of stuff that the world currently wastes can bring immense economic gains that can compensate for a reduction in production and consumption. For example, if we can eliminate global food wastage, we could produce the same amount of food as today with 66% of the energy and resources. That's because at least a third of all food produced every year, some 1.3 billion tons, is wasted, with consumers in rich countries throwing away an amount equivalent to sub-Saharan Africa's entire annual food production (FAO, 2018). At a retail level, some food is thrown away simply due to its appearance. The world's cities produce 2 billion tons of municipal solid waste a year, which, if we do nothing about it, is due to swell to a gargantuan 3.4 billion tons by 2050. The value of the raw materials in electronic waste alone is $65 billion a year, according to World Bank figures (Kaza *et al.*, 2018). The nation that throws away the most is the United States, which, with less than 5% of the world's population, is responsible for a quarter of the world's rubbish, including a billion trees worth of paper every year (USI, 2018). In the UK, a staggering 54% of electricity is lost before it even reaches homes and businesses, due to the inefficiency of the network – that's the equivalent of the output of 37 nuclear power stations (ADE, 2015). In badly insulated British homes about a third of all heat escapes through roofs and windows. And as for water, it's been estimated that the daily needs of 21 million people could be met by the water which is wasted every day in the UK through leakage (Johnson and Burton, 2010).

Waste also causes unseen environmental costs on a massive scale. The toxic effluent that flows out of our factories, the poisonous chemicals that run off our fields, the nuclear waste dumped on countries who can least afford to dispose of it and the mountains of packaging and non-biodegradable electronic waste that fill our ever-expanding landfills sites: all these gross inefficiencies can be eliminated by a circular economy. 'Eco-efficiency' means building the idea of waste into the life cycle of every product and service that enters the market. This holistic approach aims to make high-quality products which are durable, reusable and recyclable, rather than items which satisfy a short-lived desire for novelty. It's a 'cradle to cradle' attitude, to use the phrase of path-breaking designers Michael Braungart and William Macdonough (2008), which, for example, would make it impossible for the manufacturers of plastic to ignore what happens to the 95% non-recyclable material they produce after it has been consumed (often in a single use), as has happened over the past 75 years. In a circular economy, the end becomes the beginning. Once waste is properly redefined, we can start reaping the economic rewards, taking lessons not only from eco-logically literate designers but from the armies of resourceful recyclers to be found in the world's slums and shanty towns, such as Dharavi in Mumbai, which featured in the film *Slumdog Millionaire* (Boyle, 2008).

Rebalancing public and private

This major rebalancing of economics and nature – the greatest since the Industrial Revolution – will break us out of several vicious circles and set up other much needed rebalancing flows. To begin with, we'll see a very different relationship between the public and private sectors and between the market and the state. The dynamics and structure of an economy dedicated to sustainability will look very different from the current world plan, in which everything becomes a market and the people in it no more than units of capital. Peter Barnes (2006) sees the new people-planet economy as a triadic structure, in which a dynamic, expanded commons sector transforms the traditional relationship between the state and the market. The open source, collaborative efforts of commons organizations will cross national borders and bring people together on a whole range of innovative and traditional projects. It will contain many diverse, pluralistic organizational forms as not-for-profit, cooperative social enterprises take centre stage (more about this in Step 6). The land-based economy could also emerge as a new force, with a reinvigorated, sustainable agricultural sector providing a greater portion of a nation's food and small-scale urbanization reducing the growing chasm between town and country.

Economic planning will play an important role in ensuring the transition to total sustainability, especially in the early stages. But this doesn't mean that top-down state control will dominate, as the goals of the new economics are shared across society and emerge in all forms of social enterprise. For example, at the local level we can expect a continuation of the growing pushback against privatization, which, from Barcelona to New Delhi, has produced 'at least 835 examples of remunicipalization of public services worldwide since 2000, involving more than 1000 municipalities in 45 countries' (Kishimoto and Petitjohn, 2017).

The entrepreneurial functions of the state will also be enhanced, although, as Mariana Mazzucato (2013) has incisively demonstrated, even today it plays a far more telling role in successful innovation than neoliberalism admits. Taxpayer-funded investments in research will continue, but along SEWP guidelines, and the fruits of success will be returned to the public purse, not siphoned off by private corporations. Investment targets could be set by direct democracy, with the public voting on whether to prioritize arms development or better healthcare, for example. Markets will continue to exist and will be more vibrant, with more genuinely competitive small-scale enterprises, regulated by fair legislation. Corporations will be cut down to size by fair competition measures, domestically and globally, and the need to confirm to SEWP regulations. Meanwhile, the commons sector will expand, as copyright and patent laws are reduced. With people having more time on their hands, there will be greater opportunity for people to throw themselves into economic projects that excite them.

Rebalancing work and life

One of the biggest changes will be in the nature of work. A low-work or work-free society has always been part of the utopian vision, and by now it was expected that humanity would enjoy relative freedom from involuntary work. In fact, John Maynard Keynes (1930) thought that by 2030 our biggest challenge would be what to do with all our free time. Instead the world is working harder than ever before. In Japan *karōshi*, or death by overwork, has become such a grave problem that the government has introduced legislation designed to prevent employees from putting in more than 60 hours a week.

At last we can expect a revolution in the whole concept of work, as barriers between formal and informal employment dissolve. As production contracts, a shorter working week will be necessary, as some economists have been advocating for a while (e.g. NEF, 2010). A 20-hour week could become the norm, possibly with less reduction in output than might be expected – productivity during the UK's notorious three-day week in 1974 only decreased by 6% (Simms, 2013: 294). A two-or-three-day working week would not only transform the definition of work in society but also the whole meaning of time. A four-or-five-day 'weekend' would provide ample opportunities for leisure activities, personal development, education, volunteering, community work and caring for children and the elderly. The modern era of the cash-rich time-poor – which for many has become the era of the cash-poor time-poor – would be over forever.

Increased job-sharing could be part of the mix, perhaps along the lines of legislation recently introduced in Holland which guarantees permanent, part-time jobs, not exploitative, precarious employment (Schor, 2015). Rather than aiming for full employment – the obsessive goal of all growthist economics – the circular economy will aim for selective, productive unemployment. The idea is that informal employment, such as personal- and community-based subsistence work around growing food, making and repairing goods and exchanging services, will make up any shortfall in wages.

Another innovation which will change the work landscape is the guaranteed living wage, a literally utopian concept that Thomas More advocated 500 years ago. Often referred to as universal basic income (UBI), it was successfully piloted in the 1970s in Manitoba, Canada and was found to produce no significant decrease in work motivation but a distinct increase in wellbeing, as shown by lower rates of accidents at work and psychiatric hospitalization (Forget, 2011). Today UBI is supported by economists and politicians across the political spectrum, in part because it is seen as the only solution to the mass elimination of jobs threatened by roboticization and AI-based software. This could be a risky quid pro quo in my view. Yes, intelligent machines can replace many unpleasant and dangerous jobs, but it's better to make communal decisions with SEWP principles about which jobs can be usefully retained rather than replace them in a way that could end up concentrating even more power in the hands of the global elite.

Too rapid a process of job automation looks particularly dangerous from a planetwide perspective, as it has huge implications for billions of jobs in the developing world. What happens to the 85% of all jobs in Ethiopia which are threatened by automation or the 77% in China or the 69% in India (Frey *et al.*, 2016)? Even in the USA, since 2000 only 0.5% of new jobs have shifted into the digital economy. Will digital corporations provide UBI to the millions who could be put out of work by sophisticated new sewing robots in Bangladesh, where clothing represents 82% of all exports (Stacey and Nicolaou, 2017)? With UBI, we should not fall into the old parochial trap of thinking that what works for the global North works for everybody on the planet.

That said, once work reduction is managed in a way that is fair to everybody across the world, life will be the winner. 'Work–life balance' will at last become worthy of its name, and we might even look forward to a return of the spirit of public celebration and hedonism enjoyed in the late Middle Ages, when it's claimed, more than a third of the year was taken up by public holidays and feast days (Graeber, 2011:309).

Rebalancing income and wealth

As easy profits based on mispriced natural assets disappear, some rebalancing of wealth and income will inevitably occur but achieving SEWP-type equitability targets will need more than this. High marginal rates of income tax contributed to the relatively high levels of economic equality enjoyed in the 1960s and 1970s. These could help to reduce the kinds of grotesque income inequality we examined in Chapter 1, which on current trends will see the richest 0.1% owning more wealth than the entire global middle class (i.e. the middle 40%) by 2050 (Alvaredo *et al.*, 2017). Taxing the many trillions of dollars which are currently hidden in the world's 90 tax havens would also make a significant difference – one estimate puts this sum as high as $21 to $32 trillion (Henry, 2012). This 'missing' wealth deprives societies of at least $190 billion a year in potential public spending (Zucman, 2015).

However, from a utopian standpoint, I suggest that we should also think in terms of ratios rather than rates, as this is a more rational, holistic strategy for redesigning economic equality. Most salaries are set in absolute numbers – usually by comparison with peers in a hierarchy – but ask someone how much more they think they are worth than the average worker in their organization and their salary demands often drop dramatically. In the UK, salary ratios for FTSE 100 bosses today are at least 160:1, meaning that a CEO can earn more in a few months than the average employee does in a lifetime. However, in the 1990s the ratio was 80:1 and closer to 20:1 in the 1970s (Hildyard, 2018). Much lower ratios are used by many organizations: for example, the giant Spanish cooperative Mondragon aims for a 5:1 CEO – average worker salary ratio and some new-era organizations favour pay distributions of 2:1 or even 1:1, as we'll see in Step 6.

This principle of equitable income ratios can be extended to deal with the even greater source of economic inequality, which derives from the distribution of maximized shareholder investments at the heart of the algorithms of capital. The problem of inherited wealth is increasing fast, with many of the world's multibillionaires owing their fortunes to unearned wealth, such as the Walton family of Walmart fame. Again, tax is one way to correct this imbalance. For instance, in his book *Change Everything*, economist Christian Felber argues for taxation based on an upper limit of €750,000 (although he stresses this should be decided democratically). In Germany, where inherited assets are worth up to €200 billion a year, he argues that this could mean a redistribution of wealth which would enable every person in the country to start their working life with a 'dowry' of €200,000 (2012:91).

Wealth-capping of this kind could be a way to move towards ratio-based property ownership. For example, a 5:1 ratio might grant every adult the right to own a minimum amount of accommodation equivalent to a one-bedroom flat, while permitting a maximum ownership level of the equivalent of a five bedroom house. For families with children or people with special needs a different ratio might apply. This kind of differential could initially provide some motivation for those who prize material status, although the equitability goal might be to lower the ratio over time. Banning the ownership of multiple properties is another possible measure, and one that would only affect a tiny minority in the UK. Ratio-based strategies of this kind would gradually bring about much greater equality of opportunity and outcome, reducing the vast fortunes and estates which are handed from generation to generation, often without any tax.

At this is point, you might be thinking that these proposals are too radical to ever happen in a democracy. My response would be that solutions always have to be judged in relation to the problems they set out to solve. If the utopian change plan goal of increasing equality is to be taken seriously, the measures which attempt to implement it have to be both realistic and rational. In fact, the Latin root of the word 'rationality' is *ratio*, which is also the linguistic basis of English word 'ration', in other words a share, a unit of distribution. If we are to achieve rationality in our new epoch, fair sharing has to be one of our primary goals. We're certainly not going to create meaningful equitability by persisting with the growthist myth that the only way to help the poor get a little less poor is by allowing the rich to get a lot richer. (I write this as a resident of London, one of the wealthiest cities in the world, in which vast town houses and penthouses bought for investment purposes stand empty, while record numbers of homeless people sleep on the streets.)

Rebalancing money

Like private property, money is something utopians tend to have little use for. In a twenty-first-century utopia, however, money will probably continue to exist, although rebalanced so as to have real collateral. A first step could be to compel banks to hold a 100% reserve on their loans (instead of around 7% which they are currently required to hold). This would create greater financial stability, because banks could only lend what savers have deposited. This would help to downsize banks, making them small enough to fail (but less likely to do so than today) and bring down house prices. It would also help to curtail the trillions of dollars currently traded in foreign-exchange speculation and other risky financialization activities and direct more money towards real businesses.

Another possibility, advocated by campaigning group Positive Money, would be to take the money supply out of the hands of politicians and central bankers and leave it to a democratically accountable group to decide when to increase or decrease it. This could create money that is free of debt – at present, when a debt is repaid that money is taken out of circulation – and even result in money being distributed as citizens' dividends (Jackson and Dyson, 2014). Once money is no longer controlled by bankers, people will start asking much more searching questions about its social purpose.

Local currencies are another way of bringing money back to the basics of what a community actually needs. They tend to encourage the use of local products and services, reducing transport and marketing costs and helping households to budget effectively. Ecological economist Richard Douthwaite (2010) claims that a regional currency in the North of England would have prevented the yawning gap in wealth and productivity which has opened up between it and London and the South-East since the 1980s as a result of rapid deindustrialization. Time-based currencies, where people are credited for exchanging services, will increase in popularity. Historically, David Graeber argues (2011), it's communities rather than governments which first create currencies, and whatever money looks like in the new era we can expect it to serve as a useful tool rather than as a source of entrapment and manipulation.

Perhaps the biggest surprise will be the new transparency about money. They say that money talks, but actually it's extremely discreet. It doesn't tell you anything about where it came from, whether it's dirty or clean or how long it took to earn it. The same silent sum may have been accrued by weeks of dangerous, back-breaking work or by a few seconds sitting in front of a computer screen. Freedom from debt and an end to the mystifications caused by making money out of money will increase people's real choices. Even though there will be fewer consumer goods available (initially at least), there will be greater freedom to make informed decisions, without the distortions created by our current debt-based system.

Add to that the enhanced choice-making that will come with the reduction of the subconscious and somatic influences on our purchasing decisions exercised by the advertising and marketing industry. This influence will decline as companies increasingly use word of mouth to build their reputations, (although good professional communication is always likely to be valued). This will leave companies with some of the half a trillion dollars they spend annually on advertising (Statista, 2018) to invest in improving their products and services. In any case, we need to put a stop to advertising that shamelessly exploits children, especially through repetitive TV adverts, personalized social media and child-height arrays of confectionary in retail outlets. Other aspects of manipulative consumerism will also disappear, such as gambling services that aim to create dependency and alcohol sales which deliberately target problem drinkers. Genuine, informed freedom of choice will become the norm for consumers in the new-epoch market.

Rebalancing the global economy: the Great Levelling

One huge economic task remains. Changing the growthist economics of the world's rich countries is absolutely vital both to reduce the disproportionate drain on the planet's natural resources and, crucially, to set the right example for the rest of the world to follow. But this is not sufficient to solve all of the interconnected problems of the Anthropocene. The circular economy has to add another planetwide cycle, if it is to repair the sloping world, and here we find that there is still room for economic growth in the new era, although very much along people-planet rather than profit-first lines. Up-levelling as well as down-levelling is needed to counter the forces of planetary disequilibrium over the past 500 years, which have seen Europe's and North America's shares of the world economy rise so disproportionally. The Great Levelling is the true task of utopia in the Anthropocene. And that means breaking away from the competitive, elitist, nationalistic values of our current plan and adopting a cooperative, internationalist mindset.

Ecological economists Rob Dietz and Dan O'Neill provide a matrix which can help guide this global paradigm shift (2013:184). This indentifies four economic states: desirable growth, undesirable growth, undesirable degrowth and desirable degrowth, defined in terms of the size of an economy and its use of natural resources. This categorization would enable economic planners to pinpoint where a nation is in relation to the goal of a steady-state economy which synchronizes its ecological footprint planetwide. Nations which are using too many natural resources – either directly or through importing from other nations – would need to degrow. Nations which are too low in income to provide improved wellbeing need to be encouraged to develop their own local industries, rather than remaining dependent on exporting their own natural resources and importing too much of everything else.

Global levelling of this kind gives rise to a deferential economics, which aims to help rich counties intelligently downscale and poor countries carefully upscale, until they meet in the middle in a state of total sustainability. This subtle, complex, truly 'plantetized' economics will replace the crude, one-size-fits all approach of growthism. It will inevitably involve rejecting the 'structural adjustment programmes' which since the 1980s have forced the global South to adopt neoliberal privatization and deregulation policies that mainly benefit the global North. Global levelling will also require some debt cancellation, especially where the premium has already been paid off many times and interest payments take up the majority of a country's public spending, as is often the case. Debt restructuring was voted for by the overwhelming majority of countries in the UN in 2015 but was blocked by the USA, the UK and four other creditor countries (Global Justice Now, 2017). 'Forgiving debts' is an attractive phrase, which seems to inject a much-needed dose of altruism into a global credit system, fixated on taking rather than giving. But if these debts are really long-lasting forms of exploitation, we might ask, who needs to forgive whom?

Much greater transparency around trading deals can also help the levelling process, including banning multinational corporations from using tax havens and purloining billions from developing countries by manipulating internal transfers and the practice of deliberate 'misinvoicing'. In fact, it's time to radically reappraise what we think of as foreign aid and replace it with the notion of reparation. Aid is a misnomer, as Jason Hickel stresses in his brilliant book on global inequality, *The Divide* (2017). In fact, aid is often a cover for various forms of exorbitant profit-seeking. Far from giving the developing world a helping hand, the West often uses foreign aid to justify, and perpetuate, unequal trading practices and provide lucrative, expansionary opportunities for its businesses.

The truth is that the poor countries of the world have been subsidizing rich nations since the days of the Spanish conquistadores, when the West first began to 'underdevelop' the rest of the world. And it's still happening today. For example, in 2015 Africa received $162 billion in loans, remittances from overseas workers and foreign aid, but $203 billion was taken from the continent, mainly through corporations repatriating profits or illegally transferring money (Global Justice Now, 2017). Overall, it's been estimated that $3 trillion a year flows from poor countries to rich countries but only $128 billion is granted in foreign aid (Hickel, 2017:26). Reparative finance could also compel rich countries to compensate poor countries for the global cost of climate change, which one authoritative report puts at $700 billion a year (DARA, 2013), a doubly unfair burden since many nations of the global South have contributed little or nothing to global warming. This financial rebalancing could be effected by capital transfers, loan cancellations or ecological projects such as the Great Green Wall in the Sahel region of Africa. The Great Levelling has to be the main macroeconomic goal of the new world plan, for without it total sustainability can never be achieved.

Rebalancing economics: bringing it all home

Finally, to put this new rationale into practice, we need to support radical changes in how economics is taught and measured. The first transformation is already happening, as campaigns like Rethinking Economics demand that the monoculture of neoliberal economics be replaced by feminist, ecological and other pluralistic approaches to the discipline. That will help to encourage critical thinking, as opposed to learning mathematical formulae by rote, and expose unexamined assumptions about the supposed benefits of wealth which, as we know, tend to make students more selfish.

'What we measure, we manage' is an organizational adage, and nothing can help us more to manage the Anthropocene crisis than ditching GDP as the central index of all human progress. We need a comprehensive, balanced metric which puts economic activity alongside measures of sustainability, equality and wellbeing. Many such indices already exist, such as the Happy Planet Index mentioned earlier, and they can produce startling transformations in our view of reality. For example, the General Progress Indicator shows that although world GDP has trebled since 1950, all-round progress on welfare has decreased since 1978, which means that many of the putative gains of the Thatcher–Reagan neoliberal revolution are illusory in people-planet terms (Kubiszewski *et al.*, 2013). In a more rational economic system, instead of the ups and downs of the GDP game which is bringing us to the brink of planetary collapse, we can look forward to regular, easily understandable updates on our real progress towards achieving global sustainability. This measurement of what really matters will demystify the esoteric prognostications of today's elite class of economists and bring economics home to everybody – remember *eco* means 'hearth' in ancient Greek. As Donella Meadows says (1998:viii), 'indicators arise from Values (we measure what we care about) and they create Values (we care about what we measure)'. In this way all, citizens will be able to share in making public policy, political debate and practical decision-making. In utopia, everybody is an economist.

Conclusion

To sum up, a circular economy rebalances the relationship between humanity and nature and in so doing fundamentally changes the way we deal with every aspect of economic activity. Sustainability economics marks the end of the growthist denial of natural science and the beginning of a new, evidence-based economics of 'sharing, frugality, and adaptation to natural limits ... an economics of better, not bigger' (Daly 1996:187). This shifts the balance away from the private towards the public, from work to life and from a pyramidal concentration of wealth to a much more horizontal and equitable distribution. It's a rebalancing that is most urgently needed in wealthy countries but achieving planetary sustainability will require a global economic levelling and a new differential view of economic growth. These are big, bold moves, of course, but that's what the Anthropocene crisis demands, and nobody ever said utopia was going to be easy. In Step 5, we'll explore the task of translating ecological economics into our current political discourse, but for the time being let's stick with some of the dramatic transformations this new economic vision implies in terms of practical, everyday life.

9 Step 4
Put wellbeing and community first

Step 4 is about using one of utopianism's greatest assets, the imagination, to bring ecological economics down from the macro-level to the plane of lived experience. In particular, it involves trying to picture what a circular economy would be like in terms of practical wellbeing and community life.

The new town and country

If the SEWP world plan takes effect, people around the world will gradually see a transformation in their surroundings. Towns, where over half of humanity now lives, will look, sound and feel quite different from today. Expect to see vibrant high streets full of food hubs and stalls offering multifarious products and services (Simms, 2013). People-planet urban planning will focus on designing cities which enhance community life rather than meeting business needs. This will break down the rigid barriers between work, home and leisure which exist in today's cities, many of which prioritize huge roads, single-use zones and high-rise apartments. Architectural movements like New Urbanism are already using spiral street plans, based on the winding streets of medieval towns, to provide intimate connections between where you live, shop, play and work. Circular cities – the symbol of utopia finds its way in here too – have been shown to increase social flow and face-to-face interactions between people, which in turn can bring many benefits, such as reduced crime.

People will move around in a new way, as the tyranny of communities designed around cars recedes into the past. The number of casualties of our current road world war – which results in over 1 million deaths and 50 million injuries a year (WHO, 2015) – will be dramatically reduced. Walkable towns will become the norm, with superb cycle lanes for the many new forms of pedal-driven transport which will emerge (Speck, 2012). Parents being forced to drive their children to school, because it's too dangerous for them to walk there, will become a thing of the past. Even in our vehicle-dominated world today, car ownership drops to a minimum in purpose-built, pedestrianized towns, such as Vauban, a sustainable new suburb of Freiberg in Germany.

Public transport will flourish, with electric trams and buses, light-rail transit systems and long-distance train networks. The sharing of private vehicles will become commonplace. The ambient and household air pollution that globally kills 7.3 million people a year will disappear, leaving the air fresher and cleaner (WHO, 2018b). Without the thunder of cars and lorries, cities will be much quieter, especially as there will be fewer planes droning overhead. Until such times as genuinely sustainable aviation is invented, air traffic will fall away sharply, much to the relief of those living under congested flight paths. The long-haul flights which contribute significantly to global warming – a return flight to New York dumps four tons of CO_2 into the atmosphere – will become much rarer. The global elite, before it disappears altogether, will have to wave farewell to their private jets. The vast public subsidies at present given to aviation across the world – €30 billion a year in Europe alone (Whitelegg, 2016) – can be diverted to better, more sustainable uses.

As some forms of long-distance mobility contract, communication by other means – the internet, video conferencing, holograms and other techniques – will become the priority for a new generation of internationalists and a magnet for sustainable innovation. (If this seems like going backwards, think how much our Victorian ancestors would have given to be able to talk to their relatives in other parts of the world and watch live images of them).

Ecological cities will even smell different. That's in part because an increase in carbon-absorbing street trees will dramatically reduce pollution but also because, wherever you are, you're likely to be close to open spaces. More parks and recreation areas will be a priority, and a revolution in urban agriculture will ensure that you're never too far from thriving kitchen gardens. Rooftops will house urban farms, there'll be bee hives on balconies and vegetables grown in window boxes. Urban farming, which already flourishes in many parts of the world, will change dirty old industrial towns for ever. Locally grown produce will replace the stale smell of junk food, as high-fat fast-food shops, especially those which are now permitted to cluster around school gates, vanish from the scene.

In a people-planet world, we're also likely to see a shift towards small towns and new rural communities, reversing the historical trend of endless urban sprawl and global South megacities which are largely made up of shanty towns, as Mike Davis (2006) shockingly illustrates in *Planet of Slums*. The spread to the countryside may well also take place as people commit themselves to greater self-sufficiency, especially if UBI and other changes in work liberate people from the need to cluster around areas where conventional employment is greatest.

Outside the city we'll also see some major changes to the landscape, due to climate-change adaptation and mitigation. These will include massive reforestation to absorb CO_2 and prevent flooding. Perhaps London will eventually emulate the 'deep wood' William Morris imagines in *News from Nowhere*, which extends from Kensington in the west of the city to Primrose Hill in the north and all the way east to Epping Forest. In coastal areas, we'll see the building of dykes to protect against rising sea levels and other measures to soften the impacts of extreme weather events. The countryside is also where we'll see the effects of meeting planetary boundaries around the preservation of freshwater and soil fertility, including a major shift to organic fertilizers to reduce chemical pollution. In order to meet emissions targets, reduce highly polluting methane gas and conserve water, a planned contraction of the farming of cattle and sheep will take effect. As these water-intensive practices are phased out, precious biomes will be preserved and millions of hectares of grazing land freed up for production of cereals and vegetables. Landscapes no longer blighted by pesticides will see wildlife stocks recover, which means more buzzing insects and songbirds over fields and hedgerows, as well as other species reintroduced into traditional habitats.

Housing

One of the biggest transformations will be around housing. In a people-planet utopia, housing will be a basic human right and a democratically agreed property ratio will ensure that this is a reality, not a hollow political aspiration. Growthism, which prefers to build more houses for those who already have too many, will be replaced by a new rationale. Homes will no longer be assets to be traded, but human needs at the heart of a new civilization. There'll no longer be rough sleepers on the pavement beneath empty penthouses in major cities. Shoddy temporary accommodation and exploitatively high rents in the developed world will slowly fade from memory, as will slums and shanty towns in the developing world. Minimum accommodation allocations per person will probably be decided locally and may increase as more housing stock become available.

Once housing for all becomes a right, guaranteed by society, every aspect of housing policy will change, from planning and building to home and land ownership. The availability of building skills will spread rapidly across communities, as more land is provided to build on. Making more brownfield sites available for self-build housing would leverage the construction skills which many people already possess. Some existing buildings will be reallocated, perhaps as interim measures, for example large mansions and town houses and some suitable office blocks. Co-housing is another solution which is already growing in popularity, as it combines independent living with shared facilities. Typically it involves 10 to 40 households which group together to buy large properties or build new developments, often in the form of houses clustered around a central courtyard. Other types of collective ownership will continue to develop, enabling residents to take control of their mini-communities.

Residential self-management is also likely to be a feature of the new social housing boom which could emerge, possibly comparable in scale to the 200,000 council houses a year were which were built in Britain in the 1960s. But this time the accommodation will be mainly low-rise, ecologically self-sufficient and superbly insulated. New public housing stocks will help to end the wild price fluctuations and destructive cycles of the property market. Land value taxes will also help to create balance, as is already evident in the USA from the long-term price stability of towns like Pittsburgh which use LVT, compared to the high level of foreclosure in cities that don't, such as Cleveland (Sullivan, 2010).

A world with fewer things

A society which lives within its means ecologically and with far less recourse to easy money and hard debt will also be a society where people possess fewer things. This may be difficult for some for a while but also a relief to many. How many of the 10,000 possessions, which economist Nico Paech (2012) reports that the average German owns, are essential to life or improve it in any way? Often material possessions create an oppressive prison of clutter, the very opposite of the freedom which consumerism promises.

With fewer possessions more equally distributed, there is likely to be less crime. That means less of the social misery, suspicion and isolation that crime causes – and of course lower public spending on police, security and the judicial system in general (although justice will still exist). Far fewer people will be incarcerated. Today a prisoner in the UK costs the tax payer about £35,000 a year. Reoffending rates run at around 60% (within the first year of release), which the National Audit Office (2010) calculates costs an additional £9.5 billion to £13 billion a year. And in the USA, which currently incarcerates two million people (22% of the entire global prison population), the costs to society are proportionally even higher (Lowenstein, 2015).

In a more transparent, socially cohesive world, with less personal ownership, we're also likely see a reduction in the need for lawyers, who currently sustain a global legal industry worth about half a trillion dollars a year. Fewer things means less packaging and that means savings in the flexible packaging industry which adds $400 to $500 billion to the cost of consumption. And there will definitely be fewer people requiring the current clutter-solution of paying to store things they don't really need. In the USA there are now almost 50,000 self-storage facilities, which, if combined, would occupy an area the size of Las Vegas (200 square kilometres), space that surely can be turned to far more socially beneficial uses (Strutner, 2015).

Wellbeing gains

Along with gains to the community, a sustainable, equitable world plan will also deliver major benefits to human wellbeing. Whatever we may lose in terms of consumer convenience and novelty can be more than offset by a planetwide uplift in human life satisfaction. Across the entire spectrum of HELIOS wellbeing – health, education, love, involvement, originality and sense of purpose – the rewards should be considerable.

Health

First of all, a rebalanced economy will bring huge potential health gains, as wellbeing becomes a primary goal of economics. In the UK, the National Health Service (NHS) is one of the few institutions still revered by the majority, largely because its puts human wellbeing above self-centred materialism. In a sustainable future, the NHS, or something similar, is likely to thrive but with its enormous costs reduced. This can partially be achieved by greater localization, reducing the long-distance travel of staff, patients and supplies which currently raises costs and inefficiencies and lowers the system's resilience (Whitelegg, 2016). Savings will also be made by ending the current practice whereby 'the tax payer pays twice' for drugs which are created through publicly funded research, then passed to private pharmaceutical companies for often exorbitant profit-making (Gotham, *et al.*, 2017). This new efficiency will also introduce a more future-orientated attitude to healthcare. Currently over 95% of the NHS budget is based on curing conditions once they have occurred, although the vast majority of them are preventable (Coote, 2015). Creating greater awareness of health problems in advance – rather than waiting for the heart attack to tell you are overworking, for instance – will free up many more resources. Institutions which are proactive rather than reactive build responsibility for the future into their core operations (an approach promoted by Finland's Committee for the Future).

The organizational structure of healthcare will also take a people-planet turn, with the replacement of a top-down, centralized approach by the empowerment of autonomous, self-organizing groups. This will also involve minimizing the scope of the purely commercial market in healthcare products and services. The non-profit Buurtzorg neighbourhood nursing organization in the Netherlands is a good example of both these tendencies. Founded in 2006, it employs over 7,000 nurses, who work in small, self-managing teams providing outstanding healthcare which, amazingly, requires 40% fewer hours to deliver than other forms of nursing. Management consultant Frederic Laloux (2014) suggests that scaled to the US population, this type of organization would save $49 billion year.

A sustainably managed environment will support a food revolution which will have many positive knock-on effects on human health. For example, as more people in the developed world move to vegan, vegetarian or flexitarian diets, fewer in the developing world will be lured by the status symbol of meat-eating into abandoning their plant-based diets. In the West, a culture of slow food as a pleasurable social and personal ritual will replace the hurried functionality of fast food on the run (I'll return to this theme in Step 11).

A world of rationally reduced food and drink consumption will be able to combat the current planetwide obesity epidemic. This new and terrible disease shows growth capitalism at its most grotesquely harmful. There are now several areas in the UK in which close to 50% of 11-year-olds are obese or overweight (Bodkin *et al.*, 2018) and worldwide an astonishing 1.9 billion people suffer from the same preventable condition (WHO, 2018a). The town-planning revolution will support a new healthy diet, encouraging people to walk and cycle, so providing the most effective treatment for what a report in *The Lancet* calls the current 'pandemic of physical inactivity', which it estimates costs the world $67 billion a year in healthcare and lost productivity (Ding *et al.*, 2016).

Old diseases such as smallpox and tuberculosis which have reappeared in wealthy nations will be eradicated, as will other maladies, once healthcare achieves the right degree of medicalization – not veering between too much or too little, as is so often the case today. Realistic targets will have to be set in terms of the healthcare available in old age, with the aim of reducing the gulf between the longevity of the richest and poorest countries in the world. Anti-ageing medical advances in the developing world may have to be balanced against the target of levelling global life expectancy and other sustainability goals. But progress in medicine – the late Holocene's most celebrated success story – will not end with the advent of total sustainability. On the contrary, as we focus on what is really necessary for improved health – rather than on what makes easy superprofits for Big Pharma and medical-technology corporations – we are likely to see significant medical advances. In time, progress in extending overall human longevity may well resume but this time the benefits will be shared equitably across the world.

A wellbeing-based economy also puts more resources into psychological interventions, as psychology takes over from economics as a leading driver of human progress. Less work will lead to less psychological stress, alleviating and eventually eliminating the current crisis of stress at work which opens up millions of people to a range of neurotic and psychotic conditions. Stress-free work will also help to rid us of some of our most addictive consumerist habits, liberating us from 'capitalism's squirrel cage', as Juliet Schor (1991) once called the vicious 'work-and-spend' circle of overwork leading to over-consumption. Greater public awareness of how to help mental health issues will come not only from professionals but from ordinary people trained to spot early symptoms and build resilience. In this informed, caring environment, the episodes of depression and anxiety which currently affect up to a third of the population will happen less frequently and will be far less devastating and confusing when they do occur. Supportive, challenging self-help groups helping the vulnerable will become a feature of everyday life (more of this in Step 9).

Education

Life and learning will become synonymous in utopia. Free life-long education for all will form the core of social life (we already know that the best public education in the world is to be found in relatively economically equal countries like Finland). People will move in and out of courses, some face to face, some virtual. Formal institutions will blend with informal learning groups, as knowledge, skills and interests are widely shared. There'll probably be far less emphasis on formal qualifications and certificates, although the general store of knowledge will increase markedly. Educational organizations in general will become important research centres for communities and for many aspect of practical life.

At school, education will be very different, focused on a core curriculum which makes theoretical and practical science, especially life science, available to every pupil. Understanding sustainability principles has to be something that children learn from the earliest age, so that recognition of this does not have to be forced on them in later life. Nature needs to be part of the process for urban children, bringing them into contact with agriculture and the countryside. Children's curiosity about nature and intuitive love of animals will be nurtured from the outset, bringing them an appreciation of natural economics and the advantages for animal welfare of people-planet food strategies.

The school curriculum is likely to shift towards life skills, as our definition of economics changes. Subjects such as cooking, nutrition, gardening, carpentry, sewing, furniture-making and fashion design which have all but disappeared from education at school will make a comeback. This is not backward-looking but an example of remoderning, as these activities will be updated for the twenty-first century and combined with new mechanical and digital skills. Overall, the aim will be to combat the deskilling effects of twenty-first-century consumerism, which attempts to profit from our time-poor desire for convenience, which in turn makes us increasingly helpless in life (Paech, 2016). People have become overdependent on ready-to-cook meals, pre-sliced, packaged salads or hot meals delivered to their door. Fixing any kind of machine became more difficult as devices come in complex sealed systems which only authorized experts are able to access. Subsistence education will transform children's abilities, resilience and expectations, creating a generation of 'prosumers', as adept at producing as consuming.

Apart from sustainability and subsistence skills, the curriculum is likely to be much freer than today's intensive educational programmes.

Extracurricular, informal education will probably grow, as will the peer networks and mentoring advocated by Ivan Illich (1971). Boundaries between school and community will become looser. Self-government, as pioneered in Britain by experimental schools like Summerhill, may become more common, giving children from the earliest age practical experience in making decisions about their immediate environment and learning from their mistakes (Neil, 1962). Indeed, creating rules about how discipline is handed out and what lessons are taught – and Summerhill had over 200 such rules – is symptomatic of the revolution in decision-making and rule-making, which is central to the utopian project.

Love and the care economy

A society focused on wellbeing will also recognize the huge value of human care. Reproductive labour, the process of bearing and caring for children and looking after relatives and friends is almost as undervalued by conventional economics as nature – a deficit an ecological alternative to GDP would correct (O'Neill, 2015). Supporting this largely spontaneous, self-organizing economy will help to raise the value of family life, turning it from a means of supplying employers with labour to a primary social goal.

Transvaluing the reproductive economy will help to bring about greater gender equality, transforming many aspects of our culture which we take for granted. Patriarchy has an insidious hold over growthism, promoting phallic values of size and speed and a preference for the mechanical rather than the biological, which favours a kind of stereotypical masculinity. The continued pay gap between men and women at work, which will take many decades to eliminate at the current rate of progress, is just one indication of this partially unconscious hegemony.

Fully recognizing the care economy can help to accelerate the modest gains that have been made in how men and women relate to one another over the past 40 years, which is now threatened by an authoritarian backlash. It can also bring about a new liberation for heterosexual men, as the prioritization between work and the family is reversed. Promoting the value of love and care for another can also create new possibilities for gay and transgender people and all gender identities. Greater economic equality is almost certainly the only way to make continued progress on the cultural equality agenda, although specific, measurable goals around gender, ethnicity, sexuality and age will also be required.

A society aiming to become a democracy of love will also bring new respect for the young, as the renewers of utopia. The British public has only recently started to come to terms with the horrific physical and sexual abuse of children which has long existed in many institutions, something psychologists have been aware of through first-hand clinical experience and research. And yet I believe it's not going too far to suggest that our current world plan is also abusive of children in an ecological sense. What else should we call policies which condemn children to live in a biosphere so denuded and depleted that it may not supply the means of living for some of them?

Materially, too, we're failing the young. The UK is one of the richest countries in history but almost a third of its children now live in relative poverty (60% of the median salary), according to the Social Metrics Commission (2018). Worldwide 385 million children live in absolute poverty, in households surviving on $1.90 a day (Unicef, 2016). Many children are unhappy, bullied at school and pressured into overperformance, with girls in particular experiencing a new wave of depression and anxiety. Some of this is related to the unrealistic body imagery peddled by the fashion media and the often degrading sexual roles for women promoted by easily accessible hardcore pornography.

Even a utopian society can never fully eradicate the pains of growing up or flatten the inevitable ups and downs of social and sexual life, nor should it want to, but a society which puts loving care as its highest value – expressing this not simply as rhetoric about 'family values' but as a primary economic principle – is best placed to improve the wellbeing of all its citizens. It will treat its children not as after-thoughts but as the co-creators of a society, for which they will eventually inherit full responsibility.

Involvement

Greater social involvement flows inevitably from the sustainability agenda. The circular economy cannot occur without people becoming more involved with each other. With people working 20 hours a week or less, there's more time to be spent on self-provision, growing your own food, making, repairing and bartering your own things, as well as longer hours for leisure, voluntary work and friends and family. It could mean exchanging services and goods, sharing everything from housing to tools and working together on community projects. This new form of social interaction – new at least to many of us in the developed world – can help to overcome the alienation inherent in modern society. The individualist aspiration of building a materialist fortress around yourself, where you can isolate yourself as much as possible from other people, is no longer an option. Being with others, which existentialist philosophers and others have always recognized as a crucial part of the human condition, becomes the way of everyday life, as economic necessity and human desire come together to form a new synergy.

One consequence is likely to be the end of the epidemic of loneliness that is blighting our world. It's a growing phenomenon, especially in the world's most unequal rich countries. In *Bowling Alone*, Robert Putnam (2000) charts the loss of social capital in recent years, as Americans have become more solitary at work, at home and in their leisure activities.

Older people are particularly affected, as they become a larger section of society and less integrated into shifting, dispersing communities. But younger people also suffer and can become addicted to potentially isolating social media which can further isolate some people. Where CIMENT values dominate economic interactions, a suspicion of others often thrives, creating social divisions. Establishing cooperation as the basis of human communities can help to reverse this trend. Once being involved with others is recognized as a necessity, it can also become a constant source of pleasure, surprise and self-validation.

Originality

Greater equitability can also bring greater creativity. Removing constraints on education and social mobility will bring greater opportunities for personal development and self-expression, as Danny Dorling (2017) suggests. Nobody can stop communities from doing what they have done throughout history: invent and play sports, express themselves through music, dance and art and, of course, explore the laws of nature through science. But growthism channels these spontaneous activities into profit-orientated institutions, turning talented artists, musicians and sports people into hyper-competitive, multimillionaire celebrities. Those who are 'not good enough to make it commercially' may give up altogether.

A time-rich society in which life is more important than work and education no longer an extended job apprenticeship will almost certainly see an explosion of activity in the arts, sports and science. The quality may be gloriously variable, but the quantity will be much greater. Facilities will abound – some sophisticated, some rough and ready – as opportunities expand and audiences increase. We'll see an abrupt reversal of the trend over the past few decades in Britain which has seen youth clubs, community centres and public libraries shut down, playing fields sold off, music and arts teaching in schools marginalized and small music venues closed down. New science facilities, as well as open-source technology labs and digital studios, will become more prominent, as communities focus on creating socially useful innovations within a sustainability framework.

Doubtless, the most talented will continue to shine and will be rewarded by the social esteem always accorded to those who excel at an activity, but without the stratospheric salaries that isolate them from ordinary society. A SEWP-model economy will make culture a natural expression of creativity, without the pressure of professionalism, and the constant, feverish trawl for the next superstar. Without TV programmes attempting to monetize every human skill, the revered place in society of 'the desire to produce beautiful things' which William Morris (1890/1993:xxxiii) championed, can become a reality.

Sense of purpose

A strong sense of moving towards a better world is at the heart of utopianism – and the goals of a circular global economy could have the greatest benefits for the wellbeing of all. An overarching sense of purpose lies behind many great achievements and can enable an individual to overcome the most daunting barriers. For example, psychiatrist Viktor Frankl's (1959) account of surviving Auschwitz stresses the role of a strong vision of the future in creating resilience. Visualizing himself after the war lecturing to others on his death-camp experiences gave him the sense of meaning which he needed to surmount the seemingly insurmountable.

For groups, common goals can have an even greater impact, as they are mutually reinforcing. Although exaggerated in some respects, the high morale experienced by civilians in Britain during the Second World War is not a myth (special psychiatric units set up to treat cases of trauma were closed in 1941 for lack of patients (Mackay, 2002:87)). Many people were able to survive extreme hardships without noticeably reduced wellbeing, largely because of increased social solidarity and a sense that their privations served a unified cause (Mackay, 2002). A new common purpose could be the only way to rebuild the social trust which has collapsed in the modern world – in the USA, for example, people's readiness to trust each other more than halved over the second half of the twentieth century (Putnam, 2000). Raising economic equality will help in this respect, as more equal societies inevitably have greater trust levels than societies where people are fighting individualistically for whatever will satisfy their greed and/or fear. And surely nothing will create a more invincible sense of common purpose than playing a part in creating the best world that humanity has ever known.

Conclusion

Step 4 follows on from Step 3 and offers a glimpse of the benefits that can flow from circular economics in terms of lived experience. Whatever may be lost in terms of 'consumer choice' can be more than made up for by increased control over every aspect of daily life. As Niko Paech (2012:120) says, 'self-determination depends not on having much, but on needing little'. In a properly managed economy, community life becomes safer, more rewarding and better balanced, creating potential gains in life satisfaction across the spectrum. All well and good, you might be thinking, but what will it take practically to bring about this better world? To answer that, we need to return to our current world system and step into its most bitterly contested arena.

10 Step 5
Build a circular democracy
(and champion the transvaluation
of politics)

Step 5 is about how we move towards a politics fit for the Anthropocene. Before exploring the practicalities of this transformation, let's stay with the utopian imagination for a moment and try to visualize what a people-planet democracy could be like. That's not easy, because I suspect that many of the political institutions, policies and decision-making processes of the future will be almost unrecognizable. The participatory nature of this democracy will probably be what strikes the observer first. The distinction between the electorate and the political class will be less rigid than today, with far fewer career politicians. Elections may be less frequent at a national level, but more frequent at a regional level, as politics becomes more local. Departments such as finance, healthcare, education, even foreign affairs may be directly accountable to the electorate. Permanent political parties are likely to disappear, continuing their steady decline in Western democracies from their peak in the 1950s (Mair, 2013). If they exist at all, parties in the future may be semi-spontaneous, short-lived alliances reflecting a particular set of issues or a historical moment.

And yet, the high degree of political engagement of the post-war period, when electoral turnouts of 80% or more were commonplace, will make a comeback. Political participation will be so imbued in every aspect of ordinary life that many people will cease to be aware of it. In the past, the struggle has been to bring more people into democracy; in the new epoch democracy will come to the people. The decisions that are today made in parliaments and boardrooms will be made in households, workplaces, streets and all manner of public forums. Democracy as the rule of the majority will finally come in to its own, relegating plutocracy to the distant past.

Circular democracy

In this new system, the goals of a circular economy will unite with a circular democracy, which combines the best of bottom-up community-level and top-down decision-making. Over time, the culture and psychology of total sustainability may become second nature to human beings, as advanced scientific education spreads. In these circumstances there may be no need for overarching laws and regulations or the specialist policy-makers, ecological economists and scientific experts who frame them. But initially there will be an urgent need for the decisive, forward-looking, holistic planning which is so lacking today.

In our own century, we've already seen mass movements like Occupy which combine new types of horizontal and vertical relationships and redefine political leadership around the activity of popular assemblies (Hardt and Negri, 2017). Successful democratic movements, such as Otpor in Serbia which eventually brought about the downfall of the dicta-torial Slobodan Milošević, provide clear political aims at the top of the organization, while allowing for flexible autonomy among participating groups and individuals (we'll see more examples of this in Step 12). In a future circular democracy, there will be a constant flow between those making laws and regulations and the general population. Citizens' juries may play a significant role, with assemblies of ordinary people, selected at random, proposing, reviewing and framing legislation. What starts with specialist policy-makers will go through popular debate and discussion in feedback loops which revise proposed policies and suggest new implemen-tation methods. At the same time, other policies will emerge from grass-roots groups and representative forums. These interconnecting spirals of influence will determine the final shape of legislation within the SEWP framework.

This circular decision-making will also occur in processes which criss-cross the planet. In fact, global circular democracy is likely to require something like the world government or global federation which many utopians have long advocated, in order to ensure the planetwide coordin-ation required by total sustainability. So, just as domestically we can expect to see adversarial professional party politics replaced by a more citizen-based, consensus-seeking approach, on the planetary stage we can expect universal cooperation to take over from the battlefield logic of competi-tion between nations (we'll explore the institutions needed to deliver this in the next step).

The beginnings of a political change plan

Turning to the politics of the present, we have to accept that utopian cir-cularity is still a long way off, both in form and content. The grip of grow-thism on our world plan is still vice-like and only a relatively small, if growing, minority of the electorate see the need for a radical transforma-tion along people-planet lines. So a plan is badly needed to change the content of our political conversations. At the same time, we need huge structural changes to our institutions which currently deter so many people from engaging in any kind of political activity, especially in the out-moded electoral systems of the UK and the USA.

Transforming the political conversation

The biggest challenge is to change our political consciousness. The hegemony of growthism is as much conceptual as institutional. Words matter: they frame how we think and feel and, of course, how we talk about the world. So replacing growthism, in part, is about changing the conversation we have about it, contesting its domination, exposing its contradictions and bringing to the surface its deep-lying assumptions.

In the Anglo-American world today, establishing green policies may seem almost as difficult as winning the argument against slavery two centuries ago. Some inspiration can come from the European Union, where Green parties regularly break through the 5% electoral barrier. In 2018 they went further, winning an unprecedented 18% of the vote in the German manufacturing heartland of Bavaria, tripling their MPs in the Netherlands and winning over 30% in several local elections in Belgium. Greens in Europe also have growing experience at governing in coalitions in France, Ireland and elsewhere (although this can be a bruising experience). By contrast, in the Anglo-American political oligarchies, voters remain obstinately loyal to their traditional parties (in spite of the Green Party of England and Wales winning almost 4% of the vote in the 2015 general election). This regressive situation can only improve if large numbers of supporters of the establishment parties can be persuaded to adopt an ecological position. Conservatives are natural targets in that they tend to oppose change and value the traditional countryside and yet support highly disruptive economic policies which could change almost everything about ordinary life and industrialize the rural economy. Also potentially persuadable are those on the left who fixate on wealth creation as a mean of achieving greater social equality but fail to see the transformational implications of the climate and environmental crisis.

So here are a few possible arguments which might start the change in political consciousness we urgently need.

Changing the political discourse

The first step is to expose the destructive contradiction of assuming that infinite economic expansion on a finite planet is possible. This also entails challenging the 'stealth revolution of neoliberalism which has economised everything', to use Wendy Brown's (2015) phrase, and which links all social progress to increased GDP. Instead of the all-too-familiar Bill Clinton formula about economics, we need a new mantra for the twenty-first century: 'it's the planet, Stupid'.

Sustainability arguments

In fact, sustainability is a potential conversation changer. If more people appreciated the changes that the Anthropocene crisis could bring about, our political discourse would undergo a revolution almost overnight. The same might have happened at other inflection points in history. Would the First World War have ever been allowed to start if the people of Western Europe hadn't been fobbed off with the 'over by Christmas' myth and had foreseen the years of human carnage that would follow?

Staying with a problem is never easy, especially one as complex and anxiety-provoking as the one we face today. Working with organizational leaders, I've often witnessed how keen they are to rush to the nearest solution as quickly as possible. Doggedly focusing on a problem can cause discomfort, depression, defensiveness, anger or a desire to lay the blame on somebody else, all of which make for a cocktail of negative emotions which inclines people to pull out of analysing a problem well before it has been fully understood. The result is often an inadequate solution or at best, an adequate solution to the wrong problem. And yet I've often found if people are able to stay with problem for long enough, almost miraculously the right solution will emerge.

And it's not all negative. In fact, the idea of the Anthropocene itself can be a positive argument for change. Simply understanding the concept of this new epoch – which is still not appreciated by many – can bring about a very different sense of what it is to be alive today. This unique period in the human story and the 4.5-billion-year history of planet Earth creates new opportunities for us all, along with new responsibilities.

Facing up to the challenge of the Anthropocene is about accepting our responsibility for future generations and for the children of the world living today, all two billion of them. Responsibility of this kind is something all parents understand and, it seems, electorates do as well, at least when the prospect is couched in growthist terms. For example, in the 2015 UK general election all the major political parties were committed to continued reductions in public spending, using the justification that it was grossly unfair to burden future generations with a massively increased national debt. So why should this argument not apply to the incalculably greater threat represented by the Anthropocene crisis? Debt can be cancelled by a click on a keyboard, not so the permanent or long-lasting alterations to the biosphere threatened by climate chaos, biodiversity extinction and other existential threats to life on Earth.

In this context it's patently absurd to fixate on economic growth. It's Holocene politics, which may have been justified when our science was insufficiently developed to enable us to understand our precarious relationship with our environment, but it's no longer fit for purpose. Holocene politics has had its day.

Equitability arguments

Equitability arguments can also help to breach the walls of growthism. Too often economic growth is used as a proxy for improvement in equality, disguising the achingly slow progress which is being made on social mobility, healthcare or child poverty. But the argument that economic growth and the development of democratic freedoms go hand in hand, which may have been plausible in the twentieth century, is now redundant. Remember that some of the world's most powerful economies, with booming GDPs, in China, the Middle East and Asia, are judged to be 'flawed' or 'hybrid' democracies or 'authoritarian' states by *The Economist*, which, if you recall, classifies only 12% of the world's nations as 'full democracies' (EIU, 2017). It's time to face up to the sobering thought that worshipping the god of GDP and wanting more democratic equality may be incompatible aims.

The fact that two of the world's wealthiest 'full democracies', the UK and the USA, are also two of the most economically unequal countries in the global North only underlines this point. Unequal societies increase problems for everybody, contrary to the free marketers' contention that as long as overall wealth increases, social injustice and relative poverty do not matter (Dorling, 2017). In GDP terms, the USA is the richest country in history, but it also has chronic problems of child poverty, racial discrimination, gun crime, and drug addiction which are absent from more equal societies. In the UK, increasing social mobility is meant to be a cross-party political goal, but the country's rarely criticized educational system gives 7% of the nation's children who are privately educated a hugely unfair career advantage over their state-educated peers. (Half of the UK's cabinet ministers are privately educated, as are over 70% of its barristers, high-court judges and military leaders, and even two-thirds of its Oscar winners (Sutton Trust, 2016).)

Wealth or wellbeing?

One of the reasons why our political discourse is so skewed is because it constantly values wealth above wellbeing. Enhancing wellbeing should be a structural goal of politics. As Christian Felber points out, the constitution of Bavaria states that 'all business activity serves the common good' and the preamble to the US constitution declares that it was established by the people 'in order to promote the general Welfare' (2012:141). Britain famously has no written constitution but at the dawn of a new epoch – and amid bitter disputes about the country's self-identity and place in the world – what better time to create one?

It's also vital to contest the myth that GDP – or the Great Deception Project as it might reasonably be called – gives any kind of accurate picture of a society. For example, referring to the UK as the 34th richest country

150 *The change plan*

in the world and the USA as the 108th (their respective places in the Happy Planet Index league table) has the element of surprise and might lead to a fruitful discussion of alternative economics.

What is real wealth anyway? Any politician who claims that money is more important to them than their family and friends would be unelectable. And yet that's the assumption growthist politics is based on.

We can also challenge the idea that 'business pays for public services'. This is only because we currently organize society in this way, paying some people to provide services to other people, through healthcare, education, administration and other forms of support. In fact, an appreciable portion of this help is still provided free through voluntary work. If we didn't have profit-first businesses we might be able to focus on enabling more people to pass on their skills and knowledge to others. (In this light, the price the public pays for business is a heavy one.)

Politicians' intense focus on short-term economics deprives citizens of real choice and exaggerates their feelings of helplessness and fears about their immediate financial situation. In so doing, our political leaders ignore the tsunami of change which is heading our way in the coming years. Qualitative change is inevitable in the twenty-first century. The only question is: who will decide what kind of change it should be (a theme I'll return to in Chapter 18).

Questioning technologism

Last, we need to question the implications around the world of 'the fourth industrial revolution' (Schwab, 2016). The time it takes to realize the problems with new technology is getting shorter. It took well over half a century to understand the environmental damage caused by plastics, whereas we are now seeing within a decade or so the harm that social media can cause to privacy, mental health and political freedom. All new technology is potentially hazardous, so why are we constantly seduced by it? The precautionary principle really ought to replace our uncritical, naive acceptance of novelty.

Job automation is likely to be a major political issue of the next decade, so it could be an ideal opportunity to question everything about our future. It's not just manual workers who are threatened. AI engineers actually find it easier to replicate some aspects of human intelligence than they do to imitate human mobility and perception, perhaps because abstract thought is a much more recent evolutionary development (Moravec, 1988). This paradoxical state of affairs implies that some 'easy', low-paid jobs – like serving drinks or waiting at table – will take longer to eliminate than some 'hard' well-paid occupations, such as law or accountancy. In other words, it's the professional middle class which could have most to lose from job automation.

Institutional change

Major structural changes to our political system are also needed, if we are to permanently change the quality and quantity of our political conversations. Not only do we need to upgrade Anglo-American representative democracy, we also need to move towards a much greater state of participatory democracy.

There are many measures which can help to shift decision-making from the plutocracy to the electorate. High up on the list is extending the franchise to 16- and 17-year-olds, who are often the most open to new ideas and whose future is most at stake. They're old enough to work, drive, fight in wars and become parents but not old enough to vote. What can possibly justify this? Democracy could also be strengthened by more referendums, which are becoming increasingly popular across the world (only 50 were held in the 1950s but more than 1,000 in the first decade of this century (Felber, 2012)). Properly conducted – unlike the British EU referendum in 2016 – with rule-based debates, and clear outcome choices, I believe they can help to improve political debate and close the chasm between active voters and 'the unheard third' who shun the ballot box at national elections.

At present the UK and the USA are under the sway of the worst kind of negative reinforcement cycle, in which elections are often decided by a minority of voters, an outcome which only further alienates the majority. In the 2015 British general election, it took fewer than 40,000 votes to elect a Conservative or Labour MP but on average three-quarters of a million votes were necessary to put a candidate from the Greens, Liberal Democrats or UKIP into parliament (in spite of the fact that these three parties received 24% of the popular vote). And in the following year, Donald Trump won the US presidency in 2016 with three million fewer votes than his Democrat opponent, a victory, in effect, clinched for him by the 39% of eligible American citizens who didn't vote at all, as 55% of them were Democrats (Pew Research Center, 2018b).

That's why compulsory voting could help, if only to remind people that democratic rights have been earned over many centuries by brave citizens prepared to sacrifice everything to achieve them: they've rarely been granted voluntarily by the governing elite. Democracy can never be the rule of the majority, if a substantial minority don't participate in it. Premodern egalitarian societies show that dropping out is not an option, if self-interested leaders are to be prevented from taking over (Boehm, 1999), although in a compulsory voting system, principled abstention could be an option on the ballot paper. If smoking in public can be banned, why not voting evasion? Participating in politics is also good for your health and for those around you. Compulsory voting would also highlight the need for greater voter registration. Other measures such as electronic voting are worth experimenting with, as this could increase voter engagement, especially among younger voters (this innovation now seems to be established in Estonia and Switzerland).

Proportional representation will help to break down the tyranny of the two-party system in Anglo-American politics, which restricts choice and, encourages habitual, 'zombie' voting. Having huge 'broad church' establishment parties, containing a multiplicity of different trends and positions, means that the real political decisions are often made behind closed doors and turns party feuding and in-fighting into the driving forces of politics. Coalition-forming in proportionally representative systems may be tortuous, but at least it has the virtue of greater transparency and accountability.

Levelling the information slope of politics is also vital to move towards greater freedom of choice and democratic engagement. That could involve capping party donations, restricting excessive lobbying, regulating social media influence and balancing the power of the press (both of which will still exist in utopia). We long ago replaced the secret ballots which gave landlords undue influence over their tenants, but we still accept the hugely disproportionate political influence which the super-rich exert through the media outlets which they own. TV debate, one of the only forums of national discussion, desperately needs to include more incisive questioning of media-trained politicians and cut through the duplicity and evasiveness of post-truth politics.

Another measure that could help to propel us towards participatory democracy is sortition, selecting parliamentary assemblies by lot rather than by election. Sortition goes back to ancient Athens, where many governmental decisions were made by randomly selected councils of citizens and the drawing of lots was used to fill important civic and political positions (Van Reybrouck, 2016). Aristotle considered sortition to be the most effective and least corrupt way to promote genuine democracy, as opposed to elections which it was easy for the oligarchs to dominate. The principle is still with us today in the form of randomly selected criminal juries, who without any specialist legal knowledge are considered capable of making weighty judgements that could involve life imprisonment for a defendant or even execution, in jurisdictions with capital punishment.

Citizen juries could provide legislative advice – replacing the British House of Lords, for example – or take on decision-making roles in specialist areas, such as education or healthcare. And unlike criminal juries, these assemblies would be made up of paid posts, perhaps lasting several years, so as not to discriminate against low-income citizens. They would promote equality in other ways, spreading governmental expertise and responsibility throughout society, as people returned to ordinary life after assembly duty. They could also provide sound, unbiased decision-making, as the deliberative process shows just how well non-experts can master complex subjects if they are given the opportunity (more about consensus decision-making in Step 7). A case in point is the successful role played by citizens'

groups selected by lot in Ireland in 2017 in recommending highly conten-
tious changes to the Irish constitution in respect of abortion and gay marriage (Citizens Assembly, 2018). In fact, 'Lottocracy', as it has been called,
could be one of the best cures for the afflictions currently affecting democracy worldwide (Guerrero, 2014).

Civil society and circular democracy

Major structural changes like these can help to expand the elements of
circular democracy which have always existed in the West. The flow of bottom-up influence on top-down policy has been at the root of much democratic progress from the beginning. The great historical changes in our
democracy have come as a result of ordinary men and women fighting for
their rights, often at the cost of persecution, imprisonment and death.
And it is still true today that considerable political power resides in civil
society, outside of the formal institutions of politics. The world is full of
micro-political entities, small groups spontaneously forming and reforming, campaigns on single issues or multiples issues, all agitating for change
on a myriad of different platforms. Some of these political organizations
disappear quickly; others form into new, durable institutions, often with
astonishing speed.

In the recent past, we've seen the difference popular campaigning can
make on issues such as global warming. For example, in September 2014
the mobilization of the climate movement saw people in 156 countries
take part in over 2,000 co-coordinated marches, alerting the world to the
significance of the UN climate talks the following year (BBC, 2014). In
Paris during the conference itself, tens of thousands of us kept up the
pressure on our leaders, exuberantly marching to the Eiffel Tower, in spite
of a terrorism-related police ban on demonstrations in public places.

The engagement of civil society goes beyond simply influencing conventional political parties or establishment policy-makers. It's also about
creating practical structural change. As Hilary Wainwright (2016) says,
feminist initiatives in the UK since the 1970s represent more than 'protest'
politics:

> What has been decisive is women organising themselves to find col-
> lective solutions through mutuality and collaboration – in providing
> childcare, setting up domestic violence or rape crisis centres, and
> achieving changes in health provision. These initiatives have subse-
> quently been the basis for leftwing councils using public funds to
> support this de facto expansion of public services.

This flow of circular democracy, where the bottom not only influences
top-down policy but itself creates new institutions, is also evident in the
hundreds of major international non-governmental organizations

(NGOs), such as Oxfam and Greenpeace, originally formed by small groups of concerned citizens. Nowadays, tens of thousands of campaigning groups exist in the UK and throughout Europe, and citizens can counter the secretive power of corporations with transparent lobbying of their own through online campaigning.

The new subjects of history in the Anthropocene

Change plans need change agents, people who can be relied on to champion transformations. Paul Mason (2015) suggests that 'networked individuals', cosmopolitan, techno-literate and largely millennial, are the new agents of political and economic change, replacing the proletariat whom Karl Marx defined as 'the subjects of history'. This is a good start but the appeal of utopia needs to be much broader. Worldwide, for example, it needs to include indigenous peoples and others in countries which have not yet even experienced industrialization and are still working the land in traditional ways.

Circular democracy also needs to be intergenerational. This is not easy, because for many the twenty-first century looks like a conspiracy of the old against the young. Economically, young adults have never had it so bad. They are the first modern generation to be poorer than their parents, less likely to be able to afford a home or to have a state pension before 70 (if then). Politically their views are often ignored or marginalized. If the votes of young adults carried the day, internationalism would have been the winner in the 2016 EU referendum, as over 70% of under-25-year-olds voted against Brexit. In 2015 under-25s were four times more likely to vote for the Green Party than the 65+ group. The same trend exists in the USA where Democrat millennials outnumber Republican millennials by almost two to one (Pew Research Centre, 2018a). Trapped in a world that is not of their design many feel that they are not only living in a corporate plutocracy but also in a gerontocracy, suffering the rule of the old.

Yet the idealism of the young has to be one of the greatest sources of hope for a utopian future. The fact that growth capitalism on its own economic terms is so demonstrably failing many young people only adds to the sense that a radical change is on the way. The establishment's ability to stifle the desire for a very different world cannot last for ever (as long as younger people don't themselves embrace plutocratic gerontocracy as they grow older).

Having said that, we cannot afford give up on older people, even though they are increasingly making crucial decisions about a future in which they will not participate. The later years of life are a period characterized by what psychoanalyst Erik Erikson (1985:267) termed 'generativity', 'the concern in establishing and guiding the next generation' and leaving a fitting legacy. The years beyond retirement can no longer be considered a time for easing into death. It's potentially a very rich period, freed of many family and work responsibilities (at least for some). This second youth of the old provides an opportunity for attempting to right some of the wrongs the baby boomer generation has caused. This cohort, born in 1940s and 1950s, is the original Anthropocene generation, the first in history to live entirely in an epoch dominated by humanity's influence over the planet. Baby boomers still have a chance to be remembered not as the selfish generation which benefited from neoliberalism but as the champions of twenty-first-century change, who helped to steer humanity towards the countercultural utopia many of them dreamed of in their rebellious youth.

What do we really want?

All of these issues of practical change come together in a new initiative around the profound question at the heart of the new politics of the Anthropocene: what do we really want?

For organizations, especially in crisis or at a formative stage, I've found that this can be an immensely useful question for people to ask themselves. The answers are likely to be diverse but illuminating and the discussions animated and often heated. In fact, 'what do we really want?' is just about the most emotionally charged question we can ask of ourselves and others. Existential psychiatrist Irvin Yalom (1989:3) writes of the explosive effect it can have on a large group, as people pair up and ask each other the question repeatedly:

> Could anything be simpler? One innocent question and its answer. And yet time and time again, I have seen the group evoke unexpectedly powerful feelings. Often, within minutes the room rocks with emotion.

Why? Yalom suggests it's because we are getting to the core of what we live for – our need for love, purpose, interrelationship, our care for others and fear of death. This psycho-social project could be a key driver of the great political transvaluation. It goes straight to the centre of the Anthropocene choice, the first time in human history we have been able to answer this question and perhaps the last time will have the chance to do so. Getting used to asking and answering this question should be a salient feature of our new political discourse. It needs to be answered in the broadest definition of 'we', by as many the people on this planet as possible. At the moment, it is being answered by the narrowest number, by a few political and corporate leaders acting largely in the interests of a minority. Simply asking the question could begin to revive democracies and even spread them where they don't yet exist. If rooms 'rock with emotion', then this is exactly how it should be, given the magnitude and significance of the subject. It could be raised in large public gatherings, run by psychologically trained mediators, in citizen juries and popular assemblies, as well as in much smaller settings. In fact, every conceivable forum should be used, from family discussion, to small work groups, street discussions, schools, universities, councils, governments and international bodies.

In practical terms, this could turn into the biggest psychological enquiry of all time. Carefully designed questionnaires can help to channel discussions in the right direction, narrowing down from the most general questions to more specific answers. An instrument like the Personal Construct Psychology grid could help here by offering choices between opposed pairs of values, such as cooperation or competition, wealth or wellbeing, stability or novelty, until a series of top values emerges (Fransella *et al.*, 2003).

Another part of the project could be a mass, planetwide exercise in market research, with, say, 1,000 opinion polls based on representative samples of 1,000, enough to cover all the countries and regions of the world. It would be expensive – perhaps costing tens of millions of dollars – but this would be a drop in the ocean in terms of world GDP and it would provide data for extensive statistical analysis to establish our desired future. Inevitably, social media would also play a major role in stimulating this worldwide debate.

And what of the answers? If it turns out that people value cooperation above competition, sustainability above novelty, wellbeing above material success, we have a mandate for the kind of changes that this book's utopian scenario envisages. Personally, I would wager that if the debate is framed so as to encourage genuinely informed choice, this is the decision that the majority of people would opt for. If, on the contrary, the conclusion tends towards continued economic growth and technological development at any cost, so be it. At least, we will have a better idea of what the majority wants and in a way that establishes intelligent, worldwide, democratic decision-making as a viable ongoing process.

This form of profound public self-questioning can also help us solve one of the most urgent problems we face in the twenty-first century: defining our deep human identity. At a time when nationalist and ethnic interpretations of being human are emerging as the most popular challengers to the neoliberal definition of a human as a unit of capital in a universal market, we need to make progress on what George Monbiot calls our 'species identity' and the 'nationhood of human beings' (2004:112). We need to move beyond our passport identities and our membership of this or that trading bloc to see that we are all citizens of this planet, and all heirs to 200,000 years of human history and to billions of years on life on Earth.

This human identity politics is far from being abstract and vague: it's actually historically precise and pressing. A flurry of recent research shows that this feeling of connectedness to humanity or 'global belonging' is already present for many people across the world (e.g. Der-Karabetian *et al.*, 2014). The Identification with All Humanity scale asks respondents how much they identify with 'all humans everywhere' and 'people all over the world. The average score is 3 out of 5, with 7% scoring 4 or more (McFarland *et al.*, 2013). It suggests that global consciousness or 'citizenship of everywhere' could be a natural corollary of the advent of the Anthropocene, which will grow as people become more familiar with this unique moment in time and the unprecedented decisions it calls on us to make. If you want a big idea for a new, transformative politics, nothing gets much bigger than this. And yet the Anthropocene challenge, unlike many so-called big political ideas, derives its moral urgency from conclusive evidence in social and natural science. It could just be enough to start the revolution of values and the transvaluation of political institutions we so desperately need.

Conclusion

Step 5 is about changing the current political conversation by moving from a Holocene politics around economic growth to an Anthropocene politics focused on achieving a circular democracy which is dedicated to equitability and people-planet balance. That means putting forward new arguments which debunk the myth of GDP, advocate wellbeing above wealth and heed Günter Anders's (1956:1) chilling warning that 'technology has actually become the subject of history, alongside of which we are merely "co-historical"'.

Instead, we need to engage all citizens in a new human mission, perhaps starting with the 'what do we really want?' project. Creating a genuinely participatory democracy also involves supporting a structural transformation in the institutions of voting, decision-making and policy implementation, uniting civil society and policy-makers in a continuous feedback loop. How this circular democracy can tackle the problems we face on a planetwide basis is the next challenge we need to address.

11 Step 6
Embrace utopian internationalism

Step 6 is about taking circular democracy on to the global stage and embracing internationalist solutions to the Anthropocene crisis. At a time when varieties of nationalism, based on ethnicity, nativism, sectarianism and racist supremacisim, are threatening to create a geopolitical hurricane, we need to stand by the vision of 'one people on one planet'. This offers the best chance of averting a chain of catastrophes which could stain the history of humanity for centuries to come. Initiatives which take internationalist utopianism at its word may seem impractical and counterintuitive, when judged by the battlefield logic of our current world plan. But in reality they can provide surprisingly effective and progressive turnarounds to seemingly intractable problems.

The 'miracle cure' for overpopulation

Take one of the most alarming aspects of the Anthropocene crisis, the issue of overpopulation in some of the poorest parts of the global South, which I referred to in Chapter 1. Most at risk is Africa, where the population is on course to double to 2 billion by 2050, in part driven by unexpectedly high fertility rates in several sub-Saharan countries (UN, 2015a). Combined with the effects of severe climate change, environmental degradation and continuing economic inequality, this could produce a perfect storm of famine, disease and civil war. The resulting mass migrations to wealthy countries, if the recent past is anything to go by, would be met with heightened fences, aggressive border patrols and a horrific reinforcement of the very worst CIMENT values of competitive, elitist nationalism. We could expect vociferous calls for forced sterilization and even more inhumane responses such as 'population reduction'. Overall it's a crisis that could make the casualties of the twentieth-century world wars pale by comparison.

So what's the utopian internationalist response? Simple: make a huge investment in education, wellbeing and gender equality in the poorest countries in the world. This is not based on evidence-free idealism but on rigorous research, which suggests that the world population can be stabilized at around 9 billion by mid-century and experience a steady reduction to even more sustainable levels after that (Dorling, 2017).

Here are three of the strategies for sustainable population development advocated by Robert Engelman (2012:122–5), president of the World-watch Institute and some of the evidence he uses to back them up.

Ensure universal access to safe and effective contraception for both sexes

The evidence suggests that access to contraception decreases family size across the world, partially because some 40% of pregnancies are unintended. Engel-man (2012:122) also suggests that 'a conservatively estimated 215 million women in developing counties are hoping to avoid pregnancy but not using effective contraception'. He estimates that this measure would cost about $25 billion worldwide, less than the world currently spends on pet food.

Guarantee education through secondary school for all, with a special focus on girls

In every culture in which girls have at least some secondary education, women have fewer children. Remarkably, the World Bank has estimated that women have 0.3 to 0.5 fewer children for every secondary school year they complete, compared to women who have not had this amount of schooling (Abu-Ghaida and Klasen, 2004). A massive programme of sex education, specifically around contraception – a kind of reproductive Mar-shall Plan – would be the most positive and progressive response to the overpopulation crisis, one wholly commensurate with the idea that the Anthropocene is the epoch of universal education.

Eradicate gender bias from law, economic opportunity, health and culture

In the end, gender equality and female empowerment are the best insur-ance policies against an overpopulation catastrophe. With more women in leadership positions and women everywhere able to choose their health pri-orities and family size, patriarchal and religious arguments around birth control will quickly lose much of their force. This very obviously extends to programmes for population control, which have in the past been run by men. Would women have designed the coercive sterilization programme which was introduced in India or China's draconian one-child policy? As gynaecologist and former head of the UN Population Fund Nafis Sadik says:

> If you really looked after women's needs and women's health, every-thing else would take care of itself. Not allowing them to take deci-sions for themselves is really the main obstacle to population control.
> (Quoted in Pearce, 2011:143)

Alleviating the overpopulation crisis is not just a major commitment to altruism – an example of the good things that happen when you put others before yourself – it also profoundly suits the self-interest of the global North. You don't have to be a strategic genius to work out the best solution to the unprecedented demographic problem which many of the richest countries in the world face today, as the over-65s age group rapidly expands, leaving too few younger people in the workforce. In Germany and Japan, fertility has fallen below the replacement rate, meaning that their native populations are in decline. Increased immigration from the global South will solve the West's ageing crisis by bringing together the young and the old of the world in an act of global intergenerational equality. It will also hasten the breakdown of nativist barriers, as a cosmopolitan, multi-ethnic and multinational identity becomes the norm.

In all this, we have to bear in mind that overpopulation is another symptom of our sloping world. The disproportionate use of natural resources in wealthy countries contributes to the poverty of the poorest. The average person in the richest 10% of the world has a carbon footprint 60 times larger that of their equivalent in the poorest 10% of countries (Oxfam, 2015). If developed countries used fewer natural resources, developing nations would have more of their own resources at their disposal and would suffer less of the environmental degradation caused by reckless extractivism. And if the global North stopped economically exploiting the global South in other ways, governments in Africa and Asia would be better placed to develop the healthcare, education and other public services which almost certainly would enable them to reduce their own unsustainably high birth rates.

It's no accident that countries like Niger and Burkina Faso, which have very high rates of female fertility, are also among the least economically developed nations in the world, with the some of the world's highest levels of infant and maternal mortality (Dorling, 2017). So the overpopulation crisis is really another facet of the economic Great Levelling. Once fair trade, which raises and protects local standards, is established as the global common standard (as opposed to free trade which keep standards low), the potential for a Malthusian population nightmare will rapidly recede.

This issue shows us that utopian counter-logic can bring about the revolution in values that the Anthropocene calls for. The CIMENT mindset which sees different nationalities as enemies, competitors in a deadly, zero-sum game, can only lead to disaster, whereas a holistic, cooperative approach focuses on what binds humanity together on this planet. It also tells us something else. Men and women making informed choices about their families, girls having the choices which come from better education, female career empowerment and the right of all countries to choose their own economic paths: all these factors are about increasing decision-making capacity. They indicate what the ultimate, practical goal of the Anthropocene must be: to put informed choice at the core of every aspect of human life.

Grow peace by degrowing war

Peace is another choice we've yet to master. In 1968 it was estimated that of the previous 3,421 years of world history, only 268 had been without war – that's less than 1% (Durant and Durant, 1968). And things haven't got much better since then. In fact, the *Bulletin of the Atomic Scientists* (2018) recently reset their Doomsday Clock to two minutes to midnight, suggesting that the world is closer to self-destruction than at any time since the first thermonuclear bombs were detonated in 1953. (In the optimistic, early 1990s, by comparison, the clock read 17 minutes to midnight).

These days, if not already at war, the governments of the world seem to have their finger poised on the trigger. Compared to the virtually unarmed nations of the world in 1930, which less than a decade later would fight the bloodiest war in history, the early twenty-first century is alarmingly battle-ready. There are over 27 million armed forces personnel around the world (not counting paramilitaries and militias) and annual expenditure on arms is $1.6 trillion, three-quarters of which is spent by just ten nations (World Bank, 2016). (Think how much secondary education and contraception advice you could get for $1.6 trillion) The total value of military-industrial assets (weapons, camps, installations, research departments and so on) is incalculable but is likely to run into tens of trillions of dollars.

Nations that were non-combatants in the Second World War, like China, North Korea and Saudi Arabia, now boast some of the largest, most lethal military forces in the world. In addition to the global stock of 15,000 nuclear warheads, many nations own biological and chemical weapons and cyber-warfare programmes so secret that even the governments which possess them may not be fully aware of them. And, as if any more materials for a fight were needed, there are also more than a billion civilian-held firearms out there, most of them privately owned, especially in the United States, which has more guns than citizens (Kapp, 2018).

Ending war is a goal close to the heart of utopians everywhere, but what can actually be done to turn around the continuing use, and toleration of, extreme state-based violence? Trying to understand the vicious circle of violence is a start. Just as being abused as a child increases the likelihood of becoming a child-abuser in adulthood, so other more legitimized forms of violence tend to breed violence. Take the example of the multiple shootings that take place in America almost every day (although only major incidents involving mass fatalities receive worldwide publicity). Each horrific shooting spree in a school or concert or casino promotes anguished calls for gun control. But what actually happens? There's a spike in the sales of firearms, sometimes of very same model which the shooter used. The rationale goes something like this: 'There are lunatics out there with guns so I'd better buy a gun to defend myself.' It's a terrible reinforcement cycle which most governments seem unwilling to even try to rebalance.

The best way to defeat violence is through non-violence. In a culture of aggression, where increasingly violent TV, film and video games are ubiquitous, this goes against the grain. Yet, like other utopian solutions, it draws on the well of cooperativeness which is at the heart of being human, For instance, it's well known that nowadays soldiers have to have their natural disinclination to kill other human beings trained out of them. Research by combat historian Samuel Marshall (1947) suggested that in the Second World War less than a third of American soldiers actually fired their weapons at the enemy. Yet once trained in modern military techniques and pressured into compliance, ordinary people can lose all sense of fellow feeling. Do you remember the photographs of grinning US guards posing in front of hooded, leashed or naked torture victims in Iraq's Abu Ghraib prison in 2003? Psychologist Philip Zimbardo (2007) cites this as a prime example of 'the Lucifer effect', by which good people can become evil in top-down, power-orientated environments.

By contrast, Mahatma Gandhi provides one of the greatest examples of how non-violence can overcome authoritarianism, even if it comes in the form of long-term colonial occupation and institutionalized racism. Gandhi's non-violent doctrine of *satyagraha* has been translated as 'holding on to the truth' or 'truth force'. Civil-rights campaigner Martin Luther King, who was profoundly influenced by Gandhi, called it 'soul force', urging, in his renowned 'I have a dream ...' speech, that 'we must rise to the majestic heights of meeting physical force with soul force' (King, 1963:3). For Gandhi, *satyagraha* was an example of 'the law of love' in operation, which he compared to a scientific law. 'Truth force' is not passive but extraordinarily active and assertive, which is why Gandhi believed it was 'a weapon of the strong' and that 'non-violence is the only weapon that can save the world' (Gandhi, 1991:318, 268).

As historian and UN diplomat Shashi Tharoor stresses, non-violence means much more than a simple denial of its opposite. 'Non-violence', he writes, 'was the way to vindicate the truth not by inflicting a suffering on the opponent, but on one's self'.

> This was the approach Gandhi brought to the movement for Indian independence and it worked. Where sporadic terrorism and moderate constitutionalism had both proved ineffective, Gandhi took the issues of freedom to the masses as one of simple right and wrong and gave them a technique to which the British had no response.... By breaking the law non-violently he showed up the injustice of the law. By accepting the punishments imposed upon him he confronted his captors with their own brutalization.... In the end he made the perpetuation of British rule an impossibility.
>
> (Tharoor, 2017:123–4)

Gandhi's willingness to suffer for his beliefs may be beyond most people, but other non-violent political strategies have also proved extraordinarily effective, as Mark Kurlansky (2006) illustrates in *Non-Violence: The history of a dangerous idea*. For example, he shows that in the Second World War, more Jewish people were saved by the Danish government's tactics of non-cooperation with the Nazis than by armed resistance movements in other occupied countries, such as in the Netherlands, where a quarter of the entire Jewish population died, or in Poland where 90% of Jews perished.

Kurlansky cites other instances in which extreme military violence didn't produce its desired results. For example, the deliberate killing of up to 300,000 German civilians in the Allied bombing of Dresden in 1945 seems to have done little to dampen German morale, any more than the Luftwaffe's callous targeting of civilians in Coventry reduced the British determination to fight. Kurlansky also shows that tactics such as labour strikes and non-cooperation with the authorities – most notably in Poland – played a major part in bringing down the Soviet system of government, which rather deflates the accepted competitivist claim that it was the West's aggressive use of its military and economic power that 'won' the Cold War.

Truth force surely has to be a key element in the politics of the Anthropocene, using non-cooperation to create a cooperativist revolution. It's far from being a policy of 'doing nothing' – the charge levelled against it by some – as it involves many types of assertive and committed action. Nothing emphasizes the power of human cooperation more than withdrawing it, through strikes at work, consumer strikes or even sex strikes. Economic sanctions and targeted boycotts can have a real impact, as can forms of civil disobedience, such as sit-ins and learn-ins, which aim at educating as much as disrupting. All these tactics are concerned to help others see the truth of their situation rather than to bludgeon them into submission (which only nurtures the desire for revenge). This confuses oppressors because instead of mirroring their violence, it offers something qualitatively different.

Tactics such as patience, respect and good humour pay off, as does a readiness to listen rather than indulge in impulsive, prejudiced condemnation. Think of the years of resolute negotiation and trust-building that led to the Good Friday peace settlement in Northern Ireland in 1997. This quiet diplomacy was in stark contrast to the inflammatory government rhetoric, belligerent military action and imprisonment without trial of the 1970s and 1980s, a response which turned peaceful civil resistance into something close to a full-blown civil war, in which over 3,000 people lost their lives and some 50,000 were injured.

Making real progress in overcoming war and violence can only be achieved if we rely on the first rule of utopia: trust in the human propensity for goodness. Peace workers all over the world today understand that breaking down the cycle of violence involves building up the cycle of trust.

And that means laying down some of the most dangerous weapons of war: fear, suspicion and ignorance. As psychoanalyst, peace worker and practical utopian Dieter Duhm (2015) emphasizes, creating trust requires a change of consciousness. For peace, he says, 'the way is from inside out': for too long people have been fighting for peace 'while filled with war'. Emptying ourselves of this violence means recognizing ourselves for what we really are and seeing others with the same openness and candour. 'Peace is the unconditional mutual acceptance of people that trust one another because they have perceived one another' (Duhm 2015:142).

Of course, peace also comes from the outside in, as Duhm would acknowledge. Without fundamental changes to our political and economic structures, a revolution in peace values will be extraordinarily difficult to achieve. And as Mark Kurlansky (2006) warns, time is rarely on our side. When war comes, peace efforts rapidly lose their traction. Peace-builders may even find themselves reclassified as criminals, accused of espionage and treachery, as a nation closes ranks against a (real or imagined) external enemy. This makes fighting for peace pre-emptively even more vital. So what more can be done?

First, reduce the $1.6-trillion-a-year arms trade. The more our leaders invest in weaponry, the more they are economically committed to using them, sometimes even without realizing it. In the race to stay ahead of military innovation, upgrade weapons systems, replenish depleted stocks and, of course, acquire superprofits from massive international arms sales, the algorithms of capital act as an impersonal force. To stop it, we need to end the export of arms to oppressive regimes and gradually wind down domestic arms production. This could transform engineering jobs in the defence establishment into highly skilled jobs in renewable energy, as advocated by the Campaign against the Arms Trade (2014), for example.

Second, call for transparent regulation of what's going on in our top-secret defence establishments. How much taxpayer money is going into the development of new chemical and biological weapons, for example? Killer robots are definitely on the agenda, as global expenditure on lethal autonomous weapons systems (LAWS) accelerates rapidly. Experts predict that LAWS will be impossible to control, as they are easy to hack and may be used by terrorists and rogue states against their own populations. They are the new weapons of mass destruction, according to AI professor Toby Walsh, who adds that 'one programmer and a 3D printer can do what previously took an army of people' (Busby, 2018).

Third, create worldwide Ministries of Peace committed to building peaceful relations globally, perhaps with peace-keeping troops available to it, but mainly concentrated on diplomacy, bridge-building and reconciliation. Where would the funds come from? A good place to start would have been the budget for the post 9/11 'War on Terror', which is estimated to have already cost the US taxpayer some $5.6 trillion (Crawford, 2017).

Fourth, support unilateral nuclear disarmament. This is the ultimate cycle-breaker and test of the strength and courage of non-violence. The nuclear stand-off is as dangerous today as at any time since the 1950s, and the renewed arms race gives full vent to the suspicious (even paranoid) competitiveness of some of our world leaders.

This final point brings us back to the people-planet perspective at its broadest. Even at the local level, breaking the cycle of distrust and over-coming the greed and fear syndrome of competitivism is not easy, but making real progress towards world peace will also require a wholly new set of global relationships. It's time to set utopian internationalism the biggest challenge of them all: global governance.

Towards world government?

Utopians have always dreamed of a world government. In his *Modern Utopia*, written in 1905, H.G. Wells, who would later champion the League of Nations and contribute to what became the UN Declaration of Human Rights, put a fully formed world government in charge of the future world. Edward Bellamy in *Looking Backward* (1888) didn't go quite so far but advocated a world federation, which was superior to any national government. It's hard to see how the Anthropocene crisis can be averted without a similar step change in international cooperation. If we are to steer the planet away from an ecological collapse which is wholly indifferent to national boundaries, we need to transcend our ancient dependence on parochialism and create the strong supra-national bodies, which can make circular democracy function on a global plane.

Democratizing the institutions which govern world trade, such as the WTO, the World Bank and IMF, would be a step in the right direction. As Jason Hickel argues:

> Allowing global South countries – the world's majority – to have fair and equal representation in these institutions would give them a real say in the formulation of policies which affect them.
>
> (2017:262)

He suggests equalizing national votes in the World Bank and IMF, thereby ending the effective domination that rich countries enjoy, and opening the vote for the president of these bodies beyond the USA and Europe. Making the WTO proceedings more transparent and allowing citizens to decide who represents them – as opposed to trade ministers representing the interests of corporations and international finance – would also help.

One model for a world government could be the European Union. In 1869, this was seen as a utopian dream, when a peace conference called for a united states of Europe as a way of ending war. A succession of failed peace conferences followed and Europe entered the cycle of aggression that led to two world wars, which turned out to be more devastating than the worst nightmares of Victorian peace campaigners (Mazower, 2012). Yet in the second half of the twentieth century, the eternally warring nations of Europe have formed themselves into a peaceful union which channels competition into cooperation.

Economically, the EU is still heavily influenced by neoliberalism, but its reliance on the precautionary principle provides the most effective business and environmental regulation of any comparable body in the world. Moreover, its relatively democratic structure – which assigns a significant role in policy-making to consensus voting among the member states – represents a genuine historical advance. A move towards a larger federation would reduce the domination of larger nation states. It could also pave the way for an increasingly post-national union, which grants membership to regional entities and even municipalities and city states.

However, at present the most obvious current candidate for a world government is the United Nations, which is another realization of utopian and internationalist ideals going back to the nineteenth century. Established in 1945, the UN can be considered one of the first great Anthropocene institutions, representing a possible new world order based on planetwide cooperation rather than war. It has already played a significant part in promoting planetary sustainability. Even if the UN's International Panel on Climate Change has been too slow in taking steps towards the effective climate containment it promised in the Rio Earth Summit in 1992, it still represents the best platform for making the huge changes urgently needed to avoid catastrophic global warming. For all its faults, the UN's Sustainable Development Goals programme at least gives a glimpse of what an effective SEWP plan would look like. The UN's peace-keeping role also makes a real, positive difference (although its $40 billion budget is dwarfed by the $600 billion the United States spends on arms every year). And the UN's many agencies, whether aiming to prevent sexual exploitation or improve access to safe drinking water, provide enlightened, evidence-based interventions to some of the most neglected people on the planet.

And yet the UN's progressive project is constantly subverted by its wealthiest members. The democracy of its 195 member states is constrained by the absolute veto granted to the five nations of the permanent Security Council. The USA, the UK, France, Russia and China represent less than 3% of the world's nations and under a third of its population (but are five of the six biggest global arms exporters). The Big Five, plus Japan, also wield disproportionate financial muscle, given that they provide 58% of the UN's main budget – with the USA alone contributing 22%, while the poorest 82% of member states only contribute 18% of total UN funding. This disequilibrium gives the United States considerable influence over an organization, which it has always partially viewed as a rival to its own global ambitions (Kennedy, 2006). A further imbalance is provided by the increasing influence on the UN of multinational corporations, through the role of lobbyists, in-house economists and even philanthropic donations (for example, the Bill & Melinda Gates Foundation now provides more funding to the World Health Organization than any nation except the United States (WHO, 2017)).

What can be done to correct the UN's economic and political slant? 'Everything has been globalized except democracy', writes George Monbiot (2004:83), and one of his remedies for this situation would be to open up the UN Security Council to the entire General Assembly of all member nations, whose votes would be weighted according to the size of their population and the quality of their democracy. No nation would have a veto, and major decisions would require an overwhelming majority vote. This might compel the USA to fully commit itself to the UN rather then position itself as a rival world authority. Democratizing the UN would also require internal organizational reforms, with more collective decision-making and greater transparency and accountability.

An even more radical act of equalization would be to 'right-size' national populations. In the 1950s, the economist and political scientist Leopold Kohr (1957) argued that bigness or oversize was the primary cause of world wars and economic inequality, a line of thinking that his pupil, E.F. Schumacher, would go on to characterize as 'small is beautiful'. Kohl posed the question: how can we have democracy in the UN, when China, the largest state, has a population thousands of times greater than that of the smallest state? If, instead of consisting of around 200 unequally sized nations, the UN was made up of 1,000 countries of no more than 100 million people, it could be far better placed to make choices which genuinely represented different parts of the world and the planet as a whole. It might even embody the concept of *homonoia* – the ancient Greek notion of the balance between semi-independent city states – which Kohr saw as a possible model for a new global equilibrium.

In this type of scenario, a right-sized, democratized and fairly resourced UN could become the platform for the Great Levelling, gradually erasing the economic inequalities created by 500 years of Western colonialism, self-interested growth capitalism and unfair trading relationships. This body would be a strong, global coordinating committee – to use a less emotive word than 'world government', of the kind implied by many economic theories, whether ecological or neoliberal (remember Milton Friedman's insistence that government act as the arbiter of corporate competition). As such, it could be the primary agency of the early Anthropocene's greatest achievement and the hub of a vibrant circular democracy stretching from one side of the planet to the other.

A world without borders

Finally, let's give a thought to the ultimate utopian internationalist ambition, the possibility of removing all national borders. In fact, according to anti-poverty economist Michael Clemens (2011), eliminating all restrictions on emigration from poor countries would decrease global economic inequality and boost world GDP by 50% to 150%. Even if emigration was limited to just 5% of the population in low-income countries, he claims the flow of wealth to the world's poor would still be very considerable. By comparison, currently only 3.4% of the world's population live outside their countries of birth (UN, 2017). In fact, Clemens states, the gains from this level of free movement of labour would far exceed the gains from removing every single trade barrier and capital control in the world. He claims this trillion-dollar bounty would go beyond what even the most generous reparative finance programme is likely to be able to achieve.

Of course, a move of this magnitude could not happen overnight and a sudden upsurge in unmanaged economic activity is the last thing our fragile planet requires at this point. But it gives an idea of how a gradual opening of borders could not only lead to a genuine equalization of incomes between the global North and the South, but to a wider people-planet paradigm shift.

A borderless planet – and surely this has to be the ultimate definition of utopia – would reduce economic conflict and the wars it spawns. It would also offer another solution to the problem of uncontrolled mass migrations from the world's poorest countries which represents one of this century's gravest humanitarian threats. And perhaps once people are totally free to move around the planet without passports, as they have been for most of human history, we can hope to fully realize the project of a united human identity. Only then, perhaps, will we truly feel ourselves to be one people on one planet.

Conclusion

In a nutshell, utopian internationalism can really work. Although it runs counter to growthist economics and CIMENT thinking, it can bring a progressive, equitable solution to the problem of overpopulation and help us achieve genuine peace goals through the new-epoch politics of non-violence and truth-force. By reforming bodies such as the EU and the UN, themselves the result of utopian internationalism in the past, we can step up to the higher form of international cooperation needed to manage the Anthropocene crisis and steer us in the direction of a post-national planet. This utopian spirit can even provide a viable alternative to the most powerful type of organization driving our current world system, the multinational corporation, as we'll see in the next step of our change plan.

12 Step 7
Help to grow post-growth enterprises

For someone who's worked extensively with large, hierarchical, profit-driven organizations, Step 7 is a breath of fresh air. It's a relief to get away from the cloying atmosphere of the corporation, where bullying, ego-driven executives rampage like the jealous, infighting gods of Greek mythology, contemptuous of the consequences of their actions on the mere mortals around them. We've seen how utopianism can help to transform some of the most powerful institutions of growthism. Let's now see how it can take on the mightiest of them all, the multinational corporation.

In a utopian Anthropocene, organizations will look very different from today. In a circular economy, we can expect the disappearance of many of the barriers which currently separate businesses from public services, work from leisure, employment from self-development, paid work from unpaid work and the workplace from the household and the community. Above all, the essential structures of post-growth organizations will change. Enterprises which incorporate SEWP principles will have a different orientation to natural resources built into their basic operations. They'll also have different legal constitutions and ownership structures, distinct social purposes and internationalist ways of relating to the world market.

The great news is that is that we don't have to wait until utopia to find such post-corporate enterprises. The SEWP vision is already being implemented, either partially or as a whole, in enterprises around the world which have seen through the reckless irrationality of growthist economics. The foundations for a better business world are already here.

Sustainability enterprises

Let's begin with enterprises which reject the algorithm of capital that treats natural resources as though they were endlessly renewable. Paul Hawken's classic *Ecology of Commerce* laid down some of the foundations for sustainability organizations: 'Business has three basic issues to face: what it takes, what it makes, and what it wastes' (1993:15). Creating a closed loop around these three areas involves using nature to inspire the aims, content, production process and organizational structure of an enterprise. Ecological pioneer Janine Benyus (1998) has termed this practice 'bio-mimicry', or the imitation of nature, and suggests a number of guidelines for enterprises committed to sustainability. These include using waste as a resource, diversifying, cooperating to fully use the habitat, gathering and using energy efficiently, 'optimizing rather than maximizing', using materials sparingly and running on information in order to remain in balance with the biosphere. As an example of these principles in action, she points to the virtuous circles to be found in a Danish ecopark in which an energy company pipes its waste steam to provide power to a pharmaceutical company, as well as to heat over 3,500 homes, while its cooling water, once warmed, is pumped into a local fish farm.

Achieving sustainability requires a profound paradigm shift for manufacturing companies. Take the example of American entrepreneur Ray Anderson, who says he experienced 'a spear in the heart' in 1994 when questioned on what his highly successful carpet-tile manufacturing company was 'doing for the environment'. Directly inspired by Hawken's book, Anderson decided to make his company, Interface, environmentally sustainable. This was no mean task, because as Anderson reveals in *Confessions of a Radical Industrialist* (2009:2), the carpet-tile business is 'so oil intensive you could think of it as an extension of the petrochemical industry'. Nevertheless, Interface's Mission Zero project committed the enterprise to cease taking anything from the earth that it cannot rapidly renew and included the following goals:

- Creating zero waste (e.g. the use of a simple brass nozzle, costing $8.50, saved 2 million gallons of water a year)
- Eliminating emissions from smokestacks and effluents from waste water
- Using as much renewable energy as possible
- Making transportation more resource-efficient (e.g. by reducing the weight of tiles, switching from trucks to rail and, in Europe, to barges)
- Replacing virgin raw materials with recycled or renewable materials

The final goal in the list involved finding a use for some of the 2.3 billion kilogrammes of carpet which was thrown away every year in the USA. Having found an Italian company that had invented a way of turning old clothing and mill waste into automobile door panels and dashboards, the Interface team were able to recycle the many layers of PVC and fibreglass contained in a carpet tile. A later ingenious discovery led Interface to use old fishing nets as the raw material for carpet tiles, thereby putting money into the economy of fishing communities in the Philippines and elsewhere. Another elegant way of using waste as a resource was to turn a malodorous, methane-leaking landfill site in Atlanta, Georgia into a source of energy for Interface's plant, thereby reducing its carbon footprint. It also created new capacity in the landfill, as the rubbish obligingly sank as the methane was filtered out.

A European sustainability pioneer is the family-owned German office-furniture manufacturer Wilkhahn, whose attention to detail shows what's necessary to reverse some of the basic manufacturing processes institution-alized by centuries of environmentally oblivious industrial growth. Wilkhahn eschews the throwaway culture by making its chairs modular, with clearly labelled parts that can be easily replaced. It uses high-quality eco-friendly materials, like organic wool fleeces, cork and coconut fibre. Cardboard packing is made out of renewable feedstock, replacing oil-based protective film with honeycomb cardboard. The company also reduces its solvent emissions by bonding table tops with a press heated by a hot-water system (not electrically) and recycles 98% of its waste or uses it as renewable fuels (Wilkhahn, 2017).

I have to admit that carpet tiles and office furniture may not have a major role to play in utopia, but the dedication to naturalizing their entire production process shown by companies like Interface and Wilkhahn is admirable. The danger, however, is that their conventional ownership structures keep them subject to the algorithms of capital. There is no doubt that 'green capitalism' has a hugely significant part to play in the transition to a circular economy. But when push comes to shove and profit is directly opposed to sustainability, who wins? If shareholders decide to take their investment elsewhere, what can a management team dedicated to circular economics do to stop them? And how can sustainability organi-zations resist being taken over by potentially subversive interests?

Neoliberalism has found many stealthy ways to integrate itself into the green economy, for example by favouring purely market-based economic mechanisms which erode the scope of political decision-making and the need for regulatory frameworks (Fatheuer *et al.*, 2016). Many of the same investors who sustained climate-denying fossil-fuel majors are now switch-ing to green technology, but it's questionable whether their business objectives have changed. And fossil-fuel companies continue to invest directly in the renewable energy sector (witness BP's purchase of an UK electric-car charging network in 2018).

Another caveat around green capitalism is that, although sustainability often implies a commitment to organizational equitability – and a new approach to leadership which we'll examine in the next chapter – it does not guarantee a non-hierarchical organizational structure. A top-down, corporate-style hierarchy is a perfectly feasible structure for a sustain-ability enterprise. In short, organizations authentically committed to post-growth, SEWP principles need to commit themselves to more than green technology.

Equitability: post-growth ownership structures

To fully escape the algorithms of capital, enterprises require alternative ownership structures which reject the primacy of external shareholders and the domination of profit over purpose. Here I want to look at three types of ownership which fit the SEWP model: cooperatives, social enterprises and commons-based organizations.

Cooperatives: people-first ownership

Cooperatives, or worker-owned enterprises, are a long-established way of creating shared company ownership. Britain has a fairly strong tradition of mutually owned enterprises, such as retail giant John Lewis and, more recently, Aardman (2018), the Oscar-winning animation studio behind *Wallace and Gromit*, which has announced plans to transfer the entire company into employee ownership. Indeed, across the world cooperatives are thriving. Almost 11% of Italians work in cooperatives and in the prosperous region of Emilia Romagna an amazing 40% of the region's GDP is provided by worker-owned enterprises. Proven alternatives to speculative banking exist throughout the world in the form of credit unions and mutually owned financial societies. The aggressive deregulation of this sector in the UK in the 1980s contributed significantly to the 2007/8 financial crash, with building societies-turned-banks like Northern Rock, HBOS and Bradford & Bingley going spectacularly bust. But worldwide financial cooperatives continue to grow. Germany has a thriving mutual finance sector, and, in Japan, insurance companies are among the largest cooperatives in the world, while credit unions are the main lenders to Japanese small and medium-sized businesses. Even in the USA, the home of investment banking, credit unions employ 300,000 people and have a total economic output of almost $200 billion a year (Coop News, 2017).

How do cooperatives work? One of the most impressive examples of this kind of business model is provided by Mondragon, the Spanish engineering and manufacturing conglomerate based in Aragon. Founded in 1956 in a region which was at the heart of the anarchist movement in the Spanish Revolution, Mondragon has grown into Spain's fifth largest business, employing some 75,000 worker-owners. This federation of cooperatives is run by specialist managers who are appointed by workers councils and never paid more than five times Mondragon's average salary. What is most striking about Mondragon is its triadic business model. Its manufacturing and engineering division is complemented by a university, which trains employees in the cooperative's ways and acts as a centre for cutting-edge innovation and scientific research. The crucial third leg of the model is the Mondragon bank, which specifically exists to provide patient, long-term capital for existing cooperatives and financial backing for start ups. In this way, it provides sustainable finance which protects Mondragon enterprises from the harsh winds of the global market and the predatory attentions of corporate competitors. This ingenious alternative to the algorithms of capital enabled Mondragon not only to weather the Great Recession, which hit Spain particularly hard, but also to expand beyond its national borders and develop operations in Latin America (Bajo and Roelents, 2011).

The trust is another form of public ownership, which can strengthen the non-profit sector and protect public resources from privatization. Trustees have a legal obligation to further the stated purpose of their trusts, and although they may be paid, they cannot draw profits from their activities or acquire assets. This works well for philanthropic organizations for the long-term stewardship of natural resources, such as the British National Trust and many publicly owned nature reserves across the world.

Social enterprises: beyond shareholder domination

Another increasingly popular way of ensuring that a company's ownership does not clash with the principle of equitability is to form a social enterprise which legally restricts shareholders' rights. For example, over 12,000 community interest companies (CICs) in the UK have been formed since 2004. Alongside the many traditional non-profit organizations in the public sector, such as trusts and charities, these companies build social purpose into their legal constitutions. Companies-certified-by-guarantee are the most radical form of this. They do not issue shares and contain asset locks, which means that even if the enterprise is legally dissolved its assets cannot be distributed to shareholders (although they can be transferred to another asset-locked organization). Healthcare and education are two of the most popular CIC purposes but the range of not-for-profit enterprises is growing all the time, as the following examples from over 200 CICs registered in the UK in just one month (August 2017) indicate:

> Trinity Balloons, Urban Farmers, Centre for the Study of International Peace and Security, JCM Training Centre, Greencoat Nursery, Queer Puppets Cabaret, Walk With Us, West Lothian Bike Library, Bright Copper Kettles, Living Song, Indigo Recovery Cafe, The Sporting Way, Human Kindness Food Bank, Working Woodlands Cornwall, Young Technicians, Global Sustainability, Big Sky Cinema.
>
> (Gov.UK, 2017)

I can't claim first-hand acquaintanceship with any of these enterprises, but I have to admit that the impression their mere names make on me is inspiring. They certainly seem to embody Paul Hawken's (1993:2) philosophy that 'the promise of business is to increase the well-being of humankind through service, creative invention and ethical action'.

Some social enterprises use models which allow for the issuance of shares (and have no asset lock). For instance, multi-stakeholder models may issue different classes of shares for founders, employees, supporting organizations and investors. This kind of legal structure may make it easier to attract certain types of outside investor, for example philanthropists who want a degree of control over their investments, although this can create the all-too-familiar risk of prioritizing the interests of shareholders over those of all other stakeholders (Ridley-Duff and Bull, 2011).

The commons enterprise: enter the third force

The third type of post-growth enterprise is a prime example of remoderning. The commons is one of the most ancient forms of work organization, dating back at least as far as the agricultural revolution, yet it's highly relevant today. It's a form of self-organization among workers which is based on values that are in complete opposition to materialist, possessive–aggressive behaviour. As I suggested in the Introduction, the enclosure of common land, against which Thomas More protested in *Utopia*, has a long history in Britain. Following Henry VIII's appropriation of the monasteries, the period from the late 1600s to the mid-1800s saw many 'natural' owners thrown off their own land and the privatization of a seventh of all commonly owned land in England. The notorious Highland clearances brought the mass evictions of tenant farmers, as aristocratic land owners carved out vast private estates (half of all private land in rural Scotland is still owned by just 432 landowners or '0.008% of the population' (Gov. Scot, 2014)). Today, this is the potential fate facing half a billion people in sub-Saharan Africa who have no statutory title to their lands, even though they may have farmed them for generations (Bollier, 2014:46).

One of the best known myths of the commons has been perpetrated by Garret Hardin (1968), who in an article called 'The Tragedy of the Commons', suggested that all common resources are inevitably destroyed by self-interested exploitation. What Hardin describes, as commons scholar David Bollier (2014) points out, is not a commons but a no-man's-land. Far from being an unorganized, disputed resource waiting for a hyper-competitor to take it over, commons have highly coherent, complex codes of behaviour governing exactly how a community should use them – and punishments for these who ignore these rules.

Throughout history, commons communities have sustainably managed their precious resources, using rigorous, communally developed rule systems and protocols. Commons economist Elinor Ostrom studied many cases of this phenomenon. For instance, she observed the extraordinary efficiency of the system of water irrigation used by farmers in fifteenth-century Valencia in Spain. Although selfish behaviour by farmers such as drawing water illegally would be economically rewarding, and community-appointed guards could only patrol a third of the farms, the actual rate of infraction was less than 1% (Ostrom, 1990:75). Regular community courts arbitrated all conflicts, handing out enforceable penalties if necessary. (This is also a salutary reminder that the privatization of water represents one of the greatest dangers for our own century.)

The fast-growing commons movement translates the agricultural commons of the past into a powerful third force for the twenty-first century. The entities which can be managed by commons organizations not only include natural resources such as air, water, oceans, photosynthesis, seeds, aquifers, rivers and forests but also human-made assets such as streets, playgrounds, libraries, museums, laws and political institutions. As Peter Barnes notes (2006), cultural commons resources even extend as far as language, religion, music and medicine, while the physical commons includes vital, commercially valuable areas such as the broadcast spectrum. All this holds out the promise of what Richard Swift (2017) calls

a commons-based democracy based on collectively managing and expanding what we hold in common (from air to air waves), rather than watching them ruined through privatization.

One of the most exciting areas is the digital and knowledge commons, which features many highly successful enterprises that work on an open-source, non-profit-making basis. For example, Linux is one of the world's most influential operating systems, which was developed collectively by hundreds of programmers, and now runs on the world's ten largest supercomputers (Mason, 2015). Ubuntu is another open-source operating system that runs on desktops. Mozilla's Firefox is a non-profit search engine, used by almost a quarter of all search-engine users, and WordPress is a free and open-source content-management system providing around a quarter of all websites on the internet.

The open-source movement believes in liberating the development of software and hardware by making it possible for anybody to participate in a project, as long as they obey its protocols and abide by copyright laws which forbid people from commercially profiting from it. The idea of a transnational, state-of-the-art enterprise, which is owned by nobody but which is based on carefully constructed and monitored rules promises a complete revolution in how we think about work organizations. It's inspired by the same countercultural philosophy which led to the formation of the internet in the first place and the subsequent development of the World Wide Web. Indeed, it's worth noting that had the internet been created using commons copyright protocols, it would not have been possible for many of today's high-tech billionaires to use this common resource to amass some of the largest personal fortunes in history.

Nor are commons enterprises limited to software and knowledge production; increasingly they are aiming at creating physical objects through

3D printing and other innovations. Peer-to-peer production advocate Michel Bauwens (2009) asks us to imagine the development of 'a global community of physical production houses', producing highly personalized goods, ranging from cars to electronics to furniture. With the development of self-organizing, open-source facilities such as fab labs, this community can continue to develop as a genuine alternative to conventional growthist manufacturing.

Making it planetwide

What about the planetwide role of SEWP enterprise? Of course, in a people-planet economy, much support would be given to all organizations to extend their international relationships and establish equitable global trade deals. Mondragon shows that cooperatives can rival traditional corporations in their international reach (although managing across borders is proving to be a challenge to the group's managerial principles and values (Bretos and Errasti, 2018)). Commons organizations are even more capable of bursting out of the nationalist constraints of the growthist economy. In particular, knowledge and digital commons criss-cross national and ethnic boundaries as though they weren't there.

Take online encyclopaedia Wikipedia, which across the world has nearly 500 million users a month and editions in 303 languages. Less than 12% of its 40 million articles are in English and almost as many are in Cebuano, one of the main languages of the Philippines (Wikipedia, 2019). For an enterprise only founded in 2001, it gives a sense of just how far and how fast digital non-profit ventures can go, as the internet spreads to the 2 billion people in the world who still have no access to it. Visualize this open-borders dynamic, in combination with long-term relationships created by fair traders, in states and regions committed to promoting global levelling, and it's easy to see how millions of truly international, sustainable, equitable enterprises can emerge.

Another planetwide solution is to commit your enterprise to fair trade rather than free trade. As we've seen in previous chapters, free-trade deals are often mechanisms by which the rich countries of the world take advantage of poorer nations. Free-trade deals typically revolve around low-cost products and produce – reflecting the neoliberal faith in the price of everything and the value of nothing. How this low cost is achieved is not stipulated. Often it comes about by a combination of speculative commodity markets driving prices down, poorly paid jobs in unsafe working conditions and weak or non-existent environmental protection. For example, free-trade arrangements make no mention of child labour, in which over 150 million children are engaged (half of them aged between 5 and 11 years), often in export-orientated sectors (ILO, 2017).

This secretive, exploitative, 'no questions asked' approach is rejected by enterprises entering into the fair trade business model, which grew out of the agrofood sector. As Laura Raynolds and Douglas Murray (2007:227) explain:

> This model proposed that egalitarian North/South trade links could be created by eliminating middlemen, providing better and secure prices, supporting farmer cooperatives and fostering development in impoverished communities.

Fair trade enterprises aim for highly transparent relationships with producers and farmers, based on a fair price, which reflects the market price but contains a 'floor'. This usually gives workers a minimum wage with good health and safety provisions and ensures that goods can be produced in an environmentally sustainable way. Fair trade businesses have to certify that no child labour or other forms of exploitation have contributed to the production of their goods. An additional fair trade premium is usually invested into a democratically administered fund which is dedicated to local community projects, such as building health and education facilities.

Farmers are often prohibited from using synthetic pesticides and are encouraged to take measures to improve their soil fertility. Indeed, as fair trade campaigner Ryan Zinn (2017) argues, fair trade offers one of the most viable pathways to regenerative agriculture, supporting traditional small-scale farming practices such as crop rotation, mulching and livestock integration. These techniques are more climate resilient, and often more productive, than modern industrial agricultural methods.

A British example of this approach is Fairtrade, which imports coffee, tea, chocolate, bananas and other produce. Established 25 years ago, it's recognized by 80% of UK shoppers and represents 1.6 million farmers and workers in 73 countries, mainly in Latin America and sub-Saharan Africa (Fairtrade International, 2016). It acts as a bridgehead, bringing some of the poorest and most vulnerable enterprises in the global South into equitable trading relationships with the powerful retail corporations of the developed world. Fairtrade guarantees its suppliers a minimum price, no child labour, gender pay equality, a commitment to sustainable development and a social premium to be spent on pensions, education and healthcare. Prices may be higher but how many people realize what the real cost to producers is of low-priced supermarkets products? It can only be hoped that the current attempts by some UK supermarkets to replace the Fairtrade ethical brand with their own 'fair trade' certifications is not a duplicitous cover for driving down prices and restoring normal free-trade conditions (Vidal, 2017).

These recent threats underline the fact that the fair trade movement has not yet become 'the new globalization' that some had hoped for before the 2007/8 financial crash (Murray and Raynolds 2007:4) – and like any evolving system it still has its flaws. Nevertheless, it represents one of the best hopes for a genuine alternative to the existing global supply chain, which is dominated by aggressively profit-centred supermarket chains, working on biased trade deals which reflect the interests of finance capitalists and commodity speculators (Simms, 2007).

Worldwide networks of every kind, from trade bodies to academic associations, can also help to bring together those who want to conduct business in a way that encourages global solidarity rather than a zero-sum race to the bottom. And in a future ecological democracy, all enterprises will be able to rely on the support of a state actively promoting fair, equal, reciprocal relationships with suppliers and businesses across the world.

Examples: utopia is already starting to happen

Putting all the pieces of the people-planet model in place is still a work in progress for many progressive enterprises. Not every sustainable organization is equitably structured; not every equitable organization is run on sustainable principles; and establishing any organization on a truly planetwide basis remains a challenge. That said, there is growing evidence that the SEWP enterprise is not simply a utopian ideal but an increasingly widespread commercial reality.

Two very different examples must suffice to make my point.

The first example takes us to Canada, where the not-for-profit sector is a powerful third force which is growing fast. In Quebec, for example, this sector already makes up 8–10% of the province's GDP. To illustrate this, commons scholar Jay Walljasper (2017) takes us on a tour of not-for-profit Montreal. He points out the credit union Desjardin, which is Quebec's largest financial institution; Technopole Angus, a sustainable village which already hosts 56 businesses and is set to build 500 affordable homes; and Recyclage Vanier, a recycling company which for 20 years has been competing successfully with for-profit companies, even though it often takes on people who would struggle to find jobs elsewhere. Other stops on the tour include UTILE, a student housing cooperative; Nataskinam, an Inuit-run clothing manufacturer; and Fiducie, which has invested some $50 million of long-term, patient capital in small- to medium-sized non-profit enterprises.

The presence of a mutual finance outfit in this mix of collectively owned and non-profit organizations is pivotal (remember Mondragon's unique access to friendly capital). It shows that even in a market-based economy, it's possible for new-paradigm enterprises to flourish. Indeed, you have to ask, what would stop post-growth organizations from eventually supplanting traditional corporations altogether, in a future state based on ecological economics, which actively promotes, supports and frames favourable legislation around them?

The second example of SEWP in action is rural rather than urban, a commons-based agrarian enterprise which is reviving old methods of sustainability and inventing new ones. Potato Park is situated in Peru, in the highlands of the Andes. It's home to almost 4,000 indigenous people from six communities who jointly manage over 9,000 hectares of communal land. One of the original sites of the wild potato which made its way to Europe after the Spanish conquest of the Incas, the area now grows 2,300 types of potato, over half of the world's known varieties. In addition, regional crops such as beans, maize, and quinoa are grown. The project's commitment to biodiversity has repelled attempts by corporations to patent these rare seeds. The communities are involved in all decision-making related to the management of the park, mainly through village councils. The park's economy is not based on money, although barter does take place, usually conducted by women, who play a very prominent role in the enterprise.

The Potato Park commons relies on a powerful Andean cultural tradition of *allyu*, a holistic moral and spiritual political economy, which is based on a positive reciprocal relationship between humans and their natural environment. According to Wong and Argumedo (2011), the aim of *allyu* is to achieve *sumaq qausay*, which can be translated as 'good living' or 'to live beautifully' and 'to live with others' (Florentin, 2016). It's recently been incorporated into Ecuador's constitution as *buen vivir*. This totalizing, equitable philosophy of sustainable living is based on the positive assumption of planetary abundance and aims at enhancing wellbeing and celebrating the virtues of being human. It's a belief system, which goes back hundreds of years – some claim to the Inca Empire itself – and is born out of living in the high Andes, one of the world's harshest environments, although also one of its most beautiful. Potato Park's pre-modern egalitarian ethos has seamlessly blended with twenty-first-century sustainability practices. The enterprise is classified as an Indigenous Bicultural Heritage Area and as such it 'incorporates the best of contemporary science and conservation models and rights-based governance approaches' (Wong and Argumendo, 2011). In many ways, it comes close to being a living embodiment of the SEWP model, albeit in rather unique circumstances.

Conclusion

To conclude, post-growth organizations are growing fast. Many exemplify more than one aspect of the SEWP model, and some are already putting all the pieces of the puzzle together. We can expect a rapid growth in research on different models, increased communication between them, and support services for developing them, from organizations such as Community Partners in California, which provides administrative, human resources and funding backup for non-profit enterprises (Vandeventer and Mandell, 2011).

The challenge for non-profit enterprises is to gain enough critical mass to be able to repel the ferocious competition from growthist organizations, which will use the unlevel playing field of the sloping world to their advantage. Psychologically, social entrepreneurs and post-growthers also have to resist the siren call of the CIMENT values which have dominated commercial life for centuries and the temptation to escape the sometimes exacting demands of close cooperation. Nevertheless, more and more people are rejecting the for-profit corporation as the primary model of commerce and building strong eco-egalitarian foundations for an altern- ative to the growthist world plan. A profound redefinition of the twenty- first-century working environment appears to be underway. Let's now explore what this new workplace feels like and the kind of leadership, decision-making and other organizational practices it involves.

13 Step 8

Manage yourself to utopia (by democratizing leadership and other organizational practices)

Step 8 is about managing yourself to utopia at work. It's about the self-organizing practices which SEWP enterprises use to distribute power throughout an organization and the new agenda they offer around leadership, environmental awareness, open communication and increased well-being. These practices can apply not only to workplaces but to households, places of learning, political forums and to society in general. Together, they can help to surmount the crisis of mismanagement our epoch is facing.

So let's leave behind the top-down structures of corporate or public-sector organizations, dominated by supposedly heroic leaders, who make decisions in secret and pass them down the ranks in cultures that encourage competition, divisiveness and Machiavellian brinkmanship. As before, we do not have to invent utopian alternatives from scratch. Our change plan can draw on existing eco-egalitarian practices, which emerge when maximizing shareholder values ceases to be the number-one purpose of an enterprise. These practices include new-epoch ways of making decisions and managing teams and new forms of communication, transparency and remuneration. This organizational transformation can't happen without a paradigm shift in leadership, so let's start with that.

A revolution in leadership

One of the key characteristics of SEWP-type leadership is a profound awareness of the significance of the Anthropocene, which contrasts sharply with the comparative ecological illiteracy of many leaders and managers today. Psychologist Steven Schein has extensively examined the mindset of executives charged with promoting environmentalism within organizations. He found a set of attitudes very different from those of conventional, profit-driven managers. Among these new-epoch attitudes is an awareness of the vulnerability of the earth's ecosystems (described by one interviewee as a question of 'how are we going to go from a consumption society to a balanced system?' (Schein, 2015:75)). A belief in the intrinsic value of nature and what Schein calls 'earth-centric identity' is another trait of this new leadership mentality, resulting in 'a heightened awareness of the entire global community', especially the plight of people in under-developed countries (Schein, 2015:83).

I find this striking because this attitude so closely corresponds to the CANDID values of cooperation, democracy and internationalism. It's a planetwide vision that involves an awareness of 'the part of us that identi-fies our self as literally part of nature' (Schein, 2015:66). Encouragingly, the mindset of these executives encompasses other aspects of the plane-tude approach to knowledge which I sketched in the SEWP model, such as a systems-based commitment to holism and balance. For instance, 'finding an appropriate balance between all three areas: economic, social and environmental' is how one manager formulates his organizational goals (Schein, 2015:126). New-epoch leaders also favour longer-time horizons, as a corrective to the short-termism which dominates our current leaders' thinking and which prevents them from understanding the scope of the Anthropocene crisis. This usually involves long-term business strategies, which may draw on a sense of the deep history of the planet.

Also noteworthy is an attitude that Schein calls, 'a widening circle of care', which includes considering developed countries in the same breath as the developed world, as it were, and a determination to smash current gender hierarchies. One interviewee called this the recognition of 'the need to move towards a more matriarchal society from the dominant patri-archal model' (Schein, 2015: 128). This commitment to equality confirms the circular, balancing impetus of this new leadership psychology, in strik-ing contrast to the conventional corporate executive's desire to charge onwards whatever the cost. In line with the CANDID values, this new mindset favours cooperativism over competitivism and elitism, or as one executive puts it, 'you're not command and control, you're not omnipo-tent. Practicing sustainability has allowed me to collaborate at a higher level' (Schein, 2015:113).

We can see here the beginnings of a psychological integration of sustainability and equitability, combined with a concern for employee well-being and the needs of the entire planet. It's an approach that rejects the self-interested, power-based philosophy which dominates current leader-ship practice. For SEWP leaders, the goal is to empower employees rather than to exercise power over them.

Of course, some leadership virtues will never go out of fashion. Natural leaders will always come to the fore and have a significant role to play. The courage to stand your ground is a trait utopia will always need, as is the readiness to speak up for what you believe is right, even though others may disagree. The bravery to go against the grain when necessary will always be valued. Authentic leaders are able to ask searching questions and deal with robust criticism without taking it personally. Sometimes they're able to see what is coming sooner than others, which can put them one step ahead of the group, but often they are willing to follow others and simply be part of the team. Their preference is always likely to be to help others make key choices rather than impose their own.

New-paradigm decision-making

In a SEWP enterprise, you're drawn into a very different atmosphere of decision-making, which recalls some of the practices of pre-modern egalitarian societies, as well as very contemporary alternative systems to authoritarian choice-making, such as the citizen juries and political assemblies we touched on in Step 5. The people-planet way is to make choice-making a reality for everybody, rather than to endorse a hierarchy in which your decision-making status rises or falls according to your organizational level. Building a SEWP organization is to construct a theatre of creative, group-based decision-making.

One way of envisaging this circular organizational democracy is to imagine the whole enterprise sitting in a circle formulating polices. Instead of electing representatives to make decisions, as in most parliamentary democracies, or appointing senior managers to do so, as in conventional organizations, the aim of consensus decision-making is to directly empower the entire group. This form of participatory democracy gives the whole group direct responsibility for making the decisions which most affect them.

Searching for agreement to a proposal means getting the involvement of all participants. It discourages assertive individuals from exerting undue influence over the decision-making and passive members from opting out of the process altogether. In this way, it builds up people's confidence in contributing to discussions and making difficult choices. This in turn enhances collective responsibility, which is vital when it comes to implementing agreed policies.

In order to work, consensus requires patience, mutual respect, trustfulness and a spirit of openness. It involves circling around, gathering up opinion, moving back and forth until objections are satisfied and misunderstandings removed. It's a rounded process quite different to the arrow-like rush towards a conclusion, which is typified by first-past-the-post voting systems or the often impulsive, individualistic choice-making of an all-powerful CEO. Of course it can be frustrating: in my experience, your patience can be stretched at times. But the process is also very rewarding, creating a new depth of understanding of the issues and personalities involved, which often pays off later in a project.

A typical consensus process, as described by campaigning group Seeds for Change (2017), may progress from the starting circle into smaller groups, which are free to identify the proposals for discussion, without the potentially inhibiting effects of a large group. The whole group may then reassemble to discuss the proposals, and, if necessary, make amendments. Then comes 'the test for agreement', in which the facilitator checks that everyone understands the proposal and asks if anyone has any objections to it. If a member disagrees they are asked whether they wish to block the proposal, in which case it is vetoed (although further amendments may be called for).

The 'block' is a powerful instrument and needs to be used responsibly. If the objector is prepared to register their disapproval but still allow the group to go ahead with the proposal, the process can continue. This 'stand-aside' option reduces the time spent on consensus decision-making but can change the dynamic, so it's vital that people are not pressured into accepting it. If no blocks are presented, and any stand-asides have been articulated, the group can move to an action plan in the normal way, by clarifying timelines and assigning the roles needed for successful policy implementation.

In practice, some enterprises may reserve consensus decision-making for major organizational choices and opt for a different method for day-to-day, operational decisions. Sociocracy is one tried-and-tested system of organizational democracy, first developed by Gerard Endenburg for use in his electrical engineering company, and described by Jack Quarter in his excellent history of socially innovative companies, *Beyond the Bottom Line* (2000). Sociocracy organizes an enterprise in a series of interlinking circles, consisting of work-based groups, which make policy, and councils of representatives from all areas of the business, who are elected by open discussion. This allows the specialization of functions within an organization, while ensuring there is a sufficient degree of interconnection, so that workers are aware of key decisions and directly or indirectly able to intervene in them if they so desire. Sociocracy's version of the stand-aside is described as consent rather than consensus, meaning that a member may have to decide if she 'can live with' a proposal, even if she doesn't fully agree with it (Quarter, 2000:57).

A contemporary alternative to top-down organizational decision-making, which has developed out of sociocracy, is holacracy, which aims to define the roles in an organization and carefully specify the autonomous decision-making power appropriate for each role. Holacracy aims to break down the conventional hierarchy, reducing the leader's role to just one among many, and giving executive power to whoever has the information and expertise to the make the best decisions (Robertson, 2015). Rules-based systems remove the automatic rights of managers to make important decisions, regardless of their expertise – one of the greatest current sources of organizational inefficacy – but they also reduce the power of the group, elevating individual specialisms to a high status. A more rough-and-ready, bottom-up decision-making technique is the 'advice method', used by US entrepreneur Dennis Bakke (2005), who pioneered many self-management principles in endeavouring to make 'joy at work' the mission of his multinational electricity corporation. The advice method enables an employee to make an operational decision for a team, without necessarily requiring its approval. The key stipulation is that the employee must ask advice from a number of other colleagues before settling on a choice.

Other self-organizing practices

Teamwork

As organizations make an increasing commitment to people-planet principles, we can expect many more versions of self-organizing decision-making to evolve. The same can be said of other pivotal Anthropocene social technologies such as teamwork. Essentially, utopia unleashes the power of the team. After all, cooperation is simply teamwork by another name. The kind of collaborative attitudes and practices which organizational psychologists and others have had to work hard to introduce into the modern cooperation have been understood by communities since the dawn of time. It's only in an individualistic, dog-eat-dog economy that we need a reminder that 'there is no 'I' in 'Team'.

There's no such requirement in a SEWP-type organization, which first and foremost sees itself as a team and organizes itself in terms of interconnecting groups, which often have a high degree of autonomy. The superiority of self-managing teamwork to traditional 'divide and conquer' supervision methods has been demonstrated even in ferociously competitive, global manufacturing industries. For example, through their use of semi-autonomous teams or 'work circles', Japanese car-makers like Toyota and Honda long ago outstripped the productivity of top-down, micromanaging US automotive behemoths like General Motors. Work circles are low on hierarchy and high on open interaction between team members with different specializations. Ideally, contractors and other companies in the supply chain are seen as partners in the process, rather than vendors who are forced to compete among each other to drive prices down (Benkler, 2011:206). In a utopian economy, when short working weeks become common, self-managing skills of this kind will become the norm, as teams constantly change shape, placing a premium on multi-skilled flexibility and the ability of every team member to lead whenever necessary.

A culture of transparency

In contrast to today's corporate cultures based on competition, control and concealment, the new-paradigm enterprise flourishes on openness and transparency. This implies a qualitatively different set of organizational relationships. Everything changes once you draw back the screen concealing organizational decision-making and the information on which it's based. For the average employee, it not only creates a very different point of view, it also brings a new form of active participation, which requires her to engage in, and take responsibility for, many aspects of organizational life.

The commons is one organizational form which cannot exist without transparency. Producing open-source software, for example, requires complete openness about codes and protocols as a fundamental condition of its existence. Secrecy or copyright restrictions would quickly destroy a project. Hierarchies work through a limited distribution of knowledge – or 'selective secrecy' – which bolsters the power of the elite. It deliberately deprives most employees of the most crucial resource they need to organize themselves: access to the truth. In reality, the power of the corporate manager often resides in nothing more than his knowledge of what is really going on. That's why transparent communication can have such an equalizing effect. It flattens the hierarchy, creates symmetries of knowledge and potentially produces a level playing field for everybody.

That's not to say that transparency is always easy. We all wish to hide certain aspects of ourselves, especially those things which expose us to criticism. But a culture of transparency is incompatible with a blame culture. A willingness to understand, rather than to rush to judgement, is vital if organizations are to be open. Transparency is not just about how individuals treat each other, it is also something enshrined in the legal constitution of many new-epoch organizations. In this way, openness is their default position. They operate in the bright sunlight rather than in the fog of secrecy which shrouds so many corporations and which could destroy them if it ever lifted.

Communication by dialogue

Open communication leads to dialogue, which is the primary language of the people-planet enterprise. This is in stark contrast to the monologue which is the primary dialect of the transnational corporation, often in the form of priorities and imperatives designed to maximize shareholder value. New-epoch communication rejects the idea of a monologue being passed down from the boardroom in favour of open, horizontal conversations around a shared purpose. The post-growth organization uses dialogue to search for agreement and avoid degenerating into the raucous, mutually deaf monologues of conflict. Enquiry, interrogation, curiosity, moving towards new solutions, engaging rather than alienating, opening rather than closing: these are the characteristics which distinguish the culture of the post-corporate enterprise from today's mainstream organizations.

Cooperation is the key value here, as might be expected. Competitive dialogue is often nothing more than an exchange of monologues. At best, it's a contest between two fixed positions, hitting words back and forth, probing for a weakness in the other's defence. Cooperative dialogue is quite different: it's about opening up to the other, sharing experiences and opinions, being prepared to explore new and uncertain positions and ending in a possible search for a truth which did not exist at the beginning of the dialogue. It's yet another example of the constructive circularity of utopianism, as distinct from the destructive linearity of growthism.

A revolution by listening

Embracing cooperative dialogue means assigning a new role to listening. Telling the truth involves seeking it and recognizing it when you hear it and that can only happens if you have the ability to listen well. Throughout my career in psychology, I've been aware of the liberating power of listening. So much injustice in society and incoherence in organizations derive from the simple fact of people not listening to each other. When a person is listened to, a movement from confusion and conflict to clarity and openness can occur. This entails moving from the part to the whole, an exercise in holism which connects to the totality of a situation. Otto Scharmer (2009) has recognized the transformational power of listening in his organizational 'Theory U'. He provides compelling evidence of its ability to help groups to 'sense the future' and make their way through the daunting fields of the unknown to decisions which previously had seemed impossible.

Open-minded listening is a key leadership skill for leaders and citizens alike. It's a skill that narcissists and psychopaths cannot master because it requires empathy, a quality, incidentally, which was greatly admired by the classical economist Adam Smith, who defined it as a person's ability 'to put himself in the situation of the other' (quoted in Sennett, 2012:20). This essential dialoguing capacity emerges from having the courage and steadfastness to listen closely not only to what is being said but also to what is *not* being said. This, in turn, involves emotional intelligence, the ability to understand and connect with another person's emotional rhythms. We should be truly frightened by those who cannot listen – and yet many of them are in charge of the most influential organizations on our planet, making the decisions which are shaping our future. Indeed, the entire Anthropocene crisis could be described as a case of non-listening on a historically epic scale.

That's why I suggest organizations fit for our new epoch can benefit from a coaching culture. By this I don't mean that numerous, specialist psychological coaches should be employed, although one or two may be useful. Their main role should be to help other employees to develop their coaching skills. That means having the expertise to identify a colleague who is experiencing work-related or psychological difficulties and listen to them thoughtfully and non-judgementally, in order to help them find the best solution to their issues.

Wellbeing-centred enterprises

For utopians, work should always be a source of personal development and enhanced wellbeing. In *News from Nowhere*, William Morris defined the ideal as 'easy-hard work', of the sort 'that sends you pleasantly weary to bed but which isn't trying in other ways' (1890/1993:195). E.F. Schumacher, in his celebrated essay on 'Buddhist economics', pointed out that work enables a person 'to overcome his egocentricness by joining with other people in a common task'. But he criticized work that was organized in such a way that it became meaningless or stultifying, as stemming from 'an evil lack of compassion and a soul-destroying attachment to the most primitive side of this worldly existence' (Schumacher 1973:39).

For an organization committed to SEWP principles, the pleasure of working together should be an end in itself. In other words, it's not primarily about building a business case for the superior effectiveness of good teamwork or the fact that happy workers are easier to retain and more productive. These propositions may be true, but they miss the point. The point is to have fun for its own sake, unconditionally. Work is – or should be – a celebration of being human. It's an opportunity for people not only to work together but to *be* together and overcome the separations caused by a materialistic, CIMENT-based culture which isolates and alienates individuals.

Of course, some wellbeing initiatives can be used cynically to push workers harder or to make them exploit their personal relationships. We have to be wary of managerial fads which can sometimes fool employees into failing to spot that the purposes of the new boss are essentially the same as those of the old boss. That's why the ownership structures we explored in the previous chapter are so important. Nothing absolutely guarantees an end to human exploitation but having an organizational constitution that prohibits it can definitely help.

A proper procedure for conflict resolution is another vital asset for ensuring that real organizational wellbeing is achievable. In any workplace some interpersonal conflict has to be expected (remember, utopia is not Elysium). From time to time open, passionate interactions will inevitably reach an impasse. This type of conflict should be faced fairly and squarely, not driven underground or crushed from above, as it might be in a conventional organization. In a SEWP context, professional resources and widespread interpersonal skills should be available to prevent a conflict from turning sour and potentially poisoning a situation. Coaching is one effective tool for this kind of conflict resolution, mediation is another.

Properly constituted and staffed, the wellbeing-centred enterprise can be a place where pleasurable creativity can be enjoyed for its own sake and this can undoubtedly contribute to the development of innovations that have a practical application. In fact, the creative rewards for society as a whole from organizations focusing on collective and individual wellbeing as an intrinsic value may turn out to be considerable. Once we debunk the myth that only certain individuals are capable of innovation – an argument too often made by professional 'creatives' defending their turf – huge, hidden resources of creativity could be opened up. Just as well, since we'll need all the problem-solving capacity we can get, if we are to find the right solutions to the Anthropocene crisis.

Remuneration: freedom from money?

Self-managing yourself towards a better organizational life can also involve new remuneration practices. A cure is desperately needed for the wealth virus, which, as we saw in Part II, creates cultures obsessed with financial reward. Enterprises which are purpose-led rather than profit-led often try to separate the intrinsic meaning of a job from its financial compensation. They see payment as essential to provide workers with a decent standard of living, but it is by no means the be-all and end-all of work. 'Enough' rather than 'more' should be the employee's real priority. The logic of enough may be implemented by employees setting their own salaries, by agreeing a single salary for all employees or by setting salaries according to need (taking into consideration family commitments, for instance). In some cases, the market rate for a job may be taken into account, but, in general, a modest pay ratio between the highest and lowest paid employee in an organization is likely to be used.

In some areas of the commons, unpaid work is the norm, as in the vast majority of Wikipedia's collaborators, and in the countless millions of volunteers who work for organizations across the world. But even where work is paid, as in some areas of the digital commons – bear in mind that 'free software' often means free from copyright restrictions rather than something which is provided gratis – efforts are made to separate remuneration from work. Legal professor Yochai Benkler explains this deliberate disconnection:

> As many examples from the software world repeatedly show, looser, more indirect forms of payment that are not specifically linked to specific actions are far better at motivating participation in collaborative projects. A direct appeal or a pay-for-performance model ... simply deters those who are seeking to pursue their own intrinsic interests.
>
> (Benkler 2011:185)

Defining actions in terms of their financial incentives not only reduces the pleasure of the creative process, it can also have a drastic affect on human altruism. Psychologists have observed that the altruism of very young children is often substantially reduced by extrinsic rather than intrinsic rewards (Hepach *et al.*, 2013). And for many this preference survives in adult life. For instance, Benkler notes that when the USA switched from a system of paid blood donations to an entirely volunteer system in the 1970s, donations increased in quantity and quality. When Sweden experimented in the opposite direction, offering payment for blood in what had been a voluntary system, donations by women decreased significantly (although the contribution of men was unaffected). In short, if we can see through the wealth fallacy and let people do what they believe in, rather than what they are paid to do, we could tap into a huge new source of human energy. Getting clean from the money drug can bring reinvigorated creativity for organizations and for society in general.

Planetwide practices

In the people-planet enterprise, the unconditional attitude to promoting wellbeing will also apply to planetwideness. Both these organizational purposes need to be part of a SEWP enterprise's charter, built into its constitution as an intrinsic goal, not simply as a means to an end. Thinking, analysing, planning and strategizing using a planetude knowledge frame is likely to come easily to those who see themselves as part of the new global project. For locally orientated service companies (the majority in the UK), which have no clear overseas remit, achieving planetwide connections may be more complicated, although exchanging best practice on sustainability and equitability with like-minded organizations and associations across the world will help them in this respect.

Enterprises committed to planetwide principles can also start at home, by maximizing the number of cultures, ethnicities and nationalities represented in the workplace. Diversity is not simply a recruitment practice – which may well involve positive discrimination and quotas if necessary – it's also about nurturing a culture of diversity which is important in its own right. The plurinational character of modern cities is an asset in this respect. In London, for example, with its multicultural demographics and over 300 spoken languages, it's not always necessary to go abroad to connect to the world, as the world has already come to London (BBC, 2014). But too much of this diversity exists in ethnic and national silos, so connecting disparate cultural groups within a single organization is a positive act, creating a microcosm that mirrors the greater world.

Encouraging sexual diversity is also part of the post-growth workplace, with full support for LGBTQ people and sensitivity to the needs of those who don't conform to whatever the sexual norm is assumed to be. New-epoch organizations have to become incubators for a new world of identity equality, which goes beyond anything humanity has so far achieved. This revolution in values will almost certainly bring 'business benefits' – whatever this comes to mean, as new frontiers are crossed and new markets discovered. But this is a secondary consideration. The first is to pioneer workshops for a better, safer, sounder and more rewarding world, a goal which will always be uppermost in the minds of those building SEWP enterprises.

Conclusion

To sum up, the practices of SEWP organizations promise to transform the lived experience of the workplace, encouraging everybody to become leaders. Instead of acting as the incubator of CIMENT values, the utopian workplace will enable the CANDID ethos to flourish, by developing confidence and competence in decision-making and showing how cooperative and altruistic values can work in everyday practice. It will nurture the intrinsic satisfactions of work and create stress-free opportunities to celebrate the pleasures of being with others in an culturally diverse, globally integrated environment.

All of this has to be seen in the context of a people-planet economy which actively supports ecologically democratic organizations and discourages enterprises arranged on traditional hierarchical and unsustainable principles. From state-sponsored start-ups to commons-based enterprises to larger organizations reorientating themselves from within, this powerful movement towards self-organizing, inter-connecting autonomy can gradually repopulate the corporate landscape. This new institutional reality will provide a very different psychological environment to today's profit-hungry corporations, complementing other efforts aimed at bringing about the revolution of values necessary to point us in the direction of utopia. It's time to look more closely at the role of psychology in this transvaluation.

14 Step 9

Put psychology to work on transforming our values

Step 9 is about the potential for psychology to facilitate the values revolution necessary to bring about a utopian transformation. As I suggested in the Introduction, psychology is the science of change and utopia is the ultimate change project, so the two seem to be made for each other. Indeed, one of the best known psychologists of the twentieth century, B.F. Skinner, actually wrote a utopian fiction, *Walden Two* (1948). Although the book has some positive things to say about peaceful, simple, egalitarian living, it often reads less like an evocation of a better world than a visit to one of the behaviourist psychology departments, which were once common in the universities of the West. In place of the rats and pigeons, which were the experimental subjects of behaviourism, in *Walden Two* we find a programme of 'behavioural engineering' which aims to rid the community's children of all their 'negative emotions' – 'sorrow, hate and the high-voltage excitements of anger, fear and rage' by the age of six (Skinner 1948:92). Needless to say, this distinctly dystopian practice (decried as 'sadistic tyranny' by one of the novel's characters) is not the transformative role for psychology which I envisage, although it may be a clue to why the profession has lost some of its confidence in promoting fundamental social change.

Instead of brainwashing, which deprives individuals of free choice, I want to outline a programme of expanding informed choice by means of education, therapy and discussion. Psychological interventions can be used not simply as remedial measures to prevent the worst kinds of behaviour but as tools to encourage the best in humanity. Rather than use psychological treatment to counter the most dangerously antisocial symptoms that arise from our current competitivist world system, we can try to remove the causes of that behaviour by actively promoting better ways of being. If we choose to build a society on rational principles, on the psychology of enoughism, rather than fatalistically accept the madness of an economic plan that requires multiple planets of natural resources, a world that can grow into utopia could soon emerge.

So here are some suggestions about how psychology can help to facilitate a utopian transformation. They are based on promoting the CANDID values which underlie the SEWP model, as outlined in the values grid I presented in Step 2. That means vigorously contesting the CIMENT ethos which shapes the attitudes, feelings and assumptions which perpetuate growthism. Evidence-based practices can help to transform competitivism into cooperativism, individualism into altruism and encourage non-materialist ways of being. I'll also illustrate techniques to increase confidence in democracy, promote an internationalist sense of global human identity and strengthen the serene deference to nature which puts technologism in its place. These techniques are currently used by professional psychologists, but they can easily be made accessible to non-specialists everywhere.

Promoting cooperativism

Psychological studies demonstrate very clearly how an aggressively competitive attitude can be transformed into a cooperative mindset. For instance, in a famous series of experiments in an American summer camp, Muzafer Sherif (1966) divided a collection of well-adjusted, 12-year-old boys into two groups. Initially, the boys were asked to engage in a number of cooperative activities, after which they reported almost no preference for their own group over the other group. But this peaceful coexistence was shattered when a series of competitive tasks were introduced, which offered attractive prizes to the winning group. According to one account, the boys were rapidly 'transformed into two hostile factions, never losing the opportunity to deride the outgroup and, in some instances, to physically attack it' (Brown, 1996:538). Best friends turned against each other, the groups ransacked each others' camps, stealing items, burning each other's flags and aggressively chanting their group names, the Eagles and the Rattlers. It was a state of extreme conflict which recalls William Golding's 1954 dystopian novel *Lord of the Flies*.

Unlike Golding's bleak fiction, however, Sherif's study showed that zero-sum group conflict can be reduced by the introduction of 'superordinate goals', in other words, a common purpose. Over several days, the warring groups were asked to cooperate on deliberately constructed 'emergency' tasks, such as solving a problem affecting the supply of drinking water or towing a broken-down truck. Gradually the feelings of mutual hostility subsided and in the end, the winners of the competitive tasks even used their prize money to buy the losing team a meal.

This is powerful evidence of the transformative effect of common goals. It shows in practical terms how a powerful shared vision, such as the SEWP model, can turn us into passionate cooperators. Growthism encourages us to pursue goals which bring us into abrasive conflict with each other – a state of competition which is falsely presented as the source of all progress. Competitiveness destroys the trust which cooperation requires and which the Sherif study shows can be rapidly broken, even among close friends.

Economic inequality reinforces the vicious circle. Almost twice as many people in Sweden agree with the statement that 'most people can be trusted' as in the UK, which has a much higher level of income inequality. And distrust levels are even higher in world's two most income-unequal developed countries, the USA and Singapore (Wilkinson and Pickett, 2009:53).

The psychological profile of cooperating individuals is very different from that of competitors, although, clearly, humans can easily switch between these two modes, depending on their social context. For social psychologist Morton Deutsch, the cooperativist mode stems from the recognition of human interdependence. It manifests itself through open, articulate communication, a friendly, helpful attitude and a willingness to coordinate individual tasks. Also useful are a similarity of beliefs, respect for others' ideas and needs and a readiness to define conflicting interests as a mutual problem. By contrast, the competitive mindset is characterized by power-based communication, obstructive unhelpfulness, the inability to divide up work, repeated disagreement and a tendency to reject other people's ideas.

The competitive stance often leads to the 'the view that the solution of a conflict can only be imposed by one side on the other' (Deutsch, 2006:26–7). This can cause the conflict to escalate into a power struggle or a generalized matter of principle, which can create what Deutsch terms 'autistic hostility', a total failure of empathy. As the vicious circle turns, self-fulfilling prophecies come to the fore, aggravating both parties, deepening a sense of enmity and a readiness to blame others. It's a process which can end with violent solutions that seemed unthinkable at the beginning, an outcome which all too closely resembles the possible descent into dystopia which I described in Chapter 5.

Of course, growth capitalism is not the only cause of breakdowns in trust. Family abuse, sexual harassment, racism and social bullying can all have the same effect. The goal of psychotherapy is often to restore the ability to trust people, without which it is almost impossible to live with others in a rewarding way. It involves saying 'yes' to some kinds of behaviour which involve putting your faith in others and dealing resolutely with the feelings of disappointment this may occasionally induce, while saying 'no' to forms of behaviour which may increase mistrust. Therapy often works because the therapist provides a model of authentic cooperation and trustworthiness, which some patients may never have experienced before at work, in the family or in other social contexts.

Encouraging altruism

Psychological interventions can also help to promote altruism, thereby mitigating the suspicion of others which competitive individualism reinforces. In fact, it can be surprisingly easy to achieve this values trans-formation. For instance, experiments in Japan demonstrated that count-ing your acts of kindness over a week leads to a considerable rise in reports of subjective happiness. This in turn increased the likelihood that particip-ants would engage in further acts of kindness (Otake *et al.*, 2006). A similar study in the UK also showed that acting generously increases your levels of life satisfaction (Buchanan and Bardi, 2010). Researchers in North America found evidence of a 'positive feedback loop between happiness and prosocial spending': people's mood improved as they recalled money they had spent on other people rather than on themselves (Dunn *et al.*, 2014). MRI scans confirm that altruism is a major source of pleasure for humans. Giving to charity or acting in a cooperative manner in a game can be seen in real time to light up centres of the brain associ-ated with rewards (Harbaugh *et al.*, 2007). As neuroscience reveals more about our neural processes, the idea that we are actually hardwired for altruism is rapidly catching on.

Indeed, instead of asking how we can make adults more altruistic we could reverse the questions and ask, how can we prevent children from losing the altruism they are born with? Studies reveal that infants as young as 14 to 18 months spontaneously help others to retrieve hard-to-reach objects or open cupboard doors (Warneken and Tomasello, 2009). Reviewing this and other evidence of altruism in children under the age of 3, developmental psychologist Michael Tomasello concludes that this is not the result of 'acculturation, parental intervention or any form of socialization' (2009: 29). This is backed up by Keith Jensen and his col-leagues (2014) whose comparisons between the behaviour of young chil-dren and that of primates leads them to conclude that humans have 'an emotional, possibly innate, sensitivity to the needs of others coupled with a motivation towards their welfare'. This highly pro-social propensity to help strangers and non-kin members of our species appears to be totally unique in the animal kingdom (even our nearest neighbours, chimpan-zees, treat strangers with hostility).

So what is it that spoils young children's natural generosity and impairs their delight in helping others? 'Looking after number one' has to be part of the answer. The CIMENT ethos (backed up by *Homo economicus*) views altruism as 'a mug's game', in a world where 'nice people come second'. Psychologists need to use their profession to stand by altruism – and to stand up for it. It goes to the very heart of being human. If growthism is allowed to eradicate it, what else do we have left?

Aristotle would have understood this without any difficulty, as he saw virtuous behaviour as being a part of our natural inclination towards well-being. As economist Richard Layard (2005:244) points out, this contrasts sharply with the influential philosophy of Immanuel Kant, who regarded altruism as a duty which causes no pleasure and whose individualistic, dualist approach is compatible with neoclassical economics. What our brains seem to want our current society denies. We seem to be neurologically built for helping others, and yet we live in an economic system which, at best, sees altruism as a kind of heroic act of self-sacrifice. Teaching altruism simply reinforces what we appear to intuitively desire. It suggests that a world constructed around socio-economic cooperation is not an aberration or an idle fantasy but our natural destiny, if only we choose to realize it.

Empathy is another significant attribute of altruistic, other-directed behaviour. It's the ability to see the world from another person's perspective which, as we found in Chapter 4, high-income individuals often lack. It's a trait that is disturbingly absent in psychopaths and in many of our most powerful corporations. In fact, empathy already exists in children at a very early age and simple exercises in adopting the perspective of the other can enormously strengthen this crucial skill (Harvey, 2012). Compassion, another invaluable human quality, can also be trained. For example, participants receiving a two-week training in meditation based on traditional Buddhist techniques of loving kindness were found to act more pro-socially in an experimental game than untrained participants, distributing significantly more funds to a victim of social unfairness (Weng et al., 2013).

Another powerful antidote to competitive individualism is group therapy. Nothing better explodes the myth that 'there is no such thing as society' as repeatedly sitting in a group with others, possibly with no fixed agenda, discussing opinions and feelings without the guardrails of conversational norms or institutionally directed conventions. Group work can be challenging – this is often its purpose – but it can develop empathy, compassion and a new understanding of others. Moving beyond ordinary, cautious conversation towards open, trusting emotional expressiveness is a journey which hints at a greater possible social transition. It can bring insights into self and others, and new ways of communicating with others, without unresolved competitiveness and defensive hostility. Interpersonal skills of a much higher order will be needed to reject the growthist assumption that wealth accumulation is humanity's primary goal and to embrace the conviction that what matters most in life is achieving a better balance between how people relate to each other.

Group work encourages people to confront their own prejudices and articulate their deepest feelings, qualities that are vital for overcoming the inequalities and divisions of our current paradigm. One of the radical changes in education which may occur as children are educated for life rather than work is the emergence of professionally led group counselling sessions at school in order to develop personal and interpersonal confidence at an early age.

Strengthening non-materialism

One of the biggest challenges on the road to utopia is finding a holistic philosophy of life which combines a non-materialist, ego-transcendent view of the world with a scientific, evidence-based approach to reality. Up to now religion has been humanity's preferred way of linking the inner and outer worlds, but psychology could have a significant part to play in offering an Anthropocene version of this. Psychology has always attempted to adapt traditional wisdoms – Carl Jung's work on ancient myths is an early example – as well as offering new sources of inner contemplation. For example, the repetitive mantras of cognitive behaviour therapy (CBT) act as behavioural reminders in ways that mimic the Catholic rosary or Buddhist chants. Psychology's equivalent to the church or temple may be the more prosaic room in which a group therapy or psychology workshop takes place, its confessional the one-to-one counselling session, but as a practice it has the advantage of being considerably more transparent and evidence-based than its religious counterparts.

One relatively recent development in psychology, which can strengthen the value of non-materialism, is spiritual intelligence. This draws on the persistence in human society of a need for a higher power, a sense of wholeness and a linking of the self and the non-self. One of its leading advocates, Danah Zohar, describes it as follows:

> So many of us today live lives of wounded fragmentation. We long for what the poet T.S. Eliot called 'a further union, a deeper communion' but we find little resource within our ego-bound selves or within the existing symbols or institutions of our culture. SQ [spiritual quotient] is the intelligence that rests in the deep part of the self that is connected to wisdom from beyond the ego, or conscious mind, it is the intelligence with which we not only recognise existing values, but with which we creatively discover new values.
>
> (Zohar and Marshall, 2000:9)

This need and capacity for creating values seems to exist across cultures. As I suggested in Step 5, identifying these norms is a crucial task ahead of us, which can be expressed in the cardinal question, 'what do we really want?' It may even be that the need to unite inner and outer, present and future has a basis in our brain architecture – possibly in the so-called 'God spot', neural oscillations or some other neurological centre (Zohar and Marshall, 2000). If this theory can be confirmed it would provide a thoroughly materialist explanation for why the materialism of growthism is ultimately so shallow and unsatisfying.

Mindfulness is another example of 'remoderning'. It's the application of the practice of meditation which dates back to the earliest origins of Buddhism and other Eastern wisdoms to the twenty-first-century office, factory and home in accordance with rigorous research (Chaskalson, 2014). In part, its current popularity relies on its stress-management properties, its capacity to help people detach themselves sufficiently from the pressures of the present, so as to make an often intolerable workplace slightly more bearable. Yet it's so much more than a resilience-building technique, valuable as this is: it's a powerful way of connecting with a deeper appreciation of our existence. It can provide an experience of the preciousness of being, over and beyond its instrumental value.

Psychotherapy conversations based on existential phenomenology can also bring the experience of being into sharper focus (Spinelli, 2015). Phenomenology tries to enable us to see reality as it really is, without the prejudgements and frameworks and assumptions with which we habitually interpret the world. By bracketing these perceptual frames, we can get closer to the experience of purity of being – free of the encumbrances of having and doing. In this way we can not only open ourselves to other people but also to the miracle of living.

This goal of living in the here and now is also found in the person-centred, humanist therapy associated with Carl Rogers (1967). Rogers takes 'unconditional love' as the model for the therapist's relationship with his patient, based on what he regarded as the normal attitude of a parent to a child. It's a model that he thought should be extended to other helping professions, including education, and to many interpersonal relationships. In fact, a society entirely built around unconditional love is a particularly telling way of describing utopia. It's another reason why the belief systems of many indigenous people, who have not lost a strong sense of gratitude for life, are still so appealing.

Nor should we think of non-materialism as a purely mental activity. It can be profoundly physical, as in the ancient tradition of yoga which is currently enjoying a major vogue in the West. Aldous Huxley thought so much of yoga that in his 1962 novel *Island* he based an entire utopia around it. As early as 1946 he'd envisaged an alternative to the dystopia of *Brave New World* in the form of a community in which religion, defined as 'the conscious intelligent pursuit of man's Final End, the intuitive knowledge of the Tao or logos', exists side by side with scientifically governed, environmentalist economics (Huxley, 1946:iii). Yoga and Mahayana Buddhist meditation encourage clarity of awareness and the promise of happiness, which stems in part from Huxley's advocacy of Tantric sexual practices. In the non-monogamous society of *Island*, the art of sexual union is practised extensively, using the discipline of endlessly delayed fulfilment, loosely based on the Indian techniques of *althea*. Hedonism takes practice, Huxley seems to suggest, but what better way of uniting the psychological and the physical than through sexual pleasure. In fact, in our own century, it could be humanity's best bet for preventing advanced sex robots from invading the sexual field with potentially disastrous consequences for gender equality.

Psychoanalyst Dieter Duhm (2015) takes the emphasis on liberation through love a stage further. Drawing on the work of sexual-revolution pioneer Wilhelm Reich, he advocates free love, defined as love which is 'free of fear and possessiveness' and free sexuality, 'an erotic culture based on trust, contact and solidarity' (Duhm, 2015:205). Duhm argues that it is only through this type of communion, which compliments monogamy rather than replacing it, that humanity can overcome its 'collective trauma' and achieve genuine peace worldwide. Together with the theologian Sabine Lichtenfels, Duhm has evolved a revolutionary philosophy which combines insights drawn from the world's major religions with ecology, psychology, alternative technology and field theory derived from quantum physics. This is not just a theory but a practical choice which Duhm and others have attempted to put into practice in a series of innovative intentional communities, culminating in Tamera in Portugal, which is described as a 'healing biotope' and 'global peace school'. If utopia is to happen and non-materialism is to take on a socially viable form, real-world experiments in the democracy of love such as this will play a pivotal role.

Deepening democracy

Psychology's role in promoting democracy and egalitarianism dates back to the aftermath of the Second World War, when psychologists and others began trying to identify the personality style underlying authoritarianism (Adorno *et al.*, 1950). Since the 1960s, political psychology has steadily developed – with some psychologists arguing that it's the only way to save political science from itself (Lane, 2003) – and it's certainly desperately needed today to help us understand the current crisis of democracy and why increasing numbers of people are attracted to sexist, xenophobic and authoritarian political leaders.

This anti-democratic tendency can also be countered by practical work on collective decision-making and encouraging people to have the confidence to make informed choices. Exercises in participatory democracy – perhaps in the formative stages of life at school – can help to build the vital social technology that strengthens citizenship. It can be no surprise that some people can become disillusioned with democracy if their only experience of it is to put a cross on a ballot paper once every four or five years. Moreover, research suggests that the more important a decision is, the less we rely on tried-and-tested choice-making techniques, such as cost–benefit analysis. In these circumstances, we can become more vulnerable to charismatic demagogues and unscrupulous leaders who will promise anything in order to gain access to power.

Clinical psychology and psychotherapy can also have a major role in helping people develop the independence and self-confidence necessary to be effective, choice-making, democratic citizens. Some of the profession's most successful work is in helping people to overcome the addictions of modernity, from alcohol and substance abuse to over-eating and under-eating. This includes a whole new catalogue of dependencies brought on by technologism, such as digital addictions caused by excessive use of social media, texting, online gambling and pornography and video gaming. Addictions often make cooperation with others seem impossible and encourage an obsessive, distrustful mindset. It often takes the psychologist's patience, respect and non-judgemental, empathetic attitude, combined with sound, evidence-based advice, to help the patient make the hard choices necessary to overcome an addictive behaviour.

Overall, mental health problems are on the rise in the developed world. In England, one in six of all adults (17%) are currently suffering from a common mental disorder such as anxiety or depression, with a 35% increase in the incidence of severe symptoms since 1993. Reports of self-harm among adults have doubled over the past decade – and for women they've more than tripled this century (McManus *et al.*, 2016). Children are suffering particularly acutely, with one in eight 10- to 15-year-olds reporting symptoms of mental ill health (ONS, 2015) and a quarter of 14-year-old girls and one in ten boys saying they'd self-harmed in the last year (Children's Society, 2018). We can't blame all these imbalances on growth capitalism – no doubt even in a utopian world people will experience psychological challenges. And some of the causes of psychological distress predate capitalism, such as homophobia, xenophobia or the sexism and patriarchy which underlie many cases of sexual abuse and violence against woman and girls.

Nevertheless, it is almost inevitable that the asymmetries of an economic system which strives for the unobtainable extremes of constant growth at the expense of our future on this planet are reflected in the psychological state of many people who live in this system. For capitalism is riddled with anxiety. It feeds on the stress that unfair competitiveness creates and can almost seem bipolar in the splits between what's good and what's bad, its fetishization of extreme wealth and its celebration of impossibly perfect body and lifestyle imagery. The environmental destructiveness of extractivism finds an echo in similarly selfish and exploitative attitudes to interpersonal relationships. It's no surprise, then, to find that societies with the highest levels of income inequality like the UK, the USA and Australia also have the highest rates of mental illness (Wilkinson and Pickett, 2009:67).

One way of understanding how psychologists and therapists counter the plague of mental illness in the modern world is to suggest that they already hold some of the equitable, democratic values of the CANDID ethos. Psychotherapists tend to favour cooperation over competitiveness, stressing that individuals are not alone, however isolated they may feel, and embodying a caring, altruistic attitude towards their patients. Psychotherapists are often holistic, 'reframing' a situation so that a client can see the bigger picture. Crucially, they tend to adopt a non-hierarchical stance, relating to the patient as an equal and making themselves open to all the possibilities he has to offer. Often people in need of therapy are exceptionally sensitive to the problems of the world: they feel too much and need to develop resilience to the pain the world throws at them. Helping patients to achieve a workable sense of balance in their lives is no easy matter – certainly there is no magic cure, although patience and considerate care can sometimes seem like that. When the therapy is successful, the transformation that a patient experiences, often at an emotional and unconscious level, can amount to a profound change in her belief system. Indeed, in a microcosmic context this personal revolution of values can be seen as mirroring the kind of changes at the macro-level involved in the transition to a people-planet utopia.

Spreading internationalism

Deepening the internationalist values which are essential to a majoritarian solution to the Anthropocene crisis is one of the biggest challenges we face. This is especially vital at a time of increased right-wing nationalism, xenophobia and anti-immigrant ethnocentrism. Diversity training is one area where psychology has already made a start in developing a planetwide mindset. It's an intervention which aims to increase awareness and sensitivity between people who are culturally, nationally and ethnically diverse (usually in the same society). As well as specific skills in identifying one's ethnic and cultural biases, effective cross-cultural communication involves many general new-epoch attributes, such as the ability to accept the relativity of one's own knowledge, to be non-judgemental and flexible and to tolerate ambiguity. It also emphasizes once again the importance of empathy, the perspective-taking skill which can provide a powerful bridge across national and cultural borders (McEnrue, 1993).

Anti-racism training programmes can also help participants realize that their beliefs are not neutral but often the result of cultural conditioning and that racism affects the ways in which institutions operate. This can come as a revelation to many, even those who regard themselves as non-racist, and help eliminate offensive behaviours (Webb and Sergison, 2003). Xenophobia, strictly speaking, is a fear of strangers, which can often be overcome simply by familiarizing a person with people from different cultures and ethnicities. It's noticeable that one of the most significant factors predicting the probability of voting Leave in the 2016 EU referendum was 'not having socialised with someone living in a different country in the last six months' (Demos, 2017:81–2). Unfamiliarity can breed hostility, but knowing people from different cultures and ethnicities tends to establish the common ground which we share as humans, rather than highlighting the separating factors that xenophobia fixates on.

Of course, creating awareness of cultural differences is not necessarily the same as bridging the gap between them. Psychological research into differences between nations reveals just how far apart we can be on various personality and cultural dimensions. For example, Geert Hofstede and his colleagues (2010) have analysed dimensions such as equality, masculinity/femininity, need for certainty and short-/long-term perspectives. The differences in power distance, or respect for authority, between Russia and the Nordic countries may seem depressing from the point of view of achieving greater equality, but it does at least provide an evidential launch pad for addressing these variations. On the positive side, the national averages in Hofstede's research reveal whom we should turn to for progress on these measures. For example, when it comes to possessing a long-term orientation and commitment to forward planning, countries like South Korea, Japan and China are far more adept than most European countries. Perhaps not surprisingly in the context of their leading role in the current mismanagement of the world system, both the UK and the USA score very low on this metric.

If we want to know who most agrees with the statement that 'both men and women can be tender and focus on relationships' (as opposed to men being assertive and women tender and compliant), it's Scandinavia and Latvia in Europe and Costa Rica and Chile in Latin America. As for happiness, the importance of leisure and making time for relationships, it's people in countries like Venezuela, Mexico and Nigeria who may have most to teach us about this aspect of a utopian lifestyle, in spite of whatever political and economic problems they may be experiencing .

Transcending the human tendency to prefer in-groups to out-groups and making very rapid, pre-reflective decisions about who is 'us' and who is 'them' is one of the great challenges of the Anthropocene. As we saw in Step 5, psychologists are already working to define global citizenship and ways to extend our ability to identify with all humanity. Through imaginative new research, experimentation and educational programmes, it's possible to transform the abstract notion of the human subject into a deeply felt experience. (It doesn't help that many still refer to this subject as 'man' – still less that, for some, this unconsciously means 'white man'). The task of turning all of humanity into an in-group falls to us all. Education has a major role to play in this, developing what educators Graham Pike and David Selby (1999) call 'worldmindedness'. They describe many child-centred classroom exercises to encourage observation of global interconnections, environmental holism and an awareness of personal, cultural differences. Achieving global consciousness brings us back to the idea of a common purpose which unites us more than it divides us. Superordinate goals (or should this be 'SEWPer-ordinate goals'?) are surely the only way in which an authentic people-planet identity can be forged.

Developing deference to nature

Ecological psychologists have also begun to work on the task of deepening the human sense of connectedness to nature. In practical terms, establishing this aspect of our species identity is crucial in helping us to find the right balance between humanity and the technology which is reinventing our planet and ourselves. A new type of 'techno-scepticism' is necessary, if humanity is to manage its own tools (and not surrender control to the minority that owns them). That means seeing through the hype surrounding new technology and asking what its real costs are, both in terms of what natural resources it takes to produce and in its long term effects on the environment and human health.

Techno-scepticism can lead to eco-psychology, a place where planet meets people and where we let nature into our hearts. Eco-therapists often work on bringing nature into an urban setting, holding sessions outdoors, where we can gain a better understanding of the healing power of the biosphere. Where there are streets there are (usually) trees, where there are high rises there are also parks. The tameness of nature in a city shouldn't blind us to the work it does, and the fact that we are still part of nature, however much we may concrete it over. As more people move from the country to the city – humanity's primary direction of travel over the past 300 years – eco-therapy can help to keep the presence of nature alive in towns. Shinto is another, more ancient, way of expressing reverence for nature, marked by simple, open-air shrines, featuring rocks or branches that can bring the natural world into the most crowded of Japanese cities.

An even more powerful way of propelling people into nature is wilderness therapy. Pioneer eco-psychologist Robert Greenaway (2009) claims that wilderness journeys for groups reveal the illusory nature of the dualisms which split our experiences and can restore 'our lost capacity to feel for the natural world'. Immersion in the wilderness can mean carrying all your equipment and travelling in a self-sustaining group along river courses, for instance, making decisions through consensus. This can revive a sense of the sacredness of fire and the feeling of living as a tribe or small band. For Greenaway, 'the shape of the ego changes' and an 'ecological consciousness' develops which 'connects to our surroundings, to the balances, cycles, patterns and relationships that are described by ecology'. This experience can make possible a 'deep healing' (Greenaway, 2009:137–8).

This idea of an ecological self is also articulated by Joanna Macy (2007), who sees the artificiality of a concept of a self that is divisible from its interactions with other elements in a system. We are in a constant state of interaction, she argues, which makes an 'us-and-them' attitude to nature pitifully inaccurate. Pre-modern peoples could always see themselves in nature and feel the non-human as the human, but Macy suggests that this is now becoming a modern phenomenon, which she calls 'the greening of the self'. This involves 'combining the mystical with the pragmatic, transcending separateness, alienation and fragmentation'. She cites the example of an Australian rainforest ecologist, who told her:

> I try to remember that it's not me, John Seed, trying to protect the rainforest. Rather I am part of the rainforest protecting itself. I am that part of the rainforest recently emerged into human thinking.
>
> (Macy, 2007:240)

This is a state of being which may seem extreme and one which psychology is only just beginning to understand. But the ecological self or state of deep naturalness may have a hugely significant role in helping to counter the idea that humans are simply machines manqué, as implied by some cognitive psychologists, who regard human irrationality in terms of our failure to conform to statistical norms. What also helps is cultivating a slow, deep attentiveness, an appreciation of eating or walking, as an antidote to the rapid pace of new technology, which promises instant gratification with every click and reduces patience to nano-seconds. The more this frenzy for pace grips us, the more we are captured by the technology that delivers it. And what is slow is often what is sustainable. Indeed, nature teaches long-term time perspectives in a way that nothing in modern human history can. Finding ways of experiencing the beyond-the-human without technology, digital or otherwise, may be crucial in averting the threat of a technology-led transhumanism being foisted on the majority of humanity. In fact, finding a path to an authentic Anthropocene rather than succumbing to the Technocene may just depend on it.

Conclusion

'Psychologists are always at the back of the march cleaning up the mess, whereas they should be at the front leading us towards something better.' That's the way a colleague summed up what Step 9 is about. The science of change is also the science of balance, and as such it has a potentially huge role in facilitating utopia. Through its many equalizing techniques it can help to level out the sloping world, which often makes people today feel like Sisyphus, endlessly pushing a boulder uphill only for it to roll down the other side. I believe psychology can be as influential as ecological economics in bringing about a sustainable, equitable world which puts human wellbeing at its centre. It can inject realism into idealism by providing evidence-based solutions to the problems that bedevil every aspect of human behaviour.

Across the spectrum of the CANDID values, new developments like positive psychology have a huge potential in what degrowth philosopher Cornelius Castoriadis calls 'decolonising the imaginary'. By this he means promoting profound changes in the 'psycho-social structure of people in the Western world' which replace 'that idea that the only goal in life is to produce and consume more' (quoted in Latouche, 2015:118). Setting common goals, training and other supportive, educational activities, as well as deep interventions such as personal and group-based therapy, can help to create the widespread psychological literacy which a utopian world will enjoy. Every day, psychologists work with their clients' yearning for positive transformation and this practice can help to inspire the metamorphosis that turns the Anthropocene crisis into humanity's greatest ever opportunity. It also puts psychology practitioners in closer touch than they may realize with the subject of the next step in our change plan, the utopian imagination in literature.

15 Step 10
Learn from the utopian imagination

In 2016, during the Nuit Debout social protest movement in France, a wonderful slogan from the May 1968 events was once again chanted: 'l'imagination au pouvoir'. It's a richly suggestive phrase, variously translated as 'the imagination in power' or 'power to the imagination', and a useful reminder that the ability to visualize a different world is at the heart of the utopian tradition. The status quo always tries to close down this act of imagination. Growthism insidiously tries to convince us that there is no alternative to the individualistic materialism which sets groups against each other and threatens to normalize dystopia. Step 10 is about resisting this process. It's about embracing the utopian imagination and allowing literature to lead us towards a better reality. The goal of utopianism is always to imagine the impossible into existence.

In psychology, it's well known that visualizing positive outcomes can help to turn them into realities, as demonstrated by the use of guided imagery in psychotherapy or the visualization techniques employed to improve performance skills in sport or business. Of course, utopianism goes beyond imagining an improved tennis backhand or a stress-free sales speech: it tries to visualize nothing less than an entirely new world system. What's more, this alternative society is not only presented in objective terms, as a coherent socio-economic whole, but also as a deeply subjective experience. A fictional utopia is a kind of virtual, multidimensional model that we can move around in and experience as real.

The simple, decent human rationality of utopianism lays bare the flaws in the existing world system. It can expose the mismanagement and irrationality of growthism by asking simple questions about equality, sustainability and our future goals. It's a creative exercise we could do well to encourage in education at all levels, including at the primary school stage, where adults have much to learn from children's direct and moving depictions of a better world.

Learning from fictional utopias

We also have a good deal to learn from the imagination of the greatest writers of utopian fiction – and that's what this chapter concerns itself with. So let's go back to the beginning, in true utopian style, and focus on five literary utopias, which almost exactly span the 500 years of the sloping world. They are alluring fictions which in different ways take us closer to an alternative world, in defiance of fatalism and the hegemony of wealth. They can also, as it turns out, help us to better understand the people-planet vision and what a world based on the SEWP model might actually feel like to live in.

Utopia *(1516)*

Inevitably, we must start with the original utopia, a practical and spiritual model of an alternative world, which is at once dauntingly rigorous in its logic and shot through with mischievous wit. I've referred to Thomas More's book many times but what I haven't done yet is to subject it to what we might call the SEWP test; in other words, to judge how far it advances the people-planet vision. It may seem anachronistic to talk about sustainability in relation to a work written half a millennium ago, although, as I said in the Introduction, *Utopia* seems to jump out of its historical time frame. What we now regard as environmental balance was to a great extent the norm in the late Middle Ages, before the continuum between nature and humanity was smashed. Even so, More consistently goes out of his way to acknowledge the inspiration of the natural world. And note the early example of anti-extractivism in his rejection of mining on the grounds that nature 'like an indulgent mother, has placed all wholesome things like air, water and earth itself, within our reach' (1516/2012:75).

Equitability is at the heart of More's vision, based on his Christian communalism, which rejects property and money and advocates shared accommodation and meals and a rational transparency in many aspects of social life. In Utopia, resources are distributed equally, with the result that 'while nobody possesses anything everybody is rich' (More, 1516/2012:119). Wellbeing is also respected, as Utopians' 'paramount concern is with human happiness' (More, 1516/2012:80). It's a tough kind of hedonism that More applauds, it has to be said, with no taverns, gambling, hunting or brothels, but it's based on the conviction that the greatest pleasure comes from virtue.

As for planetwideness, More presents Utopia as a self-sufficient island state, which has no ambitions to expand its influence internationally but is robustly capable of defending itself against aggressive neighbours. Utopians are not pacifists but they regard war as 'inglorious' and do everything they can to avoid it, including paying off enemies or subverting them by undercover operations. When it comes to battle, husbands and wives fight alongside one another, in order to ensure that all citizens share responsibility for the horror of war. Utopians' incipient internationalism is clearly evident in their refusal to make foreign treaties, 'since it implies that men are born as instinctive competitors and enemies who quite properly struggle to obliterate each other, unless treaties prevent it' (More, 1516/2012:98). Instead, Utopians take a cooperativist view of foreign affairs, believing that 'the shared bonds of nature are every bit as strong as a treaty, and that men are more effectively drawn together by goodwill than by pacts, by hearts rather than words'. It's a noble experiment, which our war-torn world has still not yet attempted.

News from Nowhere *(1890)*

Circularity is the signature of utopianism, as we know, and almost four centuries after Thomas More's masterpiece, we find another British visionary whom I've also referred to several times, seeking a return to the social and economic conditions which produced the first utopia. As the sloping world reached its steepest point, William Morris's *News from Nowhere* imagined a peaceful, stable alternative to the exploitative industrialism and virulent imperialism that he saw around him. The novel may have a dream-like quality, but the urgency of its call for the restoration of equilibrium with nature is unmistakeable. As Clara, one of the citizens of a civilization set in the twenty-second century, reveals, it was necessary to move beyond looking at nature and humanity as qualitatively different. 'It was natural to people thinking in this way, that they should make "nature" their slave, since they thought "nature" was something outside them' (Morris, 1890/1993:200).

The new society is based on 'the aspiration after complete equality which we now recognise as the bond of all happy human society' (Morris, 1890/1993:200). Party politics and the formal political system have been replaced (the Houses of Parliament are now only used to store horse manure). Self-organization is the principle which rules social, political and economic life. People have 'cast away riches and attained to wealth' (Morris, 1890/1993:219), working not because they are forced to but because it is a source of pleasure, derived from 'the satisfaction of the common needs of mankind' (Morris, 1890/1993:201).

Morris goes into few details about how a worldwide, libertarian utopian revolution has come about, but he makes it plain that a transformation of values has occurred, in which the spirit of human cooperation has taken over from competitivism:

> The whole system of rival and contending nations which played so great a part in the 'government' of the world of civilization has disappeared along with the inequality betwixt man and man in society.
> (Morris, 1890/1993:117)

It's a global, existential condition which prompts Morris to ask:

> Where is the difficulty in accepting the religion of humanity, when the men and women who go to make up humanity are free, happy, and

energetic at least, and most commonly beautiful of body also, and sur-
rounded by beautiful things of their own fashion, and a nature
bettered and not worsened by contact with mankind?

(Morris, 1890/1993:159)

As a statement of the people-planet vision of a world living together beautifully, it's hard to improve on this.

The Dispossessed *(1974)*

Almost a century later, it's no longer possible for utopian novelists to
turn their back on modern technology to the extent that William Morris
does. Ursula K. Le Guin, with her towering imagination and forensic
grasp of science, seeks no such thing. However, in *The Dispossessed*
(1974), she shows the same passionate commitment to a self-sustaining,
equitable society as previous utopians, even sketching an alternative language which has no need of possessive pronouns, because all property is
shared.

Set three centuries in the future, Anarres is a world based on the belief
that cooperation is the building block of human civilization. In this, Le
Guin echoes Peter Kropotkin's 1902 *Mutual Aid* essay which repudiates the
Social Darwinism that sees competition as the driver of human evolution.
In this new world, hierarchy has been rejected as the basic organizing
principle of society.

There was to be no controlling center, no capital, no establishment
for the self-perpetuating machinery of bureaucracy and the dominance drive of individuals seeking to become captains, bosses, chiefs
of state.

(Le Guin, 1974:95)

Nevertheless, this self-organizing state, 'the product of a very high civilization' is based on a unified economic policy, governed by the principle of
balance:

The special resources and products of each region were interchanged
continually with those of others, in an intricate process of balance:
that balance of diversity, which is the characteristic of life, of natural
and social ecology.

(Le Guin, 1974:95–6)

It's a society where hard work for all is necessary, although jobs are varied
and rotate according to difficultly. Work is considered 'the lasting pleasure
of life', but Anarres's Pavlic language has no separate word for work and
play (although it does for 'drudge'). Education reaches a very high

standard, but schools look quite different to our own, with 'a curriculum that included farming, carpentry, sewage reclamation, printing, plumbing, road mending, playwriting, and all the other occupations of adult life' (Le Guin, 1974:148). Children are not punished for their misdemeanours, 'though sometimes they make you go away by yourself for a while'. Indeed, crime is virtually unknown, as are prisons and police, a development which is attributed to the lack of private possessions. 'To make a thief, make an owner: to create crime, laws' (Le Guin, 1974:139), Le Guin aphorizes.

Circularity is key to life in Anarres. Communal life is arranged in circular formations, with low workshops, dormitories, learning centres and factories. 'The bigger buildings were most often grouped around open squares, giving the city a basic cellular structure' (Le Guin, 1974:97). Cities are open in other ways: there's no public advertising, for instance, and nobody feels the need to lock their doors.

At a more philosophical level, this speculative novel rejects the linear, eternally progressing notion of time, which I've described as a hallmark of the growthist irrationale. Instead, Shevek, the brilliant physics theorist who is the novel's protagonist, puts forward a path-breaking, scientific theory of circular time. This repudiates the arrow view of time 'as a meaningless succession of instants', which, Shevek argues, cannot explain, 'why things also endure' (Le Guin, 1974:224). As Lewis Call (2007) points out, this recalls Nietzsche's idea of 'eternal return', in the sense of humanity coming back to what is essential: a movement also enacted in the novel's narrative, which ends where it begins, at the airport on Anarres, as Shevek reaffirms his commitment to the society of his birth.

In Anarres, there is a relentless focus on economics and ecology, and yet, throughout, Le Guin sees psychology, ethics and politics as a single continuum. Her Taoism leads her to the holistic belief that a social and economic transformation cannot occur without an accompanying transformation in personal values. As she says, 'the revolution is in the individual spirit or it is nowhere' (Le Guin, 1974:358).

There is a snag, however, in this utopia. Anarres exists on a barren planet, which is low on natural resources, subject to extreme weather conditions, and poorly suited to human civilization. In effect, it's a mining colony of another planet, Urras, which the pacifist founders of Anarres – led by a female visionary – left some 150 years ago, preferring planetary exile to a violent rebellion against a society which they found repressive, immoral and unjust. Life on Anarres can be harsh and even ugly, compared to the sumptuous life of the elite on Urras, a hierarchical, capitalist state, which overflows with natural resources but is scarred by poverty, gross inequality and state-sponsored violence. For Shevek, the men and women of Anarres have been liberated from this tyranny, as 'possessing nothing they are free', whereas the people of Urras, as he tells a group of them, are the true dispossessed of the novel's title:

And you the possessors are possessed. You are all in jail. Each alone, solitary with a heap of what he owns. You live in prison, die in prison. It is all I can see in your eyes – the wall, the wall!

(Le Guin, 1974:229)

Urras, of course, is a portrait of our current world system – and its walls today are even higher than when the novel was written. To make it crystal clear where we could be heading, Le Guin, in a moving lament, has an inhabitant of Earth reveal our planet's possible fate:

My world, my Earth is a ruin. We multiplied and gobbled and fought until there was nothing left, and then we died. We controlled neither appetite nor violence: we did not adapt. We destroyed ourselves. But we destroyed the world first. There are no forests left on my Earth. The air is grey, the sky is grey. It is always hot.... There are nearly a half billion of us now. Once there were nine billion.

(Le Guin, 1974:347)

It's a chilling prophecy which we would do well to take to heart. Le Guin's extraordinary mixture of whole-hearted idealism and steely realism seems to predict that it's still possible to create a kind of utopia even in the harshest, worst-case, ecological conditions. What she leaves open is the best-case scenario: what would happen if ecological, egalitarian utopianism was given a fair chance on a planet with Earth's natural abundance? It's precisely this question which another fine novel written during the utopian renaissance of the 1970s attempts to answer.

Ecotopia *(1975): a people-planet society?*

Ernest Callenbach's *Ecotopia* (1975) may lack some of Le Guin's soaring imagination and philosophical largesse, but this critically overlooked novel is hard to beat as a detailed fictional account of a circular economy in action. It reveals a society that is inspired by nature and thriving on equitability and wellbeing, in which the power of love can transform the most entrenched attitudes. In fact, it gives us one of the most realized versions yet of what a society based on the SEWP model might look like – which is why it's worth examining in some detail.

Ecotopia consists of the North Western Pacific states of northern California, Oregon and Washington, which, we're told, seceded from the United States 20 years before the time of the novel, which is set in 1999. A transition to an ecological economy has occurred, largely because a wholesale flight of capital has devastated the economy (GDP dropped by a third). Having 'no real choice', the people 'began spontaneously taking over farms, factories and stores' (Callenbach, 1975:98). By democratic means, 'more deliberate economic policies' here followed on from this, creating a 'stable state' system (Callenbach, 1975:98), which mirrors many of the central tenets of modern ecological economics. Several years of painful adjustment were necessary but Ecotopians were always clear about the consequences of rejecting conventional capitalist production.

> This would mean sacrifice of present consumption, but it would ensure future survival, which became an almost religious objective, perhaps akin to earlier doctrines of 'salvation'. People were to be happy not to the extent they dominated their fellow creatures on the earth, but to the extent that they lived in balance with them.
>
> (Callenbach, 1975:47–8)

Sustainability in Ecotopia

Sustainability is at the forefront of Ecotopia's economy of balance. One of the first things noticed by the novel's narrator, the visiting US journalist Will Weston, is that sewage is being recycled, instead of being dumped in rivers and oceans (a criminal practice in Ecotopia). In fact, the entire Ecotopian energy system appears to be 'pollution free' (Callenbach, 1975:111). 'Pre-independence' fossil- and nuclear-fuel power plants have been replaced by geothermal installations, solar radiation and photo-cell systems (one is the size of an airport but quiet enough for passers by to hear the song of skylark (Callenbach, 1975:112)). All Ecotopian houses are heated by rooftop solar panels or wind-driven generators. Brilliant Ecotopian scientists are working on 'photosynthetic chemistry' by which 'your garden could then recycle your sewage and garbage, provide your food and light your house' (Callenbach, 1975:115), the ultimate in circular economics. Ecotopia has also dispensed with the internal combustion engine and with cars: transport is by trams and bikes and electric trains, which travel noiselessly at high speeds. Bays and waterways have been restored, leading to a rise in water traffic.

A massive reforestation programme helps to reduce carbon pollution and provide the plentiful timber which is Ecotopia's main house-building material, as well as the source of innovative plastics which automatically degrade when exposed to ultraviolet rays (an invention we could really do with today). No wonder that trees are the object of a kind of unofficial religion for the Ecotopians.

The population size has been stabilized (at about 14 million), partially as a result of a massive educational and medical campaign around contraception. Decentralization of power from the cities to the countryside also had a positive effect, reducing crowding in schools, hospitals and workplaces, enabling people, women especially, to think more carefully about how many children they want (Callenbach, 1975:67).

All Ecotopian organizations are based on equitability principles. Usually small-scale ('small is beautiful' is the inspiration of most economic activity), they are cooperatively owned, usually as partnerships, and non-hierarchical in structure. The 20-hour week has been instituted in Ecotopia, so work tends be pleasurable, innovative and low in stress. Weston is unable to distinguish work from play – a recurrent utopian theme – and yet productivity in Ecotopia is high. All university students combine one year of study with one year of practical work, so enterprises benefit from the services of highly educated workers. Organizations rather than individuals are taxed – and there is also a land tax which, in part, accounts for 'the remarkable compactness of Ecotopian cities' (Callenbach, 1975:99). Capital for organizations is provided by a central bank. A form of universal citizen's income has replaced the welfare system, 'a lifetime guarantee of food, accommodation and healthcare', which enables people to live without paid work, a provision much appreciated by Ecotopia's many artists and musicians.

Cities have been redesigned on a more human scale. San Francisco has been scaled down to eliminate urban sprawl, and many villages have been revived. Technology has not been abandoned. 'Picture phones' exist and video-conferencing is available, as is cable TV, although Ecotopians waste little time in watching it (even if it is free of all advertising). 'Do it yourself' is a mania among Ecotopians, who like to make things from scratch or buy products in modular form and create their own designs (this even applies to city trams). Barriers between consumption and production don't exist in this circular economy. This participatory principle extends to entertainment, where Ecotopian prefer hands-on activities such as sailing, fishing and hunting to organized sports, and to the arts where there's little difference between amateurs and professionals.

Equitability

Equitability is another major feature of Ecotopian society. Property is generally held in common, with communal housing the norm, and income levels are much more equal than in the USA. Although innovators in the country's 'mixed economy' can still earn considerable fortunes, these are not passed on to the next generation, as the inheritance of private property has been abolished.

Ecotopia is a multi-party democracy, but its political system is dominated by the Survivalist Party, which led the Ecotopian revolution. Their main political opponents, the ironically named Progressive Party, are dominated by macho, individualist, pro-Western views. The Survivalists are entirely run by women, although men are also members (the possible internal conflicts here are not explored). A form of circular democracy seems to have been achieved in Ecotopia. The system is both top-down and bottom up, and highly participatory, as Weston's attendance at typical legislative assembly demonstrates:

A meeting has no formal agenda, it opens with a voicing of 'concerns' by many participants. As these are discussed (often amid friendly laughter, as well as a few angry outbursts), general issues begin to take shape. But there are no Roberts' Rules of Order, no motion, no votes – instead a gradual ventilation of feelings, some personal antagonisms worked through, and a gradual consensual focusing on what needs to be done.

(Callenbach, 1975:93)

Interestingly, Callenbach (Callenbach and Phillips, 1985) would later elaborate on this idea of a people's parliament, proposing 'a citizen's legislature' based on random selection rather than elections, similar to the sortition model I examined in Step 5.

Gender equality is far more advanced in this novel than in most previous utopian literature. Equal pay is universal (although nurses still seem to be exclusively female, and the ritual war games are only for men). Sexism has been eliminated from personal relationships, and women have the absolute right to select the father of their children (Callenbach, 1975:70). In spite of this, the years of progress on sexual and gender equality since the novel was written make it seem too exclusively heterosexual. (Gay and transgender people don't get a look in.)

In terms of ethnic diversity, Callenbach's most consciously controversial decision, articulated in a chapter entitled 'Equality or apartheid?', was to confine African Americans to living in separate communities such as Soul City. His defence was that this segregation was what some black nationalist movements of the time were demanding, and, as he stated in 2008, 'I would probably write it quite differently at this point' (cited in Timberg, 2008). Nevertheless, it ducks one of the most crucial egalitarian aspects of the challenge of utopia, leaving the society of the novel uncomfortably – and unrealistically – white.

The wellbeing society

In terms of the HELIOS interpretation of wellbeing, Callenbach's ideal world rates very highly. Ecotopians enjoy an exceptionally high standard of health, in part because of their outdoor lifestyle and unpolluted environment, but also because they are supported by a personalized healthcare system (paid for by cradle-to-grave health insurance). Hospitals are small, with fewer than 30 patients, and nurses are allocated to patients on a one-to-one basis. Mental health is also taken very seriously. All doctors are trained as psychiatrists, and support is always available in the general population, because ordinary people are adept at listening to, and empathizing with, others. The increasingly troubled Weston discovers this when he meets Ecoptia's president, Vera Allwen, who turns their conversation into a form of therapeutic intervention.

Education is also a vital component of wellbeing in Ecotopia. Schools are compulsory but are unregulated, and children are able to switch between them. They focus on helping children 'learn how to organize their lives' (Callenbach, 1975:130), giving opportunities to those who want to pursue specialist subjects but providing everyone with practical life skills. A typical 10-year-old can construct a shelter, 'grow, catch, and cook food' make simple clothes and identify many local species of plants and animals (Callenbach, 1975:131). Universities aim at fostering independent minds and are run by college assemblies which seem to thrive on student unrest. The curriculum favours natural science over social science and focuses on practical research projects.

Love is another important Ecotopian virtue, with Ecotopians being open, tactile, and sexually liberated in way that amazes Weston. 'There are electric moments when women stare me directly in the eyes' (Callenbach, 1975:10), he notes on arrival, later observing how much Ecotopians 'enjoy their bodies' and how uninhibited and unashamed they are about making love (Callenbach, 1975:32). The novel's most impressive depiction of sexual liberation is Weston's own personal transformation, as he falls in love with Marissa. He enters Ecotopia as a cynical, sexist journalist, with a broken marriage behind him and an on/off affair with a hedonistic, 'frivolous' girlfriend. Marissa's beauty and honesty captivates him, and the sex between them is like nothing he has ever experienced. Her seriousness of purpose, combined with a spontaneous generosity of spirit, wins him over. Her reverence for nature and her extraordinary ability to live in 'a contagious state of immediate consciousness', bring about a thoroughgoing transformation of Weston's values and sense of identity. 'A new self has been coming to life within me' (Callenbach, 1975:190), he concludes at the end of the novel, leading him to commit his future to Ecotopia.

Social involvement is also a fact of life in Ecotopia, where the deliberately slow pace of things gives everybody time for each other. Older people generally live in communal groups but are involved in every aspect of life. Transparency is everywhere, from publicly available tax returns to open kitchens in restaurants. To Weston, the streets 'seem ridiculously lacking in security gates, doormen, guards or other precautions against crime' (Callenbach, 1975:13). In fact, communal life is so predominant that privacy is regarded more as a problem than a highly desirable right.

Creative originality is also evident throughout Ecotopia, where everybody has their own attractive and idiosyncratic style of dress, often made from organic materials (Weston is amazed by the absence of nylon shirts!) Houses are full of craft pottery, finely constructed furniture and handmade decorations. The arts are as important as science and are displayed confidently, competitively but not commercially, especially in the many forms of music played. 'There is hardly a young person in the country who doesn't either play an instrument, dance, act, sing, write, sculpt, paint, make video films' (Callenbach, 1975:145), and yet the Ecotopians shun professionalism, saying 'we have no art, we just do everything as well as we can' (Callenbach, 1975:147).

Ecotopia abounds in the final HELIOS component of wellbeing, a strong sense of purpose, which comes from a feeling that people live for each other, enjoying a lifestyle that is more rational, generous and virtuous than that of their US neighbours. This manifests itself not as self-righteousness but through a purposeful respect for nature and the economic stability it can bring. The cycles of nature encourage a deeper appreciation of time and can be a source of spiritual wisdom. Love for nature is also encouraged by regular camps, shrines and a natural religion in which water is particularly revered (the marsh-wading egret is Ecotopia's national emblem).

Planetwide perspective

Where *Ecotopia* can be said to fall short of the SEWP model is in its planetwide perspective. Unlike the utopias of Morris, Bellamy and H.G. Wells, Ecotopia is not part of a worldwide federation, let alone subject to a world government. Ecotopians love their world news, it's true, and there is some foreign trade – rubber is imported from Vietnam, for example – but overall the country is internationally isolated. 'Ecology in one country' eventually won the debate about internationalism and nationalism – which recalls the unfolding of the Soviet revolution – and there is little appetite to export the Ecotopian model, in a country still engaged in a vicious, undercover war with its former federal master. (We have to believe that Ecotopia's small but cunning army can continue to resist the might of the US military-industrial complex.)

Perhaps Weston's ground-breaking newspaper articles will start to breach Ecotopia's international isolation and spread a message of hope to an increasingly ravaged, polluted world, but, for the time being, Callenbach espouses a bioregional, and even separatist, political philosophy. In fact, Ecotopia represents a rejection of 'the era of the great nation states, with their promise of one ultimate world-state' (Callenbach, 1975:165). It argues that 'a small regional society can exploit its niche in the world biosystem more subtly and richly and efficiently (and of course less destructively) than have the superpowers' (Callenbach, 1975:165). This separatism extends to the internal make up of Ecotopia, as we've seen, and it seems to be spreading: we're told that Spanish- and Japanese-speaking areas of San Francisco are thinking of seceding from Ecotopia (Callenbach, 1975:164). At times, this tribalism chimes with a certain vigorous competitivism that runs through Ecotopia – the male-only ritual war games are the most obvious example of this – combined with a failure to explore how cooperation really works.

Of course, stand-alone utopias can be precious incubators of social learning and practical development but they are surely insufficient solutions to a planet facing the full fury of the Anthropocene crisis. Only an internationalist approach can solve the problems of climate change, for example, which, strangely, Callenbach doesn't actually anticipate, although he is fully aware of the dangers of environmental breakdown through chemical pollution. Another critical area which Callenbach misses is the explosion of new technology which has occurred in the four decades since the novel was published. Ecotopia is not backward technologically, it's actually a society which is thoroughly science-orientated, but, ironically for a novel set in the area that would become Silicon Valley, Callenbach fails to anticipate the digital revolution, the internet and the exponential growth of AI and robotics, as well as the medical technology which could irreversibly alter aspects of human biology. This, for me, makes the option of retreating into bioregional niches even less plausible. International solutions are all that we have, although once achieved, these will provide the basis for coordinated local development.

That said, Callenbach cannot be held responsible for failing to predict all that history has thrown at us since the early 1970s. As remarkable as his vision of the future is, there were bound to be aspects of the Anthropocene crisis which he failed to foresee. These omissions certainly shouldn't stop us from learning the lessons this inspiring utopian novel can still provide for us today.

Walkaway *(2017)*

Minimizing technological development is certainly not an accusation that can be levelled at Corey Doctorow, whose *Walkaway* (2017) is one of the tiny number of novels which merit the description of 'twenty-first century utopia' (although, to be fair, it's also a dystopia). *Walkaway* poses another crucial question: what can we do if the worst-case scenario occurs and some of the dystopian possibilities I described in Chapter 5 actually happen? Set a few decades in the future – my estimate would be around 2050 – *Walkaway* takes place in a North America where the climate has been allowed to break down (in Canada, snow is something only older people can remember). The natural environment has been ransacked and is almost devoid of wildlife. Economic inequality has increased out of all recognition, many people have died of starvation or ongoing wars and democracy is a distant memory. The mainstream world (known as 'the default') is controlled through vigilance and violence by a super-rich class of 'zottas', the '0.001%', largely composed of hyper-competitive family dynasties. Profit-based technology has run rampant, with robots providing most of the work (but with few consumers left to buy the products they make) and the rich committing much of their wealth to 'the immortality industry'. Many of them want to 'secede from humanity' altogether and live forever, an Icarian goal which runs the risk of 'bifurcating the human race into infinite Olympian masters and mayflies' (Doctorow, 2017:141).

Doctorow's response to this dystopian turn of events is two-fold. First, as far as technological development is concerned, his view seems to be 'if you can't beat them, join them' (and then perhaps you can beat them). Doctorow enthusiastically anticipates the advances in manufacturing technology, such as 3D printing, which (Callenbach and Le Guin, almost inevitably, fail to foresee), which are capable of bringing about a 'post-scarcity' state of abundance. Walkaways who have turned their back on the default world are able to use this technology to create alternative ways of living. More radically – and very weirdly in the form of 'post-death' characters who live on as software in multiple simulations of consciousness – Doctorow suggests that the only way to prevent selective immortality is to make it available to everybody. 'It's a race: either the walkaways release immortality to the world, or the zottas install themselves as permanent god-emperors' (Doctorow, 2017:142).

Doctorow's second response to mainstream dystopia is to take the self-organization ethos to its logical conclusion, and make cooperation, sharing and mutual respect the foundations of the walkaway community. Gender equality is a primary theme of the novel. Most of the main characters are female and multiple sexualities are accepted and celebrated (and a good deal of joyous sexual activity depicted). Limpopo is one of the novel's heroes, a walkaway pioneer who has co-founded a bar and community centre using 3D printing, fab labs and new construction technology which can create instant shelters, food and clothing. For Limpopo the walkaways' philosophy is that 'the stories you tell come true'. As she declares:

> If you believe that everyone is untrustworthy, you'll build this into your systems so that even the best people have to act like the worst people to get anything done. If you assume people are okay, you live a much happier life.
>
> (Doctorow, 2017:86)

For her, this means no possessions – even using clothes lockers only sends the message that 'anything else is unprotected' – and cooperative ventures using spontaneous 'bucket teams' in which people are under no pressure to work and others compensate for members' weaknesses. Limpopo, in effect, is a leader in a leaderless society, a paradox she is aware of, even confessing to the pleasurable shame of seeing statistics which show how much more work she has put in than others. (She insists this gives her no special privilege or the right to expect more of others.)

Impressively, she has developed a sophisticated time consciousness, which enables her to override her 'limbic', short-term emotional self (which can be disappointed by others acting selfishly) in favour of future-facing, delayed gratification. This is shown at its best when she comprehensibly out-argues a rapacious opportunist named Jackstraw, who issues an aggressive, sexist challenge to the walkaways' egalitarian ethos. Doctorow's exploration of the deep psychology of cooperativeness is truly ground-breaking, and his portrayal of communal wellbeing rituals, such as hot-water bathing, is also convincing. Above all, he extols the transformative, utopian virtues of working together:

> The best way to be superhuman is to do things that you love with people who love them too ... if you do more than everyone, you're still only doing it because that's what you choose.
>
> (Doctorow, 2017:121)

That cooperation is an existential choice is repeated towards the end of the novel by Gretyl, a mathematician and computer genius, who is the mastermind behind the walkaways' immortality software. Confronting the tyrannical zotta billionaire, Jacob Redwood (whose daughter is Gretyl's lover), she tells him that people like him will always exist, 'people who think you either take or get took'.

> The question is whether people like you will get to define the default. Whether you can make it a self-fulfilling prophecy, doing for all of us before we do to you, meaning we're all chumps for not trying to do you sooner.... We're not making a world without greed, Jacob. We're making a world where greed is a perversion. Where grabbing everything for yourself instead of sharing is like smearing yourself with shit: gross.
>
> (Doctorow, 2017:498)

In the end the walkaways win a military and moral victory over the forces of the default empire and embark on a journey to 'a better nation', a real utopia. It's a triumph over the battlefield mentality (literally) which sends a positive message – 'Hope's what we're doing. Performing hope, treading water in open ocean with no rescue in sight' (Doctorow, 2017:286). The novel suggests that a society based on sustainable equitability and the democracy of love – because love is at the heart of this fiction, as it is in every utopian novel – can combine with advanced technology and harness science for the benefit of all.

But, in my view, the real question that Doctorow is posing is not pitched several decades in the future – it's for now. The novel is less concerned with what we can we salvage from the wreckage when growthism has done its worst and global warming, environmental depletion and unregulated technology have been allowed to run riot. What it really asks is: how can we stop the dystopian juggernaut in its tracks while there is still time? And the answer to that question is still in our hands.

Conclusion

Walkaway and other novels in the utopian tradition show that utopianism can never die. It can, however, be wounded, not only by the insidious spread of the dystopian imagination but also by the consumerist coloniza-tion of utopia, which suggests that the good life is simply a click or a credit-card tap away. We need the imagination and courage of great writers to expose this fallacy and to show us what a better world would feel like, what kind of social and economic structures can sustain it and the revolution in consciousness necessary to bring it about.

In the next step, we'll move from imagining an eco-utopian transforma-tion to considering what individuals can do about it in the here and now. Before that, however, let's remind ourselves how utopianism can explode off the printed page into real life, with some more inspiring slogans daubed on the walls of Paris during the 1968 May events (Knabb, 2006):

- Those who lack imagination cannot imagine what's lacking.
- Open the windows of your heart.
- You can no longer sleep quietly once you've suddenly opened your eyes.
- You have to bear a chaos within you to give birth to a dancing star.
- Beneath the paving stones lies the beach.

16 Step 11
Think and act like a utopian

Step 11 is the personal part of the change plan. It focuses on some of the things you can do personally to promote the people-planet vision. Of course, we have to remember that a utopian transformation is primarily a collective issue which requires fundamental changes in goals, policies and values across the world. Utopia certainly cannot be achieved by the individual acting alone. In the past, the idea of personal behaviour – presented as consumer choice – has been used to suggest that aspects of the Anthropocene crisis can be solved without the need for profound institutional changes. For example, in the early 2000s, too much pressure was placed on individuals to reduce their carbon footprint to mitigate global warming and not enough on the political and corporate elite to make major economic changes. This shift of responsibility from the political to the moral let the leadership class off the hook and probably contributed to the egregious failure of the UN climate talks in Copenhagen in 2009.

That said, there is still a huge amount that we can all do to contribute to the utopian transformation – and to ready ourselves for a new way of living. The people-planet vision requires a multi-revolution, involving every human institution and practice, and it can start anywhere. It encompasses changes of behaviour, attitude and lifestyle, which affect everything from consumption and diet to different ways of thinking and feeling. These changes represent experiments in living which individuals can try out, finding what works for them and others in their network.

The ten steps I've already gone through suggest a wide range of practices and institutions you might engage with, in the realms of polities, economics, the workplace, healthcare and other areas of public and private life. All of these have become so thoroughly colonized by growthism that it may seem hard to realize that we still have the possibility to change them. Even relatively small steps like joining a group to talk about alternative economics, for example, or campaigning on local environmental issues can be eye-opening. If it's going to happen, utopian change has to happen in who you are, in what you do and how you feel. Above all, it has to happen where you are, especially for those living in the global North or enjoying a privileged lifestyle elsewhere.

For people in developed countries, setting a positive example is crucial if the irrationality of growthism is to be defeated. If the wealthy world, which has created so much of the Anthropocene crisis, is not seen to be pioneering a solution, how can we expect developing countries ever to follow suit? Living in a utopian way – more simply, ecologically, focusing on equality and wellbeing – sends a message of solidarity to people in developing countries, many of whom have never lived an industrialized lifestyle but who are told to aspire to Western habits which it would take many planets of natural resources to sustain. So making utopianism a reality is something everyone can experiment with, in the knowledge that innovations of this kind can provide the foundations for real political and global change.

There may be much that you are already doing to accelerate the arrival of a better world, perhaps in ways I haven't even touched on. But the utopian multi-revolution has many fronts. So here, from the serious to the frivolous, are some suggestions about how to live and act like a twenty-first-century utopian.

Embracing the truth

The truth is at the heart of utopia. Authenticity has always been a central value for utopians and grasping the truth about the Anthropocene crisis – a dense field of hyper-objects seemingly too big to comprehend – is one of the greatest challenges of our epoch. And yet today the truth is under attack as never before. Instead of rising to the occasion, the Western world is sinking to the lowest common denominators of nationalism, xenophobic populism and raw prejudice. Brexit has enveloped the UK in a fog of ignorance, duplicity and cynical manoeuvrings for power which obliterate the idea that politics is about standing up for what you believe in. In the USA, a president who violates the truth virtually every time he tweets or opens his mouth reinforces this tribal epistemology (*Washington Post* counted 2,140 'false or misleading claims' made by Donald Trump in his first 12 months in office (Kessler and Kelly, 2018)). Even genuine attempts at balance can succumb to the growthist bias towards disequilibrium. Witness the difficulty the British media has had in implementing its impartial 'principle of equivalence', with the BBC sometimes presenting climate change as a debate between evidence-based scientists and right-wing, denialist 'cranks' (Kakutani, 2018).

For utopians, embracing the truth is more necessary than ever before. 'The truth is the whole', said Hegel (1807/1931:81), and the holistic approach is the only way to combat the fragmentation of the truth into parts that have no context but themselves. As I've suggested, the people-planet vision can help with this task, by providing a dialectical starting point which shapes our perspective on all things. At one level, this is about practical internationalism, which may be strengthened by simply consulting a map of the world more frequently. Make sure you use something like the

Gall–Peters projection, which correctly represents global landmass proportions, rather than the traditional Mercator atlas which inflates the Northern hemisphere. The Mercator (which, incidentally, came into being in the feverish decades after More's *Utopia*) represents Greenland as larger than Africa (it's actually 14 times smaller), Alaska as bigger than Brazil (it's a fifth of its size) and Finland as greater in North–South extent than India (it's not).

Sustainability is another principle which helps to make the dynamic interaction between ourselves and our environment the foundation of thinking, putting inter-human divisions into perspective. And dialectical thinking can help us to see the other side of the argument, which is often obscured, by accident or design. This oppositional logic is closely related to empathy, which as we're seen, is a vital for effective leadership and the CANDID ethos in general.

Statistics, when properly applied, are also holistic instruments. Once 100% becomes the measure of the whole, the part can find its proper place. Accurate research show just how wrong public perceptions of reality can be. For example, people in Great Britain think that 24% of the nation's energy comes from renewable sources whereas the actual figure is still only 9%. We also vastly overestimate the percentage of immigrants in the country (24% average guess versus 13% actual figure) and inflate the real extent of the Muslim population by a factor of four (17% versus 4%) – and in the United States the overestimation of this ethnic group is out by a factor of 14 (14% versus 1%) (Ipsos MORI, 2018b).

Evidence-based research is the key to discovering the truth and defending it against its assailants. That means patient corroboration, searching for reliable sources, being prepared to encounter differing opinions, and having the courage to establish your own position. The trail of evidence will lead you to the truth. The Anthropocene can only be understood by looking at the evidence – it's much stranger than fiction. It doesn't necessarily conform to what 'common sense' seems to tell us. (Even Einstein thought nature couldn't be so contrary to common sense as to make quantum theory an accurate description of the structure of the atom.)

Sometimes seeing the truth isn't even that difficult, as long as you're ready to be true to yourself. In an earlier chapter, I ascribed the mismanagement of growthism to 'inattentional blindness', a phenomenon which causes us to fail to perceive what is right in front of our eyes. A classic experiment demonstrating this all-too-human foible involves asking a group to count the number of times a basketball is passed between three players in a video (Simons and Chabris, 1999). When asked, 'Did you see the gorilla?' – a person dressed in a gorilla suit who wanders between the ball players in the video – half of the observers admit that they had completely failed to notice it. They'd been so intent on their counting task that what would have been instantly obvious to any neutral viewer of the video utterly passed them by.

In other words, seeing the truth can sometimes mean doing your own thing, rather than trying too hard to do what you're supposed to do – in this case being a 'good' experimental subject. The truth is a choice and not always an easy one, especially in a growthist world constantly trying to distract us from what is really going on. So don't forget to watch out for the gorilla!

Utopian time

Utopians also need to pay attention to the truth of time. As I've previously suggested, a sense of heightened temporality is essential to people-planet thinking. As Tim Jackson (2009:203) says, 'the fundamental point about sustainability is that it's all about time'. Phillip Zimbardo and John Boyd (2008) have developed an illuminating psychological questionnaire which outlines six different time-related personalities. 'Past-positive' personalities respect what they've done in the past, while 'past-negatives' wish they'd done something else; 'present-hedonists' live for the moment, whereas 'present-fatalists' think that they have no choice over their destiny; 'future-transcendents' believe in life after death, while 'futures' plan practically for what is to come. Many of these ways of seeing the world can contribute to utopia. For instance, at a personal level, reflection on past events can be immensely helpful in revealing what is really important to us. Often this has little to do with work, money or what is expected of us. On our death bed, according to palliative nurse Bronnie Ware (2011), what we regret most is that we didn't spend enough time with friends and family, express our real feelings often enough or do more of whatever would have made us truly happy.

But of all these time perspectives, the future-orientation seems the most important to cultivate, if we are to get a grip on the truth of our epoch. That's no easy matter in a market-driven reality which envelops us in a hyper-present of consumer novelty and an illusory future based on unlimited economic expansion. Confusingly, our current knowledge system pays scant attention to future studies (popularly known as futurology), which is still a fringe academic discipline, while historical studies are omnipresent, especially in the mass media. All of this suggests that utopians need to work on their sense of the future.

In fact, Zimbardo and Boyd find that 'futures' tend to be particularly concerned about the environment and highly respectful of the biosphere. The authors go so far as to say that 'the common good is not a moral matter but a time-perspective matter' (Zimbardo and Boyd, 2010:134). The ability to put anxiety to good use is another aspect of this futurizing ability, which existential psychologists have long recognized. Worrying may be distressing but, as philosopher Søren Kierkegaard was one of the first to recognize, in *The Concept of Anxiety* (1844), it can also be constructive. Anxiety is a constant reminder that time provides no guarantees and this can help us to embrace our responsibility to shape the future in ways that benefit those who come after us.

Perceiving what has not yet happened ought to be a more widespread strength for humans: it's certainly something that we do infinitely better than any other species. And we now have not only our precious imaginations to work with but also an increasing array of scientific measuring and calculating equipment, which can help to produce the most accurate picture of the future. Of course, what comes next is always a guess – strictly speaking, it's a hypothesis which can only be verified once the future has morphed into the past – but your forecasting capacity, like an underused muscle, can rapidly be strengthened with the right exercise. Training around scenario planning – worst-case, best-case, most-likely, least-likely, and so on – is one way to develop future awareness. Sophisticated forward planning shouldn't be confined to the boardrooms of fossil-fuel corporations such as Shell and BP. It needs to be democratized so that ordinary people acquire these skills, if we are to have a chance of planning the future from a majoritarian standpoint.

Lifestyle changes: living the philosophy of balance

So much for thinking, what about action? Utopia is about taking human possibility to its furthest limits but utopians also want to get things done and convert their ideas into realities. It's a choice-making process I've described as a journey from possibilizing to probabilizing to actualizing (Harvey, 2012). Or, as Henry David Thoreau puts it in *Walden*: 'If you have built castles in the air, your work need not be lost.... Now put the foundations under them' (1854/1997:303).

Lagom

One way to put the logic of balance into practice is to learn from what people in Sweden have been doing for centuries through the everyday practice of *lagom*. Enoughism is deeply rooted in Swedish culture – and plays a big part in the Nordic tradition, which has resisted free market capitalism more effectively than many other nations. The spirit of *lagom* is usually described as 'just enough' or 'moderation is best', and the word is believed to derive from a phrase meaning 'around the team', referring to the Viking custom of passing a cup of mead around the table. The *lagom* respect for moderation expresses itself in many aspects of Swedish lifestyle, from healthy, unpretentious food to minimalist furniture and interior design and sensible work–life balance (many Swedish companies close down for several weeks in the summer). Family orientation is another aspect of this focus on balance. Sweden was the first country to introduce non-gender-specific parental leave and parents are now entitled to 480 days leave when a child is born or adopted. As Linnea Dunne (2017) stresses, we should reject the myths that *lagom* is about celebrating mediocrity, mindless conformity or stinginess. Nor does *lagom* prevent you from expressing pride and confidence in your achievements, although this should not be done in a way that is dismissive of others. A society which has pioneered social egalitarianism – and remains one of the most economically equal developed nations in the world – is now under a political pincer attack from neoliberalism and anti-immigrant populism. So what better time to stand up for the *lagom* philosophy of enough?

Simplicity

Voluntary simplicity is another expression of enoughism, which draws on a wide range of influences, including early Christianity, Buddhism, American transcendentalism, Tolstoy, Gandhi and European bohemianism. (The poet, T.S. Eliot, once lauded 'A condition of complete simplicity / (Costing not less than everything)' ('Little Gidding' V 880–1)). It's a belief system which rejects over-consumption, luxury and the 'live now, pay later' mentality of growthism. Duane Elgin (2010) has described voluntary simplicity as an 'outwardly poor, inwardly rich' lifestyle which stems from 'a deliberate choice to live with less in the belief that more will be returned in the process'.

Living simply can involve a trade-off between reduced consumption and increased time and life satisfaction. It involves a rejection of the conspicuous consumption and extravagant materialism of the rich. In a way, it's showing solidarity with billions of people around the world who have no choice but to act fugally. And yet, strangely enough, a certain kind of thrift has long been a trait of the English upper class – a threadbare shirt collar was once a curious badge of pride in the City of London – who regard throwing away perfectly serviceable goods as a sign of irredeemable vulgarity (it helps, of course, if you can afford to buy durable, high-quality products in the first place).

Opting for a simpler life is not about rejecting all technology, but it is about rejecting wastefulness. It involves trying to emulate the sensible frugality of the developing world, rather than modelling a wasteful, multi-planet lifestyle. I was suitably shamed recently by a friend from the Philippines who looked at me as though I was mad when I said I was throwing away a fan merely on the grounds that it was broken. (As my electrical skills were lacking, he took it away and fixed it for me.) Repairing may still be a choice for many of us in the West but it needs to become a necessity, as Bill McKibben (2010) has urged.

To help you indentify where you are in relation to simplicity, here's a summary of the characteristics that Elgin (2010:107–10) has found among people dedicated to simple living:

- Investing in time with a partner, family or friends and getting involved in community life.
- Developing physical, emotional and learning skills (especially where this helps to reduce dependence on specialists).
- Feeling 'a reverential concern for nature' and a compassionate concern for the world's poor.
- Preferring lower levels of personal consumption, purchasing durable products and being prepared to boycott unethical products.
- Reducing clutter and complexity by giving away seldom used possessions.
- Appreciating the simplicity of nonverbal communication, such as hugging and touching, and 'the eloquence of silence'.
- Engaging in 'livelihoods that directly contribute to the wellbeing of the world' and living and working in small-scale environments.
- Favouring holistic, preventative healthcare practices and getting around by means of public transport, biking or walking.

It's a demanding list, to be sure, and not everyone can be expected to meet all of its requirements, but it gives an impressive snapshot of the utopian all-rounder, a citizen of the Anthropocene Renaissance.

Support feminist utopianism

Another of Duane Elgin's keys to simple living is 'committing to altering male–female roles in favour of non-sexist patterns of relationships' – which is an important reminder that a people-planet utopia is also a feminist utopia. As we saw in the previous chapter, the feminist tradition in utopian fiction has always been strong. In fact, in her 1969 novel, *The Left Hand of Darkness*, Ursula Le Guin goes beyond *The Dispossessed* in terms of gender equality by envisaging a post-gender utopia in which a single sex, nominally male, is capable of taking on the reproductive, sexual and nurturing functions of both sexes. Janet Russ (1975) in her novel, *The Female Man*, also depicts a single gender utopia – although in her case, it's a female-only ideal world set a millennium in the future, after all males have been wiped out by a terrible plague. In *Woman on the Edge of Time*, published a year later, Marge Piercy (1976) traces a more anguished route from an oppressive contemporary mental institution to a future world beyond patriarchy and gender-based concepts of identity, occupation and bodily image. In her multi-racial, ecologically balanced utopia, there are no gender-specific pronouns and both sexes act as mothers to children. They also self-manage their communities and are free to change their names and sexual identities at will.

In a future world without sexual violence – currently one fifth of all women in the UK over the age of 16 report that they have experienced sexual assault (ONS, 2018) – and without gender based exploitation and discrimination, new forms of behaviour will emerge which will not only benefit women and girls. No longer will boys and men be forced to adopt 'tough', harshly competitive values, repressing their caring emotions or committing acts of physical or verbal violence in order to prove their virility.

Education has always been of special interest to utopian writers, and it's an area which many feminists are focusing on today, as the collection of essays and interviews in *The Feminist Utopia Project* reveals (Brodsky and Kauder Nalebuff, 2015). Social-justice educator Ileana Jimenez (2015:130) suggests that the aim of a feminist school should be to 'to teach young people to love' and asks: 'Wouldn't that be the ultimate goal of utopia? To live in a loving world?' That chimes with the kind of school which teacher Cindy Ok envisages, in which children don't 'sit in rows like robots' but learn from each other almost as much as from their teachers. It would involve teaching every pupil reproductive health in a multidisciplinary way, with all lessons having a feminist and anti-racist content, not just elective courses (Ok, 2015: 136). When children are taught from the very start to fully appreciate and celebrate gender differences – including the talents of skills of transgender people, who, as campaigner Miss Major Griffin-Gracy says, 'should not have to prove anything' – the possibilities for love in the widest sense open up (Bobadilla, 2015:228).

A world which transcends LGBTQ categories would release new forms of being and relating we can only dream of, including barely imaginable types of sexual experience between sensitive, reciprocating, empathizing equals. Sex in utopia could outdo all the drugs, sex robots and virtual-reality experiences made to simulate it (it may need to). At the very least, it could reverse the dramatic 14% decline in sexual activity among American adults since the 1990s which has been charted by Jean Twenge and her colleagues (2017). This trend is especially marked among young adults – over the past decade the proportion having had no sex in the past year has more than doubled, due to concerns about sexual assault and unwanted pregnancies, as well as the technological counter-attractions of social media, streamed films, online pornography and video games (Wilcox and Sturgeon, 2018). It seems that sexual intercourse could be another area of life which is urgently in need of reskilling. We might even call good sex a utopian act. At any rate, it's an natural asset utopia will unashamedly exploit as a new era of sexual freedom is initiated. Writer Lori Adelman comes to the following conclusion:

> Though good sex is never guaranteed, in a feminist utopia we would all be liberated and empowered to pursue our own erotic transcendence – and that's may be all we can really ask for. That, and maybe also, of course, 'harder, harder', 'yes', 'more' and 'right there'.
>
> (Adelman, 2015:258)

You are what you eat

Whatever you decide to do (or not do) about promoting utopian sex, let me draw your attention to another basic human need: eating. What we eat and how we produce what we eat are core issues in a new epoch in which millions of people worldwide are potentially threatened with starvation. One of the most momentous battles taking place today is between industrialized agriculture and traditional, natural farming methods. On the one side, there is US-style, profit-driven agri-business, with its often appalling treatment of animals; patented, genetically modified crops; and treeless prairies tended by robots. On the other side are many varieties of organic, free-range agriculture, which involve following natural patterns, such as the 'do-nothing', 'no-till' farming methods, pioneered by Japanese farmer and philosopher Masanobu Fukuoka. Permaculture, which encourages several layers of growth from the tree canopy down to shrubs and root crops (alongside 'verticals' like runner beans and vines), is another method of using natural ecosystem structures to grow as intensively as industrial, chemical-based farming but without the environmental damage (Whitefield, 1993).

Growing your own food is one way to put yourself on the people-planet side of the farming war. Even in urban settings, a challenge can be mounted to Big Agri and Big Food. Roof gardens, edible balconies, vegetables in window boxes or pots, food grown in small gardens or allotments: all these measures help to accelerate utopian city planning, in which buildings are designed to incorporate gardening spaces from the outset. Urban agriculture has helped Cuba survive the devastating loss of subsidized oil when the Soviet Union collapsed. In Havana, 40% of food is now grown locally, which among other things, means the city has become less of a drain on the surrounding countryside. Detroit is also attempting to overcome an industrial apocalypse, by moving 'from Mo-Town to Gro-Town', while in New York City, the epitome of high-rise metropolitanism, over 5,000 acres have recently been found for urban farming (Simms 2013:328).

So whether you live in the town, the country or the suburbs why not have a go at growing some of your own food, by yourself or with others? Remember utopia in the Anthropocene is all about growth: degrowing what is destructive in order to grow what really matters.

Cutting down on meat

The other food issue I'd highlight is eating meat. As I've said, I'm wary of putting too much pressure on individuals to alter patterns of consumption that can only be achieved by systemic changes. However, cutting out meat is a change I've made myself fairly painlessly in recent years, and it's an area where consumers really can make a difference, especially those of us in the global North. Cutting down on meat doesn't necessarily mean going wholly vegetarian or vegan – although many more people are moving in this direction. Even a flexitarian diet, which includes some poultry and fish, can make a huge difference.

That's because meat production is a staggeringly resource-intensive practice, using 10 times more kilocalories of energy than plant production and, in the case of beef, 25 times more (Simms, 2013:229). Producing a kilogramme of beef requires an astonishing 15,415 litres of water or 50 times as much as is needed to produce a kilogramme of vegetables, according to the Water Footprint Network (2018). Lamb, at 8,763 litres of water per kilogramme, and pork, at 6,000 litres, are slightly less demanding than beef, but still hugely destructive of precious water resources, when compared to starchy roots which only require 387 litres per kilogramme.

If conventional economics included land, energy, water and other ecosystem costs, the price of beef would be many times higher than it is, but this is the practical consequence of conventional economists' seemingly abstract elimination of nature from their accounting processes. Those who sit down to a steak dinner – as I've done many times in the past – are victims of the confidence trick perpetrated by the algorithms of capital, which prevents them from seeing the astronomical environmental costs of what they are eating.

What is also not reflected in meat's supermarket price tag is the huge opportunity cost of raising livestock. Producing two large steaks requires 6.5 kilogrammes of grains, such as barley, wheat, soya and corn, which could otherwise be used for human consumption. In fact, 70% of agricultural land is taken up by livestock farming and another 10% is used to grow food for ruminant animals (Worldwatch, 2014). If more people moved to plant-based diets, vast areas of land would open up for other uses. In the UK, sheep farming takes up as many hectares as all other crops put together. It's been estimated that if the entire country went vegan, it could feed up to 200 million people worldwide or release millions of hectares of countryside for rewilding (Monbiot, 2017).

Livestock farming is not only one of the major destroyers of habitats on the planet, it is also a major contributor to global warming. The belching and flatulence of cattle and sheep produces millions of tons of methane gas, which over 100 years is up to 35 times more effective as a greenhouse gas than CO_2. In total, the livestock sector produces 14.5% of global greenhouse-gas emissions, when all life cycle factors are included, such as manure and ruminant food production (Garnett *et al.*, 2017). Furthermore, meat production can be bad for your health, as it contributes significantly to antibiotic resistance, which threatens the world (four times more antibiotics are fed to cattle in the USA than are consumed by humans (Worldwatch, 2014)). Meat eating is also linked to increased risk of heart diseases, obesity and a wide range of cancers.

In the developing world, meat consumption per capita is still half of that of the West. Eating meat has not yet become institutionalized as a status symbol of wealth as it has among rich nations (although in some of them, such as Japan, this is a fairly recent occurrence). By cutting down on meat, or cutting it out altogether, we in the global North can send an important message to the rest of the world that they do not need to succumb to the madness of growthism at its most ecologically reckless.

Explore stillness

Another long-standing human need seems to be religion, although it's much harder to predict what form this will take in utopia. A multitude of personal eclecticisms may take the place of today's institutionalized belief systems, or maybe a form of world-minded awareness will develop, which can reconcile a spiritual higher authority with the methodology of science. A new human morality, a code of good living which perhaps incorporates some of the CANDID values, will almost certainly need to emerge.

All experiments with non-materialism can contribute to this new form of human consciousness, but one thing I'm sure will help is to cultivate stillness. 'Returning to one's roots is known as stillness', says the *Tao Te Ching* (Lao Tzu, *Tao Te Ching* XVI) and discovering the stillness in our-selves is surely necessary if we are to reach utopia – and stay there. Stillness can defeat the algorithms, embedded in the fabric of our world system, which constantly seek to exploit our thrill-seeking tendencies and desire for easy emotional affirmation. For growthism, if you're not consuming, you're a liability, which is why it tries to provide us with a constant torrent of fast-paced, purchase-related stimulation. Social media and the internet encourage impatience, frustration and panic in the face of anything that cannot be achieved instantly.

Growthism may even be bringing about neurological changes, which make it harder to achieve the delayed gratification associated with the adult brain. This seems to be borne out by a recent psychological study which found that a large sample of undergraduates were extremely chal-lenged by the task of sitting alone for up to 15 minutes, without any social or technological stimulation. Astonishingly, two-thirds of the men in the sample and a quarter of the women found the experience so disturbing that they elected to give themselves an uncomfortable electric shock (which they'd previously said they'd pay to avoid) rather than complete the thinking task (Wilson *et al.*, 2014).

So here's how to launch a major blow against the growthist hegemony: do nothing! Just sit alone and try to get comfortable with your own thoughts. Channel your inner Daedalus, and quell your impetuous, private Icarus. Mediation can provide a discipline for this activity, as can the prac-tice of mindfulness and other forms of non-materialism outlined in Step 9. The key point is to embrace stillness: hear it, sense it, think it and use it to subdue the anxiety that apparent inactivity can undoubtedly provoke. Slow time, as it's sometimes called, is definitely another dimension of utopian time, and very different from the rocket time of growthism. It can bring us up against boredom, which was once a perennial aspect of life, particularly for young people. I distinctly remember it from my childhood in England in the 1960s, particularly on Sundays. Back then, we were told that boredom was a failure of creativity and effort. Perhaps now we need to recultivate that idea, in order to combat the feeling that if you're not consuming you're missing out on something indispensable. The right to be bored is a human right and we should not let it disappear. It could just be essential to mastering the art of living.

William Blake (1863/1977) saw this so clearly in his poem, 'Auguries of Innocence':

> To see a world in a grain of sand
> And heaven in a wild flower
> To hold infinity in the palm of your hand
> And eternity in an hour.

Stillness enables us to appreciate the colours, lines and brushstrokes of reality. Perceiving the complexities and nuances of a situation changes time. Soon, it seems like there are not enough hours in the day to see all that there is – more time will be needed, next time. In flow situations, the clock simply cannot cope. Time that once seemed heavy is now as light as a feather. All this awaits us on the other side of the dull door of boredom. So have a go at mastering slow time – before fast time does for us all.

Have fun

Having fun is another part of being a utopian. Seriously. It's the necessary corrective to what might otherwise be seen as the dangerously puritanical aspects of living simply and in a state of balance. Conviviality is about embracing joyful exuberance and (temporary) excess in celebrating the pleasure that comes with being with other people. It also means working to overcome the profound pain which people cause one another by oppressive behaviour. So go for extravagant feasting, joyous music festivals and other celebrations of 'living together' (the Latin etymology of 'conviviality') as well as the simple pleasures of hanging out. As the European degrowth movement advocates, we can learn from indigenous peoples the importance of generous gift-giving in potlatch and other 'depense' traditions, expressed in the week-long feasts and hedonistic communal rituals of many pre-modern cultures. 'Conviviality', as degrowth theorist Serge Latouche (2009:32) suggests, 'is designed to reknit the social bond unravelled by what Arthur Rimbaud calls the "horror of economics"'.

Conviviality is an integral part of the new technology of living, as opposed to living though technology. It can include ritualistic eating and drinking, joking and prank-playing, sporting events, erotically charged music and dance, emotional storytelling or simply meeting new people in new circumstances. These fundamental tools of social existence pre-date anything that could be called a machine by hundreds of thousands of years. It's a social technology aimed at getting the most out of our social being, celebrating what we have already and sharing in the abundance which potentially comes from being alive on our exceptional planet.

One way to learn about productive conviviality is from the many intentional communities which exist around the world today. Mini-utopias have a lot to teach us about the real thing. They often focus on wellbeing, offering inspiration in the huge variety of cultural, spiritual and sporting activities. To take just one example, consider the following range of activities available to members of the well-established Findhorn intentional community in Scotland, as described by long-term resident Graham Meltzer:

> Cooking and eating shared meals, devotional and popular singing, many forms of dancing including open floor, ceilidh and biodanza, running on the beach, community-performed pantomimes and dramas, Discovery Games (in which participants reveal what's going on in their lives), taking 'a hot tub under the stars', golf, Taize meditation groups, massage sessions, support groups exploring sexuality, educational seminars and discussion forums.
>
> (Meltzer, 2015)

If, for some, this all sounds emotionally exhausting, I should emphasize that having fun is not just for extroverts. Utopia has to be for introverts too. The opposition between these personality types is another border which utopia seeks to abolish, another dualism to be transcended, as it creates a synthesis in which all personality styles can live together harmoniously. In any case, introverts' main difficulty is feeling comfortable with total strangers. Involvement with the community, a common purpose, the growth of cooperation and other aspects of the new wellbeing will help to overcome this source of inhibition. In utopia, the plaintively humorous placard I noticed recently at a protest rally in Central London, which read 'It's so bad even introverts are here', will become increasingly meaningless.

Use failure as an ally

Finally, a word on perfectionism – a growing curse of our times as social media invites us to compare ourselves to hundreds of other people living seemingly immaculate lives. For utopians, this can be a particular problem, as they set the bar very high, claiming that a better world is possible and that human perfectibility is not just a pipe dream. Utopianism rejects the pessimistic view that all we can hope for is the lesser evil, preferring to champion the greater good. But psychologically, perfectionism can cripple morale and destroy creativity, turning ambition into a weapon against itself.

So the first thing to do is realize that utopia is not a permanent place but a destination (that's another of the meanings of 'no place'). The eco-egalitarian transformation is a continuous process, even if that process ultimately takes the form of a set of stabilizing, self-correcting circularities. A second antidote to utopian perfectionism is to think of the methodology at the heart of scientific experimentation, the hypothetico-deductive approach. This is more commonly known as trial and error, and each of the terms in the phrase plays an equally crucial role. Indeed, failure is usually the only way to achieve empirical success. And accidents often turn out to greatest source of discovery, serendipity having produced many breakthroughs in science and medicine (Kingdon, 2012).

Learning from your mistakes can be alien to the wasteful, zero-sum competitivism that drives growthism, which sees failure as a shameful weakness, intolerable to those who only respect strength. Hyper-competitors risk ignoring the information that may lie buried in an experiment that goes wrong or a hypothesis that is frustrated, signs which may point towards a still unknown prize. So utopians need to learn to make the most of failure as a resource – it's one of the most abundant on the planet, and it's infinitely renewable! Used correctly, failure will never let you down.

Conclusion

In the end, a personal change plan is just that, personal. It's up to you to decide how you can contribute to accelerating the utopian transformation – and you may have ideas very different from the ones I've touched on here. But we certainly shouldn't underestimate the extent to which simple things, like getting more moderation and balance into our lives, changing basic aspects of our consumption and even having fun, can open the doors to a revolution in how we live together. The political and the private are far more intertwined than establishment politicians want us to believe. History can be changed at every level of society, and ordinary people have always played a much bigger role in transformational events than is often realized. Indeed, as we'll see in our final step, the real narratives of history offer much to encourage us about the possibility of turning a people-planet utopia into something more than a dream.

17 Step 12
Take heart from history

The final step of the change plan is about liberating yourself from the myths of the past and the distortions of a chimerical future. It's also about vigorously contesting the growthist interpretation of history. Having studied and taught in the humanities – in disciplines such as literature and political and cultural theory which are deeply historical – I'm well aware that our current knowledge system often underestimates the value of history. Looking towards the future is vital, as I've repeatedly emphasized, but we cannot hope to understand where we are going, unless we understand where we have been (and where we could have been).

The Anthropocene is a qualitatively new epoch in human and planetary history, and historical studies are beginning to reflect this. For instance, we're seeing the start of a new view of history influenced by ecology and climate science. This deep history rejects the human narcissism of treating history as though the planet was simply an inert, neutral stage on which the eternal drama of *Homo sapiens* can play out. In response to epochal change, we are also moving away from the idea of history as the creation of 'great men' or a hierarchical leadership class, which also means leaving behind history which is written and conceived by the winners. The flourishing of world history also reinforces the people-planet perspective, as more and more historians examine the past through an internationalist lens, although the traditional emphasis on national history still persists in popular studies.

You might think that history is just too big a subject to address in a single chapter but we shouldn't be put off by bigness: scale is one of the greatest intellectual challenges of the Anthropocene, but it's also a major opportunity. So let me present seven lessons from history that might encourage you to believe that a utopian transformation is possible.

Climate change can drive history

Ecological history is at an exciting time, changing our view of ourselves and our planet. John L. Brooke's *Climate Change and the Course of Global History* (2014) is an excellent example of this new approach, which emphasizes for the first time the huge impact which climate change has had on the development of humanity. Here are a few examples.

The agricultural revolution, one of the biggest transformations in human history, could not have occurred without the global warming of about 4°C which ended the Ice Age and the 2.6-million-year epoch of the Pleistocene. This brought in the climate of the Holocene 11,700 years ago, which 'has been uniquely stable, *almost surreally flat*, compared to the jagged instabilities of the Pleistocene' (Brooke, 2014:102, my emphasis). By about 6,000 years ago, the entire world was on course for agriculture, but this could only have happened in a stable, warm climate: 'it was impossible in the Pleistocene but inevitable during the Holocene' (Brooke, 2014:125).

The first political states emerged as a result of abrupt climate change. They exploded into existence out of simple tribal settlements and village communities. 'The trigger was a discrete natural catastrophe, droughts in Egypt and Mesopotamia, floods in China and Peru, that *led to population collapse and cultural crisis*' (Brooke, 2014:190, emphasis original). In other words, states can be seen as a defence against calamity rather than the evolution of a superior form of civilization.

Climate change is a major clue in the long-debated historical puzzle about what causes the rise and fall of empires. As Brooke points out, for 3,000 years in China, until the advent of the Hang dynasty, 'dynastic change would coincide with epochs of failed summer monsoons (which should bring rainfall) and intense, cold, dry winter monsoons' (Brooke, 2014:308). The final fall of the Roman Empire may have been the consequence of a massive volcanic eruption in 536 BC (probably in Central America), archaeologist David Keys (1999) has argued. This blanketed much of the globe in sulphurous clouds, bringing dark, cold days, droughts and floods, conditions which led to the development of the bubonic event known as the Justinian plague. That finally finished off Rome, which otherwise may have continued for many more centuries.

Climate change can also lead to the scapegoating of those least able to defend themselves. The Little Ice Age was a cool period in Europe and North America, which caused the Thames to freeze over in winter during the sixteenth and seventeenth centuries. (Note that the temperature variation involved here, a drop of only 1°C, was the biggest the Holocene experienced, compared to the increase of 3–4°C we are currently on course for this century.) The food shortages and other hardships caused by the Little Ice Age were often blamed on women, especially widows, as witchcraft became linked to weather control in the popular imagination. As Emily Oster (2004) has shown, up to 1 million women were executed as witches over the period, with trials increasing as the weather worsened and decreasing when it improved. It's a harsh warning about how future climate change may be blamed on the most vulnerable.

The lesson of this emerging climate-based, wellbeing-orientated approach to history is that historical change is often due to extra-human factors. Life on this planet can be fragile, and we pay a heavy price if we fail to respect the forces of climate and environment. Societies which over-shoot their ecological carrying capacity usually come to a sticky end, as is shown by the fate of the Easter Islanders, the Polynesians of Pitcairn Island or the Anasazi peoples of south-western North America (Diamond, 2005). What history can't give us are those societies which were so integrated into nature that they left no record – no waste, no monuments, nothing that squandered precious resources. These are the other winners of history, writing the invisible history of the ecologically literate. We can take heart from these past societies which go with the flow of nature rather than trying to deny it. They suggest that ecological necessity is a far better master than the algorithms of capital.

Sustainable, equitable, wellbeing-based societies may once have been the norm

The state-based hierarchies of the Holocene are not the only form of human organization. The Holocene epoch only accounts for the 5% of human history which broadly corresponds to the era of human technology known as the Neolithic or the New Stone Age. Most of the 200,000 year history of *Homo sapiens* was lived in the Pleistocene epoch, which covers roughly the same time span as the 3.3 million years of human and hominid tool-making known as the Palaeolithic archaeological era.

Life in the Palaeolithic was far from being stone age in the sense of being primitive or savage. Hunter-gatherers, foraging and horticultural societies were usually nomadic, living in close, informed connection with their environment, often in extremely equitable social arrangements. In fact, the majority of much of our human past may have been lived in egal-itarian social structures. Our best evidence for this is pre-modern, pre-agrarian societies which still exist across the world. 'Elites and class structure are virtually unknown among simple foragers' writes historian Walter Scheidel.

> In a sample of more than a thousand communities, three quarters of simple foraging communities show no signs of social stratification, as opposed to fewer than a third of those practising intensive agriculture.
>
> (2017:42)

In the Palaeolithic, the living could be easy. Anthropologist Marshall Sahlins surprised the world when he described the Stone Age as 'the ori-ginal affluent society'. He argued that whereas today's modern market economy represents the 'institutionalization of scarcity', life for hunter gatherers was quite different: 'a pristine affluence colours their economic arrangements, a trust in the abundance of nature's resources rather than despair at the inadequacy of human means' (Sahlins, 1972:29). To prove that forager societies often enjoy a high degree of wellbeing, Sahlins cited the present-day example of the Hazda, a nation of egalitarian East African foragers, who spend less than two hours a day obtaining food. Recent skeleton analysis confirms that in the Upper Palaeolithic era (50,000 to 10,000 years ago) health was better than in the Neolithic era of the Holocene. Upper Palaeolithic people were taller than Neolithic people (men up to six centimetres taller), suffered less malnutrition and tooth decay, contracted fewer animal-borne diseases and less osteoarthritis (probably caused by back-breaking agrarian work). They may also have lived longer. In fact, according to John Brooke (2014:221), 'civilizational stress' seems to have struck humanity from the very beginning of the agricultural revolution.

What also struck was the all-too-modern propensity for fear and greed. Once agriculture created a significant surplus of food, hierarchical social structures tended to replace egalitarianism. A survey of modern Native American societies discloses that whereas 86% of those with little or no agricultural surplus show no signs of political inequality, this is evident in four-fifths of those that do have a surplus (Scheidel, 2107:36). As soon as surpluses appeared, especially of crops that can be stored, minorities – families or leadership cliques – began to claim authority over their distribution and even exclusive ownership rights to them. Hierarchies replaced the generous, if sometimes precarious, affluence of hunter-gatherer life with socially induced scarcity. As Scheidel (2017:42) observes:

> States first arose in those parts of the world that had first developed agriculture: once plants – and above all cereals – and animals had been domesticated, sooner or later humans shared their fate, and inequality escalated to previously unimaginable heights.

In this light, the challenge of the Anthropocene could be this: how to recreate the lifestyle that many people in the first 95% of human history enjoyed but in the epoch of post-scarcity, technological abundance and mass populations. How to share our surpluses fairly might be another way of posing the goal of the people-planet vision of living together beautifully.

This evidence clearly underlines the importance of what I referred to earlier as 'remoderning', going back in history in order to go forwards, and it goes some way to debunking the growthist myth that human progress is simply the progress of human technology. We can take heart from the fact that sustainable, equitable, wellbeing-enhancing social organization may once have been the human norm. Why shouldn't it be again?

The Anthropocene could be the synthesis of history (but beware of the unidirectional fallacy)

One of the most influential interpretations of history – and one which has intrigued me throughout most of my adult life – is G.W.F. Hegel's *Philosophy of History*, originally published in 1836. This adopted an early and boldly internationalist perspective on human history, proposing that it has an 'ultimate design' which is revealed through 'a series of increasingly adequate expressions or manifestations of Freedom', which can be described as humanity's 'absolute goal' (Hegel, 1836/1956: 63, 23). This grand journey, which Hegel also refers to as the realization of reason, takes up all previous phases of culture, from the Orient, the Greek and Roman empires and culminates in the Germanic state – northern European, protestant and monarchical. For Marx, who was inspired by Hegel's audacious vision, the end goal of history was very different and still in the future. This was communism, a state of human freedom beyond the state, which represented the transformation of feudalism and capitalism into a new synthesis. In the 1990s, Francis Fukuyama (1992) drew heavily on the work of French Hegelian philosopher Alexandre Kojève in proposing an 'end of history', a universal condition of human reciprocity, which, he argued, would be delivered in perpetuity by market-orientated capitalism.

In the light of this, it's tempting to see the Anthropocene as the epoch which can actually fulfil humanity's destiny as a journey towards freedom and rationality. As such, it would take up the achievements of all previous phases, the egalitarian ecology of the hunter-gatherer late Pleistocene, the agricultural stability and civilization-building of the early Holocene, and the technology, democracy and personal freedoms of the late Holocene. This would be a synthesis of the best in human history: civilization without inequality, progress based on global cooperation and peace rather than on competition and war, and science that complements nature instead of seeking to transcend it. If we need a big idea to inspire the utopian transformation, they don't come much bigger than this.

At the same time, we must be wary of the complacency of the unidirectional theory of history. If neoliberals are guilty of overestimating the inevitability of the global triumph of free-market capitalism, socialists have often been guilty of over-relying on its inevitable collapse. Nothing is assured in history: it issues no warranties. Progress is not so much a one-way street as a multi-lane highway, issuing into a spaghetti junction of multiple possibilities. As I described in Part II, dystopia could be as likely an outcome of our present world system as any form of utopia, and the thesis that economic growth is inextricably linked to advances in democracy is being sorely tested by the resilience of authoritarian capitalist regimes, especially in China. Many twists and turns are possible, perhaps including some alarming U-turns, on the way to a better world.

We can explore without conquering

The great unlevelling I outlined in the Introduction was promoted by a paradigm shift in values, a negative moral and emotional revolution which we can learn from. The disequalizing impact of agricultural surpluses turned social stratification into the norm for the Holocene. But the development of the sloping world, which occurred around the time *Utopia* first appeared, initiated another dimension in human inequality. A new concept of empire came into being, one which became so normalized that even now, in a largely post-colonial world, we can underestimate the barbarity of the human values it enshrined.

As Yuval Noah Harari explains in *Sapiens*, before 1492 empires had never been based on exploring and conquering unknown territories. The Romans expanded their empire mainly to defend Rome and 'the Persians never attempted to conquer Madagascar or Spain and the Chinese never attempted to conquer Indonesia or Africa' (Harari, 2014:325). In fact, in the early 1400s, China, the largest and most ancient empire of them all, explored the world in seven great armadas consisting of ships much bigger and better equipped than Columbus's tiny vessels. They sailed from Indonesia to the Persian Gulf and East Africa. But it never occurred to them to attempt to conquer or colonize these new territories. They landed in huge numbers, exchanged gifts, satisfied their curiosity about their new cultures and then sailed on. Eventually, the great fleet was dismantled.

This tradition was shattered when the sailors of a few relatively impoverished Western European countries set out to 'discover' the New World. As Harari wryly comments (2014:325):

> The oddity is that modern Europeans caught a fever that drove them to sail to distant and completely unknown lands full of alien cultures, take one step on their beaches, and immediately declare, 'I claim all these territories for my king!'

The conquistadores didn't even know where they were on the planet – Columbus, of course, thought that the Caribbean was west, not east, of India – but that didn't stop them from claiming absolute possession of the land they found, its natural resources and the life of all its inhabitants. They saw nothing of the advanced, diverse civilizations around them except through a materialist prism which translated everything into assets: gold, silver and slaves. A new legal system was rapidly erected to justify treating humans as sub-humans, deprived of all rights.

The attitude of the occupiers led to the elimination through violence, starvation and disease of up to 90% of the indigenous population of the Americas. This event, which David Stannard (1992) has called the American Holocaust, clearly contributed to the birth of the CIMENT, battlefield mentality. To empathize with what it meant to the victims, from a British perspective, we need only to think of the genuine horror, outrage and revulsion evoked by the possibility of a Nazi occupation of Britain in 1940. Three-quarters of century later, it still provokes the most powerful negative emotions, even though, of course, it never actually happened.

What Harari calls the 'fever' of conquest is what I've been calling the irrationality of growthism. And he is right to make the link between this frenzied lust for possession in Western imperialism and the development of science. The British sent armies of ambitious agronomists, archaeologists, geologists, zoologists, botanists, anthropologists and linguists to India to help them rule the colony more effectively. And *The Beagle*, from which Darwin made many of the observations that prompted his theory of evolution, was actually a ten-gun sloop-of-war, engaged in hydrological surveys of Britain's newly acquired colonial possessions.

And the lessons from history? What was once level between nations can be level again – but this time in a way that works for everybody. Curiosity, generosity and hospitality towards strangers should not be seen as signs of foolish vulnerability, as it is for the possessive–aggressive mindset. A new internationalist code of values can promote engagement with other nations and cultures without recourse to material appropriation or economic exploitation. We can explore without conquering.

We can take heart from the 'Thriving Third'

In the history of the sloping world there has been an extraordinary period concentrated around the middle third of the twentieth century. Between 1945 and 1979 many of the indicators of human progress spectacularly started to point in the right direction. That period, which to draw attention to it, I'm calling the Thriving Third, saw a transformation in economic equality in the West, the development of the welfare state and huge progress in health, education and other aspects of wellbeing. Democracy was massively extended, with new electoral inclusions, and new heights of voter participation. The power of the plutocracy was checked by some of the highest income tax in modern history. This happened not simply in rich countries but across the world, in an unprecedented upsurge in equitability. The Thriving Third gives real substance to the claim that an economic levelling can occur planetwide and in a relatively short time frame.

The increase in economic equality in this period was remarkable. Between 1929 and 1972 what Danny Dorling (2017:78) calls a 'second American Revolution' occurred, as the percentage of national income taken by the richest 1% in the U.S. dropped from a fifth to 7.7% – an all-time record low. In the UK in 1978, the equivalent ratio plunged even lower, to 5.7%, and in counties such as France, China and India the pattern is remarkably similar. The CIMENT values significantly relinquished their hold, as cooperative altruism flooded through war-torn Europe and internationalist values came to the fore. This era should not be romanticized – there was a good deal of hard-headed business sense behind the Marshall Plan, for example – but in relative terms it represents a golden age of economic equality.

After 1945, as humanity tried to recover from the war that had come perilously close to obliterating it altogether, social equality also made extraordinary progress. It's amazing to realize that several developed countries (including France and Italy) only granted women the vote after 1945. In the UK, gay sex was decriminalized in 1967, and legislation out-lawing discrimination against people on the grounds of gender or ethni-city was introduced shortly afterwards. The social equality agenda advanced more in three decades than in some centuries – and elements of that positive trend have continued to this day (so far). We shouldn't get too carried away, however; anyone time-travelling back to the 1970s would probably be appalled by the levels of casual sexism, racism and homopho-bia they would encounter there. Nevertheless, the degree of liberation for minorities in the Thriving Third was unmistakeable. For instance, the young ceased to be seen as grown-ups manqué, mere adults in the making, and became people in their own right with a real, and increasingly rebel-lious, identity. This change culminated in the counterculture of the 1960s, when back-to-nature, anti-establishment non-conformity led to a blossom-ing of youthful self-expression and one of the most innovative and politi-cally aware periods of popular culture in history.

International cooperation moved to a higher level than ever before with the development of powerful intergovernmental bodies such as the United Nations and the European Union. For the first time since 1492, Western European imperialism went into reverse. Decolonialism initiated an unparalleled phase of global levelling, which saw the British, French, Dutch, Spanish, Portuguese and Belgian empires rapidly shrink, as territ-ories appropriated over the previous half a millennium were handed back to their rightful owners. Between 1945 and 1984, the UK alone granted independence to some 50 nations across the world, from India, Africa and East Asia to the Middle East and even Europe (Malta and Cyprus).

Even more surprisingly, these newly independent countries were allowed to develop their own economic policies, nationalizing key indus-tries, restricting capital flows and protecting their trade from their old colonial masters. This policy of developmentalism led to what Jason Hickel (2017) calls a 'postcolonial miracle'. Income in the global South shot up and was much more equitably shared than before – for example, in Latin America the gap between the richest and poorest fifth of the population diminished by 22%. Inequality between rich and poor countries was also reduced, with average income in the USA compared to East Asia shrinking by a quarter by the end of the 1970s. Advances in human wellbeing were spectacular, as Hickel explains (2017: 112–13):

Developmentalism also had an impressive impact on human welfare. At the end of colonialism, life expectancy in the global South was a mere forty years. By the early 1980s it had shot up to sixty – the fastest improvement in history. The same is true of literacy, infant mortality, and other key human development indicators.

However, the Thriving Third came to an abrupt halt at the end of the 1970s. What seemed too good to be true for the world's majorities turned out to be too bad for the world's wealthy elite to tolerate any longer. The aggressively neoliberal regimes of Margaret Thatcher and Ronald Reagan swung into action to recover the ground lost to post-war equalization. The 1980s represented a jolting return to the algorithms of capital as the driving force of global development. Extreme financial deregulation and dramatically lowered taxation on the wealthy combined to produce an explosion of new billionaires, especially under Ronald Reagan's presidency. Newly confident CIMENT values rapidly re-inserted themselves into the fabric of contemporary social, political, economic and cultural life.

There followed the huge shift of wealth from the public to the private realm which I've referred to in earlier chapters. Welfare spending contracted and privatizations proliferated, hitting the developing world hard. The World Bank alone privatized over $2 trillion worth of public assets from 1984 to 2012 in the global South (Hickel 2017:171). Developmentalism was slowly crushed by the emergence of a free-market international trade order strongly biased towards the global North. By 2014 in the United States, the CEO-to-average-worker pay ratio, which had shrunk to around 20:1 in the mid-1970s, had steepled to as high as 949:1 (according to an analysis of actual take home pay by Lazonick and Hopkins (2016)). In many other countries the share of national income of the richest 1% reverted to pre-1929 Wall Street crash levels (Dorling 2017:43). The sloping world had returned with a vengeance.

It's intriguing to think what might have happened had climate breakdown and biodiversity extinction emerged as major dangers in the 1970s. Would free-market economics still have won the battle between labour and capital which was fought out in that decade? Of course, the Thriving Third was heavily influenced by the growthist assumption that economic growth is an unalloyed good, but even so, it's worth speculating on how much easier it might have been to build a utopian transformation on the political, social and economic foundations of the 1970s. As it is, we have to take heart from the fact that a kind of equality revolution really did occur, bringing widespread transformation across many of the areas of the SEWP model. This is the most positive message recent history can send us, suggesting that the Anthropocene – which, if you remember, probably dates from 1945 – actually got off to a great start, even if too many of its assumptions (fairly inevitably) were still rooted in the Holocene. Second time round, things could be very different.

History can change fast; ideas and civil society can be the key

Who anticipated the fall of the Berlin Wall in 1989? Hardly anybody in authority. Who foresaw the collapse of the Soviet Union two years later? Very few experts. Most Cold War academics, politicians and intelligence analysts thought that Mikhail Gorbachev's perestroika reforms would stabilize the country. The defeat of a coup against him in August 1991 was widely seen as averting the crisis, and yet, by December of that year, the Soviet Union had ceased to exist.

The truth is that the status quo is often much more fragile than it seems. As the lonely, crumbling statue of Ozymandias, in Shelley's famous poem, reminds us, once-mighty rulers can soon become forgotten irrelevances. And when history changes, it can change at lightning speed. Those in the establishment are often the least able to predict it. In part, that's because these changes often come from below. Authorities are simply not used to taking into account street demonstrations of the kind which led to the collapse of the Berlin Wall, and they consistently underestimate the power of civil resistance.

Non-violent, peaceful movements can have a transformative effect, as we've seen in the case of Gandhi's role in Indian independence. In *This is an Uprising*, Mark Engler and Paul Engler (2016) cite many more examples, such as Martin Luther King's civil-rights movement, which brought about a sea change in attitudes to racism in the United States. In 2011, in Egypt, outrage at rigged elections brought millions of people on to the streets of Cairo and Alexandria and a few weeks of non-violent protest was enough to terminate the corrupt 30-year regime of Hosni Mubarak. Otpor, the peaceful civil-resistance movement in Serbia, which I mentioned in Step 5, also brought down an autocratic ruler, the so-called 'Butcher of the Balkans', Slobodan Milošević. Otpor's sophisticated alliance with traditional parties enabled it to secure a democratic future for its country in a way that proved impossible for the less organized popular movement in Egypt. Another noteworthy example of successful civil resistance is provided by Earth First, a small-scale, volunteer-only, environmental group, which in the 1980s took on the American logging corporations and helped bring about a 78% reduction in logging in US national forests.

Behind popular movements are ideas which reframe the status quo, first in people's minds, then in reality. Revolutionary ideas are often expressed in simple terms – 'liberté, égalité, fraternité', 'black is beautiful', 'we are the 99%' – but these slogans are drawn from careful, patient theoretical formulations, which seemingly overnight can erupt on to the political and cultural stage. At the moment, the people-planet vision, utopian transformation and even, to a great extent, the Anthropocene are still only ideas. But they can rapidly move from the unthinkable to the possible and then the actual, once tipping points are reached. Psychological change can also be like this: a long period of stubborn resistance, followed by a life-changing revelation, an epiphany, a change of heart and mind. When the time is ready, the idea will emerge from the chrysalis of change. And the more it has been worked on, the better it will fly.

We need to learn from dystopia

Finally, a short point on a very long subject: we have to learn from dystopia how not to do utopia. Too many social transformations begin in dialogue and end in monologue. The French, Russian and Spanish revolutions all started in a state of fervent diversity and democratic dissent, driven by a passion for a better world. But they ended ossified in uniformity and centralized hierarchy, governed by a party line that could not be overstepped. At any stage of a political transformation a leadership cult can set in, which institutionalizes groupthink, suppresses alternative voices and punishes dissent by the most extreme measures. Authoritarian leaders may even be prepared to sacrifice the revolution rather than risk losing control of it.

A utopia needs to maintain its ability to disagree with itself agreeably. Of course, it's never going to be easy to balance the need to preserve what has been won against the fearful dangers of losing it all. This can mean choosing between holding your nerve when times are tough and cutting your losses before it is too late. The viability of utopia will depend on getting this balance right. Failure can mean losing all access to the truth as discussion and debate turn into bitter warfare. Once the right to disagree has been sacrificed for the need to preserve the new status quo, utopia is in grave danger of being permanently hijacked. It can be an agonizing choice, but, once inner democracy is lost, everything is at risk.

That's why we always need to keep the possibility of dystopia alive at all times. David Graeber (2004:27) underlines the importance for the egalitarian Tiv society of Nigeria of a lurid mythology of 'occult horror', which helps to prevent anyone from grabbing too much political power. The possibility of dystopia is a vital cognitive tool against tyranny, a reminder of the dark side of the planet that we can't see and of the otherness which we always need to keep in mind. This evil twin of a better world can stop utopia from turning into its opposite. Used correctly, pessimism can be optimism's best ally.

Conclusion: the Anthropocene challenge

So that's the final step of the utopian change plan and I suggest we can be encouraged by what history has to say about its chances of coming to fruition. We've seen that history is full of periods of sustainability, enhanced wellbeing and equalizing change, when many elements of the SEWP

model seem to come into alignment. Putting them all together permanently is what has eluded us so far.

We need to be realistic about the task, of course. In the past, as Walter
Scheidel (2017) has argued, gains in equality have often come about less
by political design than through catastrophes such as war, famine, disease
and violent revolution. It's generally taken something outside human
control to shake the power of the ruling elite. But that's the challenge of
the Anthropocene, to take advantage of our historical epoch to create a
conscious design to replace our current mad world plan, one that allows
the rationality of freedom to return to itself, as Hegel might say. We don't
need the Black Death to bring about the social equality which formed the
remote backdrop to More's *Utopia*, still less the 100 million deaths in the
Second World War which jolted the world into doing something very
different in the Thriving Third. The opportunity exists for us to prove we
have matured sufficiently as a species to bring about the pre-emptive
equalization which will break the power of the Horsemen of the Apocalypse once and for all. What sociologist Ulrich Beck (2016) calls 'emancip-
atory catastrophism' can free us from what we're accustomed to doing, to
do what is right.

This is the challenge that faces us in the Anthropocene. It means rising
to the occasion, rather than sinking in it. It means progress by common
goals and cooperation rather than history by catastrophe. It amounts to
something close to the conscious history-making that would finally prove
Malthus wrong and could even prompt a form of human evolution by
design, rather than by freakish accident. Those who are fittest for the
Anthropocene would turn out to be those who are most able to cooperate
rather than to compete.

Personally, I think we'll get there in the end. We'll keep circling back to
the goals of planetary sustainability (what alternative is there?) and equality (because this will never die out as long as humans are around), until
these goals are achieved. The only questions are: how long it will take
(decades, centuries, millennia?) and what will the cost be in terms of
human and environmental loss. Put like that, the lesson of history for our
now complete change plan could be very simple. If we're heading for
utopia anyway, why take the long way around?

Part IV

Conclusion

18 Make the choice
Utopia versus dystopia

The 13th step

In Part I of this book, I attempted to describe the problem of our current world system (the Anthropocene crisis). In Part II, I provided my analysis of what drives this system (growthism and the CIMENT ethos) and why its business-as-usual trajectory could lead us towards the worst-case solution of a dystopian world. I've now also presented my optimal solution to this unprecedented problem, trying as best I can to describe a utopian change plan for the twenty-first century in 12 steps. All that remains is the most important stage of all, the 13th step, if you will.

The 13th step is the moment of choice. Change is produced by choice – not just a single choice but a succession of decisions. A change plan is not an action plan – it's more general and less detailed– but if it doesn't lead to a decision to act, a strong resolution to turn a set of ideas into reality, it's failed in its purpose.

So to help you make that choice – to decide whether my utopian proposal is a real action you want to engage with in some way, let me step back a little and try to describe this choice in a slightly different way. I'll let you into a secret: this book was originally entitled *Utopia or Dystopia: Our twenty-first-century choice.* As the writing evolved, a new format emerged which concentrated more on the positive and less on the negative, but now that the book is almost finished, I have to admit that my original title, indicating a choice between extremes, still says a good deal about where we are today and the decisions we have ahead of us.

For many readers, it's the extremism of this choice which may be what is most problematic about this change plan. I know it provokes many questions: is the problem we face really so desperate, so potentially dystopian? Can't we continue to have the benefits of economic growth in the West without sacrificing so much? In time, can't the developing world have a Western lifestyle too? And why does the utopian, cooperativist solution have to be so stretching, so demanding, so extreme, in fact?

I'm familiar with these responses. I know that significant changes can provoke anxiety, defensiveness and even anger. This is not only because of my experience as a psychologist in helping people make changes which can sometimes seem like leaping into the unknown, but also because I myself would have harboured many of these doubts a few years ago. So it might help you in making your choices about the future if I give a brief account of how I arrived at my current view of our world situation.

My journey to the Anthropocene crisis

My journey to the Anthropocene crisis began in around 2007, with the first rumblings of the earthquake which would become the 2007/8 financial crash. Major economic breakdowns are paradigm shifters in their own right, and this one ripped aside the veil of stability and the illusion of growing equality which we'd been encouraged to believe in during the long economic boom that began in the early 1990s. In the depressing, distressing, chaotic years of the Great Recession which followed the crash, I began to try to anticipate other possibilities in what now seemed like an increasingly unreliable and uncertain new millennium.

As a psychologist coaching and training leaders in organizations, I devised various strategic exercises for interrogating possible futures. One of these involved bundling together under the mnemonic CAPIT what I thought were largely unconnected problems: climate change, the attrition of nature, population issues, inequality and technology. This acronym (which I've spared you in this book, preferring the broader rubric of the 'Anthropocene crisis') seemed fitting at the time, not least because it was the Latin root word for 'leader' and, as it turned out, even more appropriately, for 'capitalism'. CAPIT first appeared in written form in the final chapter of my book on leadership (Harvey, 2015), which was essentially a meditation on the crisis in leadership in the new century.

The more I pondered the future, the more pressing these problems became, and I found myself being wrenched out of my comfortable professional role as a writer-practitioner. I started to engage with activists, campaigning for action on what I saw as the most urgent and alarming of the CAPIT issues, global warming. Working intensively with climate-change campaigners in the run up to the UN climate conference in Paris 2015, I helped to organize marches, make educational videos and set up fundraising cultural events. Seeing people freely giving their time, energy and talents to a cause in which they passionately believed was an eye-opener in itself, after my years in the money-obsessed corporate world. The open, vibrant commitment to changing the world for the better, which I found in London and Paris, re-invigorated my jaded, professional mindset. It was the start of an intellectual and emotional journey that changed my view of the world, reviving values I'd not held since my younger days.

This new milieu also brought about another revelation: the linkage between the CAPIT issues. What I initially took to be a single issue – the failure to adequately communicate to the general public the dangers of climate change – turned out to be a symptom of a much bigger problem. Action to contain global warming was being blocked by many other considerations, some of them CAPIT issues. As I learned from experienced and dedicated environmentalists, there were many other dangers to our planet beyond what was superficially known. The economic system itself prioritized profit above the wellbeing of the natural world and was creating inequalities and injustices affecting many vulnerable people across the world. Having been involved in high-tech innovation as an entrepreneur in the 1980s, I became increasingly aware of something that even some environmentalists were missing, the possibility that new technology could bring about changes to human life which were comparable in scale to climate collapse and biodiversity devastation. Indeed, as I became aware of the concept of the Anthropocene, a dreadful apprehension began to emerge of a worst-case scenario that could play out in the coming decades. At the same time, a new sense of urgency strengthened my confidence in the best in humanity and inspired me to revive my early interest in literary utopianism and commit myself to the years of research which led to this book.

This was my change of mind and change of heart, and like any personal transformation, it brought about a new professional and behavioural agenda, and a new hierarchy of personal choices and priorities. Radical changes of this sort can be difficult to decipher in retrospect: the totality of the experience blurs the precise identity of the factors involved in the transformation and the relationship between them. So to help you make your decision about what you should take from this book – because that's what really matters here – let me try to break down the complex choice between utopia and dystopia into seven dimensions. Hopefully, these points will also serve as a summary of, and conclusion to, the book.

The Anthropocene choice (waking up to the extremism of our new epoch)

It's almost impossible to understate the significance of the Anthropocene epoch. The human activity which has forged it is raising the stakes for virtually every aspect of life on this planet. Simply understanding the magnitude of these changes is one of the biggest issues that humanity has ever faced. 'Too big to comprehend' could be our greatest challenge in managing the Anthropocene. After all, geological epochs don't come along very often. The Holocene lasted 11,700 years and before that the Pleistocene endured for over 2.5 million years, so this new epoch of ours really should command our full attention, especially as the Anthropocene is likely to continue for as long as human beings inhabit Earth. For the first time in its multibillion year history, our planet has entered into a dynamic, two-way interaction with a force other than that of 'blind' natural phenomena, namely purposeful human intelligence. But just how coherent is that intelligence, and what is its true purpose?

The greatest potential changes are to our climate. That's because a planet doesn't so much *have* a climate: it *is* a climate. Change the temperature of a planet and you have a totally different geological entity, which, for example, could be as cold as Mars or as hot as Venus, and as devoid of anything we would call life as these planets appear to be. It bears repeating that the 3–4°C of warming Earth is heading towards this century, unless urgent action is taken, will create a planetary environment which has not existed for over 10 million years (since the Miocene epoch). Much of what we know about *Homo sapiens* from the past could become irrelevant as we hurtle towards this unknown future.

Even without global warming, the poisoning of the Earth's sea, air, fresh water and soil would be a major threat to our future, and the mass extinction of wildlife, fauna and habitats poses an unprecedented problem. The industrialized agriculture revolution of the past few decades averted the population bomb predicted in the 1960s but at a terrible environmental cost, which threatens the subsistence security of a population likely to pass the 10 billion mark in the course of the century.

Growthism has also produced economic inequality which is now as extreme as anything humans experienced in the Holocene. (The greatest fortune of the Roman Empire was 1.5 million times greater than that of the average Roman citizen or about as rich as Bill Gates is compared to the average American (Scheidel, 2017:4).) But before the Enlightenment, there was no social or political commitment to human equality (the constitution of the Roman Empire did not begin 'all men are equal'). In the Anthropocene, the gap between the theory and practice of economic equality has reached untenable extremes, weakening that other Enlightenment triumph, democracy, and giving new vigour to its ancient enemy, plutocracy. Meanwhile, the cries for simplistic, nationalist solutions to problems of unparalleled international complexity become shriller, appealing to the most primitive emotional prejudices. All of which means that war, that most indefatigable of the Four Horsemen of the Apocalypse, is today busier than ever in many parts of the world, but now armed with fearful new weaponry including lethal drones, cyber sabotage and internet-directed, suicide-based terrorism.

Finally, and incredibly, even if many of the above problems could somehow be magicked away, the twenty-first century would still be left with a voracious institutionalized need for technological development, which threatens to change not only nature but human nature. To complete the picture of a species under unique pressure, we have to factor in potential changes to almost everything we know about what it is to be human, a tsunami of new technology driven not by social need but by the needs of capital. Job automation – replacing not only brawn jobs but also brains jobs – is a step change for humanity in itself and other scientific advances threaten to revolutionize human biology – and perhaps dispense with it altogether, if the transhumanists have their way. Human existence, at its most practical, foundational level, is in question as never before.

In short, our ingenuity, industriousness, curiosity and seemingly incurable desire to make a difference have brought about the most extreme situation humanity has ever experienced. What will be the consequences of the human activity that has created our new epoch for the billions of children alive today, many of whom are expected to outlive this century? What choices will we make and what actions will we take?

This is the Anthropocene crisis – I make no apologies for reminding you of it. This is the problem and we need to keep coming back to it, circling back to the beginning until it can be resolved. Once you glimpse the awesome magnitude of the Anthropocene, you might think it's impossible to forget it. In a sense, the revolution has already happened; the old paradigm has been shattered and everything has changed utterly. But it still needs to be seen – and seeing is itself a kind of choice. It's a choice which growthism wants to keep hidden, as its continued existence probably depends on our not seeing it.

So the first and most important message of this book is simple: stick with the problem, keep exploring it until you have made sense of it. If this book convinces you of the extent of the challenge posed by the Anthropocene, it will have achieved its purpose. You may disagree with my analysis of growthism or my attempts to find a solution to it: that's fine by me. By all means, come up with a more viable version of utopia or whatever you choose to call it. But your solution needs to be commensurate with the problem it addresses. Don't disrespect the problem by minimizing it. Trust in its wisdom. See it for what it is, and the solution will come.

The political choice (who chooses, the leadership class or us?)

The second choice provoked by the Anthropocene crisis – the first being whether to see it at all – is about who should make the decisions that will shape our future. Democracy is intended to be the process whereby the majority of the population make the choices that matter, but my insider experience confirms what many researchers have suggested, that it's a tiny global leadership elite which is making the decisions that shape our future. The so-called wealth creators – corporate bosses, entrepreneurs, super-rich investors and shareholders – have a firm hold on the levers of power and are steering the world in a direction that primarily satisfies their self-interest. This is likely to diverge sharply from the interest of the majority of people on this planet, especially in the poorest parts of the world. This is not necessarily because our leaders are evil – although we've examined the disturbing prevalence of psychopathic behaviour among them. It's primarily because the leadership class simply obeys the rules of a game, which demands the maximization of investor returns and their unequal distribution, without regard for nature.

The global elite can choose to disobey the algorithms of capital, to be sure, and hopefully some of its members will act in a way that is genuinely altruistic. But it's questionable how free a choice this can be for individuals who have often grown up in a bubble of wealth, which is exclusively populated by their friends, families and peers, and separated from the world in which the vast majority of people live. Add to this the feverish irrationality created by the pursuit of wealth, which as we've seen, can turn cooperators into cheating competitors, replace altruism with dishonest sleaziness and even weaken one's cognitive abilities, especially the capacity to see the world from another's person point of view, which is so crucial to good decision-making.

All of this tends to support the view that the global elite will continue to do what they've become accustomed to doing, looking after number one, and being lavishly rewarded by growthism for doing so. In the face of crises, they are likely to prioritize whatever it takes to hold on to what they have – again simply playing by the rules of the sloping world, whose legal system jealously protects unequally distributed private assets. No doubt the ultra-wealthy will take out more insurance policies, in the form of executive boltholes, corporate security forces, private islands and super yachts (which are not merely status symbols but useful in the event of rising sea levels). If global meltdown approaches, the prospect of planetary exit – I have to call it Plexit – will become increasingly attractive to those to whom money is no object. Many billionaires are already investing heavily in space travel and, in particular, in the colonization of Mars. Plexit is the ultimate escape clause for those determined to pursue to the bitter end the mad growthist plan of infinite economic growth on a finite planet.

For the time being, at any rate, the super-rich will continue their normal practice of wealth-planning, making strategic choices to enhance and protect their assets, and taking the bold future-facing decisions which our governments have become increasingly poor at. The global elite will make their choices – be sure of that. The real question is: will the majority let them? Do we go along with these choices, some of which are being made even now in the world's penthouses and boardrooms? Or do the majority make choices of their own, demanding that governments act responsibility in the long term for the good of all, and participating in the bottom-up actions which ensure that a democratic transformation also occurs at a regional and community level? Lead the change or follow the change: that's the political dimension of the Anthropocene choice in a nutshell.

The economic choice (enough tweaking, we need a new system and new goals)

The economic dimension of the choice ahead of us is just as pressing. We need nothing less than a revolution in our economic thinking and practice to live up to the demands of Anthropocene. (And, as I've previously indicated, recognizing the significance of ecological economics has been one of the greatest turnarounds in my adult life). I won't rehearse all the arguments I laid out in Step 3 in favour of a natural economics, which can correct the dangerous imbalances of our current, irrational world system. I'll simply state that tweaking the growthist economic system is no longer viable for the paradigm-shifting situation we find ourselves in. Extreme historical crises present extreme opportunities, and one of these is to replace an economic system which is based on the assumption that multiple planets of natural resources are available to us, as this betrays all of us who exist on the only planet we actually have.

Capitalism, in its mercantile and industrial forms, has been around for at least 500 years and for most of that time humans have been trying to reform it to better suit the needs of the majority. In recent decades the pace of the neoliberal reversion to a nineteenth-century model of capitalism has been so rapid that it would take something close to a revolution simply to return us the mixed-economy capitalism of the 1970s. After the collapse of the global financial system in 2007/8, a golden opportunity for root-and-branch economic reform was spurned in favour of protecting those who caused the crisis. Many different versions of growth-based capitalism have been attempted, but the algorithms of capital have not been dislodged, and the system is now in danger of abandoning its claim to provide the best guarantee of democracy in a world where authoritarian variants of capitalism are becoming increasingly powerful.

Any project reaches a point where cutting its losses and starting again is the only viable option. The millions of hours of engineering time that have gone into trying to rid the internal combustion engine of the toxins that it emits from its exhaust pipe have been wasted. Change the design – for example, to an electric engine – and the problem disappears instantly: nothing comes out of the tail pipe except clean air. As we've seen, 'too little, too late' reformism threatens to facilitate rather than halt runaway climate change. The same goes for tweaking economic inequality. Why invest the massive effort and political capital it would take to decrease the ratio of bosses' pay to the average employee from 150:1 to, say, 120:1? Much more effective would be to start thinking in terms of the Mondragon cooperative's 5:1 ratio or even asking why should there be pay differentials at all. Investing in new social technology of this kind is a more efficient use of our creative resources than expecting machine technology to make up for our failings. Far better to trust in a new economic design, which can bring about permanent, long-lasting improvements, than try yet again to patch up an old system which is bound to crash once more anyway.

That's not to decry attempts at reform – I've been engaged in them myself for many years. Many people in profit-driven companies put major efforts into making these organizations more democratic, ethical and emotionally intelligent. All this is noble work. The revolution in values needed to create a post-growth economy desperately requires these innovative beginnings. In the end, however, you need the right goals to produce the right results. In Step 2, I referred to the almost miraculous transformation which goal-setting can bring about, and often brave new objectives are all that is needed to bring a new paradigm into being. When a system is broken sometimes the only sensible course is to let it break. Every dystopia has a utopia inside it trying to get out; a new economics can enable this liberation to take place.

The authenticity choice (no change is not an option)

My fourth point is that we're heading for dramatic change in the next few decades whatever happens. Staying still is not an option. The extremism of the Anthropocene crisis, and the extremism of growthism's pursuit of unlimited economic expansion ensure a white-water ride to the future. Contemplating discontinuous change can be very anxiety-provoking but breaking with the past is the hallmark of our new epoch. In this context, the changes involved in a utopian transformation can seem less daunting: they're demanding changes, to be sure, but in the West we've become so adept at speedy adaptation that it's strange that we should still underestimate our ability to cope with it.

All transformations involve loss, as one reality is sacrificed for another. This is why making decisions can be so hard for us in life. We are heading for a period of disruption and creative destruction that can't be avoided. But what kind of disruption and creative destruction and in whose name will it be made? These are the core questions. Growthist business-as-usual will almost certainly lead to the loss of climate stability, species depletion and habitat loss, as well as job losses through automation, the disappearance of the traditional countryside and possibly even the fracturing of the genetic unity of the human race. You name it, we could be about to lose it, if growthism has its way.

A people-planet solution will also lead to losses, such as fewer consumer goods, fewer full-time jobs, less luxury and less freedom for the wealthy minority to do whatever they want. But it will also bring gains, such as a greater emphasis on sharing and working together, taking collective responsibility for our planet and our future. Utopian creative destruction degrows what needs to be destroyed and grows something much better: it's disruption that leads to stability which is rational and satisfying, rather than to more disruption for the sake of profit. We're facing hard choices either way. The 'no loss option' is not on the table. We just have to decide which loss is greater – and which gain.

I could put it another way and say what's ahead of us is a choice between utopias, one fake, the other real. After all, growthism claims to be bringing about a techno-utopia, where consumerist luxury is available to all, but how this comes about on a planet heading for climate chaos and environmental depletion is not explained. At best it's likely to be a utopia for the few (and remember every dystopia is a kind of paradise for those at the top), rather than for the many. It's reckless rocket ride to the future, which prides itself on its ability to cause constant disruption and turn mere mortals into billionaire 'emperor-gods', to borrow Cory Doctorow's phrase.

By contrast, people-planet utopianism is for the many, not the few. It's based on rationality – the Latin root of which is *ratio*, you may recall, implying a share of the whole – as well as care for others, respect for the truth and deference to nature. It happens in real, long-term time, not in the magical time of endless novelty; on a real physical planet, not an imaginary, dematerialized environment, which is somehow impervious to brutal economic exploitation; and it happens for real people in every corner of the globe. In aiming to make all its new developments compatible with SEWP-type goals, an eco-democracy sets the bar far higher than lazy technologism, which is careless of the consequences of its innovations. This is the real ambition our historical moment summons forth from humanity and it calls for the highest levels of creativity of which we are capable. In the end, the Anthropocene choice boils down to a question of authenticity. Why choose the phoney utopianism of growthism when you can have the real thing?

The psychology choice (the revolution of values is up to us)

The fifth dimension of choice relates to the psychological revolution in values necessary for a genuine utopian transformation, which throughout this book I've presented somewhat schematically as an opposition between the CIMENT and the CANDID values. What I want to emphasize now is that the difference between these ways of being is essentially a matter of agency. We are capable of both sets of behaviour: what determines whether we take one course or another is not primarily down to nature or nurture but to personal decision-making, although it can be influenced by the way in which these opposing values have been culturally institutionalized.

We've seen, for example, just how easy it is to switch between full-blown competitivism and cooperativism: a simple competitive task can transform the best of friends into the worst of enemies and a common purpose can turn them back again. So which do we choose to be, competitive or cooperative? The same is true of altruism, which can be easily stimulated in people, as can aggressive selfishness. A culture that promotes individualistic materialism above communitarian altruism creates an emotional bias towards CIMENT-type values but we can choose to resist this cultural influence. We can decide to favour, and even contribute to, a culture which celebrates generosity and selflessness.

Even nationalism is simply an interpretative choice about the affection for the people, places and customs which most people grow up with. Is this fondness something that should incite hatred of others who are 'not like us', taking delight in blaming or even punishing them, or should it inspire solidarity with all humans who share this affection? Global consciousnesses can be learned (for some, it's already a reality) but our readiness to commit ourselves to developing the internationalism which our new epoch urgently needs is up to us. Is it nationalism or internationalism that we turn into a self-fulfilling prophecy? There is no more important choice than this facing us in the coming decades.

Utopia is about rationality, as I've argued, but that doesn't mean some kind of machine logic, because without emotions people are unable to make even basic decisions. It may seem crazy, in another sense, to think that human cooperation can ever go so far as to create a world based on equality, peace and harmony with nature. But that's partially because we've allowed the gap between the goal of equitable rationality and our current world system to become so extreme that it's easier to dismiss the goal as mad (or whimsical, delusional or subversive) rather than accept that it's the status quo that is the true source of the madness. Indeed, when compared to the craziness of a system which believes in never-ending material consumption, the desire for a sustainable, equitable world begins to look immeasurably more rational. At the very least, utopianism is a distinctly better class of madness.

The ethical and philosophical choice (utopia is a worthy goal in itself)

Regardless of growthism, or any other relativity, there has always been an absolute case for utopia, a case derived from basic human ethics. The principle of valuing others as much as yourself existed long before the Anthropocene and well before Thomas More coined the term 'utopia'. The goal of a world based on reciprocal respect for human dignity, self-expression and freedom has always been there and will probably remain as long as human beings exist. From this perspective, the Anthropocene crisis is simply a long-awaited opportunity to address humanity's most outstanding piece of unfinished business: how to live together well.

This task has a significant philosophical dimension, in that it requires answers to some of the basic questions which humanity has always asked about itself. The Anthropocene demands a cognitive revolution in all branches of human knowledge, and philosophy, which was once the most central of them, is no exception. The big questions it has always focused on remain unanswered. What is truth? What is the self? What is the purpose of humanity? What is the true role of science? Philosophy has become increasingly marginalized over the past 50 years but these fundamental, existential questions now have a new urgency. No longer can they be interpreted as intriguing intellectual puzzles: they are questions of the most practical, everyday relevance, which should be at the heart of public policy-making. If intelligent machines make all our decisions and provide all our labour, what will humans be for? What responsibility do we have for non-human species in a climate we are altering? Are there any limits as to how far human inequality should be allowed to go? These and many other urgent dilemmas, should force philosophy back to where it started, the public arena, as in the open-air forum in Athens, where Socrates and other distinguished thinkers in the world's first democracy conducted passionate, public debates with their fellow citizens.

At the level of public policy, this is the thinking behind the 'what do we really want?' project I put forward in Step 5. This mass opinion-polling event and worldwide public debate about human identity could open up a true festival of choice and the kind of profound human self-exploration that the Anthropocene requires of us, one way or another. It's a chance – perhaps our last for some time – to decide how we want to use the extraordinary inheritance we all receive by being born human on the only planet in the cosmos which is synonymous with life.

Of course, the results of such a project could be controversial, and perhaps discontinuous and disruptive, in the manner of our new epoch. We may lose some of the philosophical relativism which has enabled us to appreciate that people, to a considerable extent, are who they choose to be. A form of human essentialism may emerge, perhaps recognizing the need for environmental sustainability and socio-economic equality. This wouldn't mean that multiple definitions of subjectivity would have to be abandoned, but it would imply their subordination to overarching, common goals. This choice of the human project would, I believe, be very different from the technologist and transhumanist interpretations of humanity as a species destined to conquer nature which are currently in play. And this human essentialism may prove temporary as the Anthropocene moves out of its early crises into a mature, confident, increasingly diverse future.

In fact, once planetary sustainability has been achieved, a new fluidity of humanity is likely to emerge. By this time, the old middle way may have gone, but as humanity radically decentres itself, a new consensus may begin to flourish. In place of the sloping world, we'd see a more balanced, rational, shared world, a planetwide community which transcends dualisms and all inequalities of gender, class, ethnicity and sexuality. Ursula Le Guin, in *The Left Hand of Darkness*, gives us a tantalizing glimpse of what this utopia would be like:

> Anyone can turn his hand to anything.... Burden and privilege are shared out pretty equally, everybody has the same risk or choice to make.... There is no division of humanity into strong and weak halves, protective/protected, dominant/submissive, owner/chattel, active/ passive.

> (Le Guin 1969:93–4)

Once planetary sustainability is established as a principle driving all science and commerce, and something like the CANDID ethos becomes a lived reality, who knows what technological development may be possible? The Anthropocene may evolve into an epoch that enjoys the best of all that democratically directed science can offer. It could witness the evolution of many compatible forms of sustainable and equitable living. 'Polyutopia' may become the global norm, a flourishing of different models in different contexts, and, yes, in a state of planetwide economic cooperation, bioregionalism could well take over. In fact, a balanced world, centred on common goals, will almost certainly develop a diversity of life and living which is totally beyond our comprehension today.

The optimism choice (the time is right for utopia)

Finally, let's come back to now, the only time zone we can never escape, and where all our choices have to be made. My ultimate argument about the decisions facing us in this century is that the time is right for utopia. In a way, time is on our side. I don't mean by that that we have infinite time to make the right choices. On the contrary, we don't have generations or even decades to make the changes necessary to avoid irreversible climate collapse. The writing of this book has taken place over the four hottest years ever measured on this planet (WMO, 2018), culminating in a year of sweltering heat, raging hurricanes, floods and forest fires. It's a year that has also broken all records for the amount of greenhouse gas deposited in the atmosphere, after a short period of relative stabilization (Le Quere *et al.*, 2018). So it's clearer than ever that we need to make rapid progress towards total global decarbonization in the next decade. As Bill McKibben (2017) says of the struggle against global warming, 'winning slowly is just another way of losing'. And we also desperately need to regulate many aspects of digital, military and medical technology before we completely lose democratic control of it.

No, what I mean by the claim that time is on our side is that it's there is no better stimulus to choice-making than limited time. A bounded temporal frame is often the best ally we have in making tough calls, providing deadlines without which nothing would be completed, concentrating minds, removing distractions and strengthening the will to action. Under the pressure of necessity, the right choices often get made.

Indeed, I believe we are lucky to be alive at this moment in human history. Millions of years have brought us to precisely this point, this unique set of crossroads, where we can see the past and the future, spanning millennia of human endeavour. It's the ideal time to make the epic decisions which can change the future. 'We are the first generation to know we are destroying the planet and the last generation to be able to do something about it', as Tanya Steel of the World Wildlife Fund puts it (World Wildlife Fund, 2018a). Now is the right time for optimism, for believing in humanity, for celebrating the human activity which has created the Anthropocene and for wholeheartedly embracing the best-case scenario for what is to come.

Now is the time for making the right kind of human impact on our planet. The human propensity for altruistic, pro-social behaviour, which I referred to in Step 9, which manifests itself in a desire to help strangers that no other species possesses, could be the foundation for a new era of human kindness. It's time to see our new epoch not as an accident waiting to happen, but as a happy accident, a golden opportunity for the serendipity which has brought about some of humanity's greatest breakthroughs. It could be just what we need to truly start living as one people on one planet.

Setting off on the road to utopia won't be easy. We should be under no illusions about that. It involves a multi-revolution affecting every human institution and practice, from how we work and how we eat to how we relate to one another and how we think about ourselves. But every road to the future is full of uncertainties and every one of them is a gamble. So why not bet on the best in humanity, on our ability to fulfil our creative potential and achieve a democracy of love on our uniquely wonderful planet? To be sure, there will be pitfalls as well as pleasures on the path to a genuinely sustainable and equitable world. But once we are on our way, why would we ever turn back?

References

Aardman (2018) 'Oscar-winning studio Aardman determines its own future through employee ownership', 19 Nov. 2018, www.aardman.com/oscar-winning-studio-aardman-determines-its-own-future-through-employee-ownership (retrieved 14 Dec. 2018).

ABC (2018) 'Syrian War: The boy at the centre of conflicting tales about alleged Douma chemical attack', www.abc.net.au/news/2018-04-28/hassan-becomes-face-of-information-war-surrounding-syria-douma/9705538 (retrieved 27 Oct. 2018).

Abu-Ghaida, D., and Klasen, S. (2004) 'The costs of missing the millennium development goal on gender equity', *World Development*, 32:1075–107.

ADE (2015) '54% of energy used in supply of UK electricity wasted', Association for Decentralised Energy, www.theade.co.uk/news/press-releases/54-of-energy-used-in-supply-of-uk-electricity-wasted (retrieved 1 Sept. 2018).

Adelman, L. (2015) 'Finding an erotic transcendence: Sex in a feminist utopia'. In A. Brodsky and R. Kauder Nalebuff (eds), *The Feminist Utopia Project: Fifty-seven visions of a wildly better future.* New York: Feminist Press.

Adorno, T., Frenkel-Brunswik, E., Levinson, D., and Sanford, R. (1950) *The Authoritarian Personality.* New York: Harper and Row.

Ahir, H., and Loungani, P. (2014) '"There will be growth in the spring": How well do economists predict turning points', https://voxeu.org/article/predicting-economic-turning-points (retrieved 10 Sept. 2018).

Ahmed, N. (2014) 'Exhaustion of cheap mineral resources is terraforming the earth', *Guardian*, www.theguardian.com/environment/earth-insight/2014/jun/04/mineral-resource-fossil-fuel-depletion-terraform-earth-collapse-civilisation (retrieved 11 Sept. 2018).

Allen, M. (2018) 'Sean Parker unloads on Facebook: "God only knows what it's doing to our children's brains"', Axios, 2 Nov. 2018, www.axios.com/sean-parker-unloads-on-facebook-god-only-knows-what-its-doing-to-our-childrens-brains-1513306792-f855e7b4-4e99-4d60-8d51-2775559c2671.html (retrieved 10 Nov. 18).

Allen, M., and Fried, I. (2018) 'Apple CEO Tim Cooks calls new regulations "inevitable"', Axios, 18 Nov. 2018, www.axios.com/axios-on-hbo-tim-cook-interview-apple-regulation-6a35ff64-75a3-4e91-986c-f281c0615ac2.html (retrieved 27 Nov. 18).

Alliance of Democracies (2018) 'Democracy perception index 2018', www.allianceofdemocracies.org/wp-content/uploads/2018/06/Democracy-Perception-Index-2018-1.pdf (retrieved 17 Jul. 2018).

Alvaredo, F., Chancel, L., Picketty, T., Saez, E. and Zucman, G. (2017) 'World inequality report 2018', https://wir2018.wid.world/files/download/wir2018-full-report-english.pdf (retrieved 15 Oct. 2018).

Anders, G. (1956) *Die Antiquiertheit des Menschen Bd. II: Über die Zerstörung des Lebens im Zeitalter der dritten industriellen Revolution.* Munich: C.H. Beck. (Translated into English as 'The Obsolescence of Man', https://libcom.org/files/Obsolescence ofManVol%20IIGunther%20Anders.pdf (retrieved 6 Jan. 2019)).

Anderson, K., and Bows, A. (2011) 'Beyond "dangerous" climate change: Emission scenarios for a new world', *Philosophical Transactions of the Royal Society*, 369:20–44.

Anderson, R. (2009) *Confessions of a Radical Industrialist: How interface proved that you can run a successful business without destroying the planet.* New York: St Martin's Press.

AP (2018) 'Mark Zuckerberg apologies for "major breach of trust"', Associated Press News, https://apnews.com/c8f615be9523421998b4fcc16374ff37 (retrieved 3 Sept. 2018).

Babiak, P., and Hare, R. (2006) *Snakes in Suits: When psychopaths go to work.* New York: HarperBusiness.

Bajo, C.S., and Roelants, B. (2011) *Capital and the Debt Trap: Learning from cooperatives in the global crash.* Basingstoke: Palgrave Macmillan.

Bakan, J. (2004) *The Corporation: The pathological pursuit of profit and power.* New York: The Free Press.

Bakke, D. (2005) *Joy at Work: A revolutionary approach to fun on the job.* Toronto: Viking Canada.

Banerjee, N., Song, L., and Hasemyer, D. (2015) 'Exxon's own research confirmed fossil fuel's role in global warming decades ago', Inside Climate News, https://insideclimatenews.org/news/15092015/Exxons-own-research-confirmed-fossil-fuels-role-in-global-warming (retrieved 20 Oct. 2018).

Bardi, U. (2014) *Extracted: How the quest for mineral wealth is plundering the planet.* White River Junction, VT: Chelsea Green Publishing.

Barnes, P. (2006) *Capitalism 3.0: A guide to reclaiming the commons.* San Francisco: Berrett-Koehler.

Bar-On, Y., Phillips, R., and Milo, R. (2018) 'The biomass distribution on Earth', *PNAS*, 115(25):6506–11.

Barrat, J. (2013) *Our Final Invention: Artificial intelligence and the end of the human era.* New York: Thomas Dunne Books.

Bauwens, M. (2009) 'The emergence of open design and open manufacturing', we-magazine, www.we-magazine.net/we-volume-02/the-emergence-of-open-design-and-open-manufacturing/#.V6MtrfkrLIU (retrieved 4 Aug. 2016).

BBC (2014) 'Languages across Europe', www.bbc.co.uk/languages/european_languages/definitions.shtml (retrieved 1 Sept. 2017).

BBC (2017) 'Climate change summit: Global rallies demand action', www.bbc.co.uk/news/science-environment-29301969 (retrieved 20 Aug. 2017).

Beck, U. (1992) *Risk Society: Towards a new modernity*, New York: Sage.

Beck, U. (2016) *The Metamorphosis of the World.* Cambridge: Polity.

Bellamy, E. (1888) *Looking Backward: 2000–1887.* Boston: Ticknor and Company.

Bellfield, C., Cribb, J., Hood, A., and Joyce, R. (2016) 'Living standards, poverty and inequality 2016', Institute of Fiscal Studies, www.ifs.org.uk/uploads/publications/conferences/hbai2016/ahood_income%20inequality2016.pdf (retrieved 9 Sept. 2018).

Benkler, Y. (2011) *The Penguin and the Leviathan: How cooperation triumphs over self-interest.* New York: Crown Business.

Benyus, J.M. (1997) *Biomimicry: Innovation inspired by nature.* New York: William Morrow.

Berners-Lee, T., and Clark, D. (2013) *The Burning Questions: We can't burn half the world's oil, coal and gas, so how do we quit?* London: Profile Books.

BIS (2016) 'Triennial Central Bank survey of foreign exchange and OTC derivatives markets in 2016', Bank of International Settlements, www.bis.org/publ/rpfx16.htm (retrieved 23 Oct. 2018).

Blake, W. (1863/1977) *The Complete Poems,* ed. A. Ostriker. London: Penguin Books.

Bobadilla, S. (2015) 'Interview with Miss Major Griffin-Gracy'. In A. Brodsky and R. Kauder Nalebuff (eds), *The Feminist Utopia Project: Fifty-seven visions of a wildly better future.* New York: Feminist Press.

Bodkin, H. (2016) 'Sex will be just for special occasions in the future as robots will satisfy everyday needs', *Telegraph,* www.telegraph.co.uk/science/2016/12/19/rise-sex-robots-will-make-people-appreciate-real-thing (retrieved 12 Nov. 2018).

Bodkin, H., Scott, P. and Lowe, Y. (2018) 'Revealed: The first UK area where majority of children are overweight or obese', *Telegraph,* www.telegraph.co.uk/news/2018/04/25/majority-children-now-overweight-areas-official-data-reveals (accessed 2 Nov. 2018).

Boehm, C. (1999) *Hierarchy in the Forest: The evolution of egalitarian behavior.* Cambridge, MA: Harvard University Press.

Bollier, D. (2014) *Think like a Commoner: A short introduction to the life of the commons.* Gabriola Island, BC: New Society Publishers.

Bosely, S. (2018) '"Ultra-processed" products now half of all UK family food purchases', *Guardian,* www.theguardian.com/science/2018/feb/02/ultra-processed-products-now-half-of-all-uk-family-food-purchases (retrieved 20 Oct. 2018).

Bostrom, N. (2014) *Superintelligence: Paths, dangers, strategies.* Oxford: Oxford University Press.

Boulding, K. (1966) 'The economics of the coming spaceship Earth'. In H. Jarrett (ed.), *Environmental Quality in a Growing Economy.* Baltimore, MD: John Hopkins University Press.

Bourdieu, P., and Passeron, J.-C. (1990) *Reproduction in Society, Education and Culture,* trans. R. Nice. Thousand Oaks, CA: Sage.

Bowles, S., and Gintis, H. (2011) *A Cooperative Species: Human reciprocity and its evolution.* Princeton, NJ: Princeton University Press.

Boyle, D. (dir.) (2008) *Slumdog Millionaire.* USA: Warner Brothers.

Braungart, M., and Macdonough, W. (2008) *Cradle to Cradle: Remaking the way we make things.* New York: Vintage.

Breitburg, D. *et al.* (2018) 'Declining Oxygen in the global ocean and coastal waterset', *Science,* 359(6371), http://science.sciencemag.org/content/359/6371/eaam7240 (retrieved 25 Nov. 2018).

Bretos, I., and Errasti, B. (2018) 'The challenges of managing across borders in worker cooperatives: Insights from the Mondragon cooperative group', *Journal of Co-operative Organization and Management,* 6(1):34–42.

Bridge, M. (2018) 'NHS to open addiction clinic for young online gamers', *The Times,* www.thetimes.co.uk/article/nhs-to-open-addiction-clinic-for-young-online-gamers-plqr9fd8s (retrieved 23 Dec. 2018).

Bridle, J. (2018) *New Dark Age: Technology and the end of the future.* London: Verso.

Brodsky, A., and Kauder Nalebuff, R. (2015) *The Feminist Utopia Project: Fifty-seven visions of a wildly better future.* New York: Feminist Press.

Brooke. J. (2014) *Climate Change and the Course of Global History: A rough journey.* Cambridge: Cambridge University Press.

Brookings Institute (2017) 'Maximizing the local impact of federal R&D', www.brookings.edu/research/maximizing-the-local-economic-impact-of-federal-rd (retrieved 12 Nov. 2018).

Brown, M. (2014) 'Peter Thiel: The billionaire tech entrepreneur on a mission to cheat death', *Telegraph*, www.telegraph.co.uk/technology/11098971/Peter-Thiel-the-billionaire-tech-entrepreneur-on-a-mission-to-cheat-death.html (retrieved 20 Oct. 2015).

Brown, R. (1996) 'Intergroup relations'. In M. Hewstone, W. Stroebe and G. Stephenson (eds), *Introduction to Social Psychology*, 2nd edn. Oxford: Blackwell.

Brown, W. (2015) *Undoing the Demos: Neoliberalism's stealth revolution.* New York: Zone Books.

Buchanan, K., and Bardi, A. (2010) 'Acts of kindness and acts of novelty affect life satisfaction', *Journal of Social Psychology*, 150(3):235–7.

Bulletin of the Atomic Scientists (2018) 'It's two minutes to midnight: 2018 Doomsday Clock statement', https://thebulletin.org/sites/default/files/2018%20Doomsday%20Clock%20Statement.pdf (retrieved 5 Nov. 2018).

Busby, M. (2018) 'Killer robots: Pressure builds for ban as governments meet', *Guardian*, www.theguardian.com/technology/2018/apr/09/killer-robots-pressure-builds-for-ban-as-governments-meet (accessed 6 Nov. 2018).

Caballos, G., Ehrlich P., Barnosky, A., Garcia, P., Pringle, R. and Palmer, T. (2015) 'Accelerated modern human-induced species losses: Entering the sixth mass extinction', *Science Advances*, 1(5):e1400253. DOI: 10.1126/sciadv.1400253.

Cadwalladr, C. (2017) 'Robert Mercer: The Big Data billionaire waging war on mainstream media', *Guardian*, www.theguardian.com/politics/2017/feb/26/robert-mercer-breitbart-war-on-media-steve-bannon-donald-trump-nigel-farage (retrieved 25 Oct. 2018).

Call, L. (2007) 'Postmodern anarchism in the novels of Ursula K. Le Guin', *Substance*, 36(2):87–105.

Callenbach, E. (1975) *Ecotopia: The notebooks and reports of William Weston.* New York: Bantam.

Callenbach, E., and Phillips, M. (1985) *A Citizen's Legislature.* Berkeley, CA: Banyon Tree Books.

Campaign against Climate Change (2014) *One Million Climate Jobs: Tackling the environmental and economic crises*, 3rd edn, ed. J. Neale. London: Campaign against Climate Change.

Campaign against the Arms Trade (2014) 'Arms to renewables: Work for the future', www.caat.org.uk/campaigns/arms-to-renewables/arms-to-renewables-background-briefing.pdf (retrieved 6 Nov. 2018).

Carbon Brief (2016) 'How BP's energy outlook has changed after the Paris Agreement', www.carbonbrief.org/analysis-how-the-bp-energy-outlook-has-changed-after-paris (retrieved 5 May 2017).

Cave, A. (1991) 'Thomas More and the New World', *Albion: A Quarterly Journal Concerned with British Studies*, 23(2):209–29.

CfA (2016) 'Google's revolving door (US)', Campaign for Accountability, www. googletransparencyproject.org/articles/googles-revolving-door-us (retrieved 30 Oct. 2018).

Chaskalson, M. (2014) *Mindfulness in Eight Weeks: The revolutionary 8 week plan to clear your mind and calm your life.* London: HarperThorsons.

Children's Society (2018) 'The good childhood report 2018', www.childrenssociety. org.uk/sites/default/files/the_good_childhood_report_full_2018.pdf (retrieved 26 Oct. 2018).

CIA (2018) 'The world factbook: Life expectancy at birth', Central Intelligence Agency,www.cia.gov/library/PUBLICATIONS/the-world-factbook/rankorder/2102 rank.html (retrieved 25 Oct. 2018).

Citizens Assembly (2018) 'The eighth amendment of the constitution', www. citizensassembly.ie/en/The-Eighth-Amendment-of-the-Constitution/The-Eighth-Amendment-of-the-Constitution.html (retrieved 18 Dec. 2018).

Clemens, M. (2011) 'Economics and emigration: Trillion-dollar bills on the sidewalk?', *Journal of Economic Perspectives*, 25(3):83–106.

Climate Transparency (2018) 'Brown to green: The G20 transition to a low carbon economy 2018', www.climate-transparency.org/wp-content/uploads/2018/11/ Brown-to-Green-Report-2018_rev.pdf (retrieved 14 Nov. 2018).

CNBC (2017) 'Stephen Hawking says A.I. could be "worst event in the history of our civilization"', CNBC TV, www.cnbc.com/2017/11/06/stephen-hawking-ai-could-be-worst-event-in-civilization.html (retrieved 10 Nov. 2018).

Coady, D., Parry, I., Sears, L. and Shang, B. (2015) 'How large are global fossil fuel subsidies?', *World Development*, 91:11–17.

Coates, J. and Herbert, J. (2008) 'Endogenous steroids and financial risk taking on a London trading floor', *PNAS*, 105(16):6167–72.

Cohen, D. (2007) 'A desired epidemic: Obesity and the food industry', *Washington Post*, www.washingtonpost.com/wp-dyn/content/article/2007/02/20/AR200702 2001336.html (retrieved 15 Oct. 2015).

Common Cause Foundation (2016) *Perceptions Matter: The Common Cause values survey.* London: Common Cause Foundation.

Coop News (2017) 'How co-ops have a financial and non-financial impact across the US', www.thenews.coop/122909/topic/co-ops-financial-non-financial-impact-across-us (retrieved 9 Nov. 2018).

Coote, A. (2015) *People, Planet, Power: Towards a new social settlement.* London: New Economics Foundation.

Crawford, N. (2017) 'Costs of war: US budgetary cost of 9/11 wars through FY2018', Watson Institute International and Public Affairs, https://watson. brown.edu/costsofwar/files/cow/imce/papers/2017/Costs%20of%20U.S.% 20Post-9_11%20NC%20Crawford%20FINAL%20.pdf (retrieved 1 Oct. 2018).

Credit Suisse (2018) *The Global Wealth Report 2018*, http://publications.credit-suisse.com/tasks/render/file/index.cfm?fileid=77A4E912-A32D-8E84-CC8C 21144CEE52E2 (retrieved 29 Dec. 2018).

Crouch, C. (2004) *Post-Democracy.* Cambridge: Polity Press.

Crowley, J. (2011) '10 junk food brands that made a buck in Iraq', *Business Pundit*, www.businesspundit.com/10-junk-food-brands-that-made-a-buck-in-iraq (accessed 15 Oct. 2018).

Csikszentmihalyi, M. (1992) *Flow: The psychology of happiness.* New York: Harper & Row.

CTSKR (2018) 'Who wants to ban fully autonomous weapons?', Campaign to Stop Killer Robots, www.stopkillerrobots.org (retrieved 1 Jan. 2019).

Czech, B. (2013) *Supply Shock: Economic growth at the crossroads and the steady state solution.* Gabriola Island, BC: New Society.

Daly, H. (1996) *Beyond Growth: The economics of sustainable development.* Boston: Beacon Press.

Daly, H. (2008) 'A steady-state economy', paper presented to the Sustainable Development Commission, UK, 24 Apr. 2008, http://steadystaterevolution.org/files/pdf/Daly_UK_Paper.pdf (retrieved 3 Jan. 2019).

Damasio, A. (1994) *Descartes' Error: Emotion, reason and the human brain.* New York: G.P. Putnam's Sons.

DARA (2013) 'Climate vulnerability monitor: A guide to the cold calculus of a hot planet', https://daraint.org/wp-content/uploads/2012/10/CVM2-Low.pdf (retrieved 12 Dec. 2016).

Dasgupta, S. (2018) 'Risk of sea-level rise', http://blogs.worldbank.org/eastasiapacific/risk-of-sea-level-rise-high-stakes-for-east-asia-pacific-region-countries (retrieved 25 Mar. 2019).

Davies, N. (2014) *Hack Attack: How the truth caught up with Rupert Murdoch.* London: Vintage Books.

Davis, M. (2006) *Planet of Slums.* London: Verso.

Demos (2017) *Mapping and Responding to the Rising Culture and Politics of Fear in the European Union: Nothing to fear but fear itself?* London: Demos.

Der-Karabetian, A., Cao, Y. and Alfaro, M. (2014) 'Sustainable behaviour, perceived globalization impact, world-mindedness, identity and perceived risk in college examples from the United States, China and Taiwan', *Ecopsychology,* 6(4):218–33.

Deutsch, M. (2006) 'Cooperation and competition'. In M. Deutsch, P.T. Coleman and E.C. Marcus (eds), *The Handbook of Conflict Resolution: Theory and practice.* San Francisco: Jossey-Bass.

DeWall, C., Pond, R., Campbell, W. and Twenge, J. (2011) 'Tuning in to psychological change: Linguistic markers of psychological traits and emotions over time in popular U.S. song lyrics', *Psychology of Aesthetics, Creativity, and the Arts,* 5(3):200–7.

De Zavela, A.G., Guerra, R. and Simao, C. (2017) 'The relationship between the Brexit vote and individual predictors of prejudice: Collective narcissism, right wing authoritarianism, social dominance orientation', *Frontiers in Psychology.* DOI: 10.3389/fpsyg.2017.02023.

Diamond, J. (2005) *Collapse: How societies choose to fail or survive.* New York: Viking Penguin.

Dietz, R., and O'Neill, D. (2013) *Enough is Enough: Building a sustainable economy in a world of finite resources.* London: Routledge.

Ding, D., Lawson, K., Kolbe-Alexander, T., Finkelstein, E., Katzamarxyk, P., van Mechelen, W. and Pratt, M. (2016) 'The economic burden of physical inactivity: A global analysis of major non-communicable diseases', *The Lancet,* 388(10051): 1311–24.

Dittrich, M., Giljum, S., Lutter, S. and Polzin, C. (2012) 'Green economies around the world? Implications of resources use for development and the environment', www.boell.de/sites/default/files/201207_green_economies_around_the_world.pdf (retrieved 17 Nov. 2018).

Doctorow, C. (2017) *Walkaway.* London: Head of Zeus.

Dorling, D. (2017) *The Equality Effect: Improving life for everyone.* Oxford: New Internationalist Publications.

Douthwaite, R. (2010) 'The supply of money in an energy-scarce world'. In R. Douthwaite and G. Fallon (eds), *Fleeing Vesuvius: Overcoming the risks of economic and environmental collapse.* Dublin: Feasta.

Dubois, D., Rucker, D. and Galinsky A. (2015) 'Social class, power and selfishness: When and why upper and lower class individual behave unethically', *Journal of Personality and Social Psychology,* 108(3):436–49.

Duhm, D. (2015) *Terra Nova: Global revolution and the healing of love,* trans. M. Winiecki, D. Silverman and J. Baigler. Bad Belzig: Verlag Meiga.

Dunn, E., Aknin, L., and Norton, M. (2014) 'Prosocial spending and happiness: Using money to benefit others pays off', *Current Directions in Psychological Science,* 23(91):41–4.

Dunne, L. (2017) *Lagom: The Swedish art of balanced living.* London: Gaia.

Durant, W., and Durant, A. (1968) *The Lessons of History.* New York: Simon & Schuster.

Dutton, K. (2012) *The Wisdom of Psychopaths: What saints, spies and serial killers can teach us about success.* London: William Heinemann.

Dyer, G. (2008) *Climate Wars.* Toronto: Random House Canada.

Easterlin, R. (1974) 'Does economic growth improve the human lot? Some empirical evidence'. In P. David and M. Reder (eds), *Nations and Households in Economic Growth: Essays in Honor of Moses Abramovitz.* New York: Academic Press.

Easterlin, R., McVey, A., Switek, M., Sawangfa, O. and Smith Zweig, J. (2010) 'The happiness–income paradox revisited', *PNAS,* 107(52):22463–8.

ECIS (2009) 'Microsoft: A history of anti-competitive behaviour and consumer harm', European Committee for Interoperable Systems, 31 Mar. 2009, www.ecis.eu/documents/Finalversion_Consumerchoicepaper.pdf (retrieved 25 Oct. 2018).

EIU (2017) 'Democracy index 2017: Free speech under attack', Economist Intelligence Unit, https://pages.eiu.com/rs/753-RIQ-438/images/Democracy_Index_2017.pdf (retrieved 12 Aug. 2018).

Elgin, D. (2010) *Voluntary Simplicity: Towards a life that is outwardly simple, inwardly rich,* 2nd edn. New York: Harper.

Ellis, E. (2018) *The Anthropocene: A very short introduction.* Oxford: Oxford University Press.

Engelman, R. (2012) 'Nine population strategies to stop short of 9 billion'. In the Worldwatch Institute, *State of the World 2012: Moving towards sustainable prosperity.* Washington DC: Island Press.

Engler, M., and Engler, P. (2016) *This is an Uprising: How nonviolent revolt is shaping the twenty-first century.* New York: Nation Press.

Equality Trust (2017) 'The Equality Trust Wealth Tracker 2017', www.equalitytrust.org.uk/sites/default/files/The%20Equality%20Trust%20Wealth%20Tracker%202017.pdf (retrieved 5 Aug. 2018).

Erikson, E. (1985) *Childhood and Society,* 2nd edn. New York: Norton.

Fairlie, S. (2009) 'A short history of enclosure in Britain', *The Land,* www.theland magazine.org.uk/articles/short-history-enclosure-britain (retrieved 10 Oct. 2018).

Fairtrade International (2016) 'Monitoring the scope and benefits of fair trade', www.fairtrade.org.uk/~/media/FairtradeUK/What%20is%20Fairtrade/

Documents/Policy%20and%20Research%20documents/Monitoring%20 reports/Fairtrade%20Monitoring%20Report_9thEdition%202016.pdf (retrieved 7 Aug. 2017).

FAO (2016) *The State of World Fisheries and Aquaculture 2016*, Food and Agriculture Organization of the United Nations, www.fao.org/3/a-i5555e.pdf (retrieved 12 Dec. 2018).

FAO (2018) 'Save food: Global initiative on food loss and waste reduction', Food and Agriculture Organization of the United Nations, www.fao.org/save-food/ resources/keyfindings/en (retrieved 12 Dec. 2018).

Fatheuer, T., Fuhr, L. and Unmüssig, B. (2016) *Inside the Green Economy: Promises and pitfalls*. Munich: Green Books.

Fehr, E., and Fischbacher, U. (2003) 'The nature of human altruism', *Nature*, 425:785–91.

Felber, C. (2012) *Change Everything: Creating an economy for the common good*, trans. S. Normi. London: Zed Books.

Florentin, D.B. (2016) 'Between policies and life: The politics of buen vivir in contemporary Ecuador', Centre for Wellbeing in Public Policy working paper 5, www.sheffield.ac.uk/polopoly_fs/1.538160!/file/CWiPP_WP_201605_Florentin. pdf (retrieved 12 Nov. 2018).

Foa, R.S., and Mounk, Y. (2016) 'The danger of deconsolidation: The democratic disconnect', *Journal of Democracy*, 27(3):5–17.

Forbes (2015) 'The world's most powerful people 2015', www.forbes.com/sites/ davidewalt/2015/11/04/the-worlds-most-powerful-people-2015/#61e3b64f1868 (retrieved 15 Dec. 2018).

Forbes (2018) 'The billionaires: Meet the members of the three-comma club', www. forbes.com/billionaires/#10516930251c (retrieved 15 Dec. 2018).

Forget, E. (2011) 'The town with no poverty: The health effects of a Canadian guaranteed annual income field experiment', *Canadian Public Policy*, 373:283–305.

Forth (2018) 'Great Britain and stress: How bad is it and why is it happening?', www.forthwithlife.co.uk/blog/great-britain-and-stress (retrieved 11 Dec. 2018).

Frank, B., and Schulze, G. (2000) 'Does economics make citizens corrupt?', *Journal of Economic Behavior and Organization*, 43:101–13.

Frank, R., Regan, D. and Gilovich, T. (1993) 'Does studying economics inhibit cooperation?', *Journal of Economic Perspectives*, 7(2):159–71.

Frankl, V. (1959) *Man's Search for Meaning: An introduction to logotherapy*. Boston: Beacon Press.

Fransella, F., Bell, R. and Bannister, D. (2003) *A Manual for Repertory Grid Technique*, 2nd edn. Chichester: Wiley.

Freedom House (2018) 'Democracy in crisis', Freedom in the World 2018 report, https://freedomhouse.org/report/freedom-world/freedom-world-2018 (retrieved 12 Dec. 2018).

Freud, S. (1920/1984) *On Metapsychology: The theory of psychoanalysis*, trans. Angela Richards. London: Penguin books.

Frey, C., and Osborne, M. (2013) 'The future of employment: How susceptible are jobs to computerisation?', www.oxfordmartin.ox.ac.uk/downloads/academic/ The_Future_of_Employment.pdf (retrieved 10 Nov. 2018).

Frey, C. *et al.* (2016) 'Technology at work 2.0: The future is not what it used to be', www.oxfordmartin.ox.ac.uk/downloads/reports/Citi_GPS_Technology_ Work_2.pdf (retrieved 10 Nov. 2018).

Friedman, M. (1962) *Capitalism and Freedom*. Chicago: University of Chicago Press.

Friedrich, T., Timmerman, A., Tigchelaar, M., Timm, O. and Ganopolski, A. (2016) 'Nonlinear climate sensitivity and its implications for future greenhouse warming', *Science Advances*, 2(11). DOI: 10.1126/sciadv.1501923.

Fukuyama, F. (1992) *The End of History and the Last Man*. New York: Free Press.

Galinsky, A., Magee, J., Inesi, M. and Gruenfield, D. (2006) 'Power and perspectives not taken', *Psychological Science*, 17(12):1068–74.

Gandal, N., Roccas, L., Sagiv, S. and Wrzesniewski, A. (2005) 'Personal value priorities of economists', *Human Relations*, 58(10):1227–52.

Gandhi, M. (1991) *The Essential Writings of Mahatma Gandhi*, ed. R. Iyer. New Delhi: Oxford University Press.

Garnett, T. *et al.* (2017) 'Grazed and confused? Ruminating on cattle, grazing systems, methane, nitrous oxide, the soil carbon sequestration question – and what it all means for greenhouse gas emissions', Food Climate Research Network, www.fcrn.org.uk/sites/default/files/project-files/fcrn_gnc_report.pdf (retrieved 3 Jan. 2019).

Gino, F. and Pierce, L. (2009) 'The abundance effect: Unethical behavior in the presence of wealth', *Organizational Behavior and Human Decision Processes*, 109 (2009): 142–155.

Global Justice Now (2016) '10 biggest corporations make more money than most of countries in the world combined', www.globaljustice.org.uk/news/2016/sep/12/10-biggest-corporations-make-more-money-most-countries-world-combined (retrieved 15 Oct. 2017).

Global Justice Now (2017) 'Honest accounts 2017: How the world profits from Africa's wealth', www.globaljustice.org.uk/sites/default/files/files/resources/honest_accounts_2017_web_final_updated.pdf (retrieved 1 Nov. 2018).

Godwin, R. (2018) 'Triathlons, ultramarathons and ambitious baking: Why is modern leisure so competitive?', *Guardian*, www.theguardian.com/lifeand style/2018/nov/21/triathlons-ultramarathons-and-ambitious-baking-why-is-modern-leisure-so-competitive (retrieved 12 Dec. 2018).

Goldsmith, M. (2007) *What Got You Here Won't Get You There: How successful people become even more successful*. New York: Hyperion Books.

Goodwin, S., Gubin, A., Fiske, S. and Yzerbyt, V. (2000) 'Power can bias impression processes: Stereotyping subordinates by default and by design', *Group Processes and Intergroup Relations*, 3(3):227–56.

Gotham, D., Redd, C., Thaysen, M., Ha, T., Chow, H. and Athersuch, K. (2017) 'Pills and profits: How drug companies make a killing out of public research', www.globaljustice.org.uk/sites/default/files/files/news_article/pills-and-profits-report-web.pdf (retrieved 10 Nov. 2018).

Gov.Scot (2014) 'The land of Scotland and the common good', Scottish Government, www.gov.scot/publications/land-reform-review-group-final-report-land-scotland-common-good/pages/61 (retrieved 12 Nov. 2018).

Gov.UK (2017) 'Community interest companies registered in August 2017', UK Government, www.gov.uk/government/uploads/system/uploads/attachment_data/file/641613/companyListMonthly_Aug2017.csv/preview (retrieved 12 Sept. 2017).

Graeber, D. (2004) *Fragments of an Anarchist Anthropology*. Chicago: Prickly Paradigm Press.

Graeber, D. (2011) *Debt: The first 5,000 years*. Brooklyn: Melville House.

Gray, A., and McLannahan, B. (2018) 'US banks poised for $17billion in share-holder payouts', *Financial Times*, www.ft.com/content/bcf77ea2-6ff3-11e8-92d3-6c13e5c92914 (retrieved 15 Nov. 2018).

Greenaway, R. (2009) 'The wilderness experience as therapy: We've been here before'. In L. Buzzell and C. Chalquist (eds), *Ecotherapy: Healing with nature in mind*. Berkeley, CA: Counterpoint.

Greenfield, D., Inesi, M., Magee, J. and Galinsky, A. (2008) 'Power and the objectification of social targets', *Journal of Personality and Social Psychology*, 95(1):111–27.

Guerrero, A. (2014) 'The Lottocracy', *Aeon*, https://aeon.co/essays/forget-voting-it-s-time-to-start-choosing-our-leaders-by-lottery (retrieved 15 Nov. 2018).

Hansen, J. (2009) *Storms of my Grandchildren: The truth about the coming climate catastrophe and our last chance to save humanity*, London: Bloomsbury.

Harari, Y.N. (2014) *Sapiens: A brief history of humankind*. London: Harvill Secker.

Harari, Y.N. (2016) *Homo Deus: A brief history of tomorrow*. London: Harvill Secker.

Harbaugh, W., Mayr, U. and Burghart, D. (2007) 'Neural responses to taxation and voluntary giving reveal motives for charitable donations', *Science*, 316(5831):1622–5.

Hardin, G. (1968) 'The tragedy of the commons', *Science*, 162(3859):1243–8.

Hardoon, D. (2017) 'An economy for the 99%: It's time to build a human economy that benefits everyone, not just the privileged few', Oxfam, www.oxfam.org/sites/www.oxfam.org/files/file_attachments/bp-economy-for-99-percent-160117-en.pdf (retrieved 17 Oct. 2018).

Hardoon, D., Fuentes-Nieva, R. and Ayele, S. (2016) *An Economy for the 1%: How privilege and power in the economy drive extreme inequality and how this can be stopped*. Oxford: Oxfam.

Hardt, M., and Negri, A. (2017) *Assembly*. Oxford: Oxford University Press.

Harvey, M. (2012) *Interactional Coaching: Choice-focused learning at work*. London: Routledge.

Harvey, M. (2015) *Interactional Leadership: The art of the choice-focused leader*. London: Routledge.

Hawken, P. (1993) *The Ecology of Commerce: A declaration of sustainability*. New York: Harper Business.

Hawking, S. (2018) *Brief Answers to the Big Questions*. London: John Murray.

Heede, R. (2014) 'Carbon majors: Accounting for carbon and methane emissions 1854 to 2010: Methods and results report', Carbon Mitigation Services, www.climate accountability.org/pdf/MRR%209.1%20Apr14R.pdf (retrieved 10 Nov. 2018).

Hegel, G.W.F. (1807/1931) *The Phenomenology of Mind*, trans. J.B. Baillie. New York: Harper & Row.

Hegel, G.W.F. (1836/1956) *The Philosophy of History*, trans. J. Sibree. New York: Dover Publications.

Heidegger, M. (1927/1962) *Being and Time*, trans. J. Macquarrie and E. Robinson. Oxford: Blackwell.

Helliwell, J., Layard, R. and Sachs, J. (2018) 'World happiness. Report 2018', https://s3.amazonaws.com/happiness-report/2018/WHR_web.pdf (retrieved 1 Jan. 2019).

Henry, J. (2012) 'The price of offshore revisited: New estimates for "missing" private global wealth, income, inequality and lost taxes', www.taxjustice.net/cms/upload/pdf/Price_of_Offshore_Revisited_120722.pdf (retrieved 12 Nov. 2017).

Hepach, R., Vaish, A. and Tomasello, M. (2013) 'A new look at children's prosocial motivation', *Infancy* 18(1):67–90.

Hern, A. (2015) 'Experts including Elon Musk call for research to avoid AI "pitfalls"', *Guardian*, www.theguardian.com/technology/2015/jan/12/elon-musk-ai-artificial-intelligence-pitfalls (retrieved 5 May 2017).

Hickel, J. (2016) 'Global inequality may be much worse than we think', *Guardian*, www.theguardian.com/global-development-professionals-network/2016/apr/08/global-inequality-may-be-much-worse-than-we-think (retrieved 10 Sept. 2018).

Hickel, J. (2017) *The Divide: A brief guide to global inequality and its solutions*. London: Heinemann.

Hildyard, L. (2018) 'The new pay ratio rules: How they'll work and why they're needed', http://highpaycentre.org/blog/the-new-pay-ratio-rules-how-theyll-work-and-why-theyre-needed (retrieved 5 Jan. 2018).

Hitchcock, A., Laycock, K. and Sundorph, E. (2017) 'Work in progress: Towards a leaner, smarter public-sector workforce', *Reform*, www.reform.uk/wp-content/uploads/2017/02/Reform-Work-in-progress-report.pdf (retrieved 11 Feb. 2018).

Hobbes, T. (1651/1968) *Leviathan*, ed. C.B. Macpherson. London: Pelican Books.

Hofstede, G., Hofstede, G.J. and Minkov, M. (2010) *Cultures and Organizations: Intercultural cooperation and its importance for survival*. New York: McGraw Hill.

House of Commons (2016) 'Employment practices at Sports Direct: Third report of session 2016–17', Business, Innovation and Skills Committee, https://publications.parliament.uk/pa/cm201617/cmselect/cmbis/219/219.pdf?utm_source=219&utm_medium=module&utm_campaign=modulereports (retrieved 2 Jan. 2019).

HSE (2018) 'Work related stress, depression or anxiety', Health and Safety Executive, www.hse.gov.uk/statistics/causdis/stress/stress.pdf (retrieved 5 Dec. 2018).

Huxley, A. (1946) *Brave New World*. New York: Harper & Brothers.

Huxley, A. (1962) *Island*. London: Chatto & Windus.

IEP (2018) 'Global peace index 2018: Measuring peace in a complex world', Institute for Economics & Peace, http://visionofhumanity.org/reports (retrieved 22 Oct. 2018).

Illich, I. (1971) *Deschooling Society*. New York: Harper and Row.

ILO (2017) *Global Estimates of Child Labour: Results and trends 2012–2016*. Geneva: International Labour Office.

IMO (2014) 'Third International Maritime Organization GHG study 2014', www.imo.org/en/OurWork/Environment/PollutionPrevention/AirPollution/Pages/Greenhouse-Gas-Studies-2014.aspx (retrieved 1 Aug. 2016).

International Rescue Committee (2007) 'Mortality in the Democratic Republic of Congo: An ongoing crisis', www.rescue.org/report/mortality-democratic-republic-congo-ongoing-crisis (retrieved 12 Nov. 2018).

IOM (2018) 'Migration, climate change and the environment: A complex nexus', International Organization for Migration, www.iom.int/complex-nexus#estimates (retrieved 6 Nov. 2018).

IPCC (2014) 'AR5 synthesis report: Climate change 2014', Intergovernmental Panel on Climate Change, www.ipcc.ch/pdf/assessment-report/ar5/syr/AR5_SYR_FINAL_SPM.pdf% (retrieved 12 Aug. 2018).

IPCC (2018) 'Special Report: Global warming of 1.5ºC', Intergovernmental Panel on Climate Change, https://report.ipcc.ch/sr15/index.html, (retrieved 1 Dec. 2018).

Ipsos MORI (2017) 'Veracity index 2017', www.ipsos.com/sites/default/files/ct/news/documents/2017-11/trust-in-professions-veracity-index-2017-slides.pdf (retrieved 11 Nov. 2017).

Ipsos MORI (2018a) 'Fake news, filter bubbles and post-truth other people's problems', www.ipsos.com/ipsos-mori/en-uk/fake-news-filter-bubbles-and-post-truth-
are-other-peoples-problems (retrieved 8 Sept. 2018).

Ipsos MORI (2018b) 'The perils of perception 2018', www.ipsos.com/ipsos-mori/
en-uk/perils-perception-2018 (retrieved 29 Dec. 2018).

Jackson, A., and Dyson, B. (2012) *Modernising Money: Why our monetary system is
broken and how it can be fixed.* London: Positive Money.

Jackson, T. (2009) *Prosperity without Growth: Economics for a finite planet.* London:
Routledge.

Jacobson, M. *et al.* (2017) '100% clean and renewable wind, water and sunlight all-
sector roadmaps for 139 countries of the world', *Joule,* 1(1):108–21.

Jimenez, I. (2015) 'Interview with Ileana Jimenez'. In A. Brodsky and R. Kauder
Nalebuff (eds), *The Feminist Utopia Project: Fifty-seven visions of a wildly better future.*
New York: Feminist Press.

Jensen, K., Vaish, A. and Schmidt, M.F. (2014) 'The emergence of human proso-
ciality: Aligning with others through feelings, concerns, and norms', *Frontiers in
Psychology,* 29 July. DOI: 10.3389/fpsyg.2014.00822.

Jha, P. (2009) Avoidable global cancer deaths and total deaths from smoking,
Nature Reviews Cancer, 9(9):655–64.

Johnson, A., and Burton, J. (2010) 'Water torture: 3 billion litres of water are lost
every single day through leakage', *The Independent,* www.independent.co.uk/
news/uk/home-news/water-torture-3300000000-litres-are-lost-every-single-day-
through-leakage-2034999.html (retrieved 2 Jan. 2019).

Jordhal, H. (2007), 'Economic inequality'. In G.T. Svendsen and G.L.H. Svendsen
(eds), *Handbook of Social Capital.* Cheltenham: Edward Elgar, 2009.

Kakutani, M. (2018) *The Death of the Truth.* New York: Tim Duggan Books.

Kaplan, R. (2000) *The Coming Anarchy: Shattering the dream of the post Cold War.* New
York: Random House.

Kapp, A. (2018) 'Estimating global civilian-held firearms numbers', www.small-
armssurvey.org/fileadmin/docs/T-Briefing-Papers/SAS-BP-Civilian-Firearms-
Numbers.pdf (retrieved 5 Nov. 2018).

Kasser, T. (2002) *The High Price of Materialism.* Cambridge, MA: MIT Press.

Kaza, S., Yao, L., Bhada-Tata, P. and Van Woerden, F. (2018) *What a Waste 2.0: A global
snapshot of solid waste management to 2050.* Washington DC: World Bank Publications.

Kelley, C., Mohtadi, S., Cane, M., Seager, R. and Kushnir, Y. (2015) 'Climate
change in the Fertile Crescent and implications of the recent Syrian drought',
PNAS, 112(11):3241–6.

Kennedy, P. (2006) *The Parliament of Man: The United Nations and the quest for world
government.* New York: Allen Lane.

Kessler, G., and Kelly, M. (2018) 'Donald Trump made 2,140 false or misleading
claims in his first year', *Washington Post,* www.washingtonpost.com/news/fact-
checker/wp/2018/01/20/president-trump-made-2140-false-or-misleading-
claims-in-his-first-year/?utm_term=.dc86d38032d8 (retrieved 12 Oct. 2018).

Kets de Vries, M. (2012) 'The psychopath in the C-Suite: The SOB redefined',
INSEAD Faculty and Research working paper, https://sites.insead.edu/
facultyresearch/research/doc.cfm?did=50923 (retrieved 25 Oct. 2017).

Kets de Vries, M. (2014) 'Pity the super-rich', INSEAD Knowledge, 10 Dec. 2014,
https://knowledge.insead.edu/blog/insead-blog/pity-the-super-rich-3739
(retrieved 20 Oct. 2018).

Keynes, J.M. (1931) 'Economic possibilities for our grandchildren'. In J.M. Keynes, *Essays in Persuasion*. London: Macmillan. Available online at www.executiveshift. org.uk/images/site_graphics/downloads/John_Maynard_Keynes.pdf (retrieved 10 Oct. 2018).

Keys, D. (1999) *Catastrophe: An investigation into the origins of the modern world*. London: Century.

King, M.L. (1963) ' "I have a dream …": Speech by the Rev Martin Luther King', www.archives.gov/files/press/exhibits/dream-speech.pdf (retrieved 5 Nov. 2018).

Kingdon, M. (2012) *The Science of Serendipity: How to unlock the promise of innovation in large organizations*. Chichester: Wiley.

Kishimoto, S., and Petitjohn, O. (eds) (2017) *Reclaiming Public Services: How cities and citizens are turning back privatization*. Amsterdam and Paris: Transnational Institute.

Klein, N. (2007) *The Shock Doctrine: The rise of disaster capitalism*. London: Allen Lane.

Knabb, K. (2006) *Situationist International Anthology*. Berkeley, CA: Bureau of Public Secrets.

Knight, L. (2012) 'The psychology of the rogue trader', BBC Business News, www. bbc.co.uk/news/business-19849147 (retrieved 20 Oct. 2018).

Kohr, L. (1957) *The Breakdown of Nations*. London: Routledge & Kegan Paul.

Kristensen, H., and Norris, R. (2017) 'Worldwide deployments of nuclear weapons, 2017', *Bulletin of the Atomic Scientists*, 73(5):289–97. DOI: 10.1080/ 00963402.2017.1363995.

Kubiszewski, I., Costanza, R., Franco. C., Lawn, P., Talberth. J., Jackson, T. and Aylmer, C. (2013) 'Beyond GDP: Measuring and achieving genuine global progress', *Ecological Economics*, 93:57–68.

Kuhn, T. (1970) *The Structure of Scientific Revolutions*, 2nd edn. Chicago: University of Chicago Press.

Kurlansky, M. (2006) *Non-Violence: The history of a dangerous idea*. New York: Modern Library.

Kurzweil, R. (2005) *The Singularity is Near: When humans transcend biology*. New York: Viking Penguin.

Laloux, F. (2014) *Reinventing Organizations: A guide to creating organizations inspired by the next stage of human consciousness*. Brussels: Nelson Parker.

Lammers, J., and Stapel, D. (2010) 'Power increases dehumanization', *Group Processes and intergroup Relations*, 14(1):113–26.

Lammers, J., Stapel, D. and Galinsky, A. (2010) 'Power increases hypocrisy: Moralizing in reasoning, immorality in behavior', *Psychological Science* 21(5):737–44.

Lane, R. (2003) 'Rescuing political science from itself'. In D. Sears, L. Huddy and R. Jervis (eds), *Oxford Handbook of Political Psychology*. Oxford: Oxford University Press.

Latouche, S. (2009) *Farewell to Growth*, trans. D. Macey. Cambridge: Polity.

Latouche, S. (2015) 'Decolonization of the imaginary'. In G. D'Alisa, F. Demaria and G. Kalis (eds), *Degrowth: A vocabulary for a new era*. London: Routledge.

Layard, R. (2005) *Happiness: Lessons from a new science*. London: Allen Lane.

Lazonick, W. (2014) 'Profits without prosperity: How stock buybacks manipulate the market and leave most Americans worse off', Institute for New Economic Thinking, www.ineteconomics.org/uploads/papers/LAZONICK_William_Profits-without-Prosperity-20140406.pdf (retrieved 12 Dec. 2017).

Lazonick, W., and Hopkins, M. (2016) 'Corporate executives are making way more money than anybody reports', *The Atlantic*, www.theatlantic.com/business/archive/2016/09/executives-making-way-more-than-reported/499850 (retrieved 6 Jan. 2019).

Lee, K., Ashton, M., Choi, J. and Zachariassen, K. (2015) 'Connectedness to nature and to humanity: Their associates and personality correlates', *Frontiers in Psychology*, 21 July. DOI: 10.3389/fpsyg.2015.01003.

Le Guin, U.K. (1969) *The Left Hand of Darkness*. New York: Ace Books.

Le Guin, U.K. (1974) *The Dispossessed*. New York: Harper and Row.

Le Quere, C. *et al.* (2018) 'Global carbon budget 2018', *Earth System Science Data*, 10(1):1–54.

Levine, R., Norensayan, A. and Philbrick, K. (2001) 'Cross-cultural differences in helping strangers', *Journal of Cross-Cultural Psychology*, 32(5):543–60.

Lietaer, B. (2002) *The Future of Money: Creating new wealth, work and a wiser world*. New York: Random House.

Lowenstein, A. (2015) *Disaster Capitalism: Making a killing out of catastrophe*. London: Verso Books.

McEnrue, M.P. (1993) 'Managing diversity: Los Angeles before and after the riots', *Organizational Dynamics*, 21(3):18–29.

McFarland, S., Brown, D. and Webb, M. (2013) 'Identification with all humanity as a moral concept and psychological construct', *Current Directions in Psychological Science*, 22:194–8.

McGee, P. (2017) 'How VW's cheating on emissions was exposed', *Financial Times*, www.ft.com/content/103dbe6a-d7a6-11e6-944b-e7eb37a6aa8e (retrieved 2 Jan. 2019).

Mackay, R. (2002) *Half the Battle: Civilian morale in Britain during the Second World War*. Manchester: Manchester University Press.

McKibben, B. (2010) *Eaarth: Making a life on a tough new planet*. New York: Henry Holt and Company.

McKibben, B. (2015) 'Exxon knew everything there was to know about climate change by the mid-1980s – and denied it', *The Nation*, www.thenation.com/article/exxon-knew-everything-there-was-to-know-about-climate-change-by-the-mid-1980s-and-denied-it (retrieved 1 Aug. 2018).

McKibben, B. (2017) 'Stop talking right now about the threat of climate change: It's here; it's happening', *Guardian*, www.theguardian.com/commentis free/2017/sep/11/threat-climate-change-hurricane-harvey-irma-droughts (retrieved 28 Nov. 2018).

McManus, S., Bebbington, P., Jenkins, R. and Brugha, T. (eds) (2016) *Mental health and Wellbeing in England: Adult psychiatric morbidity survey 2014*. Leeds: NHS Digital.

Macy, J. (2007) *World as Lover, World as Self: Courage for global justice and ecological renewal*. Berkeley, CA: Parallax Press.

Maddison, A. (2007) *Contours of the World Economy 1–2030 AD: Essays in macroeconomic history*. Oxford: Oxford University Press.

Magee, J., Milliken, F. and Lurie, A. (2010) 'Power differences in the construal of a crisis: The immediate aftermath of September 11, 2001', *Personality and Social Psychology Bulletin*, 36(3):354–70.

Mair, P. (2013) *Ruling the Void: The hollowing of Western democracy*. London: Verso.

Manchester University (2013) 'Poor more generous than rich in recession, study shows', www.manchester.ac.uk/discover/news/poor-more-generous-than-rich-in-recession-study-shows (retrieved 6 Jul. 2018).

Manuel, F.E., and Manuel, F.P. (1979) *Utopian Thought in the Western World*. Oxford: Basil Blackwell.

Marshall, S. (1947) *Men against Fire: The problem of battle command*. New York: William Morrow & Co.

Maslow, A. (1971) *The Farther Reaches of Human Nature*. New York: Viking Press.

Mason, P. (2015) *Postcapitalism: A guide to our future*. London: Allen Lane.

Matthews, L. (2010) 'Cap and share: Simple is beautiful'. In R. Douthwaite and G. Fallon (eds), *Fleeing Vesuvius: Overcoming the risks of economic and environmental collapse*. Dublin: Feasta.

Max-Neef, M. (1991) *Human Scale Development: Conception, application and further reflections*. New York, Apex Press.

Mazower, M. (2012) *Governing the World: The history of an idea from 1815 to the present*. New York: Penguin Books.

Mazzucato, M. (2013) *The Entrepreneurial State: Debunking public vs private sector myths*. London: Anthem Press.

Meadows, D. (1998) *Indicators and Information Systems for Sustainable Development: A report to the Balatan Group*. Hartland Four Corners, VT: Sustainability Institute.

Meadows, D. (2008) *Thinking in Systems: A primer*. White River Junction, VT: Chelsea Green Publishing.

Meadows, D., Meadows, D.L., Randers, J. and Behrens, W. (1972) *The Limits to Growth: A report for the Club of Rome's project on the predicament of mankind*. New York: Universe Books.

Meltzer, G. (2015) *Findhorn Reflections: A very personal take on life inside the famous spiritual community and ecovillage*. n.p.: CreateSpace.

Mento, A., Steel, R. and Karren, R. (1987) 'A meta-analytic study of the effects of goal-setting on task performance, 1966–1984', *Organizational Behaviour and Human Decision Processes*, 39(1):52–83.

Merleau-Ponty, M. (1962) *The Phenomenology of Perception*, trans. C. Smith. London: Routledge & Kegan Paul.

Met Office (2015) 'Global average temperature 2015', www.metoffice.gov.uk/research/news/2015/global-average-temperature-2015 (retrieved 10 Oct. 2018).

Miller, A. (1985) *For Your Own Good: Hidden cruelty in child-rearing and the roots of violence*, trans. H. Hannum. New York: Farrar, Strauss and Giroux.

Molinsky, A., Grant, A. and Margolis, J. (2012) 'The bedside manner of Homo economicus: How and why priming an economic schema reduces compassion', *Organization Behaviour and Human Decision Processes*, 119(1):27–37.

Monbiot, G. (2004) *The Age of Consent: Manifesto for a new world order*. London: Harper Perennial.

Monbiot, G. (2017) 'The meat of the matter', www.monbiot.com/2017/10/06/the-meat-of-the-matter (retrieved 19 Nov. 2018).

Moravec, H. (1988) *Mind Children: The future of robot and human intelligence*. Cambridge, MA: Harvard University Press.

More, M. (2013) 'The philosophy of transhumanism'. In M. More and N. Vita-More (eds), *The Transhumanist Reader: Classical and contemporary essays on the science, technology and philosophy of the human future*. London: Wiley Blackwell.

More, T. (1516/2012) *Utopia*, trans. D. Baker-Smith. London: Penguin Books.

Morgano, B., Potapov, P., Turbanobva, S., Stolle, F. and Hansen, M. (2014) 'Primary forest cover loss in Indonesia over 2000–2012', *Nature Climate Change*, 4:730–35.

Morozow, E. (2013) *To Save Everything Click Here: Technology, solutionism and the urge to fix problem that don't exist*, London: Allen Lane.

Morris, C. (2016) 'Share of German citizen renewable energy shrinking', Energy Transition, https://energytransition.org/2018/02/share-of-german-citizen-renewable-energy-shrinking (retrieved 11 Jan. 2019).

Morris, W. (1890/1993) *News from Nowhere and Other Writings.* London: Penguin Books.

Mulligan, M. (2015) *An Introduction to Sustainability: Environmental, social and personal perspectives.* London: Routledge.

Murray, D., and Raynolds, L. (2007) 'Globalization and its antinomies: Negotiating a fair trade movement'. In L. Raynolds, D. Murray and J. Wilkinson (eds), *Fair Trade: The challenges of transforming globalization.* London: Routledge.

National Audit Office (2010) *Managing Offenders on Short Custodial Sentences.* London: The Stationery Office.

NEF (2010) '21 hours: The case for a shorter working week', New Economics Foundation, https://neweconomics.org/2010/02/21-hours (retrieved 12 Oct. 2016).

NEF (2018) 'Happy Planet Index', New Economics Foundation, http://happyplanetindex.org (retrieved 7 Jul. 2018).

Neil, A.S. (1962) *Summerhill.* London: Victor Gollancz.

Nietzsche, F. (1888/1954) *Der Antichrist: Fluch auf das Christentum,* Munich: Hanser.

Nietzsche, F. (1889/1968) *Twilight of the Idols and the Anti-Christ,* trans. R. Hollingdale. London: Penguin Books.

NOAA (2017) 'Global and regional sea level rise scenarios for the United States', National Oceanic and Atmospheric Administration, https://tidesandcurrents.noaa.gov/publications/techrpt83_Global_and_Regional_SLR_Scenarios_for_the_US_final.pdf (retrieved 12 Oct. 2018).

Nowak, M. (2011) *Super Cooperators: Beyond the survival of the fittest: Why cooperation, not competition, is the key to life.* New York: Free Press.

NRI (2015) '49% of the Japanese working population can be replaced by artificial intelligence and robots', Nomura Research Institute, www.nri.com/jp/news/2015/151202_1.aspxt (retrieved 15 Oct. 2017).

Ochner, C., Tsai, A., Kushner, R., and Wadden, T. (2015) 'Treating obesity seriously: When recommendations for lifestyle change confront biological adaptations', *Lancet Diabetes and Endocrinology,* 3(4):232–4.

O'Connell, M. (2017) *To be a Machine: Adventures among cyborgs, utopians, hackers, and the futurists solving the modest problem of death.* London: Granta.

Ok, C. (2015) 'Interview with Cindy Ok'. In A. Brodsky and R. Kauder Nalebuff (eds), *The Feminist Utopia Project: Fifty-seven visions of a wildly better future.* New York: Feminist Press.

O'Neill, D. (2015) 'Gross domestic product'. In G. D'Alisa, F. Demaria and G. Kalis (eds), *Degrowth: A vocabulary for a new era.* London: Routledge.

ONS (2015) 'Measuring national well-being: Insights into children's mental health and well-being', Office for National Statistics, www.ons.gov.uk/peoplepopulationandcommunity/wellbeing/articles/measuringnationalwellbeing/2015-10-20 (retrieved 17 Dec. 2017).

ONS (2018) 'Sexual offences in England and Wales year ending 2017', www.ons.gov.uk/peoplepopulationandcommunity/crimeandjustice/articles/sexualoffencesinenglandandwales/yearendingmarch2017#how-prevalent-are-sexual-assaults (retrieved 17 Nov. 2018).

OPEC (2018) 'World oil outlook 2018', Organization of the Petroleum Exporting Countries, https://woo.opec.org/pdf-download/index.php (retrieved 30 Dec. 2018).

Oreskes, N., and Conway, E. (2010) *Merchants of Doubt: How a handful of scientists obscure the truth on issues from tobacco smoke to global warming.* New York: Bloomsbury Press.

Orwell, G. (1949) *Nineteen Eighty-Four.* London: Secker and Warburg.

Oster, E. (2004) 'Witchcraft, weather and economic growth in Renaissance Europe', *Journal of Economic Perspectives*, 18(1):215–28.

Ostrom, E. (1990) *Governing the Commons: The evolution of institutions for collective action.* Cambridge: Cambridge University Press.

Otake, K., Shimai, S., Tanaka-Masumi, J., Otsui, K. and Frederickson, B. (2006) 'Happy people become happier through kindness: A counting kindnesses intervention', *Journal of Happiness Studies*, 7(3):361–75.

Oxfam (2015) 'Extreme carbon inequality', www.oxfam.org/sites/www.oxfam.org/files/file_attachments/mb-extreme-carbon-inequality-021215-en.pdf (retrieved 7 Nov. 2018).

Paech, N. (2012) *Liberation from Excess: The road to a post-growth economy*, trans. B. Liebelt. Munich: Oekom Verlag.

Paine, C. (dir.) (2006) *Who Killed the Electric Car?* USA: Sony Pictures Classics.

Parliament of the World's Religions (1993) 'Declaration towards a global ethic', https://parliamentofreligions.org/pwr_resources/_includes/FCKcontent/File/TowardsAGlobalEthic.pdf (retrieved 7 Aug. 2017).

Pearce, F. (2011) *Peoplequake: Mass migrations, aging nations and the coming people crash.* London: Transworld.

Peters, T. (1997) 'The brand called You', *Fast Company Magazine*, www.fastcompany.com/28905/brand-called-you (retrieved 30 Oct. 2018).

Pew Research Center (2018a) 'Trends in party affiliation among demographic groups', www.people-press.org/2018/03/20/1-trends-in-party-affiliation-among-demographic-groups (retrieved 29 Dec. 2018).

Pew Research Center (2018b) 'An examination of the 2016 electorate, based on validated voters', www.people-press.org/2018/08/09/an-examination-of-the-2016-electorate-based-on-validated-voters (retrieved 30 Dec. 2018).

Picketty, T., and Saez, E. (2012) 'A theory of optimal capital taxation', National Bureau of Economic Research, www.nber.org/papers/w17989 (retrieved 19 Oct. 2017).

Piercy, M. (1976) *Woman on the Edge of Time.* New York: Alfred A. Knopf.

Piff, P., Kraus, M., Côté, S., Cheng, B. and Keltner, D. (2010) 'Having less, giving more: The influence of social class on prosocial behavior', *Journal of Personality and Social Psychology*, 99(5):771–84.

Piff, P., Stancato, D., Côté, S., Mendoza-Denton, R. and Keltner, D. (2012) 'Higher social class predicts increased unethical behaviour', *PNAS*, 109(11):4086–91.

Pike, G., and Selby, D. (1999) *In the Global Classroom*, vol. 1. Toronto: Pippin Publishing.

Pimentel, D., Ayamr, I. and Lawson, M. (2018) 'Reward work, not wealth', Oxfam, https://d1tn3vj7xz9fdh.cloudfront.net/s3fs-public/file_attachments/bp-reward-work-not-wealth-220118-en.pdf (retrieved 2 Jan. 2019).

Politifact (2017) 'Does Donald Trump's cabinet collectively own more than what a third of Americans do?' www.politifact.com/truth-o-meter/statements/2017/

mar/27/charles-schumer/does-trumps-cabinet-own-more-13-Americans (retrieved 18 Nov. 2017).

Pomeranz, K. (2001) *The Great Divergence: China, Europe and the making of the modern world economy.* Princeton, NJ: Princeton University Press.

Potsdam (2016) 'Sea level rise past and future', Potsdam Institute for Climate Impact Research, www.pik-potsdam.de/news/press-releases/sea-level-rise-past-and-future-robust-estimates-for-coastal-planners (retrieved 1 Oct. 2018).

Princen, T. (2005) *The Logic of Sufficiency.* Cambridge, MA: MIT Press.

Proto, E., and Rustichini, A. (2013) 'A reassessment of the relationship between GDP and life satisfaction', *PLOS ONE,* 8(11). DOI: 10.1371/journal.pone.0079358.

Putnam, R. (2000) *Bowling Alone: The collapse and revival of American community.* New York: Simon & Schuster.

Quarter, J. (2000) *Beyond the Bottom Line: Socially innovative business owners.* Westport, CT: Quantum Books.

Rand, A. (1957) *Atlas Shrugged.* New York: Random House.

Raskin, P., Banuri, T., Gallopin, G., Gutman, P., Hammond, A., Kates, R. and Swart, R. (2002) *The Great Transition: The promise and lure of the times ahead: A report of the Global Scenario Group.* Boston: Stockholm Environment Institute, https://greattransition.org/documents/Great_Transition.pdf (retrieved 10 Mar. 2019).

Raworth, K. (2017) *Doughnut Economics: Seven ways to think like a 21st-century economist.* London: Random House Business Books.

Raynolds, L., and Murray, D. (2007) 'Fair trade: Contemporary challenges and future prospects'. In L. Raynolds, D. Murray and J. Wilkinson (eds), *Fair Trade: The challenges of transforming globalization.* London: Routledge.

Rees, M. (2003) *Our Final Century: Will civilisation survive the twenty-first century?* London: Arrow.

Ridley, M. (2010) *The Rational Optimist: How prosperity evolves.* London: Fourth Estate.

Ridley-Duff, R., and Bull, M. (2011) *Understanding Social Enterprise: Theory and practice.* London: Sage.

Rigaud, K.K. *et al.* (2018) *Groundswell: Preparing for internal climate migration,* Washington DC: World Bank. Available online at https://openknowledge.worldbank.org /handle/10986/29461 (retrieved 12 Mar. 2019).

Ripple, W., Wolf, C., Newsome, T., Galetti, M., Alamgir, M., Crist, E., Mahmoud, M. and Laurance, W. (2017) 'World scientists' warning to humanity: A second notice', *BioScience,* 67(12):1026–8. DOI: 10.1093/biosci/bix125.

Robbiou du Pont, Y., and Meinshausen, M. (2018) 'Warming assessment of the bottom-up Paris Agreement emissions pledges', *Nature Communications,* 9, www.nature.com/articles/s41467-018-07223-9 (retrieved 9 Mar. 2019).

Robertson, B. (2015) *Holacracy: The revolutionary management system that abolishes hierarchy.* New York: Portfolio Penguin.

Ross, A. (2018) 'New movement aims to cajole UK wealthy to donate more to charity', *Financial Times,* www.ft.com/content/c2dbb3ca-812c-11e8-bc55-50daf11b720d?segmentid=acee4131-99c2-09d3-a635-873e61754ec6 (retrieved 12 Dec. 2018).

Rousseau, J.-J. (1754/1984) *A Discourse on Inequality,* trans. M. Cranston. London: Penguin Books.

Ruskin, J. (1860/1985) *Unto this Last and Other Writings.* London: Penguin Books.

Russ, J. (1975) *The Female Man.* New York: Bantam Books.

Ryff, C., and Krueger, R. (eds) (2018) *Oxford Handbook of Integrative Health Science.* New York: Oxford University Press.

Saez, E., and Zucman, G. (2014) 'Wealth inequality in the United States since 1913: Evidence in the form of capitalized income data', National Bureau of Economic Research working paper 20625, www.nber.org/papers/w20625 (retrieved 12 Mar. 2019).

Sahlins, M. (1972) *Stone Age Economics.* Chicago: Aldine Atherton.

Sample, I. (2015) 'Future of human gene editing to be decided at landmark summit', *Guardian,* www.theguardian.com/science/2015/nov/28/future-human-gene-editing-landmark-summit-dna-crispr-embryos (retrieved 20 Aug. 2018).

Sartre, J.-P. (1958) *Being and Nothingness: An essay on phenomenological ontology,* trans. H. Barnes. London: Methuen.

Scharmer, C.O. (2009) *Theory U: Learning from the future as it emerges.* San Francisco: Berrett-Koehler.

Scheidel, W. (2017) *The Great Leveler: Violence and the history of inequality from the stone age to the twenty-first century.* Princeton, NJ: Princeton University Press.

Schein, S. (2015) *A New Psychology for Sustainability Leadership: The hidden power of ecological worldviews.* Sheffield: Greenleaf Publishing.

Schmidt, M., and Sommerville, J. (2011) 'Fairness expectations and altruistic sharing in 15-month-old human infants', *PLOS ONE,* 6(10). DOI: 10.1371/journal.pone.002322.

Schor, J. (1991) *The Overworked American: The unexpected decline of leisure.* New York: Basic Books.

Schor, J. (2015) 'Work sharing'. In G. D'Alisa, F. Demaria and G. Kalis (eds), *Degrowth: A vocabulary for a new era.* London: Routledge.

Schumacher, E.F. (1973) *Small is Beautiful: A study of economics as if people mattered.* London: Blond and Briggs.

Schumpeter, J. (1942) *Capitalism, Socialism and Democracy.* New York: Harper & Bros.

Schwab, K. (2016) *The Fourth Industrial Revolution.* Geneva: World Economic Forum.

Sedlacek, T. (2011) *The Economics of Good and Evil: The quest for economic meaning from Gilgamesh to Wall Street.* Oxford: Oxford University Press.

Seeds for Change (2017) *Short Guide to Consensus Decision-Making,* www.seedsforchange.org.uk/shortconsensus.pdf (retrieved 12 Nov. 2018).

Sennett, R. (2012) *Together: The rituals, pleasures and politics of cooperation.* London: Allen Lane.

Shen, Y. (2018) 'Moshe Safdie's Chongqing project sets world record with highest "horizontal skyscraper"', *ArchDaily,* www.archdaily.com/889744/moshe-safdies-sets-world-record-with-highest-horizontal-skyscraper (retrieved 18 Apr. 2018).

Sherif, M. (1966) *Group Conflict and Co-operation: Their social psychology.* London: Routledge & Kegan Paul.

Silver, L.M (1998) *Remaking Eden: Cloning and beyond in a Brave New World.* London: Weidenfeld & Nicholson.

Simms, A. (2007) *Tescopoly: How one shop came out on top and why it matters.* London: Constable and Robinson.

Simms, A. (2013) *Cancel the Apocalypse: The new path to prosperity.* London: Little, Brown.

Simms, A. (2017) ' "A cat in hell's chance": Why we're losing the battle to keep global warming below 2C', *Guardian,* www.theguardian.com/environment/

2017/jan/19/cat-in-hells-chance-why-losing-battle-keep-global-warming-2c-climate-change (retrieved 20 May 2017).

Simons, D., and Chabris, C. (1999) 'Gorillas in our midst: Sustained inattentional blindness for dynamic events', *Perception*, 28(9):1059–74.

Sinclair, U. (1935) *I, Candidate for Governor: And how I got licked.* New York: Farrar and Rinehart.

Skinner, B.F. (1948) *Walden Two.* New York: Macmillan.

Smith, P., and Hofmann, W. (2016) 'Power in everyday life', *PNAS*, 113(36): 10043–8.

Social Metrics Commission (2018) 'Measuring poverty: A new measure of poverty for the UK', http://socialmetricscommission.org.uk/MEASURING-POVERTY-FULL_REPORT.pdf (retrieved 18 Nov. 2018).

Solnit, R. (2009) *A Paradise Built in Hell: The extraordinary communities that rise in disaster.* New York: Viking Penguin.

Speck, J. (2012) *Walkable City: How downtown can save America one step at a time.* New York: North Point Press.

Spinelli, E. (2015) *Practising Existential Therapy: The relational world*, 2nd edn. London: Sage.

Stacey, K., and Nicolaou, A. (2017) 'Stitched up by robots: The threat to emerging economies', *Financial Times*, www.ft.com/content/9f146ab6-621c-11e7-91a7-502f7ee26895 (retrieved 22 Oct. 2018).

Stannard, D. (1992) *American Holocaust: The conquest of the New World.* Oxford: Oxford University Press.

Statista (2018) 'Global advertising spending from 2010 to 2018', www.statista.com/statistics/236943/global-advertising-spending (retrieved 8 Aug. 2018).

Steffen, W. *et al.* (2015) 'Planetary boundaries: Guiding human development on a changing planet', *Science*, 347(6223). DOI: 10.1126/science.1259855.

Stern, N. (2006) *Stern Review on the Economics of Climate Change.* London: HM Treasury.

Stiglitz, J. (2012) *The Price of Inequality.* New York: W.W. Norton and Company.

Stone, O. (dir.) (1987) *Wall Street.* USA: 20th Century Fox.

Strutner, S. (2015) 'America has more self-storage faculties than McDonalds, because apparently we're all hoarders', *Huffington Post*, www.huffingtonpost.co.uk/entry/self-storage-mcdonalds_n_7107822 (retrieved 22 Oct. 2017).

Sullivan, D. (2010) 'Why Pittsburgh real estate never crashes: The tax reform that stabilised a city's economy'. In R. Douthwaite and G. Fallon (eds), *Fleeing Vesuvius: Overcoming the risks of economic and environmental collapse.* Dublin: Feasta.

Sutton Trust (2016) 'Leading people 2016: The educational backgrounds of the UK professional elite', www.suttontrust.com/wp-content/uploads/2016/02/Leading-People_Feb16.pdf (retrieved 4 Nov. 2018).

Swift, R. (2017) 'Whose streets? The clampdown on popular rights', *New Internationalist*, https://newint.org/features/2017/12/01/shrinking-political-space (retrieved 14 Nov. 2018).

Tannen, D. (1992) *You Just Don't Understand: Women and men in conversation.* London: Virago.

Tharoor, S. (2017) *Inglorious Empire: What the British did to India.* London: Hurst and Company.

Thatcher, M. (1987) 'Interview with Douglas Keay', *Woman's Own*, 23 Sept. 1987, www.margaretthatcher.org/document/106689 (retrieved 1 Oct. 2016).

Thoreau, H.D. (1854/1997) *Walden*. Boston: Beacon Press.

Timberg, S. (2008) 'The novel that predicted Portland', *New York Times*, www.nytimes.com/2008/12/14/fashion/14ecotopia.html?pagewanted=2&_r (retrieved 1 Jul. 2017).

Tobaccofreekids (2018) 'The global cigarette industry', www.tobaccofreekids.org/assets/global/pdfs/en/Global_Cigarette_Industry_pdf.pdf (retrieved 1 Jan. 2019).

Tomasello, M. (2009) *Why We Cooperate*. Boston: MIT Press.

TUC (2015) 'Nearly a third of people bullied at work', Trades Union Congress, 16 Nov. 2015, www.tuc.org.uk/news/nearly-third-people-are-bullied-work-says-tuc (retrieved 7 Aug. 2017).

Twenge, J., Sherman, R. and Wells, B. (2017) 'Declines in sexual frequency among American adults, 1989–2014', *Archives of Sexual Behavior*, 46(8) DOI: 10.1007/s10508-017-0953-1.

UBS (2018) 'Billionaires report 2018: New visionaries and the Chinese century', Union Bank of Switzerland, www.ubs.com/global/en/wealth-management/uhnw/billionaires-report.html (retrieved 1 Jan. 2019).

Uhls, Y., and Greenfield, P. (2011) 'The rise of fame: An historical content analysis', *Cyberpsychology: Journal of Psychosocial Research on Cyberspace*, 5(1), https://cyberpsychology.eu/article/view/4243/3289 (retrieved 1 Oct. 2018).

UN (2001) 'Urbanization: Fact and figures', *Urban Millennium, Istanbul+5*, United Nations Centre for Human Settlement, www.un.org/ga/Istanbul+5/booklet4.pdf (retrieved 7 Sept. 2018).

UN (2015a) 'World population prospects, 2015 revision', United Nations, https://esa.un.org/unpd/wpp/Publications/Files/Key_Findings_WPP_2015.pdf (retrieved 1 Jun. 2018).

UN (2015b) 'Transforming our world: The 2030 agenda for sustainable development', United Nations, https://sustainabledevelopment.un.org/content/documents/21252030%20Agenda%20for%20Sustainable%20Development%20web.pdf (retrieved 12 Nov. 2018).

UN (2017) 'The international migration report 2017', United Nations, www.un.org/development/desa/publications/international-migration-report-2017.html (retrieved 20 Oct. 2018).

UNESCO (2016) 'Global literacy trends today', United Nations Educational, Scientific and Cultural Organization, http://uis.unesco.org/sites/default/files/documents/fs38-50th-anniversary-of-international-literacy-day-literacy-rates-are-on-the-rise-but-millions-remain-illiterate-2016-en.pdf (retrieved 8 Nov. 2017).

UNFCCC (1992) 'United Nations framework convention on climate change', http://unfccc.int/files/essential_background/background_publications_htmlpdf/application/pdf/conveng.pdf (retrieved 15 Oct. 2018).

UNHCR (2016) 'Frequently asked questions on climate change and disaster displacement', United Nations High Commissioner for Refugees, http://www.unhcr.org/uk/news/latest/2016/11/581f52dc4/frequently-asked-questions-climate-change-disaster-displacement.html (retrieved 20 Oct. 2018).

Unicef (2016) 'Ending extreme poverty: A focus on children', United Nations International Children's Emergency Fund, www.unicef.org/publications/files/Ending_Extreme_Poverty_A_Focus_on_Children_Oct_2016.pdf (retrieved 1 Aug. 2017).

Urban, M. (2017) 'Ice will return but extinctions can't be reversed: We must act now', *Guardian*, www.theguardian.com/environment/2017/dec/28/ice-will-return-but-extinctions-cant-be-reversed-we-must-act-climate-change (retrieved 2 Jan. 2019).

Urbina, I. (2013) 'Think those chemicals have been tested?', *New York Times*, www.nytimes.com/2013/04/14/sunday-review/think-those-chemicals-have-been-tested.html (retrieved 11 Nov. 2018).

USI (2018) 'Paper recycling facts', University of Southern Indiana, www.usi.edu/recycle/paper-recycling-facts (retrieved 10 Oct. 2018).

Valtorta, N., Kanaan, M., Gilbody, S., Ronzi, S., and Hanratty, B. (2016) 'Loneliness and social isolation as risk factors for coronary heart disease and stroke: Systematic review and meta-analysis of longitudinal observational studies', *Heart*, 102(13):1009–16.

Vandeventer, P., and Mandell, M. (2011) *Networks that Work: A practitioner's guide to managing networked action*. Los Angeles: Community Partners.

Van Kleef, G., Oveis, C., van der Löwe, I., LuoKogan, A., Goetz, J. and Keltner, D. (2008) 'Power, distress, and compassion: Turning a blind eye to the suffering of others', *Psychological Science*, 19(12):1315–22.

Van Reybrouck, D. (2016) *Against Elections: The case for democracy*, trans. L. Waters. London: Bodley Head.

Victor, D., Akimoto, K., Kaya, Y., Yamaguchi, M., Cullenward, D. and Hepburn, C., (2017) 'Prove Paris was more than paper promises', *Nature*, 548(7663):25–7.

Vidal, J. (2017) 'Move by UK supermarkets threatens to bring Fairtrade crashing down', *Guardian*, www.theguardian.com/global-development/2017/jun/24/fairtrade-crashing-down-sainsburys-tesco-tea-growers-nairobi (retrieved 1 Apr. 2018).

Wainwright, H. (2016) 'The new politics isn't just protest, it's about change from the ground up', *Guardian*, www.theguardian.com/commentisfree/2016/sep/28/new-politics-protest-momentum-jeremy-corbyn-labour-government (retrieved 1 Jan. 2019).

Walljasper, J. (2017) 'A more equitable economy exists right next door', *On the Commons*, www.onthecommons.org/magazine/a-more-equitable-economy-exists-right-next-door-0#sthash.SdjgX7el.dpbs (retrieved 8 Nov. 2018).

Wallman, J. (2013) *Stuffocation: Living more with less*. London: Penguin Books.

Wang, L., Malhotra, D. and Murnighan, J. (2011), 'Economics education and greed', *Academy of Management Learning and Education*, 10(4):643–60.

Ware, B. (2011) *The Top Five Regrets of the Dying: A life transformed by the dearly departed*. London: Hay House.

Warneken, F., and Tomasello, M. (2009) 'The roots of human altruism', *British Journal of Psychology*, 100(3):455–71.

Water Footprint Network (2018) 'Water footprint of crop and animal products: A comparison', https://waterfootprint.org/en/water-footprint/product-water-footprint/water-footprint-crop-and-animal-products (retrieved 19 Oct. 2018).

Waters, R. (2017) 'Robot tax: Do androids dream of personal deductions?', *Financial Times*, www.ft.com/content/597fff44-fa78-11e6-9516-2d969e0d3b65 (retrieved 11 Jul. 2018).

Webb, E., and Sergison, M. (2003) 'Evaluation of cultural competence and anti-racism training in child health service', *Archives of Diseases in Childhood*, 88(4):291–4.

Wells, H.G. (1905) *A Modern Utopia*. London: Chapman and Hall.

Wells, H.G. (1933) *The Shape of Things to Come*. London: Hutchinson.

Welzer, H. (2012) *Climate Wars: Why people will be killed in the twenty-first century*, trans. P. Camiller. Cambridge: Polity Press.

Weng, H., Fox, A., Shackman, A., Stodola, D., Caldwell, J., Olson, M., Rogers, G. and Davidson, R. (2013) 'Compassion training alters altruism and neural responses to suffering', *Psychological Science*, 24(7):1171–80.

Whitefield, P. (1993) *Permaculture in a Nutshell.* East Meon, UK: Permanent Publications.

Whitelegg, J. (2016) *Mobility: A new urban design and transport planning philosophy for a sustainable future.* n.p. Createspace.

WHO (2015) 'Global status report on road safety 2015', World Health Organization, www.who.int/violence_injury_prevention/road_safety_status/2015/en (retrieved 2 Nov. 2018).

WHO (2017) 'Voluntary contributions by fund and by contributor, 2017', World Health Organization, www.who.int/about/finances-accountability/reports/A71_INF2-en.pdf?ua=1 (retrieved 6 Nov. 2018).

WHO (2018a) 'Obesity and overweight: Key facts', World Health Organization, www.who.int/news-room/fact-sheets/detail/obesity-and-overweight (retrieved 30 Oct. 2018).

WHO (2018b) 'Air pollution', World Health Organization, www.who.int/airpollution/en (retrieved 1 Jan. 2019).

Wikipedia (2018a) 'List of dystopian fiction', https://en.wikipedia.org/wiki/List_of_dystopian_literature (retrieved 25 Oct. 2018).

Wikipedia (2018b) 'List of dystopian films', https://en.wikipedia.org/wiki/List_of_dystopian_films (retrieved 25 Oct. 2018).

Wikipedia (2018c) 'Dystopian video games', https://en.wikipedia.org/wiki/Category:Dystopian_video_games (retrieved 25 Oct. 2018).

Wikipedia (2019) 'List of Wikipedias', https://en.wikipedia.org/wiki/List_of_Wikipedias (retrieved 25 Mar. 2019).

Wilcox, W.B., and Sturgeon, S. (2018) 'Too much Netflix, not enough chill: Why young Americans are having less sex', *Politico*, www.politico.com/magazine/story/2018/02/08/why-young-Americans-having-less-sex-216953 (retrieved 19 Nov. 2018).

Wilkhahn (2017) 'Consolidated environmental statement 2017–19', www.wilkhahn.com/fileadmin/user_upload/Wilkhahn-Environmental-Statement.pdf (retrieved 1 Nov. 2018).

Wilkinson, R., and Pickett, K. (2009) *The Spirit Level: Why more equal societies almost always do better.* London: Allen Lane.

Wilks, S. (2013) *The Political Power of the Business Corporation.* Cheltenham: Edward Elgar Publishing.

Williams, K., Papadopoulou, V. and Booth, N. (2012) 'Prisoners' childhood and family backgrounds: Results from the Surveying Prisoner Crime Reduction (SPCR) longitudinal cohort study of prisoners', Ministry of Justice Analytical Services, https://assets.publishing.service.gov.uk/government/uploads/system/uploads/attachment_data/file/278837/prisoners-childhood-family-backgrounds.pdf (retrieved 6 Jun. 2017).

Wilson, T.D. *et al.* (2014) 'Just think: The challenges of the disengaged mind', *Science*, 345(6192):75–7.

WMO (2018) 'The state of the global climate in 2018', World Meteorological Organization, http://ane4bf-datap1.s3-eu-west-1.amazonaws.com/wmocms/s3fs-public/ckeditor/files/Draft_Statement_26_11_2018_v12_approved_jk_0.pdf?VXUDp1UTysIkHog4_TTuiHsIzZ6A9D93 (retrieved 5 Dec. 2018).

Wong, B., and Argumedo, A. (2011) 'The thriving diversity of Potato Park', https://ourworld.unu.edu/en/the-thriving-biodiversity-of-peru-potato-park (retrieved 12 Nov. 2018).

World Bank (2016) 'Armed forces personnel total', https://data.worldbank.org/indicator/MS.MIL.TOTL.P1 (retrieved 5 Nov. 2018).

World Bank (2018a) 'GDP per capita, all countries and economies, 2001 and 2011', https://data.worldbank.org/indicator/NY.GDP.PCAP.CD?end=2011&start=2001 (retrieved 20 Nov. 2018).

World Bank (2018b) 'Poverty overview', www.worldbank.org/en/topic/poverty/overview (retrieved 23 Oct. 2018).

World Resources Institute (2017) 'The world's top 10 emitters and how they've changed', www.wri.org/blog/2017/04/interactive-chart-explains-worlds-top-10-emitters-and-how-theyve-changed (retrieved 11 Jun. 2018).

Worldwatch (2012) 'The state of consumption today', www.worldwatch.org/node/81 (retrieved 9 Mar. 2019).

Worldwatch (2014) 'Peak meat production strains, land and water resources', www.worldwatch.org/peak-meat-production-strains-land-and-water-resources-1 (retrieved 19 Nov. 2018).

World Wildlife Fund (2018a) *Living Planet Report 2018: Aiming higher*, eds M. Grooten and R. Almond. Gland, Switzerland: WWF.

World Wildlife Fund (2018b) 'Wildlife declines show nature needs life support', www.wwf.org.uk/updates/wildlife-declines-show-nature-needs-life-support-wwf-warns (retrieved 29 Mar. 2019).

Yalom, I. (1989) *Love's Executioner and Other Tales of Psychotherapy*. New York: Harper Perennial.

Yergin, D. (1991) *The Prize: The epic quest for oil, money and power*. New York: Simon & Schuster.

Zimbardo, P. (2007) *The Lucifer Effect: How good people turn evil*. New York: Random House.

Zimbardo, P., and Boyd, J. (2008) *The Time Paradox: Using the new psychology of time to your advantage*. New York: Simon & Schuster.

Zinn, R. (2017) 'Fair trade is the pathway to regenerative agriculture', https://fairworldproject.org/wp-content/uploads/2017/09/Fair-trade-is-pathway-to-regenerative-agriculture.pdf (retrieved 15 Nov. 2018).

Zohar, D., and Marshal, I. (2000) *Spiritual Intelligence: The ultimate intelligence*. London: Bloomsbury.

Zucman, G. (2015) *The Hidden Wealth of Nations: The scourge of tax havens*. Chicago: University of Chicago Press.

Index